# THE
# RETURN
## OF THE
# DANGEROUS
# CLASSES

# THE RETURN OF THE DANGEROUS CLASSES

## *Drug Prohibition and Policy Politics*

DIANA R. GORDON

*W. W. NORTON & COMPANY*
*New York    London*

The text of this book is composed in Meridien with the
display set in Radiant. Composition by PennSet, Inc.
Manufacturing by The Maple–Vail Book Manufacturing Group.
Book design by Charlotte Staub.

Library of Congress Cataloging-in-Publication Data

Gordon, Diana R.
    The return of the dangerous classes : drug prohibition and policy
politics / Diana R. Gordon.
        p.   cm.
    Includes bibliographical references and index.
    1. Narcotics, Control of—United States.   2. Drug abuse—United
States—Prevention.   I. Title.
    HV5825.G67   1994
    363.4'5'0973—dc20                                        93-42535

ISBN 0-393-03642-1

W. W. Norton & Company, Inc.
500 Fifth Avenue, New York, N.Y. 10110
W. W. Norton & Company Ltd.
10 Coptic Street, London WC1A 1PU
1 2 3 4 5 6 7 8 9 0

*To Cathie and Steven*

# Contents

# PREFACE

"Get-tough" politics on crime and drugs have animated American social policy for at least a generation. In the 1960s the tone was set in Republican Presidential nomination speeches. Barry Goldwater, in 1964, in the wake of civil rights demonstrations that turned bloody, decried "the growing menace . . . to personal safety, to life, to limb and property, in homes, in churches, on the playgrounds and places of business, particularly in our great cities." Richard Nixon, in 1968, warned that "some of our courts have gone too far in weakening the peace forces, as against the criminal forces, in this country."[1] More recently, Republican Presidents have focused the theme, with Ronald Reagan vowing tougher enforcement of drug laws in 1986 and George Bush proclaiming all-out war, announcing in his 1989 inaugural address, "This scourge will stop."[2] By the mid-1990s anti-crime rhetoric had become a bi-partisan mantra, intoned by Democratic President Bill Clinton as well as conservative Senator Alfonse D'Amato (Republican–N.Y.).

Given the conservative trends of the 1980s, it is perhaps not surprising that both the objectives and the instruments of "law and order" and the "war on drugs" have become virtually sacrosanct, backed by a consensus as broad as earlier support for the Cold War. While many believe that political announcements of future policy directions in this area are intended to draw attention to the conditions they supposedly address, the relationship is more often inverted. It has become as much the function of crime and illicit drug use to provide an opportunity for politically obligatory "get-tough" postures as it is the role of recurring drug and crime wars to point the way toward solutions.

This book is an examination of forces that sustain drug prohibition, an argument that an apparently failed policy survives because it serves many aims and interests other than the declared objective of reducing dangerous drug abuse. The audience I have in mind includes not only people who are professionally involved in drug policy and regular observers of its twists and turns, but also members of the concerned public who feel at least some dissatisfaction with a program of prohibition that (1) excludes the most dangerous drugs, (2) generates deadly violence in communities already burdened with poverty and despair, (3) contributes little or nothing to the reduction of dangerous drug abuse (and, in some cases, worsens its effects), and (4) distorts social policy debates in ways that discount many conditions that drive people to the most dangerous uses of psychoactive substances. I am hoping that my work will stimulate this audience to think about how to address the sources of drug abuse along with its effects.

A book that relies on a number of case studies requires the active assistance of many other people. More of this research project took place in living rooms and offices than in libraries; the interviewees who contributed to it ranged from junkies in Germany to congressional representatives in Washington. Although I was occasionally disturbed by their opinions, my greatest debt is to the supporters of drug prohibition who revealed their policy commitments to me. I am also grateful to their opponents, who shared with me the frustrations of swimming against a powerful current. Among the research contacts who were particularly helpful are William Bryant, Perry Bullard, Kate Godefroy, Alyce Hanley, Marie Majewske, Albert Riederer, Jerry Sheehan, and Glenda Straube.

It is easy to get carried away with the excesses of the drug wars and to indulge in hyperbole as to their methods and effects that is not dissimilar to the political grandstanding that drug abuse makes tempting. Following the political theorist C.B. Macpherson, I am grateful to friends and colleagues who not only gave me valuable information and ideas but also saved me from my enthusiasms. Thanks to Richard L. Miller, who supplied me for more than a year with a steady stream of information about Kansas City drug wars and the politics behind them. Henner Hess, Lorenz Böllinger, and Sebastian Scheerer kept me posted on developments in Germany. Tom Weisskopf gave me background on Michigan politics. Jim Dempsey, Ginny Sloan, and Eric Sterling gave me guidance to death penalty politics on Capitol Hill. Loren Siegel fed me American Civil Liberties Union perspectives, and Rachel Donaldson shared her interesting undergraduate thesis with me. Nick Dorn reviewed the chapter on European drug policies with great care. Ethan Nadelmann gave me not only ideas and encouragement, but also his Alaska file; I'm grateful to him, and to Lynn Zimmer and John Morgan, for giving me a critique of the chapter I found most challenging. I'm indebted to Stuart Scheingold for wise perspectives on the politicization of crime in general and its particular character in Seattle; Sally and Dick Parks added a personal welcome to my visits in that lovely city.

I was blessed with several competent research assistants. Many thanks to Giovanna Giorgini in Rome, who collected and helped analyze reports of Italian policy developments; Sasha Parks, who tracked down details in Seattle; and Sabrina Christiansen, who translated German documents for me at 8 A.M. on a summer holiday. Vicky Donner, whose talent at verifying (and sometimes correcting) pesky details bodes well for her future as researcher and political scientist, became a treasured friend as well as my truly indispensable helper.

Financial support came from the German Marshall Fund, the Aaron Diamond Foundation, and the Smith Family Fund. Moral support came from my women friends—Kathy and Lily especially, as well as Mary, who had a special role in continually reminding me that my sanity depended on cleaning up the piles of books and files on the floor around my desk at least every two weeks. David M. Gordon, as always, was most important of all—for his trenchant and comprehensive editorial comments, his loving assurances that I would eventually finish, and his fabulous homemade pasta.

# THE
# RETURN
## OF THE
# DANGEROUS
# CLASSES

# PROLOGUE

In 1992 when the Democrats ended twelve years of right-wing Republican reign in the White House, many Americans dissatisfied with Reagan-Bush get-tough crime and drug policies understandably sniffed the political winds for breezes of reform. It became clear almost immediately, however, that in this regard Bill Clinton would not be a breath of fresh air. His first drug budget left the Bush emphasis on law enforcement virtually intact, and he appointed an experienced police chief to head the federal Office of National Drug Control Policy. "It seems we're going to go on doing things that don't work," a drug policy consultant to the United Nations told the *New York Times* when the budget was released.[1]

As the new president began to settle into his job, priorities in this area became murkier. The national drug strategy he unveiled in October 1993 looked much like those of the previous four years, but in early 1994 a new one stressed drug treatment and prevention. The fiscal year 1995 budget proposal supplemented law enforcement funds with almost a billion dollars for public health measures to control drug abuse, but the White House thwarted Attorney General Janet Reno's efforts to get the country to back away from long mandatory minimum sentences for minor drug offenses. Though Clinton evaded direct endorsement of the tough anti-crime bill passed by the Senate in late 1993 his 1994 state-of-the-nation message hailed the "three strikes and you're out" sentencing proposal of its most fervid backers.[2]

Clinton's recent wavering may be more apparent than real. His few remarks on crime in the previous year's state-of-the-nation address, in February 1993, provide clues to the sources of his perspective both then and now. In a speech otherwise celebrating change, his message on fighting crime was more of the same. Then and again in August of that year he announced that he would embrace the legislation that had stalled in Congress in the waning days of the Bush administration, and vowed as well to put 100,000 new cops on the streets.[3] (Unlike his predecessor, however, he also committed himself to fighting hard for gun control.)

Most members of Congress knew that they would be politically compelled to vote for either the old crime bill or a new one that featured very similar get-tough provisions. And many knew—as Clinton, the policy wonk, probably did—of the large body of evidence, generated over two decades, that these measures did little to decrease crime.[4] But evaluating the president's substantive position on crime is almost beside the point. Bill Clinton probably didn't believe that the country that already puts more of its citizens behind bars than any other advanced nation, the nation that hasn't improved its rate of clearing crimes with arrest in twenty years, would curb crime with tougher sentences, enhanced police patrol, or dozens of new federal capital crimes.[5] Furthermore, it is unlikely that he raised that totem in the state-of-the-nation address because he thought his listeners believed in it. His purposes were more symbolic.

Asking Americans to cooperate in what would surely be a wrenching national endeavor to "rebuild America," Clinton needed counterpoint.[6] Granting the homely psychological truth that for most of us my enemy's enemy is my friend, he sought to identify an enemy shared with millions of viewers at the very same moment that he was asking them to make sacrifices. And he needed to show Congress that while he was asking legislators to take the political risks of supporting new taxes and reduced spending, he would endorse one policy direction that would sell well with constituents. He played scapegoat politics, and his audience in the capitol responded with the biggest hand of the night.

## THE PROBLEM AND THE PROJECT

In the last quarter-century crime and drugs have been a focal point for much public debate about morality and public safety in this country. Some social issues—abortion, sex education in the schools—call into play core religious attitudes and mobilize single-issue interest groups around polarized positions. Others—teenage pregnancy, welfare dependence—rely for their salience on the identification of a relatively narrow spectrum of targets. But issues of crime and drugs generate near-universal concern, and ordinary citizens and leaders alike often believe that how we address them reflects the moral state of the nation. Furthermore, crime and drugs implicate nearly everyone, however peripherally. The debate over crime and drugs has become less important for the possibilities of concrete public action than for its breadth as a contested terrain on which battles over power and principle rage. This book explores some of that contested territory.

My thinking about these matters evolved from an initial sense of disorientation. Several years ago, as I was trying to understand the directions in which street crime policy was moving (for another writing project), I found myself profoundly uncomfortable with both the declared definitions of the American drug problem and virtually all prevailing prescriptions for it—among them, a priority for vigorous law enforcement, a primary emphasis on public health approaches, and the proposal for legalizing adult consumption of all psychoactive substances.[7] I realized that my inability to arrive at substantive preferences in the area of drug policy derived in part from being distracted by what might be called its "surface noise." Stripping away what others were suggesting I should believe about the problems and their solutions, I discovered my own perspective. Although the research for this book has qualified and extended my views somewhat, they have not altered fundamentally. I present them now as the core observations that informed subsequent inquiries, reported in this book, as to why and how prohibition dominates drug policy.

First, I share with most people a concern with the effects of what is commonly called "the drug problem"—the consequences of the use of dangerous, psychoactive substances by several million Americans, entangled with the social disruptions brought about by the ways we have responded to (and often generated) that use. People who die of overdoses, families torn apart by the distraction and isolation that accompanies compulsive consumption of large or concentrated doses of opiates or cocaine, neighbors whose homes are burglarized so that addicts can afford a fix, innocent bystanders (and not-so-innocent participants) who are unintended victims of violent trade competition among drug dealers—I grieve for them and for the costs to the country of their losses.

Second, I view the conventional definition of "the drug problem" as profoundly confused and misguided. It leaves out damage done by legal drugs, particularly alcohol, which is at least equivalent—definitely greater in terms of lives lost; perhaps less dramatic, but no less pervasive, in terms of visible assaults on our social landscape. It confuses the effects of illegality—the ingestion of very concentrated (and therefore more dangerous) forms of drugs, the turf wars of traffickers, heightened levels of property crime, the physical deterioration of people rendered penniless by their habits—with the effects of the drugs themselves. And it loads the baggage of decades of economic disinvestment and decline onto a rickety wagon of drug abuse that simply cannot bear its weight.

Finally, whether one considers the drug problem as commonly defined or as I might more narrowly define it, drug prohibition in the United States has failed to solve it. Perhaps the simplest indicator is also the clearest: An estimated 26 million people continue to use illicit drugs each year, about 5 million of them—in the sober estimation of the most responsible public health experts—problematically enough to need treatment.[8] The evidence of failure can be found in every city; cocaine and heroin emergencies in New York City hospitals rose in each of three successive quarters in 1991 and 1992.[9] Other failures, like police corruption and the violence that too often surrounds drug transactions, implicate the prohibitionist nature of drug policy—its tendency to drive up the price of drugs and the profit from dealing in them, the necessity for a drug dealer to be armed in defense against cops and competitors. Studies of drug-related violence in Miami and New York have found that only very small percentages can be attributed to the psychopharmacological effects of drugs; most violence "is an economic side effect of drug prohibition," notes Brown University community health specialist David C. Lewis, occurring either in the course of crimes committed to buy drugs or in drug dealers' turf wars.[10]

Given these core observations, two major questions emerged to shape my research: Why is the conventional definition of "the drug problem" so inclusive, encompassing so much violence and suffering and evil that might with equal or greater logic be attributed to other harmful social conditions—poverty, inequality, urban disinvestment? And why has prohibition policy become more intense and expansive as evidence has mounted of its failures to achieved declared goals?

In order to root my exploration of these questions in the flesh and blood of contests over drug policy, I studied five cases of drug politics in action in a variety of arenas. They include

- the development of a congressional consensus supporting the death penalty for drug "kingpins," even where no murder is committed;

- the adoption and revision of a Michigan law mandating life imprisonment without parole for people convicted of possession of more than 650 grams of opiates or cocaine derivatives;
- the recriminalization in Alaska, by citizen initiative, of possession of marijuana for personal use (after fifteen years of decriminalization);
- the passage of an anti-drug sales tax, in the era of taxpayers' revolts, to fight drugs in Jackson County, Missouri (Kansas City); and
- the adoption of a Seattle ordinance making it illegal to loiter with intent to engage in an illegal drug transaction.

## DRUG POLITICS AND RATIONALITY

I began research on these case studies in a rationalist vein, trying to explain the apparent paradox of continuing support for drug prohibition in the face of its instrumental failure. If the war on drugs were really aimed at reduction of drug abuse and the misery and violence it can engender, then a rationalist perspective on drug policy—one which concentrates primarily on the explicit objectives that policy actors say they embrace—would presumably begin to consider serious and substantive alternatives to the prevailing prohibitionist pursuits. Obviously, this was not the case; prohibition is alive and well throughout the land, despite widespread awareness of its failures and some articulate dissenters.[11]

I soon discovered that even establishing the contours of the paradox was daunting. The rationalistic perspective simply did not work for an analysis of this policy area. I needed to move away from considering policy as an end that is produced by decisions made through the political process, reflecting stable, informed calculations about how best to shape the social and political world. As I interviewed people struggling to have an influence on drug policy, I saw them first and foremost defending and promoting visions and interests more deeply rooted than the rather abstract notions of what government interventions could shape human decisions about taking and distributing drugs. I began to see drug policy as a resource for furthering values—of security, order, and participation—and staking claims—to material and political success, to public goods.[12] Public policy is a means as well as an end. Viewed this way, the persistence of drug prohibition makes much more sense.

Eliminating drug abuse is not the only item on the policy agenda that produces and sustains prohibitionist policies. This book argues that a "shadow agenda"—distinct from the declared action agenda of government and the broader agenda of items for public discussion, but profoundly influencing both of them—is a normal aspect of policy politics.[13] It also explores the elements and impacts of the shadow agenda of current American drug policy, a particularly dark and volatile one, with racial and generational conflicts, as well as prospects of political and material gain, feeding prohibitionist policies. Finally, my analysis concludes that overlooking or discounting the influence of shadow agendas on public decisionmaking not only impedes progress in particular policy areas—in this case, drugs—but also distracts citizens and policymakers from addressing other, perhaps even larger, concerns.

This book, then, is as much about the fears and hopes of Americans and their political leaders in the last twenty years—beginning about the time of the passage of the "Rockefeller drug law" in New York in 1973, then considered "the nation's toughest drug law"—as it is about the particular politics of drug prohibition.[14] The political scientist Stuart Scheingold has argued that the messy and complex politics of street crime can be understood only in the context of broader cultural values and social conditions of American life—our punitive morality, our reliance on individualistic answers to social questions, the inequalities of race and class that we tolerate.[15] This book shares Scheingold's perspective and applies it to an exploration of drug prohibition politics that produce longer prison sentences and outlaw status for young minority males but provide no relief from the most destructive effects of the U.S. "drug problem."

## SLIPPERY CONCEPTS AND WORKING DEFINITIONS

Even the simplest description of this book as being about drug policy politics confronts different meanings of "politics." If the word is taken to mean both electoral contests and the larger workings of power relationships ("who gets what, when, how"), it is surely correct to say that the symbolic elements of drug policymaking are political. (In other words, it would be much too simple to allege, as some liberals do, that seeking the electoral advantage is the exclusive or primary motive behind every noninstrumental demand for prohibitionist drug policies; the domain of symbolic politics includes other impulses, issuing from citizen activists and the media as well as from political figures.) This book will attempt to trace the effect of politics in both senses on selected prohibitionist developments in recent American drug policies.

Definitional knots are common in both academic and popular writing about drugs and drug policy. To begin with, the word "drug" as it is commonly used is a legal construction, describing "controlled substances" rather than chemical combinations having psychoactive effects, which would have to include alcohol and tobacco, among others. The rubric of "narcotics," which scientific classification defines fairly narrowly, often expands in the popular mind to cover other drugs, even stimulants. And "addiction" can refer to specific physical reactions (the development of tolerance to regular and uniform doses, and the withdrawal syndrome) or more generally to almost any kind of obsessive devotion.

I cannot promise to avoid all such imprecisions. But I can at this point provide a few guides to my own use of the unruly vocabulary of drug policy.

In this book "drug abuse" refers to the regular or compulsive ingestion of illicit drugs taken in substantial doses or in concentrated form. (I use the term "illicit" instead of "illegal" because some drugs are illegal only under some circumstances—sedatives purchased without the legally required prescription, for instance.) This is the definition of those leaning toward a predominance of public health measures for addressing the condition; for those who see the problem as a moral or legal one, the definition of "drug abuse" is virtually identical with "drug use"—any ingestion of proscribed psychoactive substances. (I considered not using the term at all because of its ambiguities. But I finally decided to use it *because* of those ambiguities, rather than despite them, to remind myself and my readers of the nature of problem definition as an interpretive activity. What matters in policy politics is not the relationship of a definition of a term like "drug abuse" to some elusive objective reality, but how tenaciously large numbers of people believe that the term is sufficiently descriptive to warrant its inclusion as an item on a government agenda.)

I am choosing to divide users into two loose categories, which I shall call "casual users" and "compulsive users." The former are people who use illicit drugs irregularly and with primarily recreational aims, or regular (but not heavy) users of marijuana and hashish. The latter are those who use illicit drugs other than the hemp products with regularity and at considerable cost to their bodies and their relationships with others. I call them "compulsive users" in order to get around disputes about what constitutes addiction or dependence. As a social fact influencing criminal justice policy, whether a user experiences physiological withdrawal or psychological dependence is irrelevant.

"Prohibition" as the subject of my study is the general proscription by the criminal law (at all levels of government) of the consumption, manufacture, and distribution of selected psychoactive substances in particular forms.[16] It also includes corollary policies, such as the exclusion of those convicted of drug offenses from the benefits of the Americans With Disabilities Act or the requirement that states must enact laws suspending driver's licenses of convicted drug offenders or lose federal highway funds.[17]

Related terms expand or contract the notion of prohibition. "War on drugs" and "drug war" are narrower than "prohibition," which effectively began at the national level in 1914 with the passage of the Harrison Act, the granddaddy of federal drug control laws. These terms refer to the congeries of contemporary campaigns enforcing prohibition (beginning in the Reagan years, renewed and intensified—at least rhetorically—by Bush's explicit declaration of a war); these campaigns rely primarily on troops from federal agencies (Drug Enforcement Agency, Customs, Coast Guard, etc.) working on their own and jointly with local and state police and prosecutors, but also on some backup support from treatment and prevention programs. "Drug control" is broader than "prohibition," the ongoing effort by government at all levels to reduce or eliminate illicit drugs, whether through treatment and prevention or law enforcement, whether by private or public interventions.

The architecture of this book is simple. Chapter 1 develops my central argument that American drug-control policy is freighted with many concerns only tangentially related to drug abuse, and Chapter 2 lays out the contours of drug prohibition at the millennium. The next five chapters, which constitute Part II, briefly set the stage for each case study, introducing the sites, issues, and players of each instance of policymaking in simple narrative form. The analysis begins in Part III, using material from the five cases to inform and illustrate my examination of the strategies in the policy politics of drug control—the items on the shadow agenda of contemporary drug prohibition. By building on these specific cases, I hope that the more abstract analysis that follows will be richer and more firmly rooted in the interactions of citizens and policymakers.[18]

Readers may by now be wondering when the dangerous classes of the title enter the picture. Contemporary U.S. society seems locked in the grip of an identity crisis. The verities of the American dream and the American character turn out not to be eternal, and even if they were, we do not know where we would like them to lead us. Lacking a vision of what we want to be, we settle for the near-term goal of keeping the lid on. Our confusion emerges in social policy-making: We are ambivalent in our choice of targets, we allow the medium to define our messages, and we treat means as ends. Perhaps most troubling, we turn on each other, finding political avenues for the identification of enemies who can be blamed for our national social and economic ills. These are the "dangerous classes"—minorities, youth, sometimes immigrants and liberals—that drug-control policy helps to marginalize. I describe this process in Chapter 10; Chapter 11 discusses the crucial role of race in that dynamic.

Drug prohibition is not only a vessel for antagonisms and fears about the dangerous classes, but also a resource for political and material gain. Chapters 12 and 13 discuss ways in which those who make and implement drug policy find opportunity—sometimes on their constituents' behalf, sometimes on their own—in the national consensus that demonizes and punishes those who take and sell drugs.

As important as the intersecting social and political forces that support prohibition is the ideology that mediates between them and the policies I discuss in this book.[19] On the surface that ideology is a set of images and expectations about drugs. But here, too, we are dealing with a product, this time of other, broader ideologies. Chapter 14 traces the discourse of drugs—drugspeak—in the 1980s as an expression both of the ideology of drugs and of the broader commitment to the social conservatism that played such an important part in the domestic politics of that period, from presidential elections to neighborhood race relations. It deals with the ways in which language shapes and conveys our understanding of both the problem to be solved by prohibition and our belief in certain approaches to solving it. It explores the use of language as an exercise of policymaking power, produced from many sources but finally legitimating the state's definitions of morality and the proper measures to be taken to defend it.

Part IV looks beyond the present drug wars to other places and uncertain futures. Chapter 15 explores recent directions in European drug policy and examines the politics behind developments in the cases of Germany and Italy. It argues that as a nation we probably won't follow the more liberal policies that are taking root in some European nations, though the theme of what is called "harm reduction" or "harm minimization" may sooner or later be influential here.

Once again my conclusions are driven by the supposition that policy politics are more powerful than rational analysis in shaping the directions of drug prohibition. Shadow agendas operating in a number of European countries appear to support drug policy reform in ways that seem unlikely here. They also suggest limitations on the liberalizing trend in Europe.

The book ends with some of my own views about where American drug policy should go. Although this book is not a critique of drug prohibition as an instrumental policy, but an examination of the forces that sustain it, I feel compelled to express my concern that prohibitionists and legalizers, from opposite sides of both the libertarian and the pragmatic fence, may be making precisely the same error. Both assume that drug policy is the sole—or at least principal—tool for solving the drug problem. My orientation to policy politics leads me to the conclusion that no less important than the substance of what our drug policy should be is how we address the shadow agenda of prohibition—the racial and generational antagonisms, the yearning for order and for social and political participation, the political and fiscal insecurities of both citizens and leaders. Effective drug policy reform will require responses to these tensions as well as innovation in the ways we seek to affect the behavior of those who consume, produce, and distribute drugs.

*Part I*

# INTRODUCTION

# Chapter 1

# Drug Prohibition: More and Less Than Meets the Eye

On December 13, 1991, the Minnesota Supreme Court made national headlines by upholding the decision of a Hennepin County judge that a state law providing harsher penalties for possession of crack cocaine than for possession of powder cocaine violated the Equal Protection Clause of both the Fourteenth Amendment of the U.S. Constitution and the Minnesota Constitution.[1] The law had a discriminatory impact on African-Americans, who were disproportionately represented among crack users. The court found that there was no rational basis for the distinction between the two substances because "evidence as to the degree of dangerousness between crack and cocaine powder is based on testimony as to effects resulting from different methods of ingestion, rather than on an inherent difference between the forms of the drug."[2]

The decision received national attention for several reasons: It challenged, if only in a small way, the legitimacy of the widely supported "war on drugs"; it showed that appellate courts, even in this era of judicial and political conservatism, might occasionally apply a broad equal protection analysis to the administration of criminal justice; and it brought into an eminently respectable and mainstream forum the recognition that racism—sometimes overt, more often veiled—taints drug policy.[3] Although the five African-American men who challenged the statute did not charge that the legislature, in enacting it, had intentionally discriminated, intent is irrelevant to the law's effect. A footnote in the majority opinion also stated that statistics and legislative history "could be held to create an inference of invidious discrimination"; and a concurring opinion pointed out that the legislators must be presumed to know of the likelihood that the law would have a discriminatory impact on blacks.[4]

*15*

## POLICYMAKING AS POLITICAL STRUGGLE

If social scientists were not surprised by such a finding, it is not necessarily because they were cynics likely to believe anything negative about legislators' motives. In the last two decades American political scientists and sociologists have begun to acknowledge the degree to which policymaking is as much a site of political struggle as are electoral contests. Some of us are skeptical (as are many citizens) of traditional theory that holds that public policy reflects the informed, rational preferences of the polity as expressed through elections and run through the policy process. For one thing, we know that policymakers are not merely passive recipients of citizens' pleas for help, and that, politically speaking, all pleas are not created equal. Only rarely does grass-roots activity really define the issues, get them on the political agenda, and keep them there. And we see that political interaction around issues, or what Charles Lindblom calls "the play of power," begins long before overt political demand surfaces and bills are debated, executive orders drafted, or appeals argued, and continues long after a policy has been implemented.[5] In addition, the issues, the political messages that shape them, and the forums in which they are created all have symbolic significance, which may count for more in determining policy outcomes than the observable process of overt demand for action on stated problems.[6] Finally, the problematic nature of a social condition should not be taken as given but rather as the construction of human observers of the condition —an activity that is itself inherently political.[7] With these perspectives, a policy that reflects—inadvertently or purposefully—the racial tensions of the day seems quite normal.

Understanding the trajectories of drug prohibition, then, requires close examination of the complex agendas that shape it. An important part of the investigation of political agenda-setting is the search for multiple meanings in citizens' political demands. On the one hand, both policymakers and political analysts must take people at their word as to what they say they want from the political system. On the other hand, the complaint on which government seems to be acting is usually merely the outer layer of the policy onion. The layers beneath are claims for recognition of other values and interests, often sites of more intense conflict than mere positions on issues, and sometimes more problematic to voice in public contests. (The Lord may have been able to say, "Vengeance is mine," but the contemporary death penalty supporter had better not.) Policymakers must respond to those claims, too, of course, however indeterminate and ungenerous they may be. (In fact, as often as not, political actors have stimulated the policy demand at its covert as well as its overt levels, or at least laid the foundation for its expression.) Issues emerge freighted with concerns other than the stated grievance and headed for more complex and ambiguous outcomes than are included in declared policy goals.

Making sense of the multiple meanings of policy demand is not easy. A basic understanding of human psychology aids, of course, in understanding policy politics. More immediately relevant is attention to context; the social and political environment in which politicians and voters construct issues can tell us much about the multiple messages they exchange. But when all is said and done, the best-equipped policy analysts have a healthy skepticism about finding fixed and consistent values in the striations beneath the veneer of policy argument or about being able to trace with precision the contributions of those values to policy outcomes. They also know that policy analysis itself is a form of political argument, one of the forces shaping the construction of an issue and designating action taken on it as a "solution."[8]

Though somewhat abstract in their general formulation, these observations apply very concretely to U.S. drug policy at the end of the twentieth century. The country's strongly prohibitionist perspective is firmly rooted in American history and culture and is supported by every major segment of the electorate. It is a foregone conclusion that drug policymaking will be dominated by law enforcement measures. Yet the political demand that sustains what appears to be a popular and political consensus has many sources besides concern about reducing the physical and social harm that can occur as the result of experiences with psychoactive drugs.

The variety and depth of wants and needs that sustain prohibition are extraordinary. The near-universal yearning for personal safety gives governing elites a chance to demonstrate the social control capabilities of the state, manage the "dangerous classes" in American society, feather their own nests politically and materially, and replace the economic and political opportunities of the Cold War with others that require similar kinds of activities and expenditures. Neighborhood activists can embrace the anti-drug crusade to protect property interests and the ideology that supports them, or promote institutional growth for the local forces of order. Ordinary citizens who take up the drug-control banner can find meaning in political life by participating in reviving what many feel is a threatened moral consensus.

*17*

And all of the above actors can be genuinely committed to furthering physical security. The allure of prohibition is irresistible.

None of the above is meant to suggest that there is not a real and substantial social condition—compulsive use of some mind-altering substances (including licit drugs like alcohol and tobacco, as well as illicit ones like heroin and crack)—that is medically dangerous and socially destructive to both users and their contacts, and which people have good reason to ask government to address. And pointing out that many conditions other than drug abuse make up "the drug problem" is not to deny that drug abuse interacts with and exacerbates those ills. Furthermore, drug abuse takes on a particularly agonizing cast when it is concentrated in communities—principally the nation's inner cities—already burdened with disease and disadvantage; the drama of armed and dangerous young people dependent in one way or another on the illegal drug industry is a genuine tragedy. Finally, there is a cultural logic in the contemporary choice of a prohibitionist approach to drug-taking. Although the criminalization of opiates and cocaine derivatives, for example, is largely a twentieth-century phenomenon, the United States has been strongly punitive since before it was a nation, favoring the stick over the carrot to control behavior since its puritan days.[9]

But the chapters that follow argue that the weight and profusion of the alternate functions of our current drug policy are at least as powerful in political agenda-setting as the medical and social harm caused by drugs. And the strains that gave rise to these forces—like declining material security (for cities as well as for individuals), family instability, racial polarization, and political alienation—are likely to persist in the American polity. If no other all-purpose carrier of values and interests equivalent to the drug problem emerges to hold such a wide variety of discontents, many citizens will continue to project their yearnings for relief from these broader discontents onto drug prohibition. Its symbolic role as a response to latent political demand will be, as it is now, more important politically than targeting and conquering the most pernicious consequences of compulsive drug use.

In this context some note that the issue of drugs has become like the issue of communism in the Cold War years in its evocation of a great range of public fears. It is true that with both issues people project individual insecurities onto what is perceived to be a serious and insidious collective threat. But the similarity goes deeper than that. With communism, the danger was perhaps named more precisely; the subversives hunted by the House Un-American Activities

Committee in the 1950s and the local and national policies derided as communistic—national health insurance, fluoride supplements for drinking water—would lead to an alternative means of organizing economic production and distribution that would end our world as we knew it. But of course for those who led the anti-communist charge, the world they sought to preserve was one of hierarchies— boss and worker, market and state—both familiar and profitable. Similar layers of meaning constitute the menace of drugs, though the context is cast as social rather than economic. At a superficial level, drugs threaten addiction and depravity; what is also at stake, however, the alarmists believe, are fundamental hierarchies of authority —parents over children, the affluent over the poor, lighter races over darker ones, accumulators over dependents—and the mediating mechanisms, like law enforcement and media socialization, for reinforcing their legitimacy.

## "THE DRUG PROBLEM" DEFINED

I have already mentioned that a social condition does not constitute a problem simply by virtue of its existence or the damage it does; its problematic character is assigned through human interpretation. Political scientist Deborah Stone adapts the observation to policy analysis by noting that policy-problem definition involves the "strategic representation of situations," people's portrayal of their experiences so as to make a claim on the political process.[10] Either formulation captures the idea that discrete realities of pain and destruction become problems only when attention is paid.

The overlay of public opinion on private troubles elevates them (usually when they have aggregated and intensified and taken on the drama of televised reality) as matters demanding attention from the state. In taking this process for granted in modern political life, we may jumble cause and effect. Emile Durkheim reminds us that behavior is criminal because we don't like it, not that we find it repugnant because it is criminal.[11]

Why does the conventional definition of "the drug problem" include so many elements that might be employed in the construction of a quite different problem? It makes sense to begin that inquiry with an examination of the relevant strategic portrayals of behavior we don't like. It is not surprising that citizens, professionals, and politicians identify different problematic elements; what they see depends on where they sit. Congressional representatives on committees with foreign policy jurisdiction construct the image of rapacious cartels exploiting illiterate peasants and corrupting American law enforcement. Parents respond to reports that marijuana has become more potent and that regular pot-smoking has become more pervasive among high-school and even junior high-school students. Doctors may characterize the problem based on their work in emergency rooms, where 371,208 drug abuse episodes were recorded in 1990.[12] The media often focus on the graphic drama of gaunt black men nodding out in doorways and "crack babies" born to addicted mothers. Moralists lump together many quite separate phenomena to construct an all-encompassing "drug problem" that renders problematic any use whatsoever of an illicit substance.[13] William J. Bennett, the first Director of the Office of National Drug Control Policy, firmly declared the problem to be "experimental first use, 'casual' use, regular use, and addiction alike."[14]

Having a particular involvement with one aspect of the issue does not prevent the inclusion of other elements in one's definition of the condition to be addressed. The perspectives mentioned above barely touch on the sources of anxiety and antagonism which lead ultimately to longer sentences for drug offenses, reduced procedural protections for accused drug dealers, comprehensive drug-testing for public employees, and marijuana searches in school lockers. Citizens and their leaders also define the drug problem in more grandiose and diffuse ways—as a threat to national security; as underclass decadence; as genocide (committed against blacks); and as challenge to the individual qualities of self-denial, ambition, and initiative that "made America great." These alternative definitions flow from our less rational, more instinctual understandings of the world, the most basic level at which "the nature of man and the functioning of the [political] system are part of a single transaction."[15] Shaped by culture and social conflict as well as by universal operations of the psyche, the "other" definitions—by their breadth and weight, by the support they engender from influential people and institutions—are at least as useful in explaining the durability of our concern about psychoactive substances as are those that are more conventionally instrumental. They merge and enlarge the focused concerns of specialized publics into a more diffuse and threatening whole.

In allowing such a fulsome development of this process, we have, from time to time, fostered a national preoccupation that the very real phenomenon of drug abuse is a more pressing domestic policy problem than many others, such as a fifteen-year stagnation in the standard of living for most people; a growing gap between rich and poor; high levels of personal and corporate indebtedness and low levels of productivity; an educational system incapable of preparing students for rewarding lives as citizens and workers; inaccessible and insufficient services such as health care, child care, and public transportation; growing racial divisions; polluted air and water; and crumbling infrastructure (particularly urban). Sometimes we have even suggested that "the drug problem" has brought about these ills. We have named the river for one of its tributaries.

The definitional process constrains even as it broadens. Until recently the scope of "the drug problem" has included only illicit drugs. But the legal drugs of alcohol and tobacco damage and kill many more people than do the controlled substances.[16] Mark Kleiman vividly notes the dissonance of lethal but legal alcohol and the lesser toll of illicit drugs:

> Instead of a few thousand overdose deaths, mostly among the young, we have tens of thousands of chronic-disease deaths, mostly later in life. Instead of the disorder of street dealing, we have the disorder of public drunkenness. Both drugs produce accidents, poor employee performance, drains on the health-care system, damaged newborns, and failures to fulfill family and neighborhood responsibilities, but the total damage in every one of these categories is clearly greater for alcohol than for cocaine.[17]

Beginning in the late 1980s, this message, sent by public health experts like C. Everett Koop, the U.S. Surgeon General in the Reagan administration, began to penetrate public consciousness.[18] Adherents of the small but growing drug legalization movement have also made use of alcohol and tobacco data, hoping that they would point up the irrationality (or hypocrisy) of present drug policy and thus further the decriminalization of drugs. Such an expectation ignores the multiple meanings of political demand for drug control. If my earlier analysis is correct, official social control policy is unlikely to change merely as a result of a new perspective—no matter how "rational" or rooted in statistical truth—on the relative dangers of legal and illegal substances. Some broadening of problem definition in this direction may occur, however. Many drug prevention programs now include the objective of alcohol prevention.[19]

Determining that a social condition is problematic includes giving it greater or lesser priority for public action than other similarly labeled conditions. That this assignment of priority relies on interpretation rather than on some objective measure of reality is apparent by looking at how the salience of public problems changes in public polls over time—sometimes from year to year, sometimes in shorter time periods than that—even when the damage done by the condition remains more or less constant. The dynamic is interactive. During the summer of 1989 President Bush took full advantage of public fears about drugs in a period when he lacked more global opportunities in the spotlight, and the major media whipped up public concern about illicit drugs with a rash of broadcasts about the problem, building to the president's well-publicized announcement of a new "war on drugs" in early September. *New York Times*/CBS News polls taken between early 1989 and mid-1990 reflect a huge increase in public perception of drugs as "the most important problem facing this country today" during the summer of 1989 and a sharp drop in the succeeding months.[20]

The definitional anomalies discussed here strongly suggest that we don't distribute concern for public problems by simple measures of relative damage wrought by different conditions. Instead, it is often asserted, we show the greatest concern for those problems that can be portrayed, generally in the media, as having the most dramatic and clear-cut consequences. It is certainly true that crime, drugs, and abortion can be easily dramatized, dealing as they do with acute threats of death and violence. But drama, too, is in the eye of the beholder. There is no theoretical reason why slower, more chronic losses of life, love, means, and dignity cannot also dominate public concern. (Sometimes they do; the economic anguish of millions of Americans during the Great Depression overshadowed other policy issues in the mind of the American electorate.[21]) And what gives a problem drama depends both on the way it is communicated by opinion shapers and on whether the audience resonates with the values and assumptions behind the presentation. It is at this point that determination of the importance of a problem interacts with choosing the approach to be taken to its solution.

The point isn't that illicit drugs have been exaggerated as a blot on contemporary American life. Of course they do terrible damage—at least if one specifies certain kinds and doses and frequencies of consumption. (Snorting or injecting cocaine, for instance, is dangerous in a way that chewing coca leaves is not.) The prevalence of injury, disease, despair, and death immediately attributable to drugs and activities that attend their exchange in poor urban neighborhoods is the most obvious testimony to the social damage that drugs can cause.

The point, rather, is that drugs—and particularly the activity of selling them—have become the organizing metaphor for debates about other, more constitutive issues: the causes and effects of urban blight, the collapse of community, intergenerational tension, interpersonal violence. The metaphor is voracious—the symbol that ate Chicago, as the rock group Winchester Cathedral might have sung. And its magnetic qualities of logical simplicity and moral clarity lure us away from messier and more demanding confrontations with larger collective failures.

## CHOOSING PROHIBITION

Just because people have decided what hurts them does not mean that they have chosen a particular kind of remedy. Moving from grievance to demand involves making key political choices, even if, in the conscious mind of the petitioner, the course of action to be prescribed may seem self-evident. As Lindblom notes, "There exist no bedrock fixed political wants or preferences; all are acquired from society and, for every individual, depend on society: what it teaches, asks, and offers."[22] The acquisition of those preferences sets the direction of policy, the limits of what the political system will handle (at least for the time being) as well as the possibilities.

The choices made in this second step of agenda-setting often reflect both root principles of governance and power relationships in the larger society. They touch on such matters as the proper balance between state and private activity, how widely or narrowly policy costs—financial and social—will be spread, what groups are to bear the benefits and burdens of state action, and whether the policy may further equality at the expense of freedom or vice versa (not always a trade-off, but often). Policy directions, as opposed to particular proposals, are only rarely and marginally altered by the later formulation and adoption of measures spurred by them. They also often provide clues to future trends in other policy areas; libertarian or egalitarian or authoritarian tendencies emerge with some consistency in areas as diverse as labor, crime, and the arts. It would be a mistake, however, to assume that because policy directions seem to express a "national mood," a true consensus exists around the underlying assumptions of the policy.[23] If drug prohibition truly expressed a collective mind-set, there would presumably not have been an estimated 26 million people—nearly one-eighth the population ten years or older—who used legally forbidden drugs (most of them casual users of marijuana) at least once in 1991.[24]

The get-tough perspective on drugs is neither culturally nor historically inevitable. After the Hague Convention of 1912 first defined opiates as an international problem, Great Britain, the country whose general culture has most influenced ours, treated drug addiction as a public health issue, leaving it up to physicians to distribute opiates and cocaine.[25] And in this country it was not until well into the twentieth century that the criminal conception of drug abuse and addiction became the dominant force in public policy.[26] Opium products for medical treatment (including "quieting the nerves") were common from colonial times, patent medicines containing cocaine were widely sold in the nineteenth century, and marijuana was an ingredient in candy and other foods. A leading historical account of drug use in the United States describes attitudes toward opiates in the late nineteenth century:

> Employees were not fired for addiction. Wives did not divorce their addicted husbands, or husbands their addicted wives. Children were not taken from their homes and lodged in foster homes or institutions because one or both parents were addicted. Addicts continued to participate fully in the life of the community. Addicted children and young people continued to go to school, Sunday school, and college.[27]

Why, then, in the late nineteenth century, did we start down the repressive path for drug policy? It wasn't because of new discoveries about the dangers of opium and cocaine, nor was it based on evidence that compulsive use of those drugs was increasing so rapidly that only measures as dramatic as criminal penalties would communicate the dangers of the drugs. Opium use began to decline on its own, before federal controls were instituted, and the perception that opiates could be dangerous spread only gradually.[28] The explanation for prohibitionist directions lies elsewhere, in the extent to which the initial definition of "the drug problem" was determined by cultural, economic, organizational, and political imperatives only tangentially— and sometimes not at all—related to the physical and social harms caused by drugs; and in the nature of those imperatives.

The first drug prohibition law was a 1875 San Francisco ordinance prohibiting opium and aimed at Chinese workers, who were no longer needed to bring the railroad west and who were blamed for taking jobs of whites during a depression.[29] And the 1914 Harrison Act, the linchpin (until the 1970 passage of the Controlled Substances Act) of federal prohibitionist action, was not aimed primarily at social or health problems caused by drugs. Instead, it was the culmination of a foreign policy struggle in which the ambitious adventurer-diplomat Hamilton Wright had put the United States in the embarrassing position of telling other countries to do as it said, not as it did.[30] The legislative impetus for passage was the need for the United States at least to give the appearance of regulating its drug trade in order to comply with an international treaty that sought to keep any one nation from acquiring dominance in the profitable opium trade with China.[31]

The early measures restricting and criminalizing drug use and distribution had two elements in common, neither of which had anything to do with the prevalence of opium use or its dangers. Both were fueled by racial and economic antagonisms in the larger society, and both obscured the role of elites as sources of conflicts that generated policy. By importing and exploiting the Chinese, the railroad barons had brought American workers to heel and fostered racial bigotry and economic discord. And Hamilton Wright, wheeling and dealing at home and at international trade conferences, was not only furthering commercial relationships between the United States and China (regulation of the opium trade would relax other trade barriers) but finding expression for his own personal, all-embracing racism.[32]

It stands to reason that such forces would beget policies of exclusion, relying on law enforcement, rather than policies of nurturance that would treat drug abuse as a problem with medical solutions. The criminal law seeks to separate the wrongdoer from the respectable community he or she is presumed to taint. "If the Chinaman cannot get along without his 'dope,' " said a committee of the American Pharmaceutical Association in 1902, "we can get along without him."[33] Themes of racism and nativism, as well as methods of elite manipulation of social conflict, run through the subsequent history of drug policy and reinforce its prohibitionist tendency. Marijuana became a concern only when associated with "degenerate" Mexicans working on farms (and therefore taking scarce jobs from Americans) during the Great Depression in the Southwest.[34] Cocaine, a medical blessing when used as an anesthetic in the Civil War, came to be viewed as a dangerous stimulant when associated with blacks in the first two decades of the century, despite contemporary evidence that African-Americans were rarely users.[35] Over and over since then, political entrepreneurs have orchestrated drug scare campaigns in Congress and the press. Harry Anslinger, head of the Federal Bureau of Narcotics from 1930 to 1970, introduced Americans to "narcotics gangs" long before the emergence of South American cocaine cartels but just when Senator Estes Kefauver was unveiling the underworld of Sicilian organized crime.[36] In 1970 President Richard Nixon claimed to have succeeded in persuading television producers to include anti-drug themes in their series. His administration also promised to convict the top ten dealers in every city if Congress would enact new, tougher drug laws and spend more money on federal law enforcement agents to catch them.[37]

By this time the messages of nearly a century had turned prohibition (except as applied to marijuana) into an apparent inevitability supported by popular consensus. Liberals as well as conservatives—the harshest state drug laws of the day were supported by a liberal Republican, New York Governor Nelson Rockefeller—could make political capital out of get-tough positions on drugs. In the public mind, drug-taking and drug-selling had become unassailably criminal activities and drug policy was part and parcel of the criminal law.

The war on drugs thus signals the return of the dangerous classes. The designation of "dangerous classes" is not limited to particular regimes or eras, nor does it necessarily reflect the social harm they cause. Dangerous classes emerge in times of social or economic upheaval, created by the search for stability, and often quite independent of actual social harm caused by the groups so identified. In the United States the idea of dangerous classes sprang up in the second half of the nineteenth century, spurred by migration and immigration—the flow into cities of people displaced from farms by agricultural mechanization and from far-off lands by poverty and pogrom. Not until the Progressive Era, with its greater prosperity and ability to conceive of structural, or at least sociological, causes of civic disorder, did the notion fade.

Although the most visible and immediate dangers posed by "dangerous classes" were what we now call street crimes, behind them lay the shadows of a greater danger—the challenge to conditions that bred robbers and vagabonds. Labeling identifiable groups as pariahs, attributing their sins solely to individual agency, reduced the likelihood that respectable people would perceive social disorder as a reminder of the ways in which the social and economic arrangements of their society were failing them. For both kinds of danger, control supplied the solution.

## THE PROHIBITIONIST FUTURE

By defining "the drug problem" as primarily a target for law enforcement and loading it up with so many other social tensions, officials and early anti-drug activists broadened the appeal of joining the crusade beyond the original circle of moral entrepreneurs. Even otherwise politically uninvolved citizens could blame drugs for many real and imagined ills, and as a corollary, seek to exorcise them as relief from those other pains. Overt racism and political opportunism—while they still flourish in drug politics—are no longer necessary to sustain prohibitionism. A wider variety of concerns can now be packed into prohibition by a much wider range of political actors, especially as drug policy has remained an area where state and federal laws operate concurrently. The citizenry now plays as important a role in keeping drug policy on the political agenda as do the official actors in the policy game. Parents' groups all over the country constitute a formidable lobby in the crusade against marijuana. Public opinion surveys show that most people are willing to pay higher taxes to support tougher penalties for drug-dealing, and the National Punishment Survey found in 1987 that a representative sample of Americans supported prison sentences of more than ten years for cocaine wholesalers and more than five years for users.[38]

The establishment of this solid base of support, with its diverse sources, makes modification of the general trend, or even minor deviations from it, difficult even to discuss in public forums. The declared goal of drug prohibition at the federal level is a "drug-free America," as the most prominent national ad campaign puts it. This theme goes largely unchallenged, even though most Americans acknowledge the futility (or downright silliness) of seeking total eradication of drugs through abstinence, as measured by polls which show that a majority believe that some amount of drug use is here to stay.[39] Yet few political leaders have been unwilling to endorse more modest aims, increasingly popular in Europe, of reducing the physical and social harm that compulsive drug users do to themselves and others.[40] The policymaking process seems immune to evaluating the properties of drugs or distinctions between different dosages and methods of ingestion if such an investigation might tend to cast doubt on the fairness or effectiveness of the prohibitionist policy direction. Even projects that have been unequivocally shown to be life-saving, like the exchange of clean needles for dirty ones to protect intravenous drug users from acquired immunodeficiency syndrome (AIDS), have been rejected at the national level as out of step with the war against drugs, though that may change as more and more cities, like Seattle and New York, undertake such projects.

Whether this situation will change in the foreseeable future does not depend principally on the quality of drug research, or the persuasiveness of policy dissenters, or which party dominates Congress, state legislatures, or the White House. With its symbolic underpinnings, prohibition has become a monument to the larger projects of the cultural right: the veneration of the nuclear family and its traditional hierarchies, the (selective) conditioning of political benefits on standards of personal moral behavior, and the retreat from efforts to guarantee social equality for groups previously outside the white, middle-class, male-dominated mainstream. This association of the policy with a more general ideology means that while that perspective commands widespread attention, prohibition will continue to have powerful proponents. Only rejection of the cultural right—something which, again, can be achieved only in the agenda-setting aura of the policy process, not in legislative debate or program administration— or the discovery of a symbolic substitute will weaken the prohibition edifice. Repudiation of the rightist program won't come easily, since even those political elites and mass audiences who do not embrace it as a whole are attracted to some of its parts—as is evidenced by Clinton's embrace of a "get-tough" crime bill much like that of his Republican predecessors. One does not have to endorse the cramped social vision of former Vice President Dan Quayle to associate the images of home and hearth he evokes with longed-for material security, family stability, and community harmony. People will need to find alternative routes to the ends they yearn for to weaken prohibition's symbolic allure.

We will of course never be able to strip drug policy—or any other, for that matter—of its shadow agenda, nor should we want to. Symbolism contributes richness to political life, as dreams give meaning to sleep. By their very nature, all political acts carry latent meanings, many of which sustain in us our best hopes for civil society. (Think of the U.S. Constitution.) But giving equal weight to the hidden policy messages and thereby addressing the other, pressing social policy issues that they reveal might free us from our national obsession with illicit drugs, dilute the demonization of drug takers and sellers, and minimize the damage done to human beings and their environments by compulsive drug use. We might even, in the process, discover that we had reduced drug abuse.

# CHAPTER 2

# *Getting Tough on Illicit Drugs*

The morality plays of the late Middle Ages served more than a homiletic function. They reflected and perpetuated a larger medieval culture that integrated the realms of theology, economics, law, and social life.[1] The pains of death, the villainy of the usurer, the benevolence or calumny of the feudal lord—all were channeled into abstract contests of good and evil, metaphors of ruin and redemption. American drug prohibition at the end of the twentieth century has a similar dual role. Its scope and content not only set moral boundaries but also express fears, antagonisms, and ambitions beyond the usual reach of the criminal law.

For both sets of actors in the policy drama—policymakers and voters—the drug dealer is a politically certified demon. Scapegoats are most useful when not blameless. The young punk on the streets of Harlem can be attacked with impunity because his law-abiding neighbors are attacking him too; the Colombian or Turkish "kingpin" who deploys planes and boats and oversees a chain of command of hundreds of people cannot credibly claim bias on the part of those seeking to wipe him out. Both serve as the frightening (and alluring) link between unrewarding reality in ordinary life and the dramatic, glamourized images of television entertainment. They are highly visible stand-ins for underlying problems that citizens and leaders alike shrink from confronting.

Earlier American drug wars have left a legacy that colors the current one; the theme of racial antagonism and the device of demonizing users and sellers are recurring.[2] But the drug war that began in the 1980s is more complex than those of earlier periods. It is being fought on more fronts—in foreign countries, on inner-city streets, in farm fields and office rest rooms—and it is costlier, in both economic and social terms. Most significant for understanding prohibition as a symbolic vehicle, the weapons employed have great variety and are wielded within all institutions of social control—schools and families, as well as the traditional institutions of criminal justice.

## WEAPONS OF WAR

Today's efforts to realize the general prohibitionist aim are comprehensive and tough, aimed at both cutting off the supply of illicit drugs and eliminating demand for them. As "a lineal descendant of the war on crime," prohibitionist drug policy is high on the agendas of governments at all levels and is strongly supported by the general public, business, and interest groups associated with such fields as education and criminal justice.[3] Despite protests that drug enforcement is ineffective at reducing the most destructive forms of drug abuse, often takes liberties with individual rights, and selectively targets poor and minority populations, the war on drugs also gets support from urban minority constituencies who are hardest hit by compulsive drug use. It includes both corrective and preventive elements, though the line between them sometimes blurs.

During the 1980s U.S. prison and probation populations, already on the rise during the previous decade, took off. In 1980 state and federal prisons held 315,974 sentenced prisoners, at a rate of 138 per 100,000 residents (already a record); by 1992 the number had risen to 883,593, for a rate of 329.[4] In the second half of the decade alone, the number of people in some form of correctional custody—prison, jail, probation, or parole—increased by 48 percent, from 2.9 million to 4.3 million. By 1990, according to the U.S. Department of Justice, 2.35 percent of the adult resident population of the country was under correctional supervision.[5]

Although we don't have perfect data for tracing the mechanisms that produced this situation, it is clear that drug prohibition has been the lump in the boa constrictor of the decade's get-tough crime-control program. More than other mandates of the criminal law, it brought people into prison and onto probation. And the increase in time served in prison for violation of drug laws outstrips increases for other crimes.

During the 1980s estimated arrests nationwide for violations of drug laws almost doubled, from 581,000 in 1980 to 1,090,000 in 1990.[6] While we lack complete data for a decade-long national picture of trends in convictions and sentences for drug offenses, what we do

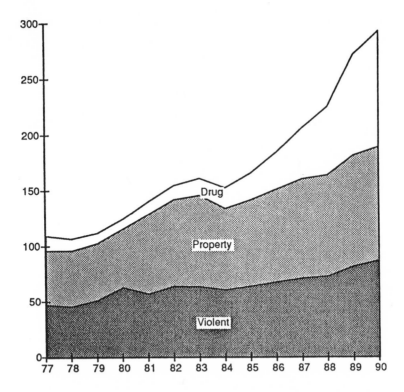

*Fig. 1.* Surge in drug convictions: Number of new court commitments by offense (in 1,000), 1977 to 1990. *Source: U.S. Department of Justice, Bureau of Justice Statistics. ''Prisoners in 1992.''* Bulletin, *May 1993, Fig. 1 (and underlying data kindly provided by Bureau of Justice Statistics staff).*

have suggests an even greater jump than for arrests; while we apprehended more suspects, we were even more vigorous in prosecuting them. Figure 1 shows the surge in court commitments to prison for drug convictions relative to other types of offenses during the 1980s. Figure 2 demonstrates that a drug arrest was five times more likely to result in a court commitment to state prison in 1990 than ten years earlier.

The punitive trend in drug enforcement is particularly striking in the federal correctional system, where national drug legislation has its most immediate impact. The number of defendants sentenced to prison for federal drug offenses increased by 298 percent between 1980 and 1990, while the number sentenced for all offenses rose by 111 percent.[7] By 1990 there were 25,311 drug offenders in federal

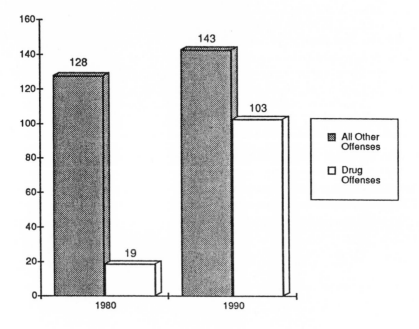

*Fig. 2.* Turning drug arrests into convictions: Frequency of court commitments to state prisons per 1,000 arrests, 1980 to 1990. *Source: U.S. Department of Justice, Bureau of Justice Statistics. "Prisoners in 1992." Bulletin, May 1993, Table 12.*

prisons, more than the total number of prisoners in 1980.[8] More than half of all federal inmates (54.2 percent) were in prison for drug offenses.[9]

The difficulties of collecting comparable data from fifty states preclude knowing just how many state inmates are doing time for drug offenses, but recent data documenting the flow of felony cases during the latter half of the decade are revealing.[10] The Department of Justice estimates that there were 274,613 state felony drug convictions in 1990; the 168,360 of those judgments that were for trafficking constituted a 120 percent increase over the number in 1986, just four years previously.[11] (By contrast, the increases in convictions for robbery and aggravated assault over that period were 12 percent and 41 percent, respectively.) State courts sent 87,859 drug offenders to prison in 1989, an increase of 665 percent over 1981, while commitments for all offenses in that same period doubled.[12] In some states the increases are even greater; data from California for the decade show a tenfold increase in felony drug offenders sent to prison.[13] In 1980 about one in fifteen offenders sent by courts to state prisons had been convicted of a drug law violation; by 1990 the proportion had risen to one in three.[14]

The contribution of drug prohibition to increases in the country's incarceration rate comes not only from sending more people to prison but also from keeping drug offenders there for longer periods. Tougher federal drug laws and changes in federal sentencing practices (particularly the advent of mandatory sentences and the abolition of parole) have shifted sentencing in federal courts away from probation and toward more prison terms. Between 1986 and the first half of 1990 the share of federal sentences to probation for drug offenses dropped from 40 percent to 17 percent.[15] Federal drug prisoners are being incarcerated for longer periods, also; between 1980 and 1989 federal drug sentences lengthened by 59 percent, while the comparable increase for all offenses was 23 percent.[16] Mandatory minimum sentences drove up actual time served by 40 percent in just the years between 1985 and 1990. (The period of incarceration also increased for other federal crimes, but by less.[17]) It is fair to conclude from federal sentencing trends of the past twenty years that where drug law violations were formerly treated in district courts like property crimes they are now treated like violent crimes.[18]

State drug policies vary a good deal, but the trend in the late 1980s was definitely toward tougher treatment of drug defendants. A National Criminal Justice Association report found that between 1987 and 1990 at least fourteen states increased penalties for drug possession and at least fifteen for manufacturing and distribution; all but one state increased penalties for distributing drugs to minors.[19] Estimates tallied by the Department of Justice of the minimum time that newly sentenced state drug offenders would spend in prison increased from a mean of twenty-seven months in 1986 to thirty-seven months just three years later.[20] Reflecting the relative priority of drug sanctions, the Department of Justice also estimated that time served would actually go *down* for felony offenders sentenced in 1986 and 1990 to state prisons for the crimes of rape, robbery, aggravated assault, burglary, and larceny.[21] (In the federal system average sentences for some of these crimes have gone down in recent years, also.[22])

What this attenuated statistical picture leaves out is the dramatic randomness of the extremes. On the one hand, mandatory penalties for even minor crimes mean that some prisons are filling up with the plankton of the drug business, nonviolent adolescents who finance their purchases of athletic shoes (and sometimes their families' rents) with occasional employment selling drugs on the street.[23] On the other hand, dealers farther up the line may evade prison terms altogether by agreeing to cooperate in law enforcement investigations of their colleagues or bosses.[24] Life sentences without possibility of parole are imposed in some jurisdictions—Michigan and the federal system, for example—for mere drug couriers as well as for career criminals.[25] The 1990 survey of state drug laws by the National Criminal Justice Association found that in Idaho, Kansas, Louisiana, Michigan, Montana, Nevada, Oklahoma, and Rhode Island, a first-time drug offender can be sentenced to life imprisonment.[26] Almost a thousand people received life sentences in state courts for drug offenses in 1989.[27]

Punishing drug offenders has become a feature of neighborhood life, too. Putting more people in prison and keeping them there longer has crowded the institutions and spurred building programs; loading drug offenders into various forms of community supervision is transforming what used to be relatively straightforward penalties. More than 3 million people were on probation and parole in 1990, up almost 150 percent since 1979.[28] We do not have data on how many of this number had been convicted of drug abuse violations, but a survey of felony convictions in state courts in 1986 revealed that more than three-fifths of convicted drug traffickers were assigned to probation.[29] Anecdotal evidence from large cities suggests that lower-level drug-dealing is an extremely common offense among probationers.

The need for nonincarcerative sentences for felony drug offenders as the prisons ran out of room was probably the principal stimulus for the development of new "intermediate punishments." These are forms of community supervision that are cheaper and more readily available than prison but tougher than conventional probation. Most common is intensive probation, where more is required of the probationer—common conditions include holding down a job, submitting to unannounced drug tests, performing community service, and paying restitution to one's victim—and the probation officer drops by frequently to check on the probationer's whereabouts and behavior (and, in the best cases, to offer moral support and concrete assistance).[30] Day fines (which relate the offender's financial obligation to ability to pay), home confinement, and electronic monitoring (connecting offenders through a plastic bracelet or anklet to a computer to keep track of their whereabouts) are also increasingly popular as "interventions that are beginning to fill the sentencing gap between prison at one extreme and probation at the other."[31]

## ADDING CIVIL PENALTIES TO THE ARSENAL

Criminologists have developed a variety of rationales for criminal punishment. During most of the twentieth century, utilitarian perspectives, justifying punishment with its potential for reducing criminal behavior, have been theoretically more acceptable than the purely moral argument that punishment has only to be deserved, that the offender's culpability demands societal response to restore moral balance.[32] But in the last twenty years, the sentencing philosophies of incapacitation and rehabilitation have come under a cloud that refuses to dissipate. It has become apparent that in many areas of crime there is an almost endless supply of potential offenders to take the place of those who were sent away and that providing inmates with counseling and job training only rarely alters their life chances sufficiently to keep them from getting into trouble once released.

One response to this dilemma has been to give more prominence to retribution (sometimes called "just deserts") and to the deterrence rationale, which holds that punishment will send a message to those contemplating crime (and to the person being punished, who will presumably someday resume a life where relatively unfettered behavior choices can again be made). The perspectives are evident not only in the intensification of traditional criminal punishments but also in some of the more innovative features of the drug war.

Taking a cue from the occasional practice of requiring civil commitment for treatment of drug abuse, prohibition now encompasses a variety of civil penalties as well as the more usual criminal ones. The Anti-Drug Abuse Act of 1988 includes "user accountability" provisions that allow (or require) a judge to strip a convicted drug offender of such federal benefits as a student loan, a research grant, or a mortgage guarantee.[33] Federal and state courts—most notably, the courts of Rhode Island—have begun to impose these penalties.[34] Many states now suspend the driver's license of a drug offender, whether convicted of possession or dealing and even when the offense is not driving-related.[35] The federal government has expanded the theme of civil punishment beyond offenders themselves by threatening to punish states that do not enact such laws by withholding their highway funds.[36]

One of the most visible recent penalties—often imposed before any determination of guilt, and sometimes instead of it—has been civil asset forfeiture, the seizure of cash and cars (most commonly), boats, and even farms and businesses where law enforcement officers suspect that manufacture, sale, or purchase of illicit drugs has taken place.[37] The rationales of this policy choice are that it "attack[s] the economic foundations of crime," in the words of the federal official in charge of the program, and that news of the confiscation will spread quickly among potential drug buyers or sellers, driving them to another jurisdiction or, in the case of dealers, out of the business entirely.[38] Then–Attorney General Dick Thornburgh merged the rationales when he said, in 1990, "It is poetic justice when money seized from drug dealers is now going to be used to help wipe out the stain of drug trafficking. Our new message to drug profiteers is 'You make it, we'll take it.' "[39] The message to potential purchasers, like the spectacle of medieval hangings conducted in the town square, also seems to drive the practice of forfeiture; banners erected across city streets make proclamations like, "Car Seizure Program in Progress: Drive In for Drugs and Walk Out."[40]

The seizure of drug offenders' assets—often done at the time of arrest—is one of several drug war measures where a penalty is imposed by civil law long before the completion of any disinterested and constitutional process of apprehending possible culprits and determining their guilt.[41] The practice of asset forfeiture originates in English common law and is justified as less oppressive than conventional contemporary punishments without trial (and therefore not carrying with it the baggage of due-process protections) because action is taken against the *res,* rather than the person. But the line between deprivations of liberty and mere property can be very blurry, as when a car needed for employment is confiscated, or businesses thought to be fronting for drug operations are shut down without the cumbersome niceties of criminal court proceedings. And asset forfeiture often rides roughshod over the rights of the person whose property was used for drug activity without his or her knowledge, the "innocent owner," in legal jargon.[42]

As with the "get-tough" street crime program of the 1970s and 1980s, the perceived state of drug abuse emergency, with its requirement that law enforcement become more efficient at capturing and confining offenders, has justified a significant narrowing of procedural protections for defendants suspected of or charged with drug crimes.[43] Prime among constitutional icons that the drug war is toppling is the Fourth Amendment prohibition against unreasonable search and seizure.[44] The Supreme Court has become increasingly indulgent of extraordinary measures taken in the investigation of drug cases, such as drug-sniffing dogs and electronic tracking of persons and things.[45]

Narrowing the definition of what constitutes a search has combined with a permissive attitude toward requiring a warrant for police searches to result in effectively abandoning the protection of a warrant for vehicle searches.[46] And the Supreme Court recently ruled that a police chase is not a seizure requiring Fourth Amendment protection if it neither exerts physical force on the suspect nor involves a "show of authority" on the part of police.[47] This means that drugs or other evidence tossed aside by someone who takes off at the sight of police can be admitted in evidence in a later trial even if the police giving chase did so without the reasonable suspicion constitutionally required for a seizure.

This case is one of many that illustrate the whittling away of the principal means of enforcing the Fourth Amendment, the exclusionary rule, which requires that illegally seized evidence (which these days often means drugs or their profits or the paraphernalia used in consuming or making them) be excluded from trial. The break came in 1984, when the Supreme Court ruled that illegally seized evidence—in one of two companion cases it was indeed drugs—could be admitted in court if the police genuinely and reasonably believed the warrants they had obtained to conduct the search were valid.[48] The "good faith exception" technically applies only to searches pursuant to a warrant; for nonwarrant searches (where a suspect has consented to being searched or there is no time to obtain a warrant) admissibility of the evidence depends on the "totality of the circumstances" under which the seizure was made, a discretionary judicial evaluation which, in effect, permits good faith mistakes in that circumstance, too.[49]

Although some of the policies described above (such as asset forfeiture) are intended in part to make drug consumption and distribution more difficult, their principal effect is to deal with malefactors. The war on drugs also includes efforts that focus primarily on interfering with the market mechanisms of drug businesses.

The preventive policies include the federal commitment to protecting national borders from drug importation, as well as international cooperation (and, in the case of Panama, military intervention) to deter foreign growers from finding American markets. But the policies that are most likely to enlist ordinary citizens and grass-roots activists in prohibition enforcement are those most immediately aimed at thwarting supply and demand. Examples include local ordinances that prohibit loitering for the purpose of buying and selling drugs; enhanced penalties for drug-dealing in particular locations, like near a school; and programs that facilitate closing down inner-city buildings suspected of harboring the drug trade.[50] It is also in this area that prohibition enforcement reaches beyond the criminal justice system. Not only the neighborhood-watch groups that co-operate with police are involved; suburban parents, for example, and high-school teachers have become, privately and collectively, enforcement agents. Their efforts are usually directed at potential rather than actual markets—drug screening, for example, to keep the trade out of schools and offices and public housing.[51]

## COSTS OF WAR

Even a brief exposition of the scope of prohibition should include a glimpse at the economic and political commitments the policies entail. Identifying "the drug problem" as a high-priority matter for government action and choosing to address it primarily with law enforcement measures has meant that extraordinary amounts of public resources have been devoted to it in recent years, especially for a period when the federal deficit is also a major concern and governments at lower levels are in a constant state of fiscal crisis.[52]

Unlike most public services, criminal justice became a better and better source of employment in the 1980s, thanks largely to the drug problem. Jobs in police agencies (federal, state, and local) increased by 36 percent between 1982 and 1990; judicial and legal services personnel (judges, court officers, prosecutors, and publicly supported defense lawyers), by 46 percent; and corrections staffs, by 86 percent.[53] (Total government employment—federal, state, and local—increased by only 16 percent during that period.[54]) Specialized drug units in state and local police and sheriffs' departments employed almost 19,000 officers full-time in 1990.[55] The U.S. Labor Department has designated the job of correction officer one of the fastest growing occupations and predicts that it will remain so for the rest of the decade.[56] At the national level, the number of federal judges almost doubled during the decade between 1981 and 1991. When it became clear that eastern European spies no longer constituted a domestic threat, the Federal Bureau of Investigation (FBI) reassigned the more than 300 agents in its foreign counterintelligence unit to the investigation of urban street gangs—in other words, drug punks.[57] The explosion in federal drug cases has necessitated a huge increase in the time of U.S. attorneys and federal investigators spent on those cases. The Drug Enforcement Administration (DEA), the largest specialized police force in the federal government, grew like kudzu

1980s, from a budget of under $200 million at the beginning of the decade to $719 million for 1993.[58]

All of this adds up. The federal budget for drug control exceeded $13 billion for fiscal year 1994, about two-thirds of it for law enforcement—as distinct from "prevention" and "treatment"—at home and abroad.[59] Precise figures on state and local expenditures for the drug war are unavailable, but Peter Reuter, a distinguished American researcher on the economics of drug control, estimates that in 1990 (when the federal drug budget was a mere $6.7 billion) those governments spent about $18 billion, 80 percent of it for law enforcement.[60] We should also consider that much of the rest of expenditures at all levels of government are part of the commitment to prohibition. "Prevention," "education," and "treatment" are often misnomers, as funds earmarked for these activities may be spent on exhortation not to take the drugs that are legally prohibited and "information" (outright propaganda) on the dangers of those drugs, rather than on the presentation of scientifically verifiable information on such subjects as the pharmacology of psychoactive substances and the physiological and psychological consequences of ingesting various substances with varying frequency. Some prevention and education programs—like DARE (it stands for Drug Abuse Resistance Education), which sends "patrol-hardened, veteran police officers" into schools to "shore up the classroom teacher's anti-drug instruction" —have such close links to law enforcement that they must at times serve a surveillance function, identifying "at-risk" youth for later drug enforcement attention.[61]

The commitment to drug prohibition has consequences for political structure as well as for political contests and the definition of individual liberties. For most of our history, law enforcement has been primarily a local function, with significant variations in the criminal laws of the states and the key discretionary decisions of the criminal process made by local judges, prosecutors, and police forces. In the twentieth century that pattern began to erode, however, with drug prohibition leading the trend.[62] In 1914 the Harrison Act set national standards for the regulation of psychoactive substances, and the Comprehensive Drug Abuse Prevention and Control Act of 1970 (as well as more recent legislation extending that Act) widened federal jurisdiction over drug offenses. Drug law violations constitute a larger and larger proportion of criminal cases handled by U.S. attorneys' offices, the federal government has half-a-dozen agencies with substantial responsibility for drug control, and Zimring and Hawkins argue plausibly that 70 percent of drug law enforcement now takes place at the national level.[63] Federal initiatives also spurred the war on street crime that began with the Safe Streets Act of 1968—with activities like joint national-local task forces of police and prosecutors and grants to local law enforcement for such specialized programs as career criminal units. As variants on these programs became standard features of criminal justice at the local level, a pattern has emerged: National government dominates, local governments cooperate and imitate.[64] The result is that, at least in the cities, a subtle mix of domination, cooperation, and imitation is gradually rendering local and national law enforcement virtually indistinguishable.

## VISITING THE BATTLEFIELDS

The data in the previous pages serve as a kind of aerial reconnaissance of the war on drugs. As general surveys of trends in the drug war's arsenal, however, they do scant justice to the various and interdependent forces shaping commitments to drug prohibition. To deepen our understanding, we need to hover over the actual fields of battle. My case studies of drug policymaking, which comprise the next five chapters of this book, are intended to give us a closer look.

In choosing particular engagements I sought to focus primarily on the earliest and most seminal stages of drug prohibition policymaking. All three branches of government make public policy. The image of courts as dealing only with the relations of contesting parties and resolving past disputes collapses when appellate decisions touch on far-reaching questions with implications for the future, like the constitutionality of economic regulation or the scope of civil rights laws. And administrative agencies go far beyond their textbook role of implementation when their task is to give meaning to some broad legislative mandate such as the income tax or the prohibition against price-fixing. Nonetheless, there is a sense in which legislative enactment constitutes primary policymaking, collective action from which rule-making in the other branches derives its authority. The site of democracy is the statehouse, not the judge's chambers or the executive agency. It is in legislation that we envisage citizens or their representatives coming together to set public rules for future conduct.

If the study of legislative activity is set in a broad sociopolitical context, we can learn from it not only "who gets what, when, how" but why its subject captured the attention of the legislators.[65] Even if answering this question does not give us immediately generalizable information—we are learning, after all, only a little about how one particular policy came to be—it does so at the stage of the process where social and political life overlap. In championing the consent of the governed, democracy holds forth the possibility for every group and individual that what start out as private troubles may become matters of public concern and action. Whether the promise is realized depends in large part on the core exercise of power at the point of conversion—on the forces that create an issue, characterize it, and designate its sponsors. Later battles of a judicial or administrative kind may be more likely to determine a particular policy outcome— consider court decisions on abortion or school prayer and Food and Drug Administration (FDA) rulings on drugs for AIDS or cancer. But the first impulses for public action are usually legislative.

For this reason I have chosen for my case studies five examples of legislative process in action, at national, state, and local levels. The players are not always professional legislators; one citizen initiative and a ballot proposition are included, to capture direct as well as representative policymaking. Furthermore, legislation is rarely the last word. Administrative regulations may refine legislative directives al- most beyond recognition, and implementation may suggest ends that were not acknowledged in a policy's enactment; police in Anchorage have been notably cool toward their new license for controlling mar- ijuana use. In the case of the Michigan drug possession law, the policy has been rejected in part by a court of last resort, and the U.S. Supreme Court may throw out a loitering law very similar to the one in Seattle; the recriminalization of marijuana possession in Alaska is also being tested in the courts. But whether these policies survive or not, their genesis can tell us something about the culture—political and otherwise—that spawned them and the twists and turns of transfor- mation from individual and collective worry into someone's idea of the appropriate state solution. In watching the drug policy agenda take shape, we also encounter a culture that is generating other social policy initiatives—welfare reform, for instance—heavily freighted with moral concerns.

Referring to the importance of understanding the motivations of political activists and leaders, Harold Lasswell wrote, "Political science without biography is a form of taxidermy."[66] I think of the cases that follow as policy biographies, stories that can enliven the abstractions that explain the policy process and provide context for the instru- mental and symbolic politics that characterizes policymaking in social policy areas. In the service of drug prohibition these policy campaigns

THE RETURN OF THE DANGEROUS CLASSES

illustrate the formulation and application of legislative command, the marshalling of threat and incentive to mobilize general and interest-group support, the manipulation of organizational and political imperatives, and the creation and dissemination of propaganda. They also show us why change is so elusive in our solidly prohibitionist drug policy.

*Part II*

# SNAPSHOTS
## OF
# AMERICAN DRUG
# PROHIBITION

# Chapter 3

## The Kingpin Must Die

As this book goes to press, the American death row population is at an all-time high. It is primarily a state-sentenced group; only 5 of the 2,802 occupants of death rows in January 1994—all of them convicted of murders related to their illicit drug businesses—were federal inmates.[1] If Congress has its way, this pattern will change.

The death penalty in the United States is imposed in only a very small fraction of murder cases, and it is even more infrequently carried out. In 1988, for example, there were 9,340 convictions for murder (including non-negligent manslaughter) in state courts—only one federal capital sentence was imposed between 1960 and 1990—but only 296 death sentences—one-thirtieth the number of murder convictions—and only eleven executions.[2] Ten of the executions were carried out by southern states, reflecting the disproportionate imposition of the death penalty in the South and on blacks.[3] Of the total death row population nationwide as of January 1994, 1,117 (39.86 percent) were black; 1,557 (55.57 percent) had been sentenced in southern states.[4] The death penalty is now generally reserved for murders where aggravating circumstances are found—though this does not mean that it is applied only to the most heinous crimes.

This picture of relative parsimony is fairly recent, established since state death penalty statutes were rewritten in light of the 1972 Supreme Court case of *Furman v. Georgia*, which found the death penalty statutes of Georgia and Texas (and, by implication, those of thirty-seven other states, the District of Columbia, and the federal government) cruel and unusual punishment in violation of the Eighth and Fourteenth Amendments.[5] Post–Civil War executions had peaked at 190 in 1938, but then began to decline, although until the 1950s there were always more than 100 executions in the country each year.[6] Capital punishment was less strongly regional in the past, though the pattern of southern predominance, in part a legacy of slavery, still existed.[7] The racial disproportionality now observable in the imposition of the death penalty was even more striking in the early decades of the century; in every year of the 1940s executed blacks outnumbered whites.

At the time of the *Furman* decision the death penalty was imposed for rape as well as murder, and occasionally for other offenses, like robbery or kidnapping; in 1971 sixteen states and the federal government still included rape among capital offenses.[8] During the 1940s, 17 percent of executions around the country were for crimes other than murder; 198 people were executed for rape (only 19 of them white).[9] In 1977, however, the Supreme Court, in a plurality opinion, ruled that "a sentence of death is grossly disproportionate and excessive punishment for the crime of rape and is therefore forbidden by the Eighth Amendment as cruel and unusual punishment."[10] Presumably, as a corollary of this decision, such crimes as robbery or arson would also come within the prohibition. But a decade later the Court permitted the imposition of the death penalty on two brothers who were convicted with two other men of murdering a family of four, even though they did not intend to kill the victims and did not actually take part in the killing.[11]

A number of recent cases, in fact, suggest stronger judicial support for state discretion in imposing the sentence of death, a trend that may lead to a rise in executions in the 1990s and beyond. (In 1993 there were thirty-eight executions in the United States, the largest number in more than thirty years.[12]) The Supreme Court has refused to find it constitutionally cruel and unusual to execute defendants who were mentally retarded or still juveniles at the time of their crimes.[13] And it has ruled that statistical evidence of racial bias in jury decisions to impose the death penalty does not pose a "constitutionally significant risk" of bias in the imposition of an individual sentence; racial influence on the imposition of capital punishment violates due process only if bias can be shown in that specific case.[14] The Court has further upheld state procedures for capital cases even when they refuse to take into account evidence of innocence that came to light after trial.[15]

A bulwark sustaining continued Supreme Court endorsement for the death penalty has been public support for it. In *Gregg v. Georgia*, the 1976 case that established the two-stage process (separate determinations of guilt and penalty) now required in capital cases, the plurality noted "society's endorsement of the death penalty for murder"—expressed through state legislation, jury decisions, and one state referendum—as an appropriate consideration in deciding whether it was unconstitutionally cruel.[16] Although support, as measured by the Gallup Poll, fell in the late 1950s and 1960s, it began to rise again in the late 1960s (ironically, just as courts briefly showed concern about the constitutionality of the death penalty) and grew steadily until the 1980s.[17] In recent years it appears to be holding steady at between 70 and 80 percent of the population (according to which survey you read). Data from the National Opinion Research Center show little variation in support by age, educational level, or type of occupation; and regional differences are probably now less pronounced than they once were. While gaps exist between the generations, between men and women, Republicans and Democrats, whites and blacks, rich and poor, it is striking that, with the exception of blacks, a majority of even those groups less likely to favor capital punishment—women, Democrats, low-income people, and the young—do so.[18] Apparently anger at violent crime, impatience with what is perceived as unnecessary delay in meting out justice, and belief in the deterrent value of capital punishment outweigh any commitment to individual rights in this area and public awareness that capital sentencing is often arbitrary.

## THE DEATH PENALTY RETURNS TO WASHINGTON

The history of the development of congressional consensus for making drug kingpin trafficking a capital offense has three stages: (1) the discovery of the political utility of "the drug problem" for furthering the development of a general federal death penalty; (2) the addition of drug-related murders when committed by kingpins to the list of capital offenses to be included in a federal death penalty; and (3) the innovation of including kingpin activity—selling illicit drugs as a leader of a "continuing criminal enterprise" that deals in volume—on that list, even where no death resulted.

Ever since states began rewriting their capital punishment laws in the mid-1970s to make them constitutionally acceptable, the issue has had electoral significance.[19] Many candidates for state office (and sometimes mayoral candidates, too) feel it necessary to declare their position on the death penalty; candidates in 1990 gubernatorial races in Florida, Texas, and California squabbled over who was the *real* death penalty candidate.[20] Where one stands has become a test of an

47

elected official's toughness on crime and, more generally, responsiveness to deeply held moral views of constituents. Political salience
arrived late at the national level, however, reflecting in part the fed-
eralist presumption that law enforcement should be primarily a local
matter, and in part the power of liberal senior members of Congress
to stall death penalty legislation during the decade after the *Gregg*
case set out standards for the imposition of capital punishment.

Until 1988, efforts to reinstate the federal death penalty were un-
availing. The sole exception was a provision allowing a sentence of
death for homicides occurring during an act of air piracy.[21] Passed
in 1974 under conditions of momentary panic over a rash of air
hijacking incidents, the provision has never been applied. (The last
federal death sentence was carried out in 1964, imposed on an Iowa
man convicted of murder and kidnapping.)

But substantive irrelevance does not diminish symbolic utility. Supporting death penalty legislation has become a costless way for senators and representatives in Congress to demonstrate vigilance against
predatory crime, so opportunities to modify and expand the scope of
capital punishment in a high-crime era continue to be attractive.

The development of federal legislation that would more generally
recognize the legitimacy of death as the ultimate punishment and
would therefore include a much broader range of capital offenses has
become an increasingly important project for cultural conservatives.
In the years immediately following *Furman*, conservatives in Congress
attempted to include a general death penalty in the overhaul of the
federal criminal code; for two years in a row President Nixon called
for capital punishment in his State of the Union speeches and followed
it up by sending death penalty bills to Congress.[22] But comprehensive
code revision proved to be an ill-fated effort. It generated too many
controversies (including capital punishment), and it ran afoul of the
House Judiciary Committee, where Chairman Peter Rodino (Dem-
ocrat-N.J.) had staked his liberal credentials on holding up get-tough
crime legislation. Criminal code revision was finally set aside in 1982,
though chunks of it—sentencing guidelines, preventive detention—
re-emerged in the Comprehensive Crime Control Act of 1984. Support for capital punishment remained strong in both parties (though
Republicans and southerners dominated), however, and the active
death penalty proponents continued to look for another avenue.

## DEATH FOR DRUG MURDERS

During the 1980s the model for federal crime legislation was the omnibus bill. On the one hand, the idea of comprehensiveness, of legislation that takes on a problem in its entirety, appears to be responsibly policy-oriented. But combining many ideas often results in confused political messages and invites political sleight of hand. Real debate over specifics is elusive because there is so much partisan posturing over what are perceived to be the overall directions of the legislation. Bargaining and compromise on the specifics of the bill become difficult when they come to stand for the whole. It is often the fate of the omnibus bill to become stalled on one or two sticking points; its size and complexity also mean that sometimes important provisions and programs can be buried in it and passed with little or no debate.

The omnibus approach attracts policy entrepreneurs whose favorite issues are homeless. In 1986 a handful of minority congressional staffers were working with the legislative counsel's office in the Department of Justice to figure out ways of reinstating a federal death penalty. One important opportunity arose out of highly publicized evidence of the ravages of drug abuse: the death in June of Len Bias, a University of Maryland basketball star, from a cocaine overdose; the appearance of crack cocaine on the streets of big cities; and drug-related killings of law enforcement officers, including the kidnapping and torture in Mexico of Enrique Camerena, a federal Drug Enforcement Administration agent. Drug politics played a role, too. House Minority Leader Robert Michel (Republican-Ill.), searching for a banner for Republicans to wave during the upcoming congressional elections, had set up a task force to develop a tough and sweeping set of legislative proposals; and in late July Speaker Thomas P. O'Neill (Democrat-Mass.) announced that a tough anti-drug package would be a priority for passage in the fall.[23]

Although the idea of a federal death penalty for drug-related murders had been floating around for some time, the Reagan administration position on expanding the death penalty for drug crimes was as yet undeveloped. The President had told *Newsweek* in May 1986 that executing drug dealers "would be counterproductive," while Vice President Bush, who was then in charge of the White House drug policy, disagreed, noting that drugs were "a great threat to our society."[24] But President Reagan and the First Lady were preparing the announcement in September of a "national crusade against drugs," and the atmosphere of urgency about the drug problem suggested that few proposals would be regarded as unduly harsh.[25] A large majority of respondents to a *New York Times* poll made public in early September said they would be willing to pay higher taxes for imprisoning drug dealers.[26] "The time has come to turn some of the screws," commented Representative Glenn English (Democrat-Okla.), whose role in oversight of federal drug programs—he was Chairman of the Government Operations Subcommittee on Government Information, Justice and Agriculture—made him a key player in the development of the omnibus bill.[27]

The $2 billion crime package that zipped through legislative review in the House in the late summer—it cleared twelve committees in seven weeks—was an ideal vehicle for a drug crime death penalty. Its hard-line proposals included mandatory life sentences without parole for selling drugs near schools; a major exception to the exclusionary rule, which prohibits evidence seized in violation of the Fourth Amendment from being used in a criminal trial; and authorization for military involvement in drug interdiction.[28] For several months Republican Congressman George W. Gekas of Pennsylvania (first elected in 1982, a former prosecutor and state legislator) had been trying to get approval of a proposal for the death penalty for murders committed by drug dealers in the course of managing a "continuing criminal enterprise" (already called "drug kingpins"). It had been defeated on a party-line vote in the House Subcommittee on Crime, chaired by New Jersey Democrat William Hughes, and in the Judiciary Committee (though not by much; the vote was 16 to 19).[29] Now Gekas saw his chance, and he introduced the measure when the omnibus drug bill came to the House floor, where it passed, 296 to 112, in a late-night frenzy of get-tough lawmaking. Although the proposal died in the Senate, where opponents threatened to filibuster over it, the overwhelming House support, combined with Senate pro–death penalty votes in previous congressional sessions, suggested that this was an idea with a future.

It re-emerged in the omnibus drug bill of 1988, this time along with proposals for several other capital crimes, the beginning of a wider effort to establish a general federal death penalty. Senator Alfonse D'Amato (Republican-N.Y.), noting the proposal's success on the House floor in the previous session, took a leadership role this time, pushing the death penalty for kingpins who killed recklessly as well as intentionally. In the House the Judiciary Committee once again rejected a Gekas amendment—it required the traditional element of intent but went beyond the D'Amato proposal in proposing

the penalty of death for anyone who killed another during the commission of a drug felony—but the congressman took his crusade
directly to the floor, where he again prevailed.[30] Despite compromises
in the conference committee, the bill that cleared both houses on
October 22—the last day of Congress before adjournment—reflected
the pressures of pro–death penalty Republicans and the reluctance
of wary Democrats to take positions in opposition to a measure aimed
at what President Reagan had just called "vicious killers" in a national
radio address.[31] It permitted the death penalty for intentional killing
by kingpins in the furtherance of a "continuing criminal enterprise"
and for the murder of law enforcement officers by anyone engaged
in "a drug-related felony offense."[32] Legislators could now face their
constituents during fall election campaigns, having sent the message
to the nation that they supported capital punishment for some drug-
related murders. Reagan signed the drug kingpin bill into law just
after the 1988 election.

(As of this writing, the law has not been used for the Colombian
drug lords commonly perceived as the villains of the piece. In May
1990, David Ronald Chandler was the first person sentenced to death
under it—an Alabama marijuana dealer convicted of hiring someone
to kill a member of his drug ring who was said to have become an
informer.[33] Almost three years later, a federal jury in Richmond sentenced three young, black local drug gang members to death for
murders they committed to protect their crack trade.[34] In separate
cases in 1993 two Hispanic drug distributors, one in Brownsville,
Texas, and one in Muskogee, Oklahoma, were sentenced to death.[35]
Those remain the only federal capital sentences imposed for drug
murders.)

## DEATH FOR DRUG-TRAFFICKING?

In 1988, during his first presidential campaign, then–Vice President
Bush had already hinted that he might try to go Congress one better.
At a speech to the Coast Guard on the campaign trail he raised
the idea that drug-trafficking alone—at least at the "kingpin" level
—should be grounds for the death penalty. Although the idea had
not been blessed by Congress, it had, in fact, arisen there, in the
form of an amendment proposed by Representative Bill McCollum
(Republican-Fla.) to the 1988 drug bill. Despite being regarded by
most in the House Judiciary Committee as, at best, a novelty and, at
worst, an excrescence, the proposal "was not laughed out of the

room," as one congressional staffer put it. McCollum was a hardliner on crime and was part of a task force of Republican representatives that had been meeting for several months to consider tougher drug policy. They pushed particularly hard for the enactment of "user accountability" provisions, the civil penalties—curbing federal benefits, student loans, and so forth—that can supplement drug convictions; the kingpin death penalty did not then become a major priority.

After his election, President Bush did not follow up immediately on his campaign reference to support drug-dealing as a capital crime. His first crime proposals to Congress omitted it, and a Department of Justice official, in fact, testified before the Senate Judiciary Committee in September 1989 that such a measure would be constitutionally "questionable."[36] But by mid-1990, Bush was back with a broader crime bill bristling with death penalty provisions, among them one for kingpin trafficking without the requirement that death result. Essentially the president's proposal increased the existing penalty for trafficking by the leader of a "continuing criminal enterprise" (defined as a group that sells at least 150 kilos of cocaine or opiates annually) from mandatory life imprisonment to death.[37] In the House Judiciary Committee, Representatives Gekas and McCollum, joined by Representative Clay Shaw (Republican-Fla.), pressed similar proposals; the McCollum version, which ultimately prevailed, applied the death penalty more narrowly, increasing the threshhold amount of drugs transacted to double the amount that warranted life imprisonment, and he did not make attempted sales punishable by death.[38]

By 1990 the Republicans had won over a number of representatives otherwise thought to be liberal, like Charles Schumer, a Brooklyn Democrat, and Larry Smith, a Democrat from southern Florida, where drug-trafficking was rampant. Representative Hughes, something of a conservative on other criminal matters like the death penalty for homicides and mandatory prison sentences, still opposed the provision on the basis that death would be an unconstitutional penalty under *Coker v. Georgia*; the proposal failed in his subcommittee and then in the Judiciary Committee, by a vote of 14 to 22.[39] Schumer, however, had come to believe that dealing in large quantities of drugs was like terrorism and espionage, where the death penalty has been considered constitutionally acceptable because of the threat to the nation posed by the activity; and when the McCollum amendment was resurrected on the House floor in 1990, he voted for it. In the House the vote was 295 to 133, after all-night debate; the Senate's version of the kingpin death penalty passed along with the rest of the omnibus bill, 94 to 6.[40]

The proposal died in conference committee, however, victim of other disputes over the omnibus crime bill of which it was a part. At the symbolic level, the outcome didn't matter much. Both houses—and the once and future political candidates who peopled them—were on record as having supported death for high-level drug-dealing.

By 1991 death for kingpins was old hat. In May of that year then–Deputy Attorney General William Barr told the House Subcommittee on Crime and Criminal Justice that "the death penalty debate is over" and noted that provisions for capital punishment of kingpin activity in the President's new omnibus crime bill were based on those approved the previous year by both House and Senate.[41] That high-level drug-dealing would become a capital crime in the near future was considered a "settled issue," as two congressional aides put it, although Hughes and a liberal Democratic from West Virginia, Congressman Harley Staggers, did propose amendments to remove it from the death penalty provisions of the 1991 crime bill.[42]

The kingpin proposal was no longer innovative, since it had been refined and debated over a three-year period. It was not controversial either, since drug-trafficking had taken on such an aura of national threat that most legislators saw opposition to *any* step taken against it as political suicide. (In the Senate an amendment to the 1991 omnibus bill to delete the drug kingpin provisions was introduced by Judiciary Committee Chairman, Senator Joseph Biden (Democrat-Del.), but it was soundly defeated, 68 to 30.[43]

Democrats had by now jumped on the bandwagon; only 101 out of 261 Democratic representatives voted for the Hughes amendment to strike the kingpin provision from the death penalty provisions of the 1991 bill.[44] The total package passed easily in both House and Senate.[45] The House Judiciary Committee, with its new Chairman, Representative Jack Brooks (Democrat-Texas), no longer served as the institutional forum for opposition to the death penalty and other get-tough crime measures; in fact, the bill it reported out in 1991 included more capital offenses than the president's bill.[46] When the omnibus bill was brought to the House floor there was some grand-standing on the death penalty in general, and a small group of liberals refused to support the package because of the inclusion of capital punishment. But debate was perfunctory. Kingpin activity was just another of the fifty-two capital crimes proposed for inclusion in a general federal death penalty.

The ease with which Congress accepted the idea of including a crime not resulting in death within the range of federal capital offenses did not, however, ensure its enactment. What congressional staffers call the "hot-button issues" of crime-control legislation had become gun control, the exclusionary rule, and habeas corpus. Deadlocked over these issues, and bickering over what significance they had for the overall toughness of the bill, Congress recessed in 1991 (and adjourned in 1992) without giving final approval to the conference committee version, which President Bush had threatened to veto as not tough enough. The battle had assumed larger partisan significance, becoming a test of whether the Democrats could embarrass the Republican President by forcing him to veto a bill that would be generally perceived as strongly anti-crime.[47]

The pressure for national politicians to sound tough and protective on crime—and therefore on drugs—appears unlikely to let up soon. While emphasizing the importance of support for drug treatment and education in his campaign and in the announcement of his 1994 national drug strategy, Clinton endorsed the Democratic version of 1993 anti-crime legislation that included many of the same get-tough measures—dozens of capital crimes, limits on habeas corpus (later removed from the bill), federal support for increased police patrol— that have been under consideration almost continuously since the mid-1980s.[48] The expanded federal death penalty will not be an obstacle to passage of national crime legislation in the rest of the 1990s. But neither will the drug kingpin proposal retain much political value, having lost its novelty. In order for the death penalty to become once again a site for political gain, its proponents will have to widen its application still more, perhaps by extending the penalty for kingpin murders to attempts (as was provided in the Senate version of the 1991 bill), or by reaching down the ladder of crime to make the business activity of middle-level, retail street dealers punishable by death. For the time being there seems to be plenty of room for expansion.

# CHAPTER 4

# *The 650 Club*

Technically, Michigan has no death penalty. State lawmakers cannot, however, be considered soft on crime. They have endorsed gradual capital punishment, life in prison without possibility of parole, and not just for first-degree murder. In 1978, driven by many of the same forces that have spurred get-tough campaigns in Congress, the legislature enacted a mandatory nonparolable life sentence for possession or distribution of more than 650 grams—about a pound-and-a-half—of a mixture containing hard drugs. (By contrast, the same penalty for drug possession could be imposed in a federal court only for an amount of at least 600 kilos (273 pounds) of heroin or at least 1,500 kilos of cocaine, well over a ton.[1]) On June 16, 1992, the Michigan Supreme Court held that the part of that law that applied to simple possession violated the state constitution's prohibition against "cruel or unusual punishment." Because the only other crime in Michigan to receive such a sentence is first-degree murder, the court said the penalty was "unduly disproportionate" and ordered that the prisoners sentenced under it be considered for parole after serving 10 years. Still subject to it, however, are those convicted of dealing or planning to do so, whether they are "kingpins" or first-time offenders.[2]

## DRUGS IN A DECADE OF DECLINE

Michigan has a history of social liberalism. Strongly abolitionist in the nineteenth century, it did away with capital punishment in 1847, ten years after becoming a state. Although a Republican stronghold from 1855—the first state party convention in the country was held during the summer of 1854 in Jackson—Michigan became strongly Democratic when the economic base shifted from farms to automobiles, and industrial workers were hard hit by the Great Depression. Generous post–World War II welfare state policies prevailed until the state elected a Republican governor in 1990; in 1989, for instance, its average monthly Aid to Families with Dependent Children (AFDC) payment was 24 percent higher than the national average.[3]

In the last generation Michigan—principally the southeastern section—has fallen upon hard times. Faced with foreign competition and a saturated American car market, and unable to adapt to the increasing demand for smaller cars, the auto industry stalled in the early 1970s and then crashed after the gas crisis of 1979. In 1980 auto manufacturers laid off 250,000 workers, and 450,000 more lost jobs in related businesses.[4] Detroit had been in trouble long before that, with the "Big Three" building plants in the suburbs and capital fleeing to the Sunbelt and abroad.[5] By the mid-1970s the average real income of "Motor City" residents was dropping, and Detroit's population—and therefore its political power—was shrinking.[6] Between 1960 and 1980 the city lost half of its share of seats in the state legislature.[7]

In the mid-1970s the state reflected (and sometimes led) national social and cultural trends, including complex perspectives on illicit drugs. Early in the decade, going along with other states, the state legislature had drastically reduced the penalties for all drug offenses, and the decriminalization of marijuana was under consideration, as it was in a number of other states.[8] A majority of judges on the highest court in the state shared the legislature's perspective. Just before the Controlled Substances Act of 1971, reducing drug penalties, took effect, the Michigan Supreme Court ruled that the state's twenty-year mandatory minimum penalty for marijuana sale was in violation of the U.S. and Michigan constitution because it did not meet "the test of proportionality" to the crime or the "evolving standards of decency" test for cruel and unusual punishment.[9] The court found the sentence constitutionally "unusual" because it could be imposed for both small and large quantities and because it was "equally applicable to a first offender high school student as it is to a wholesaling racketeer."[10] On the same day the court threw out the state penalty for marijuana possession, finding that it was a violation of equal protection, since there was no rational basis for the classification of marijuana as a narcotic.[11] Separate opinions in that case stressed the relative harmlessness of marijuana and decried state action that would "dictate to anyone what he can eat or drink or smoke in the *privacy* of his home [italics in original]."[12] Later in the decade, when the legislature finally rejected a bill decriminalizing marijuana possession, it did so by only narrow margins.

This permissiveness, however, was largely an elite position, popular in the university towns of Michigan, where local ordinances provided for civil fines for marijuana possession. It coexisted with strongly prohibitionist sentiments on illicit drugs, including marijuana, throughout the broader population and among political elites. Legislative debate over a proposed marijuana decriminalization bill in 1976 revealed intensely polarized views. During a heated floor debate in the State House of Representatives one aroused legislator struck another, who favored decriminalization, on the head with an ashtray. After initial passage, the bill was finally defeated on reconsideration in 1977 when a representative whose son had died from the abuse of hard drugs rose on the House floor and appealed to his colleagues not to permit marijuana, the drug that his son had first used. As for harder drugs, at least one effort to find policy alternatives to comprehensive prohibition ran afoul of public antagonism. At a 1977 hearing on legislation for heroin maintenance clinics proposed by a black state representative from Detroit, angry witnesses charged that addicts would be enslaved to the drug and that the program would be used to control blacks.[13]

In 1977 Detroit was, without question, a city with a large number of heroin abusers. In 1975 National Institute of Drug Abuse figures had rated it fourth among metropolitan areas in its addiction rate.[14] Law enforcement officials declared it to be a heroin distribution center for the Midwest. As in most cities, police, the media, and the general public associated the use and sale of heroin with street crime of many sorts—assaults by out-of-control addicts, burglaries and robberies believed to be undertaken to finance a habit, occasional violence between dealers.

The political opportunity for tough drug-control proposals probably came less from specific concern about drug use and its consequences than from general street crime trends in Michigan of which drug-related crime seemed emblematic. Led by decaying Detroit, the state's rate of Federal Bureau of Investigation (FBI) Index crimes (murder, rape, robbery, assault, burglary, larceny, and motor vehicle theft) reported to the police had more than quintupled between 1960 and 1975.[15] More pronounced than the general trend was the increase in robbery, a frightening and much-publicized crime that, for many people, called up the image of the desperate addict, mugging innocent people on the street to get money for his fix. Public anxiety is apparent from local polls taken in 1978. The Michigan Poll found 13 percent of 500 adults surveyed rated crime as the most important current problem in the state, fourth in level of concern behind taxes (39 percent), unemployment (24 percent), and inflation (23 percent).[16] Citizens were apparently willing to get tough, at least for the most serious crimes; 72 percent of adults polled by the *Detroit News* in the Detroit metropolitan area favored the death penalty, reflecting the national trend.[17]

Michigan politicians were riding the crime issue. In his state-of-the-state address in early 1977 Governor Milliken stressed a crackdown on crime and called for expansion of the state police (who rarely ventured into the high-crime urban areas).[18] In the spring of 1977, citing nine recent murders by parolees in his district, L. Brooks Patterson, the Oakland County (Pontiac) prosecuting attorney, who aspired to be attorney general of Michigan, led an initiative campaign to get voters to approve the elimination of prison "good time" for those serving terms for violent offenses. The initiative did not pass, but it was a subject of lively public and media debate for several months.

## LIFE FOR POSSESSION

It was in this atmosphere that State Representative Paul Rosenbaum, Chairman of the Judiciary Committee of the Michigan House of Representatives, urged adoption of his six-bill legislative package of tough measures against drug offenders. Not to be outdone by Patterson, who was alleging that the state legislature had failed to protect the public in not eliminating "good time," Rosenbaum included such a measure in his package; but the linchpin was House Bill 4190 providing stiff mandatory penalties for drug offenders. Announced as an initiative against dealers of large amounts of heroin, the sanctions also applied to possession. The theory was that anyone holding more than a few individual doses was likely to be dealing and that it was harder to get a conviction for selling than for possession or conspiracy to distribute. Proving a sale required law enforcement officers either to observe a transaction, which was unlikely, or to set up buy-and-bust operations, which were costly and dangerous. The bill mandated life in prison for possession of 650 grams or more of cocaine or opiates, twenty to thirty years for 225 to 650 grams, ten to twenty years (or lifetime probation) for 50 to 225 grams.[19] Rosenbaum had previously introduced his package in 1975, but it had died in the state senate when the session ended in 1976. In the spring of 1977 it sailed through the state house of representatives, 84 to 11.

The mandatory penalty provisions got much less attention from both other legislators and the public than did a companion bill that gave law enforcement wiretap authority in investigating drug crimes. This measure—which ironically might have been the device that made the 650-plus law effective in snaring the big operators—roused civil libertarian concerns about privacy violations and the possibility of abuse of law enforcement authority, and failed to pass in the senate. Although law enforcement organizations predictably supported the package, neither the Michigan Attorney General nor the Department of Public Health did.

In light of subsequent litigation over the 650-plus provision, it is interesting that no one—neither political actor nor public commentator—appears to have expressed doubt, in 1977 or the following year when the mandatory penalty provisions passed the state senate, 27 to 7, about its legality under either the Michigan or the U.S. Constitution.[20] Neither excessiveness nor unequal application of the law was of concern, at least publicly. The few legislators who opposed the mandatory sentences cited a lack of faith in their deterrent effect, a concern that they would raise the price—and therefore the profits—of illicit drugs, and a belief that prohibition generally encouraged police corruption. One pointed out that existing lengthy prison terms had not ensnared many big narcotics dealers, but she did not explore the implications of the possibility that the more severe punishment might be imposed, as the current one was, only on "small fry" in the drug trade.[21] A newspaper editorial complained that the life sentence without parole would "cause a grave strain on the already bulging prisons."[22]

## ADDING CONFUSION TO CRUELTY

Twelve years after the passage of what came to be called the 650 lifer law, its effects were the subject of heated controversy. The issue went beyond the law's effectiveness in deterring major drug dealers, which most observers held to be minimal. At least as much attention was being given to broader issues of social policy, such as the proportionality of punishment, the exercise of discretion—that of the judge and the prosecutor—in the criminal justice process, racial justice in sentencing, and disparities in treatment of state and federal defendants.[23] The supreme courts of both the United States and the state of Michigan were weighing the constitutionality of the law, the state legislature was considering an amendment that would take the teeth out of it, and columnists around the state and the nation were calling for reform. Paul Rosenbaum, by then a criminal defense lawyer in Lansing, had repudiated his own creation, saying he had no idea in 1978 that the "mules" of the drug business would be those who would be principally snared by the law.

But that was certainly the situation. By the end of 1990, 138 people had been sentenced under the "over 650 law," 117 of them since 1986 when the influx of crack led to intensified enforcement.[24] Most of the "drug lifers" in Michigan prisons (serving the same life sentence without parole as prisoners convicted of first-degree murder) were low-level couriers in the cocaine trade, more than half were first offenders, and a few were under twenty when they were arrested.[25] In a state where 83 percent of the population was white in 1990, only 50 percent of the 650 lifers were white.[26] Faced with family men and grandmothers and high-school students who hardly fit the expected profile of the kingpin defendant, some judges were beginning to defy the law, imposing lesser sentences and releasing a few people on bond pending appeal of their sentences. Judge David Breck of the Oakland County Circuit Court, for instance, chose to sentence a carpenter with no prior record to seven to thirty years instead of life in prison. In an opinion that expressed the views of some of his colleagues, he wrote, "This court recognizes that the drug problem is the scourge of society, and those deserving of life imprisonment for dealing drugs should be so sentenced. However, in its zeal to clear up the drug problem, this court feels that the legislature overlooked some of those who got caught up in its web."[27]

To many, the law was unfair in other ways. Not only did it impose the same sentence on first-time offenders as on major drug dealers, but some defendants, partners in crime with the drug lifers, got around the stiff penalty by making a deal with the prosecutor to inform on others in exchange for a lesser charge; the bigger dealers benefited from this loophole, since the "mules" were less likely to have information with which to bargain. Another inequity was that federal penalties were much lighter, so that defendants charged with the same offenses received vastly different sentences depending on whether their cases went to state or federal court. The law had its defenders, but the rationale was less utilitarian and more retributive than it had been in the less pessimistic 1970s. "The punishment for that offense is not disproportionate when you compare the nature of the act with the consequences the drugs pose on society," remarked a prosecutor. Evoking more colorful images, a judge noted, "Sure, [the 650 lifers] may not have any criminal records, but these are people who smell out a chance to make a buck selling poisons that murder our babies."[28]

This image of the drug seller, however peripherally involved in the trade, is what gave legislators pause in 1991 as they considered a bill to revise the law, allowing judges faced with defendants convicted of possessing more than 650 grams to impose a lesser penalty if they found "substantial and compelling" reasons to do so.[29] Representative William Bryant, the Republican legislator who was sponsoring the bill, had become convinced that the 650 law was unfair, "severe and absolute," and an unwise deprivation of judges' discretionary authority.[30] The bill he proposed would still require that a judge who departed from the life sentence impose a minimum sentence of at least five years and a maximum of any length. While Bryant's seat (Grosse Pointe Farms) was a safe one—in 1990 he was re-elected with 73 percent of the vote—other legislators feared reprisals from the public if they supported the revision. Democrats noted that in 1988, after the mandatory penalties for drug possession of lesser amounts had been reduced by bipartisan agreement in the legislature, Republican attacks on them contributed to the narrowness of their victories in November.

Privately, many legislators hoped that the U.S. Supreme Court would solve their political problem for them. The case of Ronald Harmelin, a forty-five-year-old pool hustler and small-time drug peddler (and user) who was also a drug lifer confined for his first criminal offense of possessing 672.5 grams of cocaine, was before the justices in the 1990–91 term. The prospect that the Michigan statute would be thrown out appeared reasonably good, based on the court's 1983 ruling that a bad-check conviction leading to a life sentence without parole was "significantly disproportionate" to the crime and therefore "cruel and unusual."[31] But on June 27 the Court repudiated the earlier case and decided, 5 to 4, that Harmelin's punishment was constitutionally acceptable, though perhaps cruel, on the ground that the Eighth Amendment does not guarantee that punishments will be proportional.[32]

The story does not end here, however. The wording of the provision in the Michigan Constitution that prohibits excessive penalties is slightly, but crucially, different in that it prohibits "cruel *or* unusual" punishment.[33] A year after the *Harmelin* decision, the Michigan Supreme Court found that the punishment of life imprisonment without parole was indeed cruel in the case of Kenneth Hasson and Ruth

Bullock. They were arrested when Hasson, who had just flown in to the Lansing airport, tossed his suitcases containing thirty pounds of cocaine into the back of Bullock's car.[34] In finding that the punishment was "unduly disproportionate" to the simple charge of drug possession brought against the defendants, the court noted that "The defendants in this case have been punished more severely than they could have been for second-degree murder, rape, mutilation, armed robbery or other exceptionally grave and violent crimes."[35] The ruling directed the state to give those drug lifers who had been sentenced for drug possession only—about 30 of the total of 160 inmates— parole review after they had served ten years.

The decision has, however, added confusion to cruelty in Michigan's drug sentencing scheme. Although Republican State Senator Jack A. Welborn, chairman of the senate committee dealing with criminal justice matters, and Oakland County Prosecutor Richard Thompson issued predictable statements of outrage at the lenience of the decision, the 650-plus law remained intact for most inmates sentenced under it. The decision did not apply to drug lifers convicted of possession *with intent to deliver* or of *conspiracy* to possess or deliver drugs. This had the ironic effect of punishing someone who planned a one-kilo drug deal that never came off more harshly than someone like Hasson who was caught with a large amount of drugs but could be charged only with possession. (What might have been thought to be an oversight has now been formally endorsed; in 1993 the Michigan Supreme Court refused to apply the *Bullock* reasoning or ruling to "a delivery offense," dealing drugs or intending or conspiring to do so.[36])

At this point the reformers in the state legislature were in a real jam. The judicial branch had taken the heat, but only momentarily and marginally. The justices had thrown the political football back on the field and, if the harshness of the law was to be tempered, the legislators would have little choice but to pick it up and run with it. Bryant immediately began to consider how to finish what the Supreme Court had started. It would be necessary to go beyond the 650-plus law and revise other mandatory drug penalties. Now that some 650 lifers could be released from prison after ten years, it was clearly inequitable to impose a mandatory twenty-year sentence for possession of an amount of drugs weighing a good deal less (as little as 225 grams, half a pound). Bryant abandoned his modest reform bill for a bolder attempt to reduce all drug sentences. But he agrees that in the present political climate in Michigan, his new legislation has no chance of passage.

# Chapter 5

# *Just Saying No in Alaska*

For a time some Americans—both politicians and their constituents—seemed ready to make distinctions in drug policy between hemp products—marijuana and hashish—and "hard" drugs like cocaine and heroin. During the 1970s about a dozen states and localities decriminalized the possession of small amounts of marijuana.[1] But the trend did not go very far or have much staying power. The boldest policy change was Alaska's legalization of marijuana for personal use, and after fifteen years the state reversed itself. On November 6, 1990, Alaskans voted, 105,263 (54.2 percent) to 88,644 (45.7 percent), to recriminalize marijuana possession, despite a 1975 decision of the state supreme court that criminal penalties imposed on adults for possession of the drug for personal use violated the state's constitutional right to privacy.

## THE PIPELINE CROSSES THE LAST FRONTIER

It is hardly surprising that Alaska lives in the imagination as the land of the rugged individualist. The isolation, the permafrost, the very scale of the state—it is more than twice as large as Texas; its biggest glacier covers an area larger than Rhode Island—reward the loner stirred by elemental forces. Even though its population has more than doubled since 1960 (from 226,000 then to 550,000 in 1990) life's challenges there must often be met on one's own. Alaska remains by far the least densely populated state, with an average of only one person per square mile of land area (as compared with seventy for the United States as a whole).[2]

Accidents of geography, geology, and topography are, however, less and less likely to determine or even dominate social and political choices. Fluctuations in the price of oil matter more. As the discovery of gold was a lure attracting non-Natives to the territory in the late nineteenth century, the 1967 discovery of the 11-billion-barrel oil field off the North Slope of Alaska brought a wave of newcomers to manage the immense resource and construct the pipeline to transport it to the "Lower Forty-eight." By 1976, 41 percent of the state residents had arrived within the past five years and only 21 percent were lifelong Alaskans; Natives represented only 15.6 percent of the total.[3] Not surprisingly, the influx exposed Alaskans to new drugs and the oil boom provided money to buy them.[4] Marijuana use increased and cocaine, uncommon previously, was now easily available to those who could pay for it.

By the late twentieth century it was no longer necessary to be an adventurer to get along in Alaska. The pool of new migrants included people who relied on the technological amenities of modern transportation, communications, and household appliances. Earlier waves of arrivals came for personal reasons, to test themselves or to escape; the new Alaskans were often sent, obedient to corporate directives rather than imbued with frontier independence. Although the prospect of good pay on the trans-Alaska pipeline lured laborers eager to see (and profit from) "the last frontier," many who came were organization people, oil company managers, and technicians. And the state's potential for development was now as prominent an attraction as its rugged wilderness; "boomers" dominate both private and public sectors.

## POT AND PRIVACY

For a time, at least some aspects of the fabled individualism of Alaskans were right in step with cultural and political trends in the rest of the country. The general emphasis of the 1960s on greater personal freedom and, more specifically, its reflection in the judicial liberalism that trickled down from the U.S. Supreme Court through federal and state court systems, joined with Alaskans' traditional insistence on personal independence to influence the creation, in 1972, of a specifically enumerated right to privacy in the state constitution. Article I, Section 22 reads: "The right of the people to privacy is recognized and shall not be infringed. The legislature shall implement this section."

Such a bare-bones declaration cries out for definition, and in the years following the enactment of the right, the Alaska Supreme Court began to explore its scope. (The legislature never exercised its authority to make policy in this area.) It articulated some of the same boundaries for the right to privacy found by judicial decision in the U.S. Constitution—for example, the general limitation on privacy that a state may impose when the health and welfare of its citizens are at stake.[5] Then in 1975 it was faced with a test of the state's drug prohibition statute as it related to the possession of small amounts of marijuana for personal use.

When Irwin Ravin, an Anchorage lawyer, arranged to have himself arrested for having marijuana in his pocket in 1972, he moved before trial to have the case dismissed. He asserted that the state had violated his right to privacy under both federal and state constitutions and had failed to afford him equal protection as a marijuana user, since it was irrational to include such an innocuous substance in the prohibition of other, far more dangerous drugs. The trial judge denied the motion and that decision was affirmed by the superior court. But eleven days after the Alaska legislature had abandoned criminal penalties for marijuana possession, the state supreme court remanded the case to the district court, essentially agreeing with Ravin's privacy claim.[6] In a unanimous decision, the judges found the right to privacy of the state constitution broad enough to include "the possession and ingestion of substances such as marijuana in a purely personal, noncommercial context in the home" and ruled that the state could not intrude on that right unless it could show that to do so had a "close and substantial relationship" to the protection of public welfare— which it could not.[7] Acting on the *Ravin* decision, the Alaska legislature then excluded from its drug prohibition statute the possession by adults of less than four ounces of marijuana for use in the home.[8]

## RAIDING THEIR PARENTS' STASH?

The relationship between this lenient approach and the subsequent prevalence of marijuana use in the state, or physical and social harm caused by it, is murky but probably insignificant. Local research on adult pot consumption during the period after decriminalization (until 1991 neither of the two national surveys on drug use included Alaska and Hawaii) focused on the effects of the oil pipeline construction, which began in 1974, the same year as the *Ravin* decision. The one pre-*Ravin* study of adolescent drug use noted that drug-taking (with marijuana the most common illicit drug used) among Anchorage schoolchildren (grades 6 through 12) appeared to be more common than in two cities (Dallas, Texas and San Mateo, California) studied in the lower forty-eight states (though marijuana consumption was about the same in Anchorage and San Mateo, higher than in Dallas).[9] One cannot conclude, therefore, that later research finding relatively high prevalence of marijuana use among adolescents indicates the effects of decriminalization.[10] The most rigorous study of youthful drug-taking in Alaska found that marijuana use (defined as lifetime prevalence) statewide rose slightly between 1983 and 1988, but as its author Bernard Segal noted, responding to claims that legalization of personal use of marijuana has led to increased use, "There are many confounding factors beyond the Ravin decision that have influenced drug-taking behavior in Alaska."[11] Use was higher in Alaska than in the lower forty-eight states, as measured by the National Household Surveys of the National Institute on Drug Abuse, but this was true for every drug, including alcohol. Segal's conclusion that marijuana had "become well incorporated in the life style of many adolescents" cannot be read as a comment on the influence of decriminalization, since it could be made with equal validity in other states with more restrictive policies.[12]

Anti-marijuana activists, however, feel that a relationship between decriminalization and high marijuana use exists. "We believe use among kids mirrored the usage by adults," says Alyce Hanley, a former state legislator who supported the recriminalization of pot. "[Legal] use by adults made marijuana more accessible to kids. Students often reported [to us] that the marijuana they used they got at home from their parents' stash."[13] But it is difficult to conclude that the new law contributed to a culture in which psychoactive agents more generally were tolerated; the chain of causality surely runs the other way. Segal's study provides some indications that, in fact, the reduced tolerance for drug-taking observable elsewhere in the country was taking hold in the mid-1980s in Alaska, too. Alaska high-school seniors interviewed reported a decline between 1983 and 1988 in lifetime prevalence of marijuana, cocaine, and depressants; and students overall reported declines in the use of cocaine and depressants, suggesting that messages about the harmfulness of these substances are reaching Alaska youth.

In the past Alaska's principal public health problem has unquestionably been alcohol, and most of today's drug abusers are also heavy drinkers. Data from the State Office of Alcoholism and Drug Abuse (SOADA) suggest the relative significance of alcohol and drugs. Of 7,738 patient days for alcohol and drug treatment spent in acute-care facilities in 1982, only 4 percent were for drug problems; only 26 percent of those who were admitted to community mental health centers in 1987 for alcohol or drug treatment cited drugs as the presenting problem.[14] The specific contribution of marijuana to this picture is difficult to assess because the data combine marijuana with hashish, which is more potent and therefore likely to be responsible for a disproportionate number of problems charged to the two together. Of statewide admissions to all types of SOADA facilities in fiscal year 1988, 5.2 percent were primarily attributed to marijuana or hashish; 31.5 percent of SOADA clients in that year had some sort of marijuana or hashish use.[15] (The comparable figures for alcohol were 85 percent and 95.6 percent, suggesting that multiple drug use is common and that alcohol is usually its core.)

As for the law's effects on crime, what meager evidence exists is anecdotal and impressionistic. There are no statistical reports on marijuana's contribution to drug-related assaults or property crimes. Marie Majewske, Chairperson of Alaskans for Recriminalization of Marijuana, maintains that Alaskan teenagers were "burglarizing homes" to get money for marijuana—not because they could now buy it legally, since it had always been illegal for persons eighteen and under, but because the relaxation of the law suggested to them that ingesting marijuana was morally if not legally permissible. On the other hand, Daniel Hickey, then Chief of the Criminal Division of the Alaska Attorney General's office, stated publicly in 1986, "The legalization of marijuana for personal use has caused no problems of note and there certainly have been no negative effects on Alaska as a whole."[16] Perhaps the only thing that can be said with certainty about decriminalization's negative effects is that, if they exist, they can't be documented in any reliable way. During the fifteen years subsequent to the relaxation of marijuana possession law, use did not balloon, there were no spectacular marijuana-related crimes, and no recorded fatalities from marijuana ingestion occurred.

During the 1980s urban Alaskans worried about other drugs. A common view is that improved transportation and communications —and lonely pipeline workers—brought heroin and cocaine at least to Anchorage; but the gangs and crack houses of many American cities are notably absent. Talking with Alaskans, it is sometimes hard to disentangle evidence of an actual social condition from inchoate fears of a variety of unnamable threats from what they call "Outside."

## RESTLESS FOR RECRIMINALIZATION

The relative uneventfulness of Alaska's experience with limited legalization of marijuana possession between 1975 and 1990 did not mean it lay dormant as a political issue. Shortly after the *Ravin* decision, opponents began to pressure the legislature to do something, and once the national war on drugs was announced in the early 1980s all was not quiet on the northern front. That urban Alaskans were uncomfortable with the permissiveness of the state law became clear in 1988, when a survey conducted by the Anchorage Crime Commission for the Chamber of Commerce asked, "Do you feel possession of any quantity of marijuana by adults should be illegal?" and 61 percent of the respondents answered "Yes."[17]

Throughout the decade state legislators—particularly Republicans—had been trying to figure out how to pass legislation that would proscribe marijuana use without running up against the *Ravin* holding. Republicans in the Alaska House of Representatives realized that, regardless of the constitutionality of such legislation, supporting recriminalization would respond to the anxieties of some of their constituents—the mail they were getting strongly supported recriminalization—and enhance their image as protectors of the public welfare. It would also give them a political advantage over the Democrats, who were usually in the majority. They could profit from new vigor in the Republican Party, described by one journalist in its pre-Reagan days as "a haven for libertarians and idealistic coffee shop conservatives" but now infused with the kind of New Right sentiments that gave evangelist Pat Robertson 47 percent of the state caucuses in 1988.[18]

The Democratic leadership buried a succession of recriminalization bills in committee for several years, concerned about their constitutionality. In 1988, however, Republicans upped the political ante, making the marijuana law a hot campaign issue in state house races. The opponent of the Democratic Chairman of the Health, Education and Social Services Committee, for instance, where the recriminalization bills had stalled, attacked him as "soft on drugs."[19] (The incumbent Democrat won anyway.) The Republican-controlled senate also passed a bill that year providing a $1,000 fine and 90 days in jail for possession of small amounts of marijuana, justifying its constitutionality with the contention, opposed by some, that marijuana had become more potent since the *Ravin* decision and that the state's interest in protecting the public health might therefore now be greater and weigh more heavily against the privacy intrusion of proscribing personal marijuana use. The following year, despite support from the professional police associations, a compromise proposal, which would have made marijuana possession a violation subject to a maximum $100 fine, failed once more in the state legislature. It was rejected as inadequate deterrence and "a slap in the face" of those who supported tough drug control penalties.[20] By mid-1989 the state political community was very polarized, primarily along party lines, on the issue.

## THE INITIATIVE CAMPAIGN

At this point several Republican legislators from Anchorage were exploring another route for changing policy. Frustrated by the impasse of recriminalization legislation stuck in the House Health, Education and Social Services Committee, and seeking to challenge the Democratic majority in the house, they turned to citizen policymaking. The initiative was not novel in Alaska; in 1974 it had been the vehicle for the voters' choice—since reversed as too costly—to abandon Juneau as the state capital. Representatives Terry Martin and Alyce Hanley, sponsors of failed recriminalization bills who wished to respond to constituent pleas to make pot illegal in Alaska once again, had begun to discuss with citizen leaders the possibility of a voter initiative. Representative Fritz Pettyjohn, later selected as minority whip, and Senator Arliss Sturgulewski also publicly supported the initiative. (Sturgulewski was not known as a hardliner on drugs—in 1982 she had supported pot legalization when the Alaska legislature conformed statutory law with the *Ravin* decision—but by 1989 her views had been affected by the suicide of a nephew who had abused cocaine and alcohol. She also had her eye on the 1990 race for governor—she lost—which some observers suggest influenced her change of position.)

The legislators found the perfect ally to lead the campaign. Alyce Hanley had known Marie Majewske, a former first-grade teacher and then an Anchorage housewife—actually a grandmother bringing up her son's three children—as someone active for many years in Parent Teacher Association (PTA) activities and on school committees. Majewske was energetic, committed, thorough, and conservative—and her credentials as an honest, tenacious parent activist in the areas of education and child welfare were impeccable. She and Hanley shared a concern that young people regarded marijuana as harmless at a time when the drug appeared to have become more potent and there-fore, as Hanley puts it, "a different drug, not the innocuous drug we thought it was in the 1970s."[21] They were struck by the worries that many parents in the PTA and other community meetings expressed about the influence of marijuana in their children's lives, and they noted with disapproval the uniqueness of Alaska's partial legalization of it.

Majewske was involved from the very beginning, testing the waters for support of a possible initiative in a group she was involved with, Community Action for Drug-Free Youth, as well as with the An-chorage Crime Commission, a committee of the Anchorage Chamber of Commerce, and the Substance Abuse Network, a coalition of drug treatment and prevention groups. Nonetheless, she was initially hes-itant about taking on major responsibility for the initiative. She thought of herself as interested primarily in school curriculum issues, and she was wary of getting involved in "a political thing." As a practical matter, she didn't drive or type, two skills usually prereq-uisite to running a grass-roots campaign. On the other hand, she had worked to help start an alternative school for kids who were sus-pended from the regular program for drug use; she felt very strongly that marijuana use was both wrong and dangerous; and she genuinely wanted, as she puts it, "to do the best I could so that the people of this state could make their wishes known."[22] She agreed to chair the effort, subsequently christened Alaskans for the Recriminalization of Marijuana (ARM), and Martin's staff drew up the papers necessary to activate the initiative process.

Although there were delays and minor setbacks—the state legal department initially balked over the language proposed for the initiative—qualifying the initiative went smoothly. In order to put it on the 1990 ballot, proponents had to collect 20,343 signatures of registered voters (10 percent of the total in the state) by late 1989. Working throughout the summer on street corners, at fairs, and in shopping malls, about a half-dozen committed activists, plus some volunteers recruited for this particular task, collected more than 40,000 signatures, which the Lieutenant Governor then certified.[23] Ballot Measure #2, as finally drafted and approved, read:

> Under Alaska Law it is currently legal for adults over 18 years old to possess under four ounces of marijuana in a home or other private place. The penalty for adults over 18 years old for possessing less than one ounce in public is a fine of up to $100. This initiative would change

Alaska's laws by making all such possession of marijuana criminal, with possible penalties of up to 90 days in jail and/or up to a $1,000 fine.

Should this initiative become law?

Yes  _____

No  _____

The initiative campaign of 1990 was bitter. Proponents argued that marijuana was now a dangerous drug, that legal use sent the wrong messages about drugs to impressionable young people, and that Alaska law was out of step with the rest of the country in its permissiveness. Although the opponents countered some of these charges—they argued, for instance, that studies showing marijuana's potency were flawed and were irrelevant anyway because users could control their ingestion of tetrahydrocannabinol (THC), the active ingredient in marijuana, by simply smoking less—their principal strategy was to assert that the initiative was unconstitutional in light of the *Ravin* decision, an assault on Alaskans' right to privacy.

The policy arguments, however, were quickly supplemented with personal accusations suggesting underlying conflicts that had little to do with marijuana. Proponents of the initiative suggested that opponents were simply pot smokers whose position on the issue was self-interested; opponents accused proponents of being hypocrites, wishing to penalize use of a drug that was less physically destructive than the legal drugs of alcohol and tobacco. Each side accused the other—rather indirectly, since actual illegality was not alleged—of corruption, or at least shady dealing. Alaskans for Privacy, the group formed to oppose the initiative (and chaired by Bob Wagstaff, Ravin's original lawyer), was accused of having accepted money from "outside interests," meaning individuals and interest groups from the lower forty-eight states—principally Richard Dennis, a wealthy Chicago drug reformer, and the National Organization for the Reform of Marijuana Laws (NORML). ARM was, in turn, chastised for not having reported to the appropriate state agency some in-kind campaign resources it had received from state groups. Initiative opponents also charged proponents with having received "subtle and not-so-subtle help from the federal government"; they argued that William Bennett, the national drug czar, who came to Alaska in September to speak on behalf of the ballot measure, was using "federal tax dollars . . . to influence a state election."[24]

It was no surprise to either side that the initiative passed. The vote was at least as much a referendum on issues of authority and community that had divided Alaskans for the previous twenty years as it was a majoritarian rejection of legal marijuana use. Toward the end, the campaign was pared down to an emotionally powerful appeal to protect children by prohibiting their parents' use of marijuana. Casting a vote against the initiative became equivalent to casting a vote against the war on drugs—which, as the *Anchorage Times* put it in one of many editorials urging approval of the initiative, was "a war about attitudes—about influencing the hearts and minds of our young people."[25]

The surprise was perhaps that the measure did not pass by more; 54.3 percent voted yes, 45.7 percent no. In some districts of Anchorage and Fairbanks, and in Juneau, generally the outposts of liberals and professional people, majorities voted against the measure.[26] Even in some rural areas it prevailed by only slim margins, suggesting that many Alaskans in the bush still hold to what John McPhee has described as Alaska's "frontier code": "breathe free, do as you please, control your own destiny."[27] Bob Wagstaff immediately announced that there would be a legal challenge to the constitutionality of the new law. Supporters of recriminalization maintain that the health risk of today's more potent marijuana outweighs the privacy right that remains in force in the Alaska Constitution. A more likely basis for a decision sustaining the law is that the supreme court is widely considered to be more conservative these days; Chief Justice Jay Rabinowitz is the only remaining member of the 1975 court that ruled for Ravin.

As expected by both sides, the new prohibition has been enforced rarely, if at all; marijuana possession arrests generally occur in situations where they would previously have been made—in public, rather than in the home, and for amounts greater than four ounces. As for youthful use of pot, there is no clear indication that recriminalization has affected its incidence one way or another.

CHAPTER 6

# The Taxpayers' Revolt Meets the War on Drugs

Within the late-twentieth-century American tide of social and economic conservatism are contending currents. Policymakers are called upon, for example, to reconcile the contradictory messages of fiscal conservatism and law and order. Getting tough with criminals collides with shrinking government at the local level where most crime-fighting occurs. Among the more innovative solutions is that of Jackson County, Missouri, which covers most of Kansas City and some of its suburbs. Missourians are notoriously tight-fisted about taxing themselves for almost anything; the state's 1875 constitution set a limit on the property tax rate, and state and local politicians say their governments have had trouble raising adequate revenues ever since. Nonetheless, in November of 1989 the voters of the county decided to impose upon themselves a ¼ percent sales tax to fund their drug war, to be fought primarily with law enforcement weapons. What follows is the story of how prohibitionism came to triumph over the taxpayers' revolt in Kansas City.

## CULTURAL AND FISCAL CONSERVATISM ALONG THE MISSISSIPPI

Early in the twentieth century, Missouri was a lively entrepreneurial state, second only to California in manufacturing income for states west of the Mississippi. It slaughtered meat for the Mississippi valley region, bred and trained mules for the nation's farmers before they had tractors, led the country in the production of lead, and made most of the world's corncob pipes. Since then, however, population growth has slowed—its two major cities, St. Louis and Kansas City, in fact, lost population between 1970 and 1990—and the state's economic importance has declined. In 1900 Missouri was the fifth most populous state; by 1990, with its basic industries lagging and its defense contractors threatened by the outbreak of peace, the state had dropped to fifteenth.[1]

Politically, the state has been a bellwether for presidential elections, voting for every winner in this century except Eisenhower in 1956.[2] In the recent past it has mirrored national political trends by becoming more conservative, with Republicans holding more state offices and, since 1970, predominantly Republican governors and U.S. Senators (although, in the 103d Congress (1993–1994) six of the nine members of the House of Representatives were Democrats). Democrats remain technically in control of the state legislature, but many of them are more properly thought of as Dixiecrats, protecting rural interests and a culture that is more southern than midwestern.

On cultural issues, a conservative consensus reigns in the state legislature, transcending party lines. (Both the legislative sponsor of a tough 1989 drug bill—making the sale of more than six grams of cocaine or of any drug at all within 1,000 feet of a school punishable by up to life in prison—and the President of the Senate who strongly supported it were Democrats.[3]) Missouri is, after all, the state whose restrictive abortion statute was upheld by the U.S. Supreme Court in 1989, the case that gave the Court its first major opportunity to disable *Roe v. Wade*.[4] The statute not only prohibits abortions in public facilities and bars the use of public funds for abortion counseling, but also begins with a preamble that includes the legislative "finding" that "the life of each human being begins at conception."[5]

Conservatism on social issues is evident in other quarters. John Ashcroft, a two-term Republican governor (1985–93) who combines fundamentalist roots and leanings with an elite northern education (Yale and the University of Chicago Law School), signed the abortion law and has supported tougher tobacco and drunk driving laws, as well as capital punishment. He won re-election in 1988 with 64 percent of the vote, the biggest margin of victory for a Missouri governor since the Civil War.[6] For the first decade of his career the state's most prominent Democratic Congressman Richard Gephardt, an urban Baptist, opposed his party's prochoice position, and Representative Joan Kelly Horn squeaked into office in 1990 despite her support of it. Nonetheless, social liberals can still be found in Kansas City, a Democratic town from the days of the powerful Pendergast machine. For more than a decade the Fifth Congressional District has sent a liberal, black Democratic representative to Congress and in

1991 Kansas City elected its first liberal, black, Democratic mayor.

Another kind of conservatism is evident in both state tax policy and voting behavior. Missouri has historically been a low-tax state, and in 1980 it became even more so when the Missouri Constitution was amended to prohibit the imposition by either state or local government of new or increased taxes or fees "without the approval of the required majority of the qualified voters" of the jurisdiction where the revenue measure was being proposed.[7] The so-called Hancock Amendment—named for Republican Mel Hancock, the state legislator who led the tax revolt and who, since 1988, has represented the Missouri Ozarks in Congress—applies to all but the most trivial fee increases (like zoo admissions) as well as to general revenue measures. Missouri voters have thus had many opportunities to directly limit their collective financial burden, and limit it they have. Eight months before the vote on the anti-drug tax, Jackson County voters had rejected a proposed tax to pay for capital improvements, and since the anti-drug sales tax they have reverted to their customary anti-tax position, voting down three more revenue measures.

## EVERYTHING'S UP-TO-DATE
## WITH DRUGS IN KANSAS CITY

Missouri in the later years of the twentieth century would not be considered a high-crime state were it not for St. Louis, where the violent crime rate in 1982 (as reported by citizens to the police, which presents some reliability problems) was higher than that of New York and Los Angeles.[8] During the mid-1980s Kansas City began to catch up, with the number of robberies and aggravated assaults rising, respectively, from 2,756 and 3,504 incidents in 1982 to 3,479 and 4,230 incidents in 1988 (a period in which the city population was stable at about 450,000).[9] FBI data for that year portray it as the eighteenth most murderous city in the country, although it was only the twenty-eighth most populous.[10] Drug crimes increased, too. Kansas City and Jackson County police estimate that sixty to eighty percent of all street crime is related to drugs, though it is important to emphasize that this figure is purely speculative, and to caution that law enforcement officials are often very casual about such estimates. (Furthermore, one should not overstate the strength of a causal relationship between drug use and street crime; some unknowable percentage of, say, shoplifting and assault by drug users would have been committed by them even if they had been abstinent.) Police say that nearly 40 percent of local homicides in 1988 were drug-related—once again a number more akin to a guess than to a rigorous assessment.[11]

During the late 1980s illegal drugs became a hot media topic, as evidence mounted that Jamaican gangs had brought crack to Kansas City and were doing business openly in residential neighborhoods of the city's black community. In late 1988, for example, the local press reported that the Waterhouse posse from Kingston (reputed, among other evils, to be "tied to the People's National Party," the Jamaican socialist party) was headed by a BMW-driving, Uzi-carrying terrorist named Dogbite said to control at least fifteen local crack houses.[12] Then in early 1989 a house in a black neighborhood was firebombed, reputedly as a fatal blow in a drug feud. Six people inside, including a great-grandmother and an infant, were killed, and the city's media were full of both news reports and soul-searching features relating the incident to the larger local and national problem of illicit drugs.[13]

A particularly bad year for crime in Kansas City was 1988, conveying to many the sense that violence had exploded in their town and heightening associations between violence and illegal drugs. A record number of murders occurred that year, and a serial murderer who had killed at least six young men was arrested and prosecuted.[14] A well-publicized cocaine seizure (ten kilos) from a Los Angeles gang member lent credence to police reports that the violent and legendary gang culture of places like Los Angeles and Miami had arrived in Kansas City, making it a distribution center for the whole Midwest. But it is unclear to what extent drug activity had suddenly taken off—the *Kansas City Star* reported that in 1986 "crack went ballistic"—and to what extent a more gradual increase appeared dramatic because it was getting more attention from law enforcement.[15] When the city police department began to see more illicit drug activity in the mid-1980s it created a Drug Enforcement Unit and a Street Narcotics Unit, which, in turn, generated business for criminal justice system units down the line. According to Albert Riederer, Jackson County Prosecuting Attorney at the time, felony drug cases filed in the county increased 1,200 percent between 1986 and 1989.[16] "We kept getting more and more cases," he says of that period. "We had to put one person on full-time doing nothing but drug cases, then it was two, then four."[17]

The effects of the increase in retail drug trade were particularly visible in poor neighborhoods already suffering the decay and despair common in urban ghettos. Sales moved from the street into "drug houses," which could be either places of business or people's homes from which they sold drugs. Customers poured in from the affluent suburbs and from nearby Kansas as well as from the inner city. Kansas City has a well-organized and articulate African-American community, and its leaders not only expressed their outrage, but also took action. The leading community group, the Ad Hoc Group Against Crime—usually called just "Ad Hoc"—declared February 1989 "Report the Drug House Month" and took complaints from exasperated citizens on 222 houses, leading to the closure by police of twenty-eight houses after landlords agreed to evict tenants suspected of dealing drugs.[18] In middle-class suburbs, too, drug houses were identified and raided, and the police conducted sweeps in public housing that yielded dozens of drug arrests.[19]

## THE SALES TAX AS WINDOW OF OPPORTUNITY

Public anger at what was perceived as the city's major social crisis extended beyond the drug dealers to the institutions of criminal justice, which were seen as sluggish and indifferent. In the view of many, the police were too fastidious about civil liberties when faced with obvious drug-dealing, too few cases actually made it to trial, and sentences were too light. The media criticized Riederer for not being aggressive enough in drug cases; a three-month study conducted by the *Kansas City Times* in 1989 found that lab tests on substances found on suspects delayed arrests for as much as several weeks and that prosecutors often failed to file charges, deciding that evidence against defendants was skimpy or that another case pending against the defendant should be resolved before filing a new case.[20]

Riederer became aware of the public anger about drugs—their effect on individuals, the impact of obvious drug-dealing in neighborhoods, the inadequacies of drug enforcement—during his 1988 re-election campaign. "It didn't make any difference where I went or who the audience was," he says. "It wasn't me that was bringing this up, it was the audience. I was absolutely in awe of that." Riederer didn't need to use the issue to win re-election; after two four-year terms he was on the way to becoming, as the *Kansas City Star* put it, "an institution," and he easily defeated his challengers in both the primary and the general election.[21] But by the time he took office for his third term, he had begun to think about how he could act more aggressively against the drug problem.

Riederer's motives sprang from imperatives of both policy and politics. He was not indifferent to the future benefits a successful campaign against illegal drugs could yield. In the short run, he was thinking of challenging an old nemesis for his job of Jackson County Executive in 1990, and running for statewide office later was not out of the question. He was not above taking advantage of the "get-tough" politics that won favorable notices from the press and responded to voters' anxieties; in early 1989 he visibly supported state legislation that provided harsh penalties for juveniles who transported drugs and allowed arrests for merely being nearby when drugs were sold.[22] He was also, however, genuinely touched by the plight of inner-city residents held hostage by drug-dealing in their neighborhoods and by the fear his constituents all over the county expressed. An immediate institutional concern was also powerful. Riederer felt frustrated generally by the gap between needs and resources in criminal justice and particularly by the extra service demands that the drug crisis created. If he could come up with a funding device, he could not only respond to a problem that deeply concerned the electorate but shore up institutional resources—his own and those of police—that were inadequate even to the tasks required of them before the drug crisis. His overall approach might be simply characterized as enlightened self-interest.

The device Riederer chose for funding his drug program—the ¼ percent county sales tax whose proceeds were earmarked for fighting drugs—required initial authorization by the state legislature, followed by voter approval at the polls. He submitted only a sketchy program description to the legislators, providing for a "special trust fund" to be used "solely for the investigation and prosecution of drug-related offenses," with the possibility that the prosecuting attorney might "contract to distribute a portion of the special trust fund moneys to any not-for-profit community crime prevention organization for the purpose of preventing drug-related offenses."[23] Introduced by a friendly legislator as a Jackson County experiment, tied to the get-tough crime measures that had recently passed, and supported by the statewide prosecutors' association, the proposal passed the state legislature without difficulty for inclusion on the county ballot in November 1989. His next political contest was trickier.

Riederer now needed the county legislature to agree to submit the proposal to the voters. The stated objections he encountered in that body were tactical and programmatic. Passing such a measure might make it more difficult to raise revenue for other needs. The exclusive focus on law enforcement seemed misguided; "if you're going to arrest more people, where are you going to put them?" asked one legislator, pointing out that the program described in the state legislation would not add space to the already crowded jail.[24] Others withheld support because they wanted the proceeds from the tax to pay for treatment of drug users as well as arrest and prosecution. But the greatest obstacle to getting approval of the ballot measure lay just beneath the surface, rooted in the state's fiscal squeeze and the effects it has on political competition: The prospect of new money—the tax was calculated to bring in $14 million a year in a county whose total budget for 1990 was less than $90 million—generated competition for its control within the ranks of the policymakers. Both the legislators and the county executive, a long-standing political rival of the prosecuting attorney, could think of other functions they could support—and take political credit for—with the additional revenue. It soon became clear that Riederer was walking a tightrope: Getting an anti-drug tax on the ballot was conditional on expanding the pool of bureaucratic beneficiaries of its proceeds, but to make that concession was to risk losing his position as playmaker in a high-stakes political game.

The narrow scope of the just-passed state legislation—covering only investigation and prosecution of drug offenses—proved not to be a technical obstacle, since an alternative revenue mechanism existed in unused taxing authority granted to the county by the state in the past. Taking that path, however, abounded with political problems, quite independent of the sacrifice Riederer would have to make in sharing the take with treatment providers and corrections. The unused local authority came with no strings attached—no programmatic specifications, no earmarked fund for the money—which was an advantage to those who wanted the tax to support jail space and drug treatment. Riederer and his allies, however, worried that it amounted to an open invitation to abuse, an opportunity for the county executive to use the money to run the county in the guise of fighting the drug war, in effect evading the state's decision to bring the voters in on revenue decisions—and, not so incidentally, getting credit for leading the fight against drugs only a year before his 1990 campaign. There was the further political hazard that the electorate would see it this way too. The county executive was not popular— he was seen by many as a holdover from the bad old days of Kansas City machine politics—and, with a cynicism common in Missouri politics, the voters might assess the promise of a drug war as fraudulent and vote down the tax.

After much behind-the-scenes wrangling, the parties worked out a collaborative effort. They agreed to propose the tax using the mechanism of local authority for raising general revenue but to word the ballot measure to make clear that the tax was "solely for the purpose of investigation and prosecution of drug and drug related offenses, and the incarceration, rehabilitation, treatment, and judicial processing of adult and juvenile violators of drug and drug related offenses."[25] The proposal also called for a fiscal commission, made up of criminal justice officials and health service providers, to oversee the spending of the money and report annually to the county legislature. The estimated $14 million of proceeds from the tax were to be distributed as follows: $1.5 million each for the Kansas City Police Department and the Jackson County Drug Task Force (county law enforcement) to hire sixty new drug enforcement officers, $3 million for the prosecutor's office (for new staff and a "deferred prosecution" program for first offenders), $1 million for community crime prevention programs, $2.5 million for jail space, $1.5 for juvenile court facilities, $2.5 million for drug rehabilitation, and $500,000 for the adult criminal court.[26] Control over the expenditure of the funds was split between the prosecuting attorney and the seven-person fiscal commission (chaired by the prosecutor). The tax would go into effect on April 1, 1990, and by the time it expired seven years later it would have enabled almost $100 million of investment in the dream of a drug-free county. Riederer retained his image as architect and chief sponsor of the tax.

## MORE ANTI-DRUG THAN ANTI-TAX

From the beginning it was widely assumed by political actors and observers that Jackson County voters would approve the tax. Long before the November 7 election, community groups and law enforcement agencies began talking publicly about what they would do with the proceeds.[27] As a member of the campaign organization Citizens Against Drugs puts it, looking back, "The campaign was over the day it went on the ballot."[28] But Riederer and the friends he brought in to run the campaign—experienced compatriots from his past political life—were taking no chances. They figured that the election was theirs to lose, and they reached out for—and obtained—support in the worlds of business, labor, religion, health services, media, and government. Most voters would certainly find fighting drugs an appealing public enterprise, but, in addition to their usual resistance to taxes, many were profoundly suspicious of county government in general and of the current county executive in particular. For this reason, the campaign themes included both the law enforcement thrust of the program and the accountability of those who would run it.

Building support for the tax entailed not only defusing the anti-tax groups—Riederer's friends had contacts with the Taxpayers' Defense League, which agreed not to oppose the measure though they didn't support it either—but also co-opting service providers who might not believe in the efficacy of the weapons and troops of criminal justice in drug wars. With special-purpose tax referenda, the appropriation process precedes specification of the program, the reverse (at least theoretically) of other legislative action. The spoils are therefore available with particular prominence when sponsors are mobilizing support for this kind of legislation. Leaders of the health and social services communities needed little prodding to see their material interest in getting behind the tax; there was, after all, more than $3 million for prevention and treatment that could support both their philosophies and their agencies. Encouraged by a widely respected hospital administrator whom Riederer's people recruited to marshal support, mental health agencies and drug treatment programs contributed more than $30,000 to promoting the tax.[29] Other funds—the campaign raised a total of $200,000—came from business leaders and corporations, including an airplane parts manufacturer (and ex-bank robber) who delivered his $100,000 donation in cash in a clear-plastic briefcase at a press conference held on the steps of the Jackson County courthouse.[30]

Once the internal disputes with county legislators had been resolved, the promoters of the tax met with virtually no open opposition. The Chamber of Commerce endorsed it, neighborhood groups distributed literature in support of it, and the two most influential African-American organizations—Ad Hoc and Freedom, Inc., a powerful political club—came out in favor. A week before the election one lone public official came out against it, saying that others were privately doubtful but feared it would be "political suicide" to oppose the tax. "It's like being against the flag, motherhood, and apple pie," said Jack Hackley, a Jackson County economic development commissioner.[31] His comments probably reflected the anti-tax perspectives of his rural part of the county rather than a programmatic judgment, and in any event had no discernible effect on the election.

Materials used in the campaign capitalized on the public fear of children's exposure to drugs, an image of the drugs themselves as demonic and destructive, and the frustration that many in Jackson County—suburbanites as well as inner-city residents—felt about the intractability of drug-dealing. Although the most recent drug threat

was crack rather than heroin, the campaign logo featured a hypodermic needle as the "I" in the slogan "Fight Back"; and brochures
pictured innocent-looking teenagers with a display of ugly drug paraphernalia. Fifteen-second TV spots—produced and shown in the
last weeks before the election, underwritten by the flamboyant busi-
nessman's $100,000—reproduced a drug bust with the mixture of
drama and gritty verisimilitude found in prime-time cop shows. Foot-
age from Advertising Council anti-drug ads and police department
tapes were backed up with harsh sound effects—no text, no voice-
overs—to convey a strong law enforcement message.

As expected, the tax won easily. It carried in the county as a whole
by 60 percent; 51,907 votes for, 33,968 against.[32] The greatest margins of victory were in central city wards, but even most of the suburban areas in the eastern part of the county, where hostility to tax
measures is usually high, voted for it. As the state representative from
that area said of his constituents, "They're anti-tax, but they're anti-
drug more so." Riederer's campaign workers considered the
turnout—35 percent of the registered voters—respectable for a special
election at the county level, though it is worth noting that it was far
below the statewide turnout of 54.5 percent of the voting age population for the 1988 presidential election.[33]

## DISAPPOINTMENT AND DEFECTION

Nothing succeeds like success. Immediately after the election Riederer
was generally regarded as having brightened his political future by
taking the initiative and following through on "society's No. 1 problem."[34] "I'm excited," said Riederer about the landslide. "It gives us
an opportunity to do something about the dopers and dealers." But
fifteen months after the tax went into effect, the bloom was off the
rose. The media, some citizens, and even a few of his supporters were
charging that Riederer and his drug war had accomplished very little.

Program results were deficient at both governmental and societal
levels, critics maintained.[35] The prosecutor's office was disorganized
and self-interested, resulting in funding delays for prevention and
"deferred prosecution" programs and for the jail. Riederer had hired
new lawyers for the drug unit in his office, but he had also hired
many other kinds of employees, and the office had purchased more
new computers than there were drug fighters; was the anti-drug
money being used illegally for activities that were not drug-related?
Despite new police and prosecutorial staff, many of the usual indi-

cators of drug enforcement activity were down in Kansas City, not up: arrests of users, drug warrants issued, value of drugs seized. Police raids on drug houses, the most visible evidence that law enforcement was on the job, went from 248 in the first six months of 1990 to 182 in the same period a year later, despite the police chief's 1989 promise to increase them if proceeds from the tax enabled him to hire new officers.

Most discouraging was the anecdotal evidence that drugs were as pervasive as ever and the clear public view that the drug program had not improved the situation. "People on the street have noticed no difference," Cliff Sargeon of Ad Hoc said flatly in the fall of 1991. The view of professionals was somewhat divided. The *Kansas City Star* quoted prosecutors in the U.S. attorney's office in Kansas City as saying crack was as easy to find on the street in July 1991 as it had been a year previously, although an official of the Jackson County Drug Task Force, the drug enforcement unit operating outside the city, maintained that in general there were fewer drugs around and they were more expensive.[36] An undercover officer in the Street Narcotics Unit of the Kansas City Police Department told an interviewer for a local TV news magazine in November that "we're seeing more dope on the streets than we were a year ago"; but the head of his unit suggested the police were "holding even" and that that was all that could be expected.[37] She also defended law enforcement from the charge that its aggressive drug-fighting was meaningless if it merely displaced the drug traffic from one spot to another: "At best we may move [dealers] a few blocks, but that means something to the people on the block we move them off of." Riederer did not dispute the gloomy assessments of the drug problem in his city—nor did he defend himself vigorously against charges that the program had gotten off to a bad beginning—but he tried to keep his constituents hopeful. "We're on the right track," he said to the viewers of "Kansas City Illustrated," "you're going to see the beginnings of a real turnaround."

But Riederer did not wait to see whether his prophecy would come true. In early 1992 he surprised many by announcing he would not seek a fourth term later that year. While he says he just felt it was time, that he "wanted to serve the public and leave," even some of his close associates don't believe that's the whole story. Whether or not he really feared he would be fatally tarred by the failures of his program, it seems clear that he was troubled by the fundamental political position it put him in: the need to defend and actively promote the get-tough, law enforcement approach to illicit drugs. Freed

from immediate political imperatives, he now says arrest and prosecution won't solve the drug problem, and even that criminal justice
can't do much about crime. He has joined the Steering Committee
for the Campaign for an Effective Crime Policy, a Washington-based
reform group that includes among its proposals review of the federal
embrace of harsh mandatory sentences and a shift away from the
criminal justice emphasis in federal drug policy.[38] Speaking to a
church group in March 1992 he said, "I got caught up in it [the law
enforcement approach to drugs] and I probably believed it. It isn't
true."[39] He skirted the actual advocacy of drug legalization, but said
discussion of it should be part of the public dialogue. His audience
applauded.

# CHAPTER 7

# Loitering in
# Livable Seattle

The July 1991 issue of *The Atlantic* entitled its article on Seattle, "A City That Likes Itself." It is an apt characterization for a city with a beautiful setting, a vibrant cultural life, good schools, and low unemployment—suggesting not only the amenities of the place but also its embrace of consensus as the way to get things done. Retaining the image of "America's most livable city"—the puffery of travel brochures and postcards, which few visitors or residents dispute—is important for Seattle as it grows in commercial and cultural importance, and the arrival of open-air drug markets in the city has challenged that perspective. As part of an effort to disrupt those markets, the city council, in June 1990, passed an ordinance prohibiting "drug traffic loitering," providing that a person who "remains in a public place and intentionally solicits, induces, or procures another to engage in" a drug transaction is guilty of a "gross misdemeanor" (punishable by up to a year in jail).[1] Conflict over the drug loitering law laid bare fissures in Seattle's smooth surface and presented another challenge—to the city's social mythology of tolerance and pluralism.

## TENSIONS IN PARADISE

Since World War II Seattle has been a growing city in a generally booming state. During the 1980s the metropolitan area population increased by 23 percent, with job growth to match.[2] In 1987 its per-capita income was third highest of the fifty largest U.S. cities.[3] One reflection and celebration of the city's recent prosperity has been a concerted effort to preserve and restore commercial areas and to mingle businesses and residences in downtown neighborhoods.

*85*

While the century-old Pike Place Market retains its mixed uses, the warehouses and docks of Seattle's rough-and-tumble past as a logging and fishing town have become markets and boutiques and galleries. The original "Skid Row" (Yesler Way) is now a smart shopping street. Planning for waterfront and other large-scale development in the downtown area is underway.[4]

Seattle is not completely free of the social ills that have plagued other American cities of its size in the last generation. Housing costs escalated rapidly in the 1980s as the city's population grew, and the state's higher-than-average unemployment rates have consequences for the city.[5] Homeless people wander around the city's beautifully preserved downtown areas. Property crime rates are relatively high, though that may be attributable to a greater willingness of Seattle citizens to report such events to police than in less-trusting large cities.[6] And Seattle has not escaped the violence and disorder of the crack culture. Drug business thrives on some inner-city streets; arrests for drug law violations rose more than 800 percent between 1983 and 1989.[7] Statistics from hospital emergency rooms on drug abuse episodes and patient drug use suggest that public health consequences are not very different for Seattle than for other metropolitan areas of similar population size. Reports from city medical examiners in 1989 show Seattle with 26.92 drug abuse deaths per 100,000 population, while Minneapolis had 15.36, New Orleans 17.29, and San Francisco 54.37.[8] The vaunted livability of Seattle does not ensure immunity from misery and disease.

One response to the increase in property crime and drug activity in Seattle has been citizen crime prevention efforts. Initially organized by small businesses that felt victimized by escalating disorder, the Community Crime Prevention Councils that came into being organized residents, too. The seven councils—now with a professional staff—go beyond block watch groups (though those exist, too, and have been credited with lowering the burglary rate) to active improvement of neighborhood conditions—a volunteer graffiti brigade scrubs walls on weekends—and involvement in youth recreation programs. They also provide information on self-protection of various kinds; "Take control of your property: Prevent unwanted people and activities in your business and on your premises," reads a pamphlet for property owners and landlords. Although the spark that ignited citizen energy in several instances was perceived police ineffectiveness, the groups soon moved beyond what one activist calls the "shaking-the-fist phase."[9] Where precinct captains are oriented to the current fashion of "community policing," cooperation between crime prevention groups and police flourishes.

Police-community relations are not so smooth everywhere. Tensions in minority neighborhoods, always present, have escalated in recent years. (Of Seattle's 516,000 inhabitants in 1990, 11.8 percent were Asian, 10.1 percent were black, and 3.6 percent were Hispanic.[10]) Accusations of harassment of young black males, even brutality, are common, and residents charge that the Seattle Police Department is reluctant to investigate them and punish the officers responsible.[11] Since 1990 a group called Mothers Against Police Harassment has been investigating incidents where harassment is suspected. Unfairness seems pervasive at other levels, too. According to the public defender, most of the city's drug prosecutions are not of major dealers but of young, poor people who sell a piece of crack to an undercover officer and go to prison.[12] This pattern rankles minority residents, particularly in light of occasional scandals that reveal drug involvement—both using and dealing—on the force.[13]

In the late 1980s civic-minded Seattle took action against the "rock houses" and occasional drive-by shootings that signaled the presence of drug gangs from California and some local imitators. Police and residents of the Rainier Valley area in southeast Seattle agreed upon a drug prevention and enforcement plan that combined recreational activities for local youths with aggressive action by a special anti-crime team in the Seattle Police Department.[14] But the drug trade merely moved north, first to the Central Area, then to the downtown streets around the Pike Place Market. It wasn't that the drug raids failed to catch the dealers or close down their places of business; they ran up against the inherent limitations of repressing a low-skill, low-maintenance, high-demand, high-profit enterprise. By mid-1991 the drug bazaar had moved again—to the Denny Regrade, a mixed residential and commercial area north of downtown.

## "WE'RE GOING TO LOSE SEATTLE"

Despite police efforts to downplay the severity of Seattle's drug problem, citizens were exercised about the open-air drug markets and the violence associated with them. A poll to determine citizen concerns taken by a candidate for the nonpartisan city council during his 1989 campaign revealed that drugs and criminal gang activity in general were, as they are in many cities, at the top of the list.[15] The sensitivity created opportunities for both political leadership and political posturing. Starting about 1987, Norm Rice, then Chairman of the Public Safety Committee of Seattle's City Council, found responsive audiences when he began to crusade for more aggressive police action against drugs. When long-time Mayor Charles Royer retired two years later, Rice succeeded him—Seattle's first African-American mayor, a particularly notable fact because he was elected easily in a city with a very predominantly white electorate.[16] Among the strengths of his campaign were demands for more police and for a harder line on street crime and drugs.

When Rice took office Councilwoman Jane Noland, his successor as head of the Public Safety Committee—also ambitious to be mayor, it is said—was even more outspoken in denouncing drug activity in the city. A lawyer and long-time member of the American Civil Liberties Union (ACLU), she is widely perceived as a liberal or moderate whose sympathies have swung to the right as she has become more involved in issues of crime and justice. Although she has been a police partisan, fighting hard for generous budget allocations for them, she is very critical of police performance in reducing street drug traffic. She publicly attacked both the police chief and the mayor in 1991 when a citizen's videotape of drug-dealing in the Denny Regrade neighborhood was brought to her committee.[17]

As policy entrepreneurs both Rice and Noland were prodded by constituents, individually and in groups. When Rice was still on the city council in 1988 the South Seattle Crime Prevention Council, a community organization dominated by local merchants, came to him requesting that he sponsor a drug loitering ordinance similar to those that had recently been passed in Yakima and Tacoma. The group lobbied Noland, too. Vociferous, articulate, and well-connected, the citizen leaders were initially concerned about the "smash and grab" attacks on small businesses, but broadened their focus quickly. For the community organizations that first demanded action from local legislators, drug control was primarily a pocketbook issue; if residents and tourists avoid commercial areas because they fear encounters with drug vendors and their customers, they reasoned, businesses will fail. The concern extended beyond individual risk to the city's economic future; as one citizen activist, a merchant in the Denny Regrade area, puts it, "Unless we get the drug scene so that people who come downtown do not feel afraid—whether the threat is real or perceived—we're going to lose Seattle. . . . Financially, Seattle's tax is based on our revenues; if people are running out to Tukwila to do their shopping instead of coming downtown, we lose that revenue."[18]

At first Rice resisted the appeal for a drug loitering law. His staff consulted with police officials, reviewed a draft bill the city attorney's office had prepared, and looked at the Tacoma ordinance.[19] Unsure about the civil liberties implications of laws that targeted intent and limited association, Rice wanted to see how the Washington courts dealt with Seattle's prostitution loitering ordinance, which took an approach very similar to that proposed for drug loitering.[20] He did not address the issue in his mayoral campaign.

## THE CITY COUNCIL ACTS

Late in December 1989 the Washington Supreme Court upheld the Seattle prostitution loitering ordinance.[21] It rejected a defendant's contentions that the law was unconstitutionally broad and vague and that it discriminated against "known prostitutes." Seattle community groups immediately stepped up their pressure for a drug loitering law. By this time the merchants who led the appeal had been joined by less white and middle-class groups. Rice, who was now mayor, decided that he was comfortable with the proposal, and the city attorney tinkered with the language to model it as closely as possible on the prostitution loitering law. Introduced by Jane Noland in the city council in April 1990, Council Bill 107963 prohibited "drug-traffic loitering" and provided that the requisite intent to buy or sell drugs could be found where the suspect:

1. Is seen by the officer to be in possession of drug paraphernalia; or
2. Is a known drug trafficker; or
3. Repeatedly beckons to, stops or attempts to stop pedestrians; or
4. Repeatedly stops or attempts to stop motor vehicle operators by hailing, waving of arms or any other bodily gesture; or
5. Circles an area in a motor vehicle and repeatedly beckons to, contacts, or attempts to stop pedestrians; or
6. Is the subject of any court order, which directs the person to stay out of any specified area as a condition of release from custody, a condition of probation or parole or other supervision or any court order, in a criminal or civil case involving illegal drug activity; or

7. Has been evicted as the result of his or her illegal drug activity and ordered to stay out of a specified area affected by drug-related activity.[22]

Reaction to the proposed law was swift and polarized. Seattle's crime prevention councils favored it, as did the Seattle Police Department, but there was also a firestorm of opposition. An open letter to the Public Safety Committee of the city council from Kathleen Taylor, Executive Director of the ACLU of Washington, made available to area newspapers, summarized the two main areas of concern: "The American Civil Liberties Union of Washington urges you not to pass this bill," Taylor wrote. "We believe it will be applied in a racially discriminatory manner and will increase the incidence of HIV infection in Seattle."[23] She noted that data from the National Institute on Drug Abuse showed that nationally only twelve percent of those who use drugs are African-American, while they constitute 38 percent of drug arrests. Civil rights groups, too, sounded the theme that, as Lacy Steele, President of the Seattle branch of the NAACP, put it, "the war on drugs is in essence proving to be a war on African-Americans and other nonwhites."[24] Opponents cited the results of the drug loitering law in Tacoma, where court records showed that in its first year of operation, 91 percent of those arrested under it were minorities.[25] AIDS activists argued that the police would pick up intravenous drug users delivering dirty needles or getting clean ones from the Seattle-King County Health Department's needle exchange program, and that the law would deter addicts from using the program. The *Seattle Times* took exception to the proposed law on civil liberties grounds; "basically, the anti-loitering ordinance would make it illegal for one to be standing in a public place, 'looking suspicious,' " its editorial warned.[26] The *Times* also noted that the law would have no impact on the flow of drugs into Seattle; otherwise, the question of the measure's effectiveness at controlling drug traffic was ignored.

No one who was there is likely soon to forget the June 19 Public Safety Committee hearing on the ordinance. The small committee room was packed with angry representatives of civil rights groups and ACT-UP, the organization of AIDS activists, ready to make the most of their opportunity to participate in the public process. (Behind-the-scenes lobbying in city council offices before the hearing had been primarily by proponents of the measure.) It soon became clear that reaction to the proposal at hand was only the foam on the wave, that the hearing had exposed deep currents of more general hostility toward the police and toward what was perceived as repressive exercise of state authority in Seattle. Proponents of the measure were shouted down by those on the other side, particularly ACT-UP members, three of whom leaped over the wooden railing separating council members from the audience and railed at them. "Any council member who votes for this racist, death-promoting legislation will not be with us after the next election," promised one ACT-UP member.[27] "You've got blood on your hands, Jane Noland!" yelled another, as police hurried him out of the hearing room.

The intensity and drama of the hearing gave the issue prominence beyond the circle of those with an immediate political stake in the legislative outcome. The media played it up, though there was no bandwagon view of what should be done. "From an issue that was one among many in the back of your mind," says Tom Weeks, a councilman who had not attended the free-for-all, "suddenly it was all anyone on this floor was talking about." For Weeks particularly, drug loitering was an instant hot potato. He was the only member of the council who had decided to vote against the law, and now that the whole city was paying attention to what happened, the potential costs of breaking with the mayor and the Police Guild— former political allies—rose.

Despite the opposition, which was expressed once again at the full council meeting the following week, the ordinance passed easily, by a vote of 7 to 2. Noland had done a good job of lining up support; the other council member who joined Weeks did so only at the last minute. But postmortems by two rookie council members who found the decision agonizing—as did others on the council—faulted the process that produced the law. "I wish we had taken more time," Councilwoman Sue Donaldson told a *Seattle Times* columnist. "The mayor pushed it. The chairman of the committee pushed it. It could have been orchestrated to build more consensus."[28]

But perhaps lengthier consideration would have built tension, rather than resolving it. Enactment did not silence the conflict. At a meeting called by Rice before he signed the measure, opponents' objections once again erupted into ferocious expressions of mistrust of the police and personal accounts of harassment; even a Hispanic investigator from the public defender's office told of being harassed by the police while doing her job. The mayor also took some heat— he was called an "Uncle Tom," for instance—then and at later community meetings. African-Americans and others charged him with supporting the ordinance primarily as a tool for controlling the streets during the upcoming Goodwill Games, when Seattle, on the brink of becoming a world-class city, would be under international scrutiny for three weeks.[29]

## SAFE STREETS OR STREET SWEEPS?

Faced with suspicion of his motives and open antagonism toward those who would implement the loitering law, Mayor Rice tried to institute special accountability measures for the policy. He promised that both police and prosecutors would review all cases before proceeding beyond arrest, to be sure that they did not show evidence of harassment or discrimination. He announced that only the narcotics squad and anti-crime teams could make arrests under the law, and that they would receive special training in the law and its proper application. On the same day that the ordinance was passed, the city council acknowledged the hostility of the African-American community towards the police by passing a resolution to the effect that "the Seattle Human Rights Commission shall monitor citizen complaints regarding police harassment and shall report on the same to the Mayor and the City Council."[30]

It became apparent quite quickly, however, that concessions made to the opponents of the law would not extinguish the sources of their concerns about it. The Seattle Human Rights Commission report on investigation of citizen complaints against police, issued in November 1990, pointed out that in the first two-and-a-half months of policy implementation, twenty-nine of the fifty-seven arrestees were African-Americans.[31] Furthermore, fewer than one-third of the arrests led to drug loitering charges, seeming to substantiate the charge that the law was primarily an instrument for removing young black males, perceived as threatening to tourists and suburbanites, from city streets. A study by the ACLU of Washington released eighteen months later pointed in the same directions: Of 244 people arrested for loitering between the fall of 1990 and April 1992, 76.6 percent were black, and more than half were never charged.[32] Police and prosecutors explained the paucity of loitering charges as an indication that many arrestees had other pending charges, which took precedence over the misdemeanor for loitering; but many in the minority communities were nonetheless in accord with Gérard Sheehan, Legislative Director of the ACLU, that the law "is used as a street-sweep device."[33]

The timing of the ACLU report was not coincidental. The summer of 1992 saw a renewal of conflict over drug loitering, as the ordinance expired and arrest data provided fodder for opposition to re-enactment. Once again the issue was highly charged, and once again the law passed the city council, but this time with the slimmest of margins (5 to 4), attributable to continuing resistance from the black community and a shift in position on the part of two council members who had been ambivalent in 1990.[34] Mayor Rice went to bat for the re-enactment even more vigorously than he had in 1990, heightening speculation that he was preparing to defend himself against charges of being soft on crime and drugs in the event of a challenge from Noland in the mayoral race the following year. (She didn't run and Rice won easily, but opponents did try to tar him with a charge that he had failed to vanquish drugs and street crime.[35]) Interestingly, the council's new African-American member, elected in 1991, was the swing vote assuring victory for the ordinance. She conditioned her approval on the amendment of the ordinance to include provisions for a thirteen-member task force to address police harassment of minorities in Seattle and for regular reports on the implementation of the law, despite the failure of a 1990 request to the Seattle Police Department to maintain and circulate data on the racial makeup of arrestees under the law.[36]

The uproar over drug loitering legislation and efforts to placate its instigators began to have a ritual quality, however. It was becoming clear that laws like Seattle's were an increasingly popular recourse for other local governments around the country—not just Tacoma and Yakima in Washington but cities and counties in Florida, Michigan, Maryland, Virginia, and elsewhere—and that courts would usually support them, reasoning that as long as they had a rational basis, the fact that they had disproportionate impact on minorities did not render them violations of equal protection under the constitution. Besides, drug loitering legislation was now just one strand in a web of policies intended more to shift the geography of some of Seattle's problems than to solve them. The "aggressive panhandling" ordinance of 1988 had followed the prostitution loitering law, and a 1989 state law (like that of many other states) provided double penalties for drug dealing within 1,000 feet of a school (called "drug-free school zones").[37] In 1991 a probation condition established the SODA ("Stay Out of Drug Areas") project, designating sections of the city (sometimes quite sizable areas) "where the level of drug trafficking and associated crimes has had a substantial negative impact on the local communities involved" and from which a judge could be requested to exclude a drug offender on probation or parole.[38] Managing public space (and, some maintained, its poor, unruly citizens) had been broadly legitimized as a drug prohibition strategy.

*Part III*

# THE
# SHADOW
# AGENDA

# CHAPTER 8

# *Drug Prohibition on Demand?*

American ingenuity and pragmatism are celebrated in the context of a relatively unregulated market. We assume that products that don't catch on with consumers, whether Edsels or sitcoms, will be quickly retired, and that those that survive will be both popular and functional. Faith in this market responsiveness often carries over to the public arena; we easily assume that public policies that persist must reflect popular acceptance of the quality of government's products and continuing demand for more of the same.

Such reasoning is naive in two ways. It assumes that the policy process turns public woes into governmental action in a smooth and predictable transformation. And it credits only the overt items on the public agenda for producing the public policy under scrutiny.

Drug prohibition reveals some of the elisions in the market interpretation of the policy process. We are unlikely to retreat from the various drug wars that have constituted American prohibition even if more and more citizens recognize that these campaigns have not significantly reduced the demand for drugs or the toll drug abuse takes on bodies and minds. There are a variety of ways in which the "drug problem" generates support for law enforcement approaches to drugs. And powerful but latent agenda items shadow drug abuse to shore up prohibition. Our wars on drugs do not depend for their momentum on any popular ground swell, though they profit from —and, in turn, generate—public support. And the medical and social harm caused by drugs is a necessary but largely insufficient explanation for the nature and intensity of our commitments to drug prohibition.

## WHO LEADS AND WHO FOLLOWS?

Even sophisticated observers assume a relatively straight line between public demand and drug policy. Franklin Zimring and Gordon Hawkins, authors of an otherwise excellent book on drug policy, explain that in the second half of the 1980s tougher federal drug penalties were enacted, a federal "drug czar" was anointed, and drug wars were fought at all governmental levels "because a high level of public concern produces governmental action in a political democracy."[1] While survey data and interviews certainly document public worry about drugs, and the get-tough policy trend is undeniable, the relationship between the two is far more complex than Zimring and Hawkins suggest.

For one thing, the existence of voter concern doesn't dictate the *choice* of policy directions to address it. The identification of drugs as a problem need not automatically translate into a prohibitionist emphasis, as is evident with current tobacco and alcohol policy. The preference for law enforcement approaches over, say, a combination of taxation, regulation, treatment or services, and information about the dangers of drugs is not dictated by immutable logic. As Chapter 1 illustrated, a great variety of behaviors and effects cluster under the rubric of "the drug problem" people are concerned about. For those who worry about the relatively benign as well as the life-threatening—parents contemplating adolescent rebellion, say, who may be as concerned with experimental as with compulsive drug-taking—prohibitionist policy may be less the preferred option than the only arrow in the quiver of tired and cynical policymakers and their allies. The ease with which leaders and followers seek recourse in the criminal law is itself a thing to be explained.

Indeed, the demand-response dynamic may operate the other way around, with politicians or bureaucrats or TV personalities leading the way, sometimes finding expression for public distress, but also sometimes creating it. It is hard to locate the level of popular concern about decriminalized marijuana that one might have expected to propel the Alaska citizen initiative for recriminalization onto the ballot. The climate of public opinion (insofar as it can be ascertained; pollsters tend to steer clear of the lonely reaches of Alaska) was very unlike that of California in 1977, when the dawning of the tax revolt provided the decisive moment for Assemblyman Howard Jarvis to launch Proposition 13, the initiative freezing property taxes and tying future increases to rises in assessed valuation.[2] It was not until members of the Alaska state assembly became frustrated with a legislative process that did not respond to their interest in recriminalization and went outside that process to generate a citizen referendum that marijuana use acquired a problematic character that could be politicized. While Parent Teacher Associations (PTAs) and other parent groups had worried about pot in the schools and the exposure of adolescents to marijuana use by adults in the home, the lenient Alaska law became a target of broader public concern only as political leaders and a small group of the most intensely concerned citizens seized the day.

The linkages between citizen demand and policy formation are further distorted when politicians endorse the preferences of a small group at one end of the policy spectrum. Rather than responding directly to majority preferences, policy proponents often simultaneously manipulate public sentiment and establish themselves as leaders to be trusted. Public support for the death penalty for drug dealers not convicted of murder was ambiguous when Congress considered it—a Gallup poll recorded only 38 percent approval in late 1988, while a Times Mirror poll two years later found a sizable majority in favor.[3] But that did not keep Congress from easily and publicly arriving at a consensus on the measure. It seems reasonable to assume that the majority votes in both houses reflected less the representatives' desire to respond to the majority view of the electorate than their assumption that, in supporting a minority position, they would avoid attack from the group with the most intense preferences and be perceived as looking out for the safety of constituents even among those who might think the particular penalty unduly harsh. We might also hypothesize that by bringing capital punishment for drug-dealing to general public attention, the legislators legitimize the view often heard from law enforcement officials that drug dealers are really murderers.[4] Since the death penalty is commonly acceptable only as a punishment for murder, the creation of a minor premise that equates drug-dealing with murder may be the necessary lubricant for policy support for sentencing drug dealers to death.


## DOES POPULAR CONCERN ABOUT DRUG ABUSE FULLY EXPLAIN DRUG PROHIBITION?

The causes for concern about drugs (and the effects of their illegality) that find open expression might be grouped into the following categories: the physical or mental harm their use may cause to the user; the deleterious effects their use can have on others, not only family, friends, and colleagues of the user, but also the victims of crimes committed either to get the money for drugs or in drug transactions, and the public corruption that the illicit drug trade generates; and the violation of public morality that their use represents.

If these kinds of citizen concerns fully explained the character and dynamics of drug prohibition, we should find that those citizens who most clearly articulated them were also those who gave the strongest endorsement to aggressively prohibitionist policies. But such a direct linkage does not appear to exist. Those most directly affected by drug abuse, for example, are often least inclined toward the most repressive policies.

There are, in short, a variety of anomalies that challenge the widespread view that the public directly demands comprehensive and aggressive drug prohibition. What follows is an examination of some clues, taken from public opinion data and from the case studies, tracing departures from what one would expect if the standard policy justifications for the war on drugs were to be taken at face value.

To point to anomalies is not to suggest that public concern about drugs plays *no* role in shaping drug policy, but rather to point to a more complex dynamic. The departures from expectation demand explanation, but they are not contradictions, phenomena that cannot logically coexist. Gaps between objective social condition and public grievance should not be assumed to be either irrational or inconsistent; more elaborate (and strategic) processes than ignorance or willful misperception are at work. The currents running below the surface of policy discourse are fully as rational as those that visibly support the policy vessel; it's just that they run toward a different source.

Let us look first at those who express most anxiety about illicit drug use. Those most concerned are not necessarily those who are most beleaguered. Older people are more likely to consider drugs a national scourge than younger ones; in a Gallup poll in 1989, 31 percent of those fifty years and older identified drug abuse as "the most important problem facing the country," compared with 19 percent of those between the ages of eighteen and twenty-nine years.[5] Illicit drug use in general is overwhelmingly a youthful phenomenon, with incidence dropping off in the late twenties for most drugs.[6] (Heroin is an exception. As of 1991, usage rates were highest for those over thirty-five, a reflection of its drop in popularity over the past twenty years.[7])

One might conclude that many older people live in neighborhoods where drug abuse impinges on them directly, or that they are exposed to drug problems through children or grandchildren; but other evidence suggests that distance, as much as familiarity, breeds concern. Gallup polls taken in 1988 and 1989 found that drug use was most often cited as the "biggest problem with which the public schools in the community must deal," and that people with no children in school were more likely to hold this view (34 percent in 1988, 35 in 1989) than public school parents (30 percent both years).[8]

It might be argued that these results are not anomalous if the basis for concern about drugs is a moral, rather than a utilitarian one, that the explanation for greater concern among older people is that they have less moral tolerance. But, in fact, fewer older people than younger ones responding to the Gallup poll named "moral decline in society" as the "most important problem facing the country," and no greater concern was expressed about crime, which might have stood as a surrogate for the more general expression of concern about morality.

These observations are not intended to suggest that self-interest is generally or should be the principal basis for public concern, or that transforming concern into demands for political action is primarily the province of those with a personal grievance. The purpose here is to suggest the power of the narrative of drug abuse to attract a constituency broader than the groups who regard drug use as primarily a moral issue or those who have direct experience of shooting up or smoking crack, or walking through neighborhoods where many people do.

The Alaska case study helps illustrate how a diffuse concern about drugs can translate into specific advocacy for prohibition policy. Those who pushed hardest for recriminalizing marijuana possession were not those who had experience with problematic marijuana use, or with marijuana use at all, if interviewees are to be believed. Marie Majewske and Alyce Hanley were proud to report of their Marijuana Initiative Committee that "these were not parents of kids on drugs." While Majewske was quick to say that people with marijuana problems were welcome in her campaign, she believed that having a disinterested concern with "working for safe neighborhoods and schools" strengthened her group's legitimacy as having "no ax to grind."

Where concern is high among those most affected—people whose families and communities are directly and destructively touched by drug abuse—it does not necessarily take the punitive forms that could be expected, given the prohibitionist vigor of American public policy. Polls consistently show that African-Americans are even more concerned about drugs than whites, whether they are asked about drugs as a national problem or as observed in their own communities.[9] (Presumably this finding reflects in part the residential concentration of blacks in inner-city neighborhoods, where drug-trafficking affects daily life most pervasively.) Furthermore, blacks are significantly more likely to be victimized by those crimes—robbery and some kinds of assault—often associated with involvement with illegal drugs.[10] Nonetheless, only 28 percent of blacks (as opposed to 42 percent of whites) questioned by the *New York Times*/CBS poll in 1986 approved of giving a first-time convicted cocaine or crack dealer more than a year in jail.[11] African-Americans are also much less likely to conclude that harsher punishment is the answer to crime in general and less likely to support the death penalty for drug-dealing.[12]

Tensions also exist between perceptions of problems in the larger world and those of one's own environment. A quite small—and decreasing—percentage of Americans admit to knowing people who use illicit drugs; only 4 percent of respondents to a 1989 Harris poll said they knew anyone who used crack, and only 11 percent powder cocaine.[13] This was, however, in the same year that 61 percent of respondents to an Associated Press poll said that drugs were "the most important problem facing the country today."[14] A substantial majority of Americans appears to believe that drug abuse is rampant somewhere in the United States, but most do not seem to have direct knowledge of or contact with such abuse in their own life experiences.

Perhaps mythmaking is simply easier if its subject is not right at hand. In general, people are less prepared to believe that a negative social trend touches them than that it exists. Surveys conducted for the National Commission on Children in 1991 found that, although most adults believe that children are not getting enough direction or attention from parents, most also say that they are keeping track of their own children's whereabouts and development.[15] The tendency is also apparent in people's perceptions of street crime.[16] A 1986 Associated Press poll asked people how safe they felt walking after dark on their own street and elsewhere in the community. The tendency to feel safer near home applied to both low- and high-income respondents, to blacks as well as whites.[17] It might be thought that this perception reflects only a sense that at home one can better assess the dangers, not that those dangers are less likely to be manifested. But other data suggest that this explanation is incomplete. A 1989 Gallup poll asked people their perception of crime trends in the past year, both in the country at large and in their own area; the view that crime had increased nationally was almost a consensus (84 percent), but a bare majority (53 percent) believed that there was more crime close to home.[18]

It is thus interesting that perceptions of a link between street crime and marijuana use do not seem to explain support for recriminalization in Alaska, even though the activists believed in such a relationship. An Anchorage Crime Commission survey taken in 1988 in that city found that 76 percent felt crime had neither increased nor decreased in the recent past. Furthermore, when asked to recommend a single measure for improving police services, only 4 percent of respondents named increased emphasis on drugs; 45 percent indicated that they thought police service needed no improvement![19]

The Michigan case also suggests the fragility of the connection between public concern about a social condition and its seriousness. At the time the 650-plus law was debated and passed, in the late seventies, there were many indications of a decrease in public disorder in the state. Conforming to the national trend, reported street crime was dropping, particularly in Detroit; in 1978 the governor announced that the state's largest city had been below the national average for Federal Bureau of Investigation (FBI) Index crimes for big cities for three years in a row.[20] Officials of the federal Drug Enforcement Agency said that the flow of heroin into the country was slowing, and heroin abuse appeared to be declining, as measured by decreasing deaths from overdose and the rise in the average age of addicts in treatment (suggesting that fewer young people were becoming compulsive users who would eventually seek help).[21] Yet fear of crime and drugs remained high, with 33 percent of respondents in a 1977 statewide survey saying they were afraid to go out at night in their neighborhoods and, in a Detroit poll, 54 percent reporting they were fearful outside their neighborhoods, despite the opinion of 53 percent that downtown Detroit was safer than five years previously.[22] The fear was reflected in policy views: A 1978 *Detroit News* poll found that 72 percent of a group of adults in the metropolitan area favored the death penalty, and 75 percent of statewide respondents polled the previous year thought the criminal courts were too lenient.[23] The 1978 Michigan poll found that 13 percent of a representative sample of Michigan adults rated crime as the most important current problem in the state, fourth behind taxes, unemployment, and inflation.[24]

## DRUG PROHIBITION AND MARIJUANA USE

The prominence of marijuana in anti-drug campaigns of the last twenty years highlights the weakness of the relationship between the medical and social harmfulness of a drug and the policy priority given to eradicating it. Marijuana prohibition is enforced with extraordinary vigor (notwithstanding some urban pockets of tolerance, where use is officially punished with light fines but in practice not at all), although the drug appears to be less likely to cause death than aspirin.[25] An estimated 226,240 arrests were made for marijuana possession in 1991, and another 61,610 for sale or manufacture of the drug.[26] While most of those arrests were made by local law enforcement, the federal government has also made substantial investments in marijuana control.[27]

Can this comprehensive campaign be explained by the dangers of marijuana use? Notwithstanding the general undesirability of adolescent intoxication, smoking marijuana in moderate amounts and only on occasion—the way most of the 20 million annual users do —has not been found by respectable researchers to do serious physical or mental damage to healthy users, despite a generation of serious study.[28] And social harm cannot be compared with that of some harder drugs; as researcher Mark Kleiman puts it, "Marijuana dealers are not shooting up the cities, marijuana babies are not populating the neonatal intensive care wards, marijuana addicts are not stealing to pay for their drug habits, marijuana use and associated sexual activity are not spreading syphilis and AIDS, victims of marijuana are not clamoring for admission to treatment or flocking to self-help groups."[29]

If not by the dangers of marijuana use, can the gap between the public health implications of marijuana use and the attention given to the drug by the criminal justice system be explained by moral repugnance? It is certainly the case that the rhetoric of the marijuana crusade is instilled with precisely the same kind of moral obsessions as infused the cocaine wars. In 1990 Daryl Gates, then Police Chief of Los Angeles, testified at a Senate committee hearing that those who "blast some pot on a casual basis" should be "taken out and shot."[30] The theme of escalating villainy that justifies military involvement in fighting drug-trafficking appears in the context of marijuana as well as harder drugs. "The criminals who are growing this crop have become increasingly sophisticated, and much more violent in recent years," former U.S. Attorney General Edwin Meese asserted, warning that the armed guards and booby traps of marijuana growers threatened users of the national forests. (He instantly distanced himself from the rest of the Reagan administration, which devoted a good deal of energy to defeating regulatory activities of the Environmental Protection Agency, when he voiced concerns about environmental damage caused by marijuana growers, who, he noted, "destroy wildlife, indiscriminately cut down trees, dump pesticides in waterways and build harmful dams on creeks and streams to irrigate their illegal crops."[31])

Some of this moral repugnance may reflect more general public concerns. Poll respondents who identify themselves as belonging to a religion are more likely to oppose the legalization of marijuana than those who do not, and this pattern has held since the early 1970s.[32] Republicans are also more likely than Democrats to be against legalization, but this result—assuming that in general Republicans are likely to be more culturally conservative—may suggest more about support for authority and order than about strictly moral concerns, since Republicans are not notably more religious than Democrats.

And so, for a variety of reasons, involvement with marijuana is often penalized as severely as use or distribution of hard drugs. While penalties for possession are generally lighter for marijuana than for, say, heroin, the distinction often blurs when it comes to selling. Kleiman concludes that federal drug defendants convicted of marijuana offenses receive sentences similar to sentences for other drugs.[33] Federal legislation in 1988 permitting the death penalty for drug kingpin murders makes no distinction among the illicit drugs that are being sold or manufactured, and, in fact, the first death sentence under the 1988 law was imposed on David Ronald Chandler, an Alabama marijuana grower and dealer (white) with no previous felony convictions. (The point here is not that a murder committed by the head of a marijuana ring is any less heinous than that committed by the leader of a Colombian cocaine cartel. It is, rather, that such murders are not logically equivalent if the rationale for designating killings by major drug dealers as capital crimes is that they are committed in the course of a business that poisons and kills the consumers.)

This failure to distinguish between use of marijuana and hard drugs is further mirrored by the absence of policy distinction among occasional, moderate, and heavy drug users. In a recent article, Peter Reuter, co-director of the RAND Corporation's Drug Policy Research Center, bemoans the neglect of prevalence and consumption estimates in drug policy research and analysis but concludes that most illegal drugs are consumed by a small core of compulsive users.[34] In other words, a lot of people take small amounts of drugs occasionally, while many fewer people take large amounts continuously. That our drug policy punishes and seeks to deter both kinds of users equally suggests that its law enforcement emphasis has aims other than the reduction of use. Those who are addicted are unlikely to be deterred by the threat of arrest and prison, almost by definition, since we presume their craving renders them incapable of a rational calculation of the costs and benefits of their drug-taking behavior. Those who are casual users may be deterrable, but deterring them may not be very efficient, given the difficulties of apprehending and punishing enough of their number to send the message. In addition, those users may be deterred by less drastic means than criminal sanctions—with public health messages, for instance (though not if they present, as some do, patently absurd findings about the damage of occasional use of the milder forms of some drugs).

## DRUG PROHIBITION AND ALCOHOL ABUSE

Perhaps the most stunning anomaly of all is that, although by almost any measure of economic or social cost American abuse of alcohol is a more damaging social condition than abuse of illicit drugs, we have made peace with a mix of regulation, treatment, and social tolerance of alcohol that is still unthinkable for marijuana, cocaine, hallucinogens, and the opiates. Consider the evidence.

More than a third of American adults get drunk at least once a year; the 1984 National Alcohol Survey sponsored by the National Institute of Alcohol Abuse and Alcoholism classified 18 percent of men and 5 percent of women as heavy drinkers.[35] Young adults (including high-school seniors and college students) report that they are almost twice as likely to consume alcohol daily as smoke pot or use other illicit drugs, and more than ten times as likely to engage in what former Secretary of Health and Human Services Louis W. Sullivan called "binge drinking" within a two-week period.[36] The immediate hazards of this behavior—there are, of course, the longer-term specters of fetal alcohol syndrome and liver and heart disease—show up in the national survey of high-school seniors' drug and alcohol use, where year after year far more students who have been in an automobile accident within the previous year report that the accidents occurred after they had been drinking than after they had been smoking pot or using other drugs.[37] The National Highway Traffic Safety Administration reports that alcohol was a factor in

68,000 fatal or near-fatal accidents in 1989, and in another 148,000 where minor or moderate injury occurred; these numbers would probably have been even worse in the early years of the decade, if statistics were available, since the number of fatally injured drunk drivers dropped significantly between 1982 and 1989.[38] While we must guard against the hazards of attributing causality where mere association is present—other influences than the driver's inebriation may have contributed to or even brought about some of the accidents—alcohol is clearly the leading culprit in a very large number of highway disasters.

The association of alcohol abuse and crime is certainly as strong as for drug abuse and crime. Surveys of alcohol use among offenders (for drug crimes and others) report a high incidence of alcohol use at the time they committed the crime for which they were serving time, and male juvenile arrestees surveyed in several cities in 1990 were far more likely to report use of alcohol in the seventy-two hours preceding arrest than lifetime use of any drug other than marijuana.[39] While alcohol may not be the sole cause of a barroom brawl or domestic conflict, its contribution is often substantial.[40] The 1989 survey of inmates in local jails sponsored by the federal Bureau of Justice Statistics, which interviewed a nationally representative sample of inmates (5,675 inmates in 424 city and county jails), suggests a general tendency for drug abuse to be associated with acquisitive crime and alcohol abuse with violent crime.[41] While the proportion of inmates under the influence of drugs or alcohol was about the same for property offenses, almost twice as many said they were under the influence of alcohol when they committed violent offenses.[42] Particularly striking was the fact that a full 49.5 percent of those convicted of homicide said they were using alcohol when they killed their victim, while only 5.5 percent said they were on drugs alone at the time of the murder, and 13.7 were using both drugs and alcohol.

Comparing the harm done to others through the interpersonal violence caused or intensified by alcohol and the damage done by burglaries and muggings motivated by the need for money by drugs is a tricky business; there are simply too many confounding influences in these events. We also have no statistical measures of how much crime can be attributed to violence in the course of drug transactions. For one who lives in a large American city and pays attention to media reports of crime, such events are depressingly frequent, but we are unable to determine whether they constitute a statistically meaningful phenomenon for comparing the damage done by drugs and alcohol. The rate of overall violent crime reported in metropolitan areas to law enforcement between 1982 and 1991 increased 33.6 percent (while the reported property crime rate increased only 1.2 percent), but the rate of aggravated assault increased by 54.6 percent.[43] This rise could indicate increasing drug transaction violence, but it also might be a reflection of increasingly desperate economic circumstances—and the effects of alcohol, rather than illicit drugs— among low-income people, whose assaults are most likely to be reported to police. The murder rate, a crime often reported in the media as drug-related, rose during the same period by only 11 percent.

Alcohol and drugs combine to produce many drug episodes that those experiencing them consider emergencies. People seen for drug episodes in hospital emergency rooms in twenty-one metropolitan areas, when questioned about what they have been ingesting, are more likely to mention combinations of drugs and alcohol than any individual drug except cocaine.[44] The pattern holds for reports of drug abuse deaths from eighty-seven metropolitan-area medical examiners; alcohol is mentioned in combination with other drugs in 38.79 percent of cases reported in 1989, second only to cocaine (50.52 percent).[45]

Comparing the economic costs of alcohol and drug abuse is one way—albeit incomplete—of comparing the relative seriousness of drug and alcohol use. The Alcohol, Drug Abuse, and Mental Health Administration of the U.S. Department of Health and Human Services has sponsored several studies that make possible such estimates. They add up direct costs like the amounts spent on drug and alcohol treatment facilities, specialized training for medical personnel, and health insurance; and indirect costs like the value of lost productivity for those who die or are disabled by drug or alcohol abuse, the costs of incarceration and welfare that would not be needed if drug and alcohol abuse did not exist, and the costs of crashes and fires. Although 1985 is the last year for which complete data are available, the authors of the most recent report, written in 1990, estimate overall costs for 1988, though they note that "crack cocaine addiction and its devastating consequences are not included in the cost estimates because this major public health problem emerged after 1985."[46] AIDS costs for drug abusers are included, as well as the costs of fetal alcohol syndrome.

Overall estimates for the costs of alcohol abuse were $70.3 billion for 1985 and $85.8 billion for 1988; for drug abuse they were $44.1 billion in 1985 and $58.3 billion in 1988.[47] The cost differences reflect not only the greater number of alcohol abusers—the study assumes an alcohol abuse prevalence rate of 14.9 percent of the civilian non-institutionalized population ages eighteen to sixty-four, and a drug abuse prevalence rate of 3.6 percent—but the far greater number of alcohol abuse deaths. (The study estimated 94,768 alcohol abuse deaths in 1985 and 6,118 drug abuse deaths.) The cost gap would be even greater without drug prohibition, since almost three-fourths of the economic cost of drug abuse is incurred because drugs are illegal: police protection, legal defense, productivity losses for those who are career criminals instead of legal workers, productivity losses for those in prison for drug crimes.[48]

These figures would look quite different, of course, in the mid-1990s. With respect to illicit drugs, incarceration has shot up, increasing the costs of drug abuse and our approaches to it. The arrival of crack, the smokable form of cocaine, has added to the health care and welfare costs of drug abuse. We do not, however, know how to calculate these costs because we do not really know the size of the crack epidemic. In 1989, 39 percent of the 3,618 mentions of cocaine as a cause of death in medical examiners' reports to the U.S. Department of Health and Human Services identified a cigarette as the form in which the drug was consumed, but the "unknown" category of 48.8 percent probably includes many crack users.[49] Screening of arrestees does not distinguish between crack and other forms of cocaine; cocaine use by arrestees in many cities showed little change between 1988 and the end of 1991, according to the Drug Use Forecasting Program of the U.S. Department of Justice.[50] The National Household Survey estimated in 1991 that about a million people used crack in the year before the survey and about half that in the previous month, but we do not know to what extent those groups substituted it for another illicit drug and to what extent (or whether) such a substitution would raise the costs of drug abuse.[51]

On the other hand, estimates of lost productivity due to drugs might be lower than a decade ago, given the signs that middle-class and casual drug use has declined.[52] Alcohol abuse appears to be down too, though only slightly, and there have been larger increases in federal funding for drug abuse treatment than for alcohol treatment, two trends that make it likely that the gap between the costs of the two phenomena would be narrower than in 1985.[53] The economic bottom line, however, would surely still support the more general assertion that alcohol abuse has more damaging effects on American society than drug abuse. (This conclusion should not be read to discount the magnitude of the costs of drug abuse; the elephant is no less large an animal because we have learned about the mammoth.)

The anomaly of tolerance for a large amount of damaging alcohol abuse coexisting with prohibition of a smaller amount of arguably less-damaging drug abuse is starting to become apparent in some circles. Challenges to the tolerance for alcohol abuse have begun to emerge in the last few years, mounted by grass-roots demand for greater regulation. The movement to strengthen drunk driving laws, spurred by European examples and by the birth and growth of Mothers Against Drunk Driving and designated driver programs, has called into question the presumption that alcohol abuse, unlike drug abuse, affects individual drinkers and their intimates negatively but has little adverse impact on society as a whole. However, the concern about alcohol, limited as it is to the drunk driving situation (and to a growing awareness of fetal alcohol syndrome, which, in 1985 at least, was more costly in economic terms than drug-related AIDS), does not usually carry over to questioning the prohibitionist approach to other psychoactive substances.

The Alaskan situation illustrates both the growing awareness of damage from alcohol and the ability of prohibition activists to deny the anomaly. Johnny Ellis, co-chairman of the committee in the Alaska House of Representatives that killed recriminalization bills in 1988, was attacked as "soft on drugs" by his Republican opponent when he ran for office later that year. He won anyway, but he expressed frustration with the continuing salience of the recriminalization issue. "Why are we spending so much time talking about marijuana when there are so many more serious substance abuse problems documented in the state of Alaska?" he asked after the election.[54] By contrast, proponents of the marijuana initiative were able simultaneously to acknowledge the far greater social harm caused by alcohol in Alaska and put extraordinary amounts of energy into a prohibitionist policy that would, at best, have a marginal effect on a minor problem (even granting that marijuana abuse exists as a medically and socially significant phenomenon, which many experts would be unwilling to do). "There are already lots of laws to limit alcohol use," says Majewske, a trifle defensively, when asked why she was not interested in targeting youthful alcohol use. "I'm not out to save the world. We thought we could deal with this particular problem in this particular community."

Seattle anti-drug activists, too, recognize the toll of alcohol abuse but aren't troubled by making policy distinctions between alcohol and drugs like crack and heroin. Several interviewees told me bits of Seattle's history as a wide open logging town that tolerated public drunkenness on Skid Row and elsewhere and nowadays has alcohol emergencies comparable to those in other cities of its size. Yet the retail drug dealers, largely but not exclusively minority male teen-agers, are seen as far more appropriate targets for law enforcement control of the streets than the ragged older winos who are just as likely to accost the passerby. Lucinda Harder, head of a citizens' crime prevention group, notes that downtown Seattle has always had its "chronic drunks" who "interfere with downtown, too." But, she says, "they're easier to get along with" than the drug dealers, and "you're not in harm's way as much as you are with the drug scene."[55] Her idiom says it all: "Harm's way" is a creation of drugs' illegal status—of prohibition—not of the effect of drugs themselves.

# CHAPTER 9

# *Beyond Drug Abuse: Three Other Agenda Items*

**W**e turn now to the shadow agenda fueling prohibition policy. Some clarification and definition are necessary before analyzing its elements and effects. Drug abuse is a social condition that brings suffering and danger to many people. But if we regard prohibition as *solely* the product of concerns about compulsive use of dangerous psychoactive substances, we are missing much of what gives the policy such staying power and excludes consideration of even modest reforms by the political mainstream. Furthermore, the shadow agenda that sustains prohibitionist policies overlaps with others that drive related public activity, creating a policy culture that shapes the broad directions we take in social policy more generally. Inattention to shadow agendas potentially impoverishes our approaches to racial equality, crime control, public assistance, and employment, to name a few. "Problem solving," writes Stuart Scheingold, "is not necessarily the primary objective of public policy."[1]

By "shadow agenda" I don't mean a *hidden* agenda—a covey of items, bait for political and other conspirators, exploiting a troublesome social condition as the excuse for realizing secret (and often nefarious) objectives. The shadow agenda, rather, is more like the natural phenomenon for which it is named: now elongating, now shrinking, affected by light and angle. It is a cluster of systematic influences, deeply rooted in culture and ideology, that inhere in the pulling and tugging of policymaking. It accompanies both the institutional and the systemic agendas and helps to explain the tenacity of policies that fall short of addressing overtly defined problems.

Perhaps a helpful analogy is the image of the penumbra—the partial shadow around the full shadow of an opaque object, like planets or the moon. Justice William O. Douglas used this image to find a privacy right in the Constitution, even though it was not expressly guaranteed in the text; he reasoned that emanations from several rights that were enumerated or presumed—the right of association, the right to be free from unreasonable search and seizure, the right to refuse to incriminate yourself—formed a penumbra of privacy protection.[2] While the shadow agenda is dependent on the existence of a socially harmful condition, its components emanate from the condition, often at more than one remove. Parents' desires to retain authority over their children or their fear for the futures of young people who may be tarred in a harshly competitive world by early reputations as pot-smoking layabouts are not the same as well-founded fears of moral or physical decay caused by heavy and wide-spread marijuana use; but these concerns are linked fairly directly by a common perception that young people need both direction and vigor to succeed and that mind-altering experiences may subvert these qualities. More tangential but still related is the policy implementer's view that public sympathy for the routine services that must be pro-vided in a modern administrative state can only be mobilized with a dramatic issue or apparently simple solution; drug abuse is the engine, street crime and family counseling are the boxcars. Even the cynical politician's effort to burnish an image of leadership by embracing popularly appealing policies with little chance of passage or substan-tive effect retains a tie to the real dangers of drug abuse by its ac-knowledgment that a leader *should* be able to shield his or her constituents from the threat they perceive.

In order to identify and understand the shadow agenda, we need to look at policy politics somewhat more generally. Once having established the multiple stages and forces shaping policy, we can then turn to the specific case of the drug wars and the stages and com-ponents of agenda-setting in this particular area.

## SETTING THE POLICY AGENDA

Where to begin? With the possible exceptions of armed conflict, eco-nomic collapse, and natural disaster, objective conditions rarely bring about major changes in public policy.[3] The movement of a political system from repression to tolerance, from generosity to parsimony, from contraction to expansion, generally depends less on the state of the material world than on the way leaders and followers perceive it and the measures they take to influence each others' perceptions. This is why politics will always shape policymaking, no less in the process of defining the public problem than in the more overtly conflictual stages of enactment and implementation.

The early stages of policymaking, in fact, are crucial. Setting the policy agenda—when it is done publicly, as is most common with social issues—can excite the public as a campaign sometimes energizes the electorate. Its essence is the expression of aspirations or worries—whether those of the general public, of interest groups, or of political and economic elites—before the nitty-gritty reality of politics as the art of the possible sets in. Defining a public problem and setting general directions for addressing it is the serve in the policy game.[4]

Agenda-setting is important for several reasons. First, it is a prime exercise of power. As Harold Lasswell wrote, "The essence of power is understood to be the capacity, and usually the will, to impose one's own values as permanent or transitory motives upon others."[5] The *way* an issue is initially cast by the state and those who have coaxed it into acting—more and more often these days, the mass media— often determines not just individual measures that are taken but also basic policy themes that in turn shape future political alliances and policy debates. After an urban riot, for instance, what is most likely to determine whether the rioters get jobs or prison, or which party gets blamed for unrest, or whether macroeconomic and macrosocial arrangements will be adjusted or reinforced, is whether the event is seen by press, public, and politicians as a breakdown of authority or a *cri de coeur* from citizens abandoned by their society.

Second, policy approaches created to address an issue may outlive it, leaving an institutional legacy that will have an effect on the birth of new agendas.[6] Perhaps most important, it is at the point of issue definition that the most far-reaching—though sometimes the least visible—exercises (and manifestations) of political and social power occur. The immediate and overt clout of legislators and political executives and interest groups is, of course, very important later in the policy process in formulating particular measures and getting them adopted. Bureaucrats—either as individuals or through their institutional influence—can sometimes make (and usually break) a policy as it is being implemented. But all these later activities are colored by the initial perception of events and the determination that they are appropriate subjects for political attention—a process of constructing vehicles for political messages. Those engaged in the process have often shaped the political climate that will be receptive to these messages. Their influence may be crucial but covert, not in the sense of participating in a conspiracy but through the wordless sharing of assumptions about the way the world should work.

Drug policy is a good illustration of the hammerlock that agenda-setting has on policy. Once on the agenda, the abuse of mind-altering substances can be dealt with at later stages of the policy process only within the very limited framework that was established as part of the agenda. The prohibitionist thrust of drug policy set at the problem definition stage, with its moralistic core, allows very little room for adapting to new considerations and problems. For example, it hinders acknowledgment that transmission of the AIDS virus by intravenous drug users can be reduced by needle exchange programs. Federal drug czars have excoriated the big-city mayors and state legislatures that have endorsed these efforts to reduce the incidence of HIV spread by needle-sharing and have blocked use of federal funds for local programs. Although their adamant opposition rests to some extent on the argument that giving needles to addicts is ineffective (despite some research suggesting the contrary), the primary argument is an ideological one, based on moral premises of drug prohibition that are likely to remain impervious to mere scientific evidence of progress in slowing the rate of HIV transmission among intravenous drug users. Bob Martinez, former Director of the Office of National Drug Control Policy, underscored the tenacity of the agenda-setting aspect of policymaking in a report attacking studies of needle exchange programs that came to favorable conclusions. In the introduction he warned of the danger that we might "allow our concern for AIDS to undermine our determination to win the war on drugs" and "society's message that using drugs is illegal and morally wrong."[7]

On a broader level, the drug wars' attribution of harm and evil to individual responsibility blinds us to structural determinants of drug abuse and impedes attention that we might otherwise pay to remedying those conditions. If people who use and sell drugs are regarded primarily as agents of their own destiny, it is much easier to view drug abuse as a cause of poverty than the other way around. Casting the problem in those terms negates the possibility that drug abuse is one of the bitter fruits of deprivation and inequality.[8]

How are these early and crucial agendas established? Policy analysts usually assume that agenda-setting is an open process resulting in easily identified agenda items. Agendas are either institutional, or formal, including items for immediate government action—routine matters like budget needs; or systemic, made up of items for discussion but notable more for the controversy they generate than for the action taken on them.[9] Many conditions affecting large numbers of people—public problems—fail to reach even the systemic agenda, in this view, excluded either by "politics" (lobbying or the lack of it), by culturally determined notions of what topics are appropriate for government attention, or by the failure of powerful groups to care about them.[10]

But if a policy agenda is supposed to reflect matters of public concern upon which government is expected to act, it is important to expand the idea of agenda-setting to include items that are not even discussed, at least not openly or in recognized policy forums, but which are projected into the decisionmaking arena nonetheless and may indeed be more far-reaching than the overt items.

## THE OVERT POLICY AGENDA

Professional policy analysts tend to be rationalists, hoping and believing that public problems can be solved with the orderly application of policy-oriented premises and value-free techniques.[11] Their assessments of public activity, therefore, generally focus on the overt agendas, evaluating government activity in terms of its relationship to declared objectives or those that can be inferred from what has been declared. In the case of drug prohibition, for instance, policy evaluation is often cast in terms of a contest between those who see the American abuse of dangerous psychoactive substances (principally illegal drugs but not exclusively) as a public health problem causing disease and dependence, and those who see any abuse of illicit drugs as a moral failing, usually symptomatic of the degeneration of "traditional values," which are variously enumerated according to cultural predispositions, religious commitments, and political sympathies.[12] Both groups support prohibition, but with a different emphasis: The moralists see state sanctions as the clearest and most far-reaching expression of respect for social order and established authority. Those who define drugs as a public health problem may also believe that the sanctions of law enforcement will deter at least a few potential users and dealers and perhaps put pressure on users to get treatment. Those whose support for prohibition is based on moral grounds do not deny that programs of treatment and suasion are desirable, but their appeal rests at least as much on their value as propaganda and the discipline that they may provide as on the relief from disease and dependence that the utilitarians stress.[13]

This image of polar positions is probably overdrawn. Political leaders, who are pressured to take unequivocal stands on important public issues, frequently occupy one clearly defined camp or the other.[14] But to understand how members of the concerned public are likely to position themselves, a more revealing model might be a continuum with public health concerns at one end and moralistic ones at the other and most people perched in a spot where they can juggle both perspectives. This conclusion leads back to the point made in Chapter 1: A consensus on the seriousness of illicit drugs as a social problem does not lead to clarity as to how it should be addressed. Most Americans—even scholars, who tend to favor sharply drawn analytical distinctions—combine public health and moralistic (or legalistic) concerns in thinking about what approaches government should take. People seem prepared to live with the dissonances this duality sometimes entails—for instance, the possibility that the threat of punishment will deter users (and user-dealers at the retail level) from getting treatment and may drive people to use drugs that are more dangerous because they are consumed in more concentrated forms.

Support for drug prohibition among both moralists and public health advocates is strong. The 30 percent of respondents to a Roper survey in 1978 who said they supported legalizing marijuana had shrunk to 18 percent by 1984 (and continued at about that level at least through 1991), suggesting that proposals for greater tolerance of other drugs would receive even less support.[15] A large majority of respondents to a Gallup poll taken in 1990 thought that if drugs were legalized there would be more drugs in the schools, the number of addicts would increase, and more drug overdoses would occur.[16]

Not surprisingly, attitudes are most punitive toward drug dealers; there is strong support for more prisons to house them, and a 1988 Gallup poll found that a sizable minority of respondents (38 percent) supported the death penalty for drug dealers *not* convicted of murder.[17] In the 1987 National Punishment Survey—a little outdated, but still the most important in-depth survey of attitudes toward the seriousness of crimes—respondents ranked selling cocaine to others for resale as being only slightly less serious than intentionally setting fire to a building and causing $500,000 damage.[18] Most respondents—90 percent—favored prison for such a crime, with an average sentence length of 10½ years, a little longer than the average sentence thought appropriate for someone who committed a $1,000 robbery at gunpoint and wounded the victim enough to require hospitalization.[19] People are also prepared to punish drug users quite severely. The National Punishment Survey found that cocaine use was considered serious; a majority of respondents would impose a prison sentence, and the mean sentence length preferred (among those who approved of prison for the crime) was sixty-six months.

But severity is not the whole story. Apparently many people believe in punishment for drug offenses not because it will solve the drug problem but because it is deserved; to reduce drug abuse, many would support public health measures. Associated Press polls from 1989 to 1990 found that a majority believe that treatment is more effective in reducing drug use than punishment for users.[20] Respondents to a 1990 Gallup poll were more than twice as likely to endorse committing the lion's share of government drug-fighting resources to "teaching young people about the dangers of drugs" as to "arresting people in this country who sell drugs." Putting a major emphasis on "arresting the people who use drugs" got only 4 percent support.[21]

These are the overt influences on drug policy. But policy has costs and benefits that relate to unstated agenda items. The shadow agenda expresses anxieties and aspirations that are socially unacceptable because they clash with public morality, or don't promote what is perceived as a legitimate public purpose, or further a public purpose only remotely related to the policy to which they are attached. Its items are latent not only in the sense that they are not openly acknowledged, but also because they are often not explicitly intended; if they emanate from consciousness, it is collective rather than individual. They may be, however, at least as significant as declared and deliberate agenda items in keeping policy alive. Sometimes the shadow agenda tells us more about the national mood and general public priorities than the declared subjects of attention.[22]

## THREE COMPONENTS OF THE PROHIBITIONIST SHADOW AGENDA

To acquire a complete picture of the determinants of prohibitionist policies we must discern three principal items on the shadow agenda. They are not all present in all instances of prohibition policymaking, for several reasons. In the first place, drug control is primarily undertaken through the criminal law, which in our federal system is largely state and local—although with increasing frequency it is overridden and sometimes overshadowed by national initiatives—and is intended to reflect diversity in local conditions, attitudes, and solutions. In addition, the anxieties that propel the shadow agenda, like concern about drugs themselves, wax and wane as material and cultural forces shift. Unforeseen events—earthquakes, international conflicts—can push aside even the pressing economic and social concerns that may fuel drug prohibition, at least momentarily.

Despite the variability of policy politics, however, themes emerge from the five cases of drug prohibition policy process. They tell us a good deal about what else worries Americans besides drugs and how those worries are poured into the crucible of drug prohibition.

*Controlling the Unruly.* Critics of the recurrent drug wars often charge that they are fought against black people, or minorities more generally. They point out that penalties for the drugs (primarily crack) that African-Americans are most likely to use may be harsher than for other drugs, that black women who are drug users are more likely to be prosecuted for endangering a fetus than white women, and that state sentences are longer for black drug traffickers than for whites.[23] There is certainly a good deal of racism in American drug prohibition, and has been for more than a hundred years. The current visibility of young black and Hispanic retail drug dealers in the inner cities, and law enforcement's concentration on them, has sustained the myth of minorities as carriers of a plague of drug abuse.

But, in addition, drug prohibition feeds on a broader kind of impulse of exclusion, one that embraces control not only of minorities but also of youth and aliens and civil libertarians (or what might be called cultural liberals, who base their tolerance of alternative lifestyles less on notions of individual right than on celebration of occasional hedonism). This targeting reflects the ideology of cultural conservatism, which aims to turn back the clock to a time of greater legitimacy for public and private authority over groups who, since the dawn of the civil rights movement, have demanded greater freedom and status.[24] As with authoritarian impulses in general, it is fueled in part by the insecurities of a faltering economy.

The appeal of controlling the dangerous classes as an item on the shadow agenda depends as much on the role of the actor in the policy process as on ideology or purely political motives. I find it useful to divide policymakers into three kinds of roles that to some degree shape their perspectives on the groups who might be tamed by social policies like drug prohibition: formulators, implementers, and activists.

*Formulators* are the executive and legislative leaders who initiate policy. For them, success depends as much on the images of leadership they project in the act of delineating rules or programs as on the content of those measures. *Implementers* may be leaders, too, but their principal task is turning the initiatives of the formulators into a workable program, so the measure of their success is more likely to be performance than vision. *Activists* are individuals or groups outside the governmental institutions of policymaking who are nonetheless crucial to the process as representatives of organized interests, whether they are a small group of corporate executives or the parents of America. Their aim is to get rewards from government—rights as well as subsidy—and they have little incentive to promote, either substantively or symbolically, interests of groups other than their own.

The next chapter considers these various policy roles in controlling the dangerous classes through drug prohibition.

*Acquiring and Maintaining Political Power.* The intensity of public concern about drugs and the hammerlock of prohibition on drug policy have forced many politicians (particularly those from urban areas) to take positions on the governmental role in fighting drug abuse. But the salience of the issue can be both curse and blessing. Since support for law enforcement approaches to drugs is all but unanimous, simple endorsement of getting tough on users and dealers is not enough to give candidates for public office an advantage over their opponents; such an endorsement, in fact, is a minimum defense against being labeled soft on drugs. On the other hand, the drama that can be associated with the problem of drug abuse legitimizes what might otherwise seem like contests of braggadocio over get-tough policies, creating ample opportunity for pushing the policy frontiers into new territory, such as legislating oddball penalties ranging from the loss of a student loan or mortgage guarantee to death. (This pattern holds for street crime policy battles, too, to which drug-control debates are obviously closely related.) "The drug problem" becomes an irresistible resource for getting or keeping political power.

*Meeting Material Needs.* Since the national tax revolt combined with fiscal crises for states and cities in the mid-1970s, local services of many kinds have been severely pinched.[25] In the competition for very scarce resources, managers of public programs scramble to identify dramatic manifestations of the broader problems they seek funds to address. Drug abuse, calling up images of death and degradation, is a tempting hook on which to hang the legitimization of more routine funding needs. In the private sector a similar pattern emerges. The failure rate of American businesses (most of them small) leaped from an annual average for the four years 1973–76 of 38 per 10,000 enterprises to an average of 113 for 1983–86, a decade later.[26] This latter figure is alarmingly close to the average annual failure rate during the depths of the Great Depression (1930–33) of 127.3.[27] It is hardly surprising that in such an economic environment, business would seek maximum public assistance in reaching its markets. Pleas for protection from the general incivility of urban streets that can deter customers are particularly persuasive when couched in terms of drug transactions, activities most emblematic of larger threats to retail trade.

# Chapter 10

# *Controlling the Dangerous Classes*

The dangerous classes that threaten Americans today are not the same as those that earlier generations found menacing. But some attributes resemble those of past eras—poverty and immigrant status, for example—and the notion of associating dangerousness as much with condition as with behavior goes way back.

## YESTERDAY'S DANGEROUS CLASSES

The criminal law as an instrument for the protection and advancement of powerful interests long predates the advent of market economies in Europe. The "king's peace" imposed on offenders by Norman rulers in England was more important for the royal revenue it exacted than as crime control or punishment.[1] But the rise of capitalism displaced peasants and deposited many of them as desperate vagrants in the towns and cities, giving rise to emergent uses of law to support the new mercantilism and contain the social consequences of structural instability.[2] This process spawned the association of poverty and criminality that prevails in many western societies to this day. While the English Poor Law of 1601 provided some relief to workers suffering from rural displacement and the decline of wages in late sixteenth century England, it also forced the poor into wage labor. Furthermore, it formalized a separation between the deserving poor, for whom relief would be found, and "the many-headed monster" of vagabonds and thieves, who were sometimes also rebels.[3]

The ideological power of this distinction can hardly be overemphasized. Assigning individual and collective blame justified repression, then as now, through laws against vagrancy and theft. The sources of sin could be variously described as idleness, godlessness, and indifference to collective security, even where it was simultaneously acknowledged that structural shifts had destabilized whole communities.[4] Those held responsible for civil disorder were labeled "dangerous classes," a threat to personal safety and, if unchecked, to the social and economic order.[5]

The designation of "dangerous classes" spans regimes and eras. The stigmatized groups were also the focus of great concern in pre- and post-revolutionary France.[6] While some relationship between poverty and crime was presumed, it was incomplete, because "polite swindlers" were acknowledged to exist and were not part of the criminal class. In addition, within the ranks of the poor there were both "laboring classes" and "dangerous classes." The latter were the poor who did not work, whose idleness and desperation led them into crime. "By and large, work was the key to social acceptability. Those who did not, could not, or would not work were dangerous."[7] Those dangers—from street brawls and robberies to mass revolts of workers—obsessed both the bourgeoisie and the proletariat of Paris as crime came to be viewed, in the first half of the nineteenth century, not as aberrational and picturesque but as a normal, if troublesome, characteristic of urban social reality.[8] Both popular and elite literature reflects the preoccupation; Victor Hugo's *Les Misérables* is permeated with it, and Honoré de Balzac's later work portrays the crimes of the poor as pervasive and threatening. (Although Hugo did not publish his novel until well after 1850, it begins in 1823 and depicts social conditions of that time.)

While the "dangerous classes" label identifies groups most likely to be the immediate cause of a certain kind of social disorder, it also operates with a good deal of independence from the social harm they actually cause. Dangerous classes are constructed in the context of their role—usually, but not always, as victims—in social and economic upheavals like enclosure, urbanization, or industrialization. The source of their dangerousness, then, goes beyond the immorality of individual deviance or harm to immediate victims to the larger threat to society their actions constitute. They challenge the state's search for stability and the legitimacy of the criminal law in "maintaining bonds of obedience and deference."[9]

Although the most visible and immediate dangers posed by dangerous classes have always been what we now call street crimes, behind them lay the specter of greater challenges—sometimes overt dangers like political violence, more often passive ones like drunkenness and sloth—to an economic and social structure that bred burglars and vagabonds.[10] A deviance as obvious as thievery is easy to attribute to individual pathology or venality. Giving thieves or vagrants a derisive label and treating them as pariahs enhances the respectability of others, as Durkheim recognized. It also reduces the likelihood that respectable people will see robbery or riot as evidence of larger institutional failures in their society. The remedies for deviance were alms and punishment; then as now, they are presumed to avert both immediate harm and more general subversion.

In the United States the concept of "dangerous classes" arose with the industrialization of the nineteenth century, rooted in a moral redefinition of poverty that helped discipline workers to a low-wage market economy.[11] A missionary's description, early in the period, of tenement dwellers in New York City as "a commingled mass of venomous filth and seething sin" suggests the core association of crime with poverty.[12] Migration and immigration—the unprecedented flow into cities of people displaced from farms by agricultural mechanization and from far-off lands by poverty and pogrom—added threats of disease and dissent to those of urban crime.[13] A New York social reformer, writing in 1872, expressed a common view of the American "prolétaires" and the perils they presented:

> All the neglect and bad education and evil example of a poor class tend to form others, who, as they mature, swell the ranks of ruffians and criminals. So, at length, a great multitude of ignorant, untrained, passionate, irreligious boys and young men are formed, who become the "dangerous classes" of our city. . . . All these great masses of destitute, miserable, and criminal persons believe that for ages the rich have had all the good things of life, while to them have been left the evil things. Capital to them is the tyrant. Let but Law lift its hand from them for a season, or let the civilizing influences of American life fail to reach them, and, if the opportunity offered, we should see an explosion from this class which might leave this city in ashes and blood.[14]

After the Civil War, the ethnic cast of American dangerous classes—the big-city gangs of that era were invariably Irish, and many of the "ignorant, untrained, passionate, irreligious boys and young men" were German by birth or ancestry—was supplemented by race. The newly freed blacks could be demonized as both primitive and dangerous, and the perceived immoralities of the Chinese in the West included prostitution, gambling, and opium.[15] In the early decades of the twentieth century the association of blacks and cocaine as well as that of Mexicans and marijuana brought drug-taking within the congeries of dangers posed by the "criminal element."[16]

It is not easy to identify precisely the members of the "dangerous classes," either for a single society or over time. The category does not consist of all of the poor, nor all of the idle, nor all of the criminal, nor all of the dissenters; and it is difficult to characterize that segment of each category that *is* included. The concept is a loosely constructed amalgam of different elements that separate and connect as reflections of larger shifts in social tides. Furthermore, different observers will have in mind different combinations of these elements—always more than one, usually several, perhaps all—when they refer to the composite category. The fluidity of the concept does not, however, render it powerless. It is familiar in the discourse of deviance, less dependent on uniform definition than on the sense of shared meaning its invocation provides.

## TODAY'S DANGEROUS CLASSES

A contemporary rationalist could be forgiven for thinking that in late twentieth-century America, our greater sophistication about causality and the highly contingent nature of social threat would have buried the concept of dangerous classes. Few policy actors would now assume that the poor—even those not engaged in lawful work—are more criminal than the affluent, even if they commit disproportionate numbers of the kinds of crimes to which they have access. And the blatant nativism that enshrined the image of the foreign criminal and stimulated legislation to disarm aliens has passed.[17] Yet divisions of race, class, gender, alienage, and social ideology not only persist but seem to be deepening. They express defiance of inevitable trends of ethnic and cultural pluralism and respond to what appear to be long-term and national economic insecurities. And these divisions feed an ideology that personifies these threats in drug users, street gang members, and welfare mothers, who resurrect the blending images of poverty, idleness, and moral degeneracy that characterized earlier dangerous classes. Today's dangerous classes include segments of the diverse communities of racial and ethnic minorities; young people who exhibit some degree of independence from their elders' direction and values; and aliens and the "new immigrants" who have come to the United States from Third World countries since preferences in the immigration law changed in 1965. A fourth group is what can perhaps best be called cultural liberals—crudely, those who tolerate (and occasionally celebrate) drugs, sex, and rock 'n roll and do so in the name of individual freedom. Murray Edelman makes the point that those whose dangerousness flows from their resistance to definitions of the dangerousness of others—blacks and youth, for instance—elicit particularly intense antagonisms because explaining the awful consequences of their deviance is strategically problematic.[18]

The likelihood that the identified groups create danger—crime, urban decay, challenge to authority—is an article of faith, as both the public and the policymakers point to high levels of urban disorder, family dissolution, and unwed motherhood and low levels of productivity and patriotism. What is needed to construct them as enemies is a bridge between group identity and an experience of social threat—a neighborhood mugging or a secretive adolescent or the dramatic depiction of a murder on the nightly news—that is familiar to many people. This is where illicit drugs come in. Mediating the relationship between the designated groups and the larger dangers they signify is the symbol and the reality of illicit drug use and drug-dealing—youth who smoke pot, blacks who staff the retail levels of the drug industry in urban ghettos, Third World cocaine suppliers, liberals who deny the seriousness of all of the above (or, in the case of marijuana, who blame youthful pot-smoking on an alienating adult culture, thus insulting worried parents).

In saddling us with "the drug problem" today's dangerous classes serve as surrogates for the claimants to rights, benefits, and freedoms who have, over the past generation, fundamentally altered our cultural landscape. Racial and ethnic minorities, youth, and aliens are threatening for their demands on society, not solely their status within it. To a foreign observer it might seem that in blaming disease, urban violence, and adolescent rebellion on illicit drugs and their purveyors, we have merely embraced a set of mind-boggling fallacies, reversing cause and effect and confusing association with causality. But the distortions go deeper still. Fighting drugs in the eighties and nineties is mounting a rearguard action against full equality for racial minorities and whipping young people (and often cultural liberals) back into line after they threatened to kick over the traces in the 1960s and 1970s.[19] Resistance to race and gender equality, greater emancipation of youth, and civil liberties would be limited to the authoritarian fringe if it could not assume the cloak of righteous containment of identifiably dangerous people. Targeting druggies and kingpins ensures both legitimacy for political actors' embrace of "traditional values" and a mass following for cultural conservatism.

Both drug abuse and drug prohibition have taken a disproportionate toll on African-Americans. As a result, both the punitive policy approach to illicit drugs and proposals to legalize them are frequently attacked as racist.[20] Definitions of racism in this context and the exploration of racist elements in drug policies deserve attention beyond this general discussion; for this reason they are the subject of the next chapter. Suffice it to say here that while the implications of race for drug policy are far-reaching and complex, they constitute only a part of the more generalized shadow agenda item of taming the untamed, a single (though certainly important) manifestation of a more comprehensive force of repression and exclusion. The aim is regimentation; what Michel Foucault called the "economy of punishment" operates to restrain and inhibit those already marginalized, whether they are blacks or young people or the liberals who are sympathetic to those groups.[21]

The sins of the latest dangerous classes as they are exemplified in the "drug problem" go beyond the immorality of promoting or participating in habits of self-destruction and harm to others. They are also challenges to values of hard work and initiative or, in the case of dealers, perverters of the dream of free enterprise. Cultural and economic threats merge, as the dangerous classes are seen as responsible for declines in national productivity as well as moral righteousness. American business and competitiveness in world markets become casualties of even occasional recreational pot use. As a senior Department of Justice official put it to a group of managers in 1986, "Let's understand that the drunk or drugged worker on the assembly line or in the office isn't just cheating himself—he is stealing from the pockets of his boss, his company, and every American citizen. Defective products, lost productivity, higher costs are all part of the price we pay for drugs on the job."[22]

*Kids as a Dangerous Class*

The inclusion of young people in the category of dangerous classes may strike some as improbable, particularly as they are grouped with minorities.[23] But the combination of deviance and poverty that is often at the core of the definition has long applied equally to youth and adults. In the late Middle Ages, when an expanding market for grain shifted the locus of production from the feudal plot to a capitalist pasturage system, poverty and social disorder resulted. Bands of "vagrant children" displaced from the land roamed the streets of London from the sixteenth to the nineteenth century; "being destitute of Relations, Friends, and all the Necessaries of Life, [they] were become

the Pest and Shame of the City."[24] In this country the juvenile gangs
that flourished in big cities after the Civil War were seen as emblematic
of threats to social order generally and private property in particular.
"By 1870 the streets throughout the greater part of New York fairly
swarmed with prowling bands of homeless boys and girls actively
developing the criminal instinct which is inherent in every human
being," wrote a journalist in the early twentieth century.[25]

The traditional association appears to tar today's young. While
nationally the number of arrests of juveniles under 18 rose by only
5.2 percent during the 1980s—a much smaller percentage than for
their elders—the increase in the *rate* of arrests was much larger, since
the number of people in the age category of juvenile arrestees went
down.[26] Furthermore, arrests rose substantially for some of the most
visible crimes—auto theft, weapons possession—and for some of the
most heinous—murder, aggravated assault. (Ironically, arrests for
drug law violations declined.) Increasing deprivation among young
people precedes and parallels these trends. Between 1973 and 1983
the percentage of children under eighteen in poverty rose by 54
percent, then fell back slightly late in the decade.[27]

Of course there are different ways to cast such conditions. Arrest
data may indicate increased law enforcement attention, rather than
patterns of offending, at least partially an effect rather than a cause
of the perception of youthful criminality. Some might see structural
forces as more powerful causes of youthful deviance and desperation
than the sloth or immorality of adolescents and their parents. But
many adults express deep apprehension about youthful character. It
extends beyond behavior, to the younger generation's expectations
of rights and benefits. ("They think the world owes them a living,"
said one interviewee, speaking specifically about Seattle's hip and
mobile population of young adults but expressing a sentiment heard
in other locations and applied very broadly. "They don't care who
they hurt," said an African-American cab driver in Kansas City of
young blacks in the drug trade, even though he had just told me that
adult gangs from Jamaica and California had brought crack to the
city.)

Surveys undertaken over the past generation have consistently revealed declining public confidence in many institutions of American
life, including those assigned authoritative functions over youth
—school, family, courts.[28] Many people attribute the villainies of
youth—rising crime or earlier sexual activity or drug use—to family
breakdown, a changing labor market, and "moral decline."[29] Finding
a source in social causes rather than in individual venality may,

however, render the resulting deviance and defiance more threatening rather than less. Adults may implicate themselves in some of
the trends—the doubling of the divorce rate between 1965 and 1990,
for instance—they deem responsible for the sins of their young.[30]
The recourse to blame is an individualistic strategy that can be turned
inward as well as imposed on others.

Before the pot recriminalization initiative in Alaska, several polls
were taken to provide public information and to aid both proponents
and opponents in developing strategies for mounting their campaigns.
From the start the polls suggested that the initiative would be likely
to pass. Half of the respondents to a 1988 poll by the Anchorage
Chamber of Commerce said they felt Alaska laws did not "deal adequately with the buying and selling of illegal drugs," and 61 percent
favored making the possession of "any of marijuana by adults" illegal.[31] Two private polls taken in 1990—one throughout the state,
one just in Anchorage, where half of the state's voters are—found
similar majority support for recriminalization.[32] But between the earlier survey and the November 1990 vote, the issue was reshaped as
a referendum on the ability of the citizens of the state to correct
*youthful* behavior and use the criminal law to shape moral influences
on youth, although the law to be changed applied only to adults and
possession of pot had never been legal for persons eighteen or under.

The emphasis that prevailed was apparent in the two later polls.
Among the respondents to the Anchorage survey who supported the
initiative, 25 percent did so because they believed the current law
"condones it [marijuana] to [sic] kids" or "sends mixed messages."
When all respondents—those who opposed the initiative as well as
its supporters—were asked whether they agreed with the proponents'
argument that "making possession of marijuana in the home a crime
sends Alaska young people the right kind of moral message," 69.9
percent said they did, suggesting that even some who opposed the
initiative considered it to have positive moral weight for the young.
On the other side, even some of those who supported the initiative
were concerned about the privacy implications of enforcing marijuana
prohibition in the home.

Framing and delivering the successful campaign message was not
the work of political professionals or Madison Avenue spin doctors.
It grew out of the efforts of a few committed volunteers, led by Marie
Majewske, the retired elementary-school teacher. But Majewske and
her allies were not isolated. They had political advice and modest
amounts of administrative help from state legislators who had supported anti-marijuana legislation in the past, and supportive media

picked up the symbolic messages that the activists were sending. "Alaska is about to become the nation's most visible battle ground in the war on drugs," declared the *Anchorage Times* four weeks before the election in one of a series of editorials urging a yes vote on the initiative. "It's a serious war. A war about attitudes—about influencing the hearts and minds of our young people."[33]

Most important, however, were the contacts the activists had developed through Majewske's strong ties with the Parent Teacher Association (PTA) and the approach to drugs they had absorbed through involvement with anti-drug parent organizations around the state. PTAs from all over Alaska had been energized about the state's marijuana policy for several years; Majewske says they sent "about eighty resolutions" to the legislature before they gave up and turned to the initiative route. In Anchorage Majewske created Community Action for Drug-Free Youth "to educate parents" and form anti-drug parent committees in schools. Building on the "firm NO use philosophy" of Alaskans for Drug-Free Youth, an organization in Ketchikan, they channeled the anxieties of many Alaskans about the present and future of the state's young people into a yes vote for recriminalization.

The Alaska initiative is by no means the first or only political victory won at least partly by what is often referred to simply as "the parents' movement." In the early 1970s marijuana use became a cultural battleground, with many mainstream liberals finding it essentially harmless recreation and recommending the legalization of pot, while conservatives deplored the drug as a "gateway" to the use of narcotics and warned of the "amotivational syndrome," which would turn young people into "a large population of semi-zombies" as adults.[34] The latter bolstered their essentially moral and social arguments by applying to casual pot use marijuana research results suggesting that heavy use has medical consequences not previously understood.[35] As publicity for these views increased and polls were released showing growing use of marijuana among teenagers, parent groups around the country began to meet—sometimes through PTAs or community centers, sometimes informally—to address their concern that kids were smoking more potent pot more often, in school as well as outside, and at younger ages.[36] Some of the parents turned out to be politically skilled, and anti-pot legislators were only too glad to harness their concerns for political and programmatic ends. Pressed by several members of Congress to act more affirmatively on marijuana—Senate hearings on the new pot menace were held in early 1980—the newly elected Reagan administration encouraged and funded, directly and indirectly, a number of projects intended to mobilize parents in the fight against drugs and, more broadly, in efforts to preserve "traditional values." At the core of these efforts are PRIDE (Parents Resource Institute for Drug Education, Inc.), an international organization dedicated to fighting drugs through law enforcement and treatment, and the National Federation of Parents for Drug-Free Youth (NFP).

NFP serves as coordinator, trainer, and cheerleader for a network of thousands of neighborhood and school-based parent groups around the country. It conducts programs for secondary-school students and national drug awareness campaigns. The primary stated goal of NFP affiliates and member groups is the prevention of drug and alcohol use among the young; to this end it adopts what researchers call a "proscription model," moral exhortation and scare stories about damage to health and social life resulting from drug use.[37] (The training program for seventh and eighth graders advertises itself, in part, as "an interactional process involving refusal skills.") As is evident from the organization's name and its emphasis on the "no use message," abstinence is the only acceptable goal and all use of either drugs or alcohol is assumed to be abuse.[38] Endorsed by Presidents Reagan and Bush, with Nancy Reagan as its honorary chairperson, NFP had regular access to both William Bennett and Robert Martinez, federal drug czars appointed by Bush. Strong working relationships exist between NFP and booster groups or lodges like Kiwanis, Elks, and Junior League; locally, members work with law enforcement, media, and various service groups. Although Marie Majewske describes herself as "anti-political" and maintains that PTA pressure on the Alaska state legislature "wasn't a concerted effort," her initiative campaign and much of the anti-drug activism of other parent groups suggest the effective organization of political interests. Despite being loose-knit and ostensibly hostile to conventional politics, these groups constitute a formidable constituency for culturally conservative policy positions.

NFP and its affiliates are clearly motivated by concern for the long-term welfare of their children; their literature on marijuana stresses the lung irritation and depression they believe marijuana can cause (though no distinction is made between occasional recreational use, which most researchers have found to be relatively harmless, and heavy, frequent ingestion, which is rare). The organization aims to reach its targets with materials that are appropriate for young people—preteen activities use "raps, puppets, T-shirt design, skits and video"—although it is hard to imagine adolescent enthusiasm for the student manual that is described as "66 pages of fun and facts."

But the theme of dangerous and uncontrollable teenagers also persists. NFP literature urges parents to get professional assistance if they suspect their children of any marijuana use, and the list of suspicious behaviors that may indicate drug use is enough to terrify any parent, since it concentrates many that are only too familiar to those who live with teenagers—"aggressive, rebellious behavior," "excessive influence by peers," "low grades." The re-establishment of authority over the young is a common theme in the parents' movement. In trying to prevent drug use, NFP counsels that "discussion should evolve around setting limits for appropriate behavior for your teenagers and defining consequences for violations of those limits."[39]

A continuing theme in the messages of youth as dangerous is the threat that they may not uphold American values of hard work and initiative. Commenting in 1980 on the concern about spreading use of pot, a New York University medical school professor spoke for many parents involved in the early days of the parents' movement when he worried about "a whole generation going down the tube. . . . Are we going to see a nation of drones?"[40] In part, this concern reflects parental worries that their children will be impaired by drugs from participating successfully in what is already a cutthroat competition for jobs and education. But it also reveals a concern about their own liability as taxpayers for future support of deviants and a Hobbesian view of youth as monsters who can only be made to conform through fear.

One of the highlights of the Alaska recriminalization campaign, in the view of the activists who shaped it, was the appearance of then–drug czar William Bennett in Anchorage to support the initiative. To them he represented the highest possible authority for their policy position and the reasons behind it. Bennett's perspective on the Alaska situation is instructive as much for revealing his attitudes toward youth and their socialization as for insight into views on drug control. He publicly opposed Alaska's lenient pot law long before the initiative campaign heated up, using a TV public service announcement in the fall of 1989 to tell the Alaskan people that "recriminalization sends the right message: Drug use is wrong, and if you use drugs you'll be held accountable."[41] In an interview with Alaska's junior senator, Frank Murkowski (a committed drug warrior), at about the same time, he made clear the link between youth<sup>r</sup> d marijuana use and future American productivity: "It means they don't study, it causes what is called the 'amotivational syndrome,' where they are just not motivated to get up and go to work."[42] As for the basis of his choice to invoke the criminal law to hold young users "accountable," Bennett was very explicit in testimony before the Senate Judiciary Committee several months later: "Should we have drug education programs or should we have tough [law enforcement] policy?" he asked rhetorically. "If I have the choice of only one, I will take policy every time because I know children. And you might say this is not a very romantic view of children, not a very rosy view of children. And I would say, 'You're right.' "[43]

The success of the parents' movement has depended in part on its ability to draw in parents from many worlds, and this inclusiveness gives it the potential for a formidable political base. (The sheer numbers of young parents in the late twentieth-century United States also make them a force to be contended with—and manipulated. People between the ages of twenty-five and forty-four—the "baby boomers"—represented 78 percent of the voting-age population by 1988, an increase of 95 percent in twenty years.[44]) The rhetoric of the movement, however, has been far from politically neutral. It includes the agenda of cultural conservatives—the NFP acknowledges that parent groups affiliated with it "work toward passage of pro-family legislation"—and the authoritarian streak may be what gives political energy to the movement.[45] Bennett is forthright about the link: "The drug crisis is a crisis of authority—in every sense of the term 'authority'," he says.[46] He calls for nothing short of "the re-constitution of legal and social authority through the imposition of appropriate consequences for drug dealing and drug use."

Cast as a holy war, fighting drugs produces and expresses a wide variety of yearnings for order. At the passive end of the spectrum is the simple association of even relatively harmless drug-taking with social decay; a close second to drugs as the perceived greatest problem in the public schools is lack of discipline, far more important than curriculum deficiencies or incompetent teachers.[47] At the other end is the creation of programs like Straight, a drug treatment organization for youth with centers in several cities, where peers confronted and abused (sometimes physically) new participants in order to "break" them and, in the words of a former Straight clinical director, "remold their lives."[48] The Alaska campaign theme of marijuana control as redemption from the more general lawlessness of today's youth falls somewhere in the middle.

## Aliens as a Dangerous Class

If youth presents the dangers of the familiar, the threats of immigrants and foreigners are those of the unknown. The United States has always had an ambiguous relationship with its immigrants, welcoming them for the labor they have provided and for a certain exuberance or grace they have brought to the culture, but despising them, too, for their alien ideologies and customs and for their presumed contribution to economic hardship among the native-born.[49] Anti-immigrant feelings, dormant during fifty years of relatively low migration, have found new expression as the "new immigrants"— those who arrived after the Immigration and Nationality Act of 1965 cancelled out the biases of earlier legislation and expanded yearly quotas—have poured into the United States, and as it has proved virtually impossible to stem the flow of undocumented workers. Opposition to bilingual education programs and support for the "English-only movement" have helped legitimate the association of immigrants with deviance.

Added to hostility toward immigrants is the common view that illicit drugs are foreign substances peddled by furtive outsiders, manipulators of American innocence and gullibility. The legacy of associating drugs with forces that are un-American is an old one; it helps that many of the most common countries of origin for popular drugs are in the Third World.

In three of my case studies I encountered the same kind of recourse to antagonisms toward aliens. In each the specter of powerful and evil outsiders was used to justify aggressive action that was, however, applied far more broadly than to the small group initially labeled as threatening; and in each no drug-control effect was discernible.

In 1986 in Kansas City a task force of forty-seven federal and local officers was formed to go after the Jamaican Posses whose leaders were said to tote Uzis and drive BMWs—and manage dozens of crack houses.[50] While there is little doubt that the Jamaican drug industry found a market in the Kansas City area, the attribution of Kansas City's crack problem solely or principally to the Jamaicans is ludicrous. After many police raids on posse strongholds in 1986 and 1987, vanquishing the Jamaicans with more than a hundred federal sentences and several dozen deportations, crack nonetheless was flourishing on the streets of Kansas City. A journalist wrote late in 1988, "There are no lasting signs that in sweeping almost 200 people off the streets the authorities cut into the supply of crack here. For one thing, the price hasn't gone up. If anything, the supply is as great as ever.''[51] At that point law enforcement had moved on to another kind of outsider—the Los Angeles–based gangs, the Crips and the Bloods, who were said to have established branches in the Kansas City area.

The Caribbean area and South America are popular points of origin for those deemed most responsible for the American drug problem. The "major heroin dealers" whose threat Paul Rosenbaum invoked in Michigan came primarily from Mexico, replacing the wave of Turkish heroin that had been suppressed earlier in the decade.[52] In the producing countries both the climate and the workers' poverty and ignorance are presumed to enhance production possibilities for cocaine and opiates, and entrepreneurs can often be additionally demonized by their politically suspect associations—with guerrilla groups in countries that are friendly to the United States, with powerful regimes in countries that are not. One of the attributes of the Jamaican "Waterhouse posse" (named for the part of Kingston they came from) sometimes mentioned by law enforcement and the press in Kansas City was their supposed link to the People's National Party, the socialist party of Jamaica.

The specter of high-flying cocaine dealers from Colombia surely lubricated passage of the drug kingpin death penalty. Charles Schumer (Democrat-N.Y.) made the association explicit in floor debate in the House of Representatives:

> So I say to my colleagues that those who deal in huge amounts of drugs, the Ochoas and the Escobars [Colombian drug lords], know that they are killing people. We all know that they are killing people. We also know that they probably more than anyone else, perhaps more than a poor mule on the street who gets involved in a shooting incident, deserve society's ultimate punishment.[53]

The 1988 death penalty for drug kingpin murders has, however, not been imposed on an Ochoa or an Escobar or anyone like them.

### Liberals as "The Enemy"

Part of what makes aliens threatening is that their lack of a stake in the society gives them no incentive to respect American law. Other kinds of nonconformists are suspect, too. If a large slice of U.S. voters (not only those on the religious right) define the weakening of many kinds of authority—familial, legal, occupational—as a central social problem, an attack on those who are permissive may be the answer. With this reasoning, cultural liberals—sometimes also stigmatized as libertarians or intellectuals—become another of the dangerous classes. Groups like the American Civil Liberties Union (ACLU) and the Drug Policy Foundation, which advocates drug policy reform, are forthrightly described as "the enemy."[54] The threat liberals represent does not result from the traditionally despised combination of criminality and poverty (though they may be as law-violating or poor as anyone else) but from their apparent defiance of the sanctity of rules. Although "the deviant is one to whom that label has successfully been applied," making the label stick is more difficult where actual rule-breaking cannot be identified.[55] Perhaps for that reason, it is sometimes suggested by anti-drug warriors that liberals are self-interested drug users who wish to keep access to drugs as free as possible for themselves. When the Health, Education, and Social Services Committee in the Alaska legislature resisted the recriminalization bill, the anti-pot activists saw it as capitulation to "the drug culture," rather than recognizing the partisan competition behind the dispute or assuming that the committee was acting on some kind of principle or responding to those who were.[56]

More pervasive is the image of liberals (or occasionally intellectuals, which in this context amounts to the same thing) as having a "general hostility to law enforcement and criminal justice," as William Bennett put it.[57] Purveyors or adherents of the due-process revolution of the 1960s and 1970s, they are seen as exposing law-abiding Americans to dangerous felons now so protected by "technicalities" that law enforcement can no longer do its job. Conservative politicians at all levels pounce on this vulnerability. Frustrated citizens plagued with crack houses in their neighborhoods—even the black residents of Kansas City in the late 1980s—blame the generic liberal for search and seizure rules and other barriers to arresting and convicting drug dealers at the retail level. The association widens so that to uphold the rights and interests of the accused is to denigrate and thereby threaten those of the innocent. The Willie Horton ad in the 1988 Bush campaign was effective, after all, not only because its subject was the embodiment of black crime that people fear but because Michael Dukakis, in permitting a furlough for Horton, could be seen as failing to protect all innocent Americans if elected president.

A corollary of the liberal who is soft on crime is the liberal who appears to trivialize more traditional parental concerns with the moral implications of drug-taking and the association between drugs and youthful rebellion. Opponents of the Alaska pot recriminalization initiative infuriated the parents' groups with their message that criminalizing personal use was a violation of a privacy right; the suggestion that a civil liberties abstraction counted for more than their children's well-being was often perceived to be simply an insult, perhaps a hidden injury of class. A television ad sponsored by opponents of the initiative, portraying a middle-class mother in a well-appointed suburban kitchen earnestly explaining why she as a parent valued privacy over prohibition, may have backfired; an Anchorage nurse reported that she became a recriminalization activist upon seeing that ad.

## FORMULATORS, IMPLEMENTERS, AND ACTIVISTS MEET THE DANGEROUS CLASSES

Three different roles for policy actors—as formulators, implementers, or activists—shape the way those actors seek to control the dangerous classes. Of the three types of policy actors it is easy to see why the most aggressive demonization of drug takers and dealers comes from the *formulators*. Presidents and legislators will be judged, at least in the short run, as much on their postures of protectiveness as on the validity of their ideas. They don't have to prove the effectiveness of the standards of future conduct they propose, and they rarely get close enough to the human subjects of their policies to differentiate them within the mass category of dangerous classes. Representative Don Edwards (Democrat-Calif.), Chairman of the Civil and Constitutional Rights Subcommittee of the House Judiciary Committee, points out that for members of Congress, far removed from the responsibility for local crime control, promoting the execution of drug kingpins "doesn't cost anything," but gives them opportunity to remind their constituents that the trafficking of kingpins causes "such pain and sorrow and murder and mayhem that they deserve [the death penalty]."[58]

Paul Rosenbaum, the legislator who sponsored the 650 lifer law in Michigan, supplemented the threatening image of large heroin dealers with the menace of predatory criminals in general to persuade his colleagues to pass the bill. Painted as a contest between the "99 percent of decent, God-fearing people in this state" and the "dope dealers," his crusade was costless for him in both the short run and the long.[59] He was unlikely to be challenged by defenders of either the heroin dealers or the evil one percent, and responsibility for a policy failure would be diffused among the law enforcement implementers and within the legislative body. By the time the law was actually enacted Rosenbaum had, in effect, concluded that it would be ineffective in targeting the major dealers it was aimed at, since the wiretap provisions that he believed were essential to getting convictions had been rejected by his fellow legislators. He voted for the bill anyway, of course; he had been its principal sponsor. Besides, he was bored with his job and was running in the Democratic primary for the U.S. Senate. He wouldn't be around to deal with the proposal's ineffectiveness or any unanticipated consequences—like its application to the couriers of the drug trade—that might prove embarrassing.

The decision to support harsh prohibition policies is not so simple for *implementers*. With the exception of prosecutors, who are usually elected and whose successes often depend on public images of toughness, implementers' professional advancement is not usually furthered by taking public positions that demonize drug users and dealers. Implementers are more likely than formulators to be held accountable for the effects of policy, and their acquaintance with the operational consequences of policymaking may create greater dissonance when they are politically tempted to take strongly punitive postures. They often pay dearly for harsh penalties pushed through by formulators, carrying out directives that they see as rigid, unfair, or futile. "The mandatory sentences drive federal judges out of their minds," says Edwards. "Any time we talk with judges they say, 'For Christ's sake, what are you doing to us? We have no discretion at all.' " The judge who has had to send a welfare mother with several small children to prison for five years for possession of a small amount of cocaine and the police official who has seen that incarcerated street dealers are quickly replaced by other otherwise unemployed youth may well regard turning up the heat as compounding the problem.

Contemporary drug policy literature is starting to reflect the disillusionment of implementers with their own efforts. Jerome Skolnick reports the view of a New York City narcotics official, interviewed in 1990, on the likelihood that increased drug arrests will reduce drug trade: "Enforcement will never stop it," he said.[60] My case studies also suggest widespread ambivalence among implementers about aggressively prohibitionist policies. The Michigan Attorney General took no position on the 650-plus law; Seattle police were divided on the drug loitering ordinance; and an Alaska law enforcement official who wished not to be identified remarked, during the summer of 1991, "We've got better things to do than enforce the pot laws when we know that up on the river those guys will be growing the stuff forever."

Lower levels of support for the toughest policies do not mean that implementers are immune to using drug prohibition for less-intensive regulation of the dangerous classes. Acknowledging that suppression of drugs by the criminal law is unlikely does not preclude strategies for momentary interference with the illicit business, and many drug enforcement programs are now working on the premise that saturation patrols, making it more difficult to market drugs, have some benefits even if they only displace the problem. "We may take back a street here or a street there, but we may give up a street somewhere else," concedes Captain Rachel Whipple of the Street Narcotics Unit of the Kansas City Police Department, in the new spirit of drug-control realism.[61] But she is willing to use the law for marginal management of street drug traffic, moving the crack dealers around (and maybe others who fear getting caught up in the net of enforcement) for long enough to give those closest to the problem a brief respite. "When we show up [to close down crack houses in poor neighborhoods], people are applauding." Lowered expectations sustain the drug loitering policy in Seattle, too. It "does not stop people from taking drugs; it does not help people get off of drugs; it does not do anything except try to reduce this open-air selling activity," says Councilwoman Jane Noland.[62] And there is widespread acknowledgment in Seattle that the open-air activity is itself the product of drug policy. Law enforcement closure of crack houses begat increased street trade, which is now being driven from one neighborhood to another. "The theory is," says one community activist, "that eventually they'll go someplace besides Seattle."[63] Policies like the loitering law, the drug-free school ordinance, and the "stay out of drug area" (SODA) orders for probationers are not expected to be more than tools to encourage that departure. (Implementers' lesser commitment to punitive programs is sometimes a political resource for formulators; Noland has excoriated the police chief for "incompetence" in ridding Seattle's neighborhoods of the drug markets, and maintained that "sloppy work" in the prosecutor's office has impeded successful cases against drug dealers in the past.)

The dangerous classes ideology is most apparent in the aims of the *activists*, which are to identify the enemy and to contain named and unnamed threats. Illegal drugs have become a stand-in for both major and minor forms of social disorder; people associated with drugs are either exemplars or handmaidens of the real sources of that disorder. The youthful males—mostly black and Hispanic—who hung out in bus stops and phone booths in Seattle were to be suppressed not only because they were probably dealing drugs but also because they reminded tourists and residents of the larger incivilities of aimless, unproductive youth. The concern of Seattle merchants and crime prevention groups (the groups are overlapping but not congruent) was initially focused on idle youth who engaged in "smash and grab" attacks on stores. More intensive patrol and better citizen information could be summoned to address that problem, but the drug-dealing provided the justification for exerting new authority through law. Another aspect of the immediate aim of monitoring the streets of the city goes beyond the worry about the dangers to shoppers and residents (and hence to their profits) posed by the street drug trade and the minimal (or nonexistent, according to Jane Noland) concern with the damage done to buyers of the drugs. The local activists (backed up, of course, by the mayor and most city council members) worried about the city's tax base, its squeaky-clean image with the rest of the country and the world, and the value of their investments.

Consider also the layers of intent among the small group of Alaska state legislators and citizens who mobilized the recriminalization campaign. In part, they were moral entrepreneurs, crusaders who wanted the recriminalization of marijuana possession by adults both to convince young people that smoking marijuana was unhealthy and immoral and to mount a more sweeping battle for the minds and hearts of youth on behalf of parents and teachers and other authority figures.[64] They mobilized support by casting the problem in terms of the protection of youth—and their parents—from dangers far broader than the short-term memory loss and distraction that are the principal effects of marijuana for all but the rare compulsive users. During the period when she and her colleagues were attempting, without success, to get a recriminalization bill through the Alaska legislature, Alyce Hanley used a young girl as an object lesson: "Her aunt had introduced her at age ten to marijuana, then she used cocaine, she lied and stole, went into an institution, had sex with all the boys, had a baby and ended up addicted to some kind of drug."[65] This is the kind of story that, if accepted uncritically, not only terrifies a parent and shores up drug prohibition but also feeds the larger culture wars. (Notice that the villains here include permissive adults as well as wayward children, and marijuana as the "gateway drug" is merely the opening wedge into a life of sin, not the sin itself.) Legal authority, even if it did not apply directly to youth, would both tame and protect them.

For Alyce Hanley, stamping out pot was also a spoke in the wheel of a broadly conservative social agenda; two years earlier she had unsuccessfully lobbied against the naming of an Alaska mountain for Martin Luther King, blaming him for the violence of the civil rights movement. And Fritz Pettyjohn, the minority whip in the Alaska House of Representatives, characterized the pot initiative as "the last nail in the coffin of '60s radicalism, which we're just finishing nailing down here in Alaska."[66]

Less altruistic goals were also relevant. The minority party in the Alaska legislature was not above using marijuana recriminalization to gain the moral high ground; similarly, the Republican candidate for governor used the specter of the dangerous liberal to twist an equivocal comment made by the Democrat into a "soft-on-drugs" charge. Humanitarian and self-interested motives came together in the aim of showing the rest of the country that Alaska was no longer the odd state out, permissive and perhaps primitive, certainly resistant to the kind of team effort that was more congenial to the new dominance of oil corporation culture in what had been the last frontier.

It seems to be the formulators and the activists who are most likely to place overtolerant liberals—permissive parents, civil libertarians, "secular humanists"—among the dangerous classes. Perhaps implementers are less likely to demonize liberals because they tend to think of themselves as professionals, devoted to politically neutral ideals and removed from contests over values. They also have more to gain from winning over the liberals than from antagonizing them; they may be the next group of formulators, after all, with power to wield over police and prosecutors. Or perhaps implementers are simply less likely than other policy actors to have the public ear.

# Chapter 11

# *The Ambiguous Significance of Race*

"The whole law-and-order movement that we have heard so much about is, in operation though not in intent, anti-black and anti-underclass—not in plan, not in design, not in intent, but in operation."[1] Criminologist Norval Morris could have made a similar comment about today's drug wars, as a number of observers have. A widely publicized 1992 report explained its finding that 56 percent of young African-American males in Baltimore were under some form of criminal justice sanction largely in terms of a war on drugs that "has been racially biased and [whose] casualties have been young, male, and African American."[2] And an African-American writer charges that "the government, in engaging its drug war at home and abroad, has aimed its weapons overwhelmingly at people of color."[3]

In the previous chapter I suggested that African-Americans are not alone in constituting the dangerous classes on the shadow agenda of drug prohibition. Kids, aliens, and cultural liberals are other groups whose threatening presence and claims the drug wars aim to control. But racism—which, for the purposes of this discussion, can be defined as not only specific acts of discrimination but also efforts to maintain white dominance through perpetuating damning stereotypes and withholding remedies for past oppression—should not be underrated as an influence on drug policy, either. Patterns of the impact of drug-control policies—particularly harsh penalties for drugs associated more with blacks than whites (primarily crack), increasingly African-American prison populations, high arrest rates for minority males—should alert us to racial injustice of several kinds. While American racism is now usually less blatant than the explicit legal exclusions addressed by the civil rights cases of the fifties and sixties, its contemporary forms can be as cruel. The criminal justice system—and the attitudes that sustain its policies and practices—has become a theater where the long-running drama of resistance to racial equality is a regular feature. Nowhere is this American tragedy more evident than with drug prohibition, whether its racial themes are blatant or covert, imposed through formal statute or implemented by the law in action.

Drug use as a tool for racial polarization in this country has a long history. Until quite recently the racism was very open. The first drug prohibition law, a San Francisco ordinance prohibiting public opium dens, was enacted in an atmosphere of hostility to Chinese immigrant laborers no longer needed to build railroads. It was enforced, as the police chief put it, "to keep them [the Chinese] from opening places where whites might resort to smoke."[4] In 1910 Hamilton Wright, "the father of American narcotic laws," wrote to Congress as part of his campaign for federal prohibition legislation, "The cocaine vice . . . has been a potent incentive in driving the humbler negroes all over the country to abnormal crimes."[5]

Today's racial influences go beyond blatant acts and expressions of bias; modern racism in this area is of several types. The open association of minorities with evil or undesirable conduct—as with the depiction of "Negro cocaine fiends" in the early years of the century—has given way to the selective application of an apparently neutral criminal law, targeting blacks as more likely than whites to commit many offenses.[6] Racism also inheres in the choice to address a social problem with a particular strategy that implicates minorities disproportionately; the concentration of law enforcement resources on the inner-city retail operations of the drug trade is sometimes criticized on this basis. And an insidious indifference to policy outcomes that are particularly costly to minorities remains common. These trends often combine in ways that make it difficult to determine which is most salient.

Without question, African-Americans are as disproportionately represented in arrests for violation of drug laws as in arrests for most other common crimes. Nationally, blacks made up 41 percent of drug arrests in 1991, though only 12.3 percent of the population (but about 15 percent of the arrest-prone age group of eighteen to twenty-four); a black was *five* times as likely to be arrested for a drug crime as a white.[7] In some localities, arrests were even more lopsided; in New York City in 1989, 92 percent of people arrested for drug offenses were African-American or Latino.[8] The overrepresentation of blacks is even more striking in state prisons nationwide, where, in 1989, they accounted for 64.8 percent of new court commitments for drug offenses; a black was more than *seventeen* times more likely to be admitted to prison that year for a drug offense than a white.[9] And the trend is upward. In 1985, African-Americans constituted only 30 percent of drug arrests; between that year and 1990 the probability that a city youth under eighteen arrested for a drug offense would be black more than doubled, from 23.5 percent to 51.3 percent.[10] The proportion of blacks among state prison admissions rose 30 percent in just two years, from 1987 to 1989.[11]

The extent to which these imbalances—and other justice system statistics that could cast blacks as the major agents of "the drug problem"—can be attributed to racism is probably impossible to determine. Applying the narrowest possible definition of bias—overt discrimination in the criminal justice process—will certainly yield evidence of some racist practice—an incremental accumulation of unwarranted presumptions by criminal justice operatives at several stages. An analysis that ends there, however, overlooks contextual influences on the justice system that impose an unequal burden on blacks before they are even parties in its transactions. A broader view of the relationship between criminal justice and the larger society suggests that what otherwise appear as minor inequities in courts and precincts are really threads in a blanket of institutional and social repression. Such a perspective takes into account not only the way a particular offense is investigated and prosecuted but also how the offense was defined in the first place, how drug crimes committed by African-Americans are portrayed in the media and in political settings, and the society's willingness to live with policy outcomes that have racially disproportionate burdens—what might be called a racism of effect, rather than intent. Examining the patterns of these choices in the 1980s and 1990s reveals an unyielding lode of racial antagonism running more deeply into the bedrock of social policy than could be extracted simply through reform of police, court, and corrections. In the end, racism in the drug wars comes down to these broader and more systemic influences.

## RACIAL PATTERNS OF DRUG USE

Most illicit drug consumers in the United States are white; national self-report surveys and hospital emergency room data make that abundantly clear.[12] (For example, of the estimated 26 million people who used an illicit drug at least once in 1991, about 20 million were white, somewhat under 4 million were black, and just under 2 million were Hispanic.[13]) In the face of this reality it has become an article of faith among writers who are as appalled by the human toll of the drug wars as by the hazards of drugs that disproportionate enforcement of drug laws against blacks must therefore be attributable largely to overt discrimination or "unintended consequences" of criminal justice practice.[14] Examining that charge is difficult because once we get beyond the very general statement that most drug consumers are white, our information about the racial patterns of drug crime is incomplete and ambiguous. The best surveys we have suggest that the prevalence of illicit drug use is either somewhat more likely or somewhat less likely among blacks than among whites, according to what drug is being considered, what cohort is being studied, and which data you examine. And every data source has validity problems. Furthermore, none of the data address the demographics of selling drugs, which may be quite different from use.

The two most frequently cited sources for the conclusion that there are more white illicit drug consumers than black and no greater use prevalence among African-Americans for the most feared illicit drugs are an annual survey of high-school seniors around the country and the National Household Survey on Drug Abuse conducted by the National Institute on Drug Abuse. The high-school survey, conducted over fourteen years from 1976–1989 with nationally representative samples, consistently found lower prevalence rates—sometimes much lower—among blacks than among whites for use of both licit and illicit drugs. For the four years 1985–89 combined, for example, 25 percent of white males—but only 18.5 percent of black males—reported using marijuana or hashish within the past thirty days, while for cocaine the discrepancy was even greater, with 5.6 percent of white males reporting use, but only 2.6 percent of the black males.[15] The picture of prevalence drawn by the National Household Survey is less clear but tends in the opposite direction. For 1991 the Household Survey estimated that 12.5 percent of whites and 15.8 percent of blacks had used illicit drugs within the past year, 5.8 percent of whites and 9.4 percent of blacks within the past month. For the high-using age group of eighteen to twenty-five, however, 31.5 percent of whites were found to have used within the past year, compared with only 25.9 percent of blacks, while use within the past month was nearly the same for whites (16.0 percent) and blacks (16.7 percent).[16] Racially different use patterns become clearer when more frequent use of specific drugs is considered; 2.4 percent of whites, as compared with 4.7 percent of blacks, reported using marijuana once a week or more, while 0.2 percent of whites and 1.1 percent of blacks reported using cocaine (including crack) that often.[17]

These figures are hard to digest without others to put them in context. According to the Household Survey the 31.5 percent of whites between eighteen and twenty-five who engaged in illicit drug use at least once in the past year (maybe many times) but not in the past month—that is, casual, occasional users—represent more than 6 million people, and similar use by all age groups represents nearly 20 million people. Blacks in those categories amount to 1 million youthful casual users and just over 3½ million casual users of all ages. Looked at this way, illicit drug use appears as a common phenomenon and by no means dominated by African-Americans. If the Household Survey figures are right, blacks represent only 14 percent of the total illicit drug use in the "past year" category.[18] African-Americans make up only slightly more than one-third of the "past month" users of crack, supposedly a "black drug."[19] And the Household Survey would suggest that only about 90,000 young African-American males (age eighteen to thirty-five) consume crack as often as once a month (out of a total national population in that age category of approximately 4,750,000 as of 1989), giving the lie to what Clarence Lusane calls "the racist myth . . . that most inner-city, young black males are gun-toting, crack-smoking criminals-in-waiting."[20]

But are the high-school survey and the Household Survey accurate? Both rely on self-reporting; as accompanying notes to the Household Survey warn, "The value of self-reports obviously depends on the honesty and memory of sampled respondents . . . some under- or over-reporting may occur."[21]

African-Americans, especially younger ones, may be more likely to doubt the confidentiality of the survey and, therefore, be less candid about their behavior than whites. On the other hand, they may be more likely to regard drug use as a badge of adulthood and engage in some exaggeration. The high-school survey researchers note that they have observed over the years of the survey that more blacks than whites give inconsistent answers or fail to answer some questions and are more likely to say, in answer to a question on one form, that if they had used marijuana or heroin they would not admit it in the survey.[22] Furthermore, the samples chosen for both surveys are probably not fully representative of segments of the population where illicit drug use may be especially high: The Household Survey excludes prisoners and homeless people, and the high-school survey misses dropouts and those getting diplomas outside of the traditional day-school setting. Each survey acknowledges that omission of these groups probably results in underreporting drug use, and it seems likely that the undercount is greater for blacks, who are overrepresented among the homeless and dropouts (though not by much) and who may be less likely to trust that the survey is truly confidential.[23]

## RACIAL BIAS WITHIN CRIMINAL JUSTICE

Even if the best data available do not fully chronicle the dimensions of black drug use, the racial discrepancy between patterns of drug use and patterns of law enforcement activity needs explanation. The gap is simply too wide to be attributable primarily to racial differences in drug-taking behavior. In addition, the data problems are unlikely to change significantly from year to year, and national trend data show that while drug use is declining among blacks, as among whites, blacks represent a larger and larger share of those brought into the criminal justice system for drug offenses.[24]

Evidence of racial discrimination in drug cases dots the landscape of criminal justice. But it is not widespread at every stage of case processing, nor can it be found in every jurisdiction. Most important, it is not found in amounts that fully explain the racial cast of those most frequently processed by the system.

During the early 1980s a number of studies of criminal justice processing for all types of offenses concluded that overt discrimination could, at most, explain 20 to 25 percent of racially disproportionate outcomes.[25] Biases in sentence lengths, time served, and decisions as to which defendants would get probation and which ones prison terms were assumed to result not only from judges' discretion but also from recommendations of prosecutors and probation officers (who prepare pre-sentence reports on defendants). Equivalent research attention has not focused specifically on drug cases, but state and local studies suggest that race is a more important factor than for many other kinds of cases. A 1990 RAND Corporation study of sentencing decisions for California felons found that knowing the offender's race did not improve the prediction of which ones would be sentenced to prison and which would be given probation *except* in drug cases, where race (actually, ethnicity—the imbalance appeared in the sentencing of Latinos) was found to explain about 7 percent of the variance.[26] Research in Florida has found that convicted drug offenders are more likely to be sentenced to prison if they are black, and a study of sentencing in Texas counties suggests that blacks are given longer terms and are incarcerated more frequently than white defendants with drug convictions.[27]

Perhaps the most unlikely acknowledgment of racial bias in sentencing—unlikely because its source is the judicial branch itself —comes from a 1991 report to Congress by the U.S. Sentencing Commission evaluating the effects of requirements, enacted in several election-year bills during the 1980s, that federal judges impose mandatory minimum sentences for a number of drug and weapons offenses. The report found that 67.7 percent of black defendants convicted under these provisions (the vast majority for drug offenses) received sentences at or above the mandatory minimum, as compared with 54.0 percent of white defendants.[28] (People who got sentences below the minimum level did so because they provided "substantial assistance" to the prosecutor, because the judge found mitigating circumstances in their cases, or because of anomalies in charging.) The relationship between race and the likelihood of being sentenced above or below the statutorily indicated minimum held when statistical analysis took into account the nature of the offense and the defendant's criminal history.[29] Furthermore, disparity between blacks and whites in federal sentencing appeared to have *increased* after the mandatory minimums were implemented, although "mandatory minimums are meant to ensure that defendants convicted of similar offenses receive penalties that at least begin at the same minimal point."[30]

Discrimination in criminal justice processing surely begins before sentencing, but it is more difficult to measure in the earlier stages. The racial skew of a case probably begins with discretionary activities of police that are difficult for researchers to observe and to quantify —decisions about whom to stop, question, and arrest, and the choice of investigative and repressive techniques to employ. Matters like the choice of targets for prosecution and the factors that go into plea bargains are almost as obscure, made behind closed doors and in private negotiations. Even rigorous study cannot adequately disentangle the influence of racial attitudes from differences in resources available to different classes and races of defendants. We don't really know to what extent the judge's decision to detain a defendant pending trial, for instance, is influenced by race, partly because it is difficult to separate that influence from the weight given to a defendant's commitment to get drug treatment or to the presence of a supportive family who can keep the defendant from skipping town.[31] And it is difficult to calculate the weight of various obstacles to successful crim-

inal defense—detention pending trial, poor legal representation—
and to determine the extent to which their differential burden on
African-Americans is attributable to race rather than class. Added to
these measurement problems is the likelihood that small increments
of bias at several stages of the process result in "a substantial accu-
mulative racial differential which transforms a more or less hetero-
geneous racial arrest population into a homogeneous institutionalized
black population."[32]

In the absence of rigorous and comprehensive evidence of racism
in criminal justice, we are left to rely on impressions, plentiful and
powerful, particularly as they implicate the early stages of the process.
Police often acknowledge that arrests of blacks are disproportionate
to their involvement in drug crime, but justify it as the inevitable
result of more open-air drug markets and more visible violence in
poor minority neighborhoods.[33] But drug raids by local and federal
officers are targeted almost exclusively in black neighborhoods (with
an occasional sweep at a college campus to lend legitimacy to the
technique) and involve tactics that would be unthinkable in white,
middle-class areas. Police routinely stop, question, and search young
minority males on urban streets and in parks as though "the drug
problem" gave them license to ignore constitutional due process.[34]
They break into houses, handcuff innocent residents, and humiliate
them in front of their neighbors. "Your home is no longer your house
after that happens," said Gloria Hill of Detroit, a victim of such a
search (and a client of the Michigan Civil Liberties Union) in 1989.
"When they come in with shotguns, handcuffs and dogs, it lets you
know how powerful they are."[35] In such cases police invariably say
either that the intrusion was a mistake or, as in Hill's case, that they
had probable cause to believe that drugs were in the house. (No drugs
were found in Hill's house, and seven months after the search no
arrests had been made in the case.)

The practice of using formal or informal profiles of typical offenders
as a basis for arrests and investigations involves some racial targeting.
Federal Drug Enforcement Administration agents have developed un-
written profiles of drug traffickers to guide Customs agents and other
law enforcement officers in airports and at national borders, which
include suppositions about race and ethnicity as well as observed
suspicious behavior (nervousness, no checked baggage, returning
from the country of destination within twenty-four hours).[36] Although local police departments rarely go to such lengths to characterize those they think of as likely offenders, the principle behind
the officially approved profile shapes more informal law enforcement

decisions, both considered and spur-of-the-moment choices. A recent, documented example is the pattern of stopping motorists to search for cash acquired in drug deals in Volusia County, Florida (Daytona Beach). Videotapes of stop-and-search incidents showed that 82 percent of the occupants of the cars targeted by the sheriff's drug squad were black or Hispanic, although blacks and whites constitute nearly equal proportions of Florida drug offenders and the overwhelming majority of those using the interstate highway where the stops occurred were white.[37]

The problem here is that, while racial minorities are disproportionately represented in the total (mixed-race) group that will be found to be offenders, the odds that an individual being stopped will be a violator of the type being sought are greater for blacks than for whites—not because blacks or Hispanics are necessarily more likely to be drug offenders, but because their participation rates in this aspect (retail trade on the streetcorner, for example) of the drug business may be higher. The choice of race as a criterion for stopping someone is not, therefore, illogical. But it is certainly unfair if the standard for searches must be reasonable suspicion of a crime, or impermissible if the searches are justified as random checks, a practice that was long ago held by the Supreme Court to be the kind of "standardless and unconstitutional discretion" that should be prevented by the Fourth Amendment prohibition against unreasonable search and seizure.[38]

The accumulation of hard and soft evidence of bias in criminal justice has begun to get significant press and political attention. Not to be outdone by national newspapers' overview stories about racial imbalances in sentencing and arrests—*The New York Times, The Washington Post*, and *USA Today* have all covered the subject since 1990 —local reporters have been filing stories that document racial disparities in cities like Philadelphia and Dallas and in large states like New York and California.[39] State courts are commissioning studies of bias in their own backyards, and some judges are questioning the justice of mandatory sentencing schemes that have a disparate impact on minority defendants.[40] Even a few national political figures— including at least two congressmen, Charles Rangel (Democrat-N.Y.) and Don Edwards (Democrat-Calif.)—have spoken out. But even with conscientious reform in the treatment of minorities by police, courts, and corrections (an uncertain prospect), unintended racial inequities in drug prohibition policy outcomes seem likely to prevail. Their persistence reflects a number of influences beyond the reach of criminal justice institutions.

## RACIAL BIAS BEYOND CRIMINAL JUSTICE

It is by no means clear that the white majority either believes that the justice system discriminates or, if it did, would support measures to correct inequities. A *Washington Post*/ABC News poll conducted the day after a mostly white jury acquitted the four Los Angeles police officers charged with beating Rodney King—a moment when one might presume a high level of sympathy for blacks at the hands of law enforcement—found that, while 89 percent of black respondents thought blacks were not treated equally by the criminal justice system, only 43 percent of whites did.[41]

How to explain this response? There may be a few innocents, protected by the de facto residential segregation that persists in many cities, who believe that police harassment of blacks and judicial bias are rare events. But a more likely explanation for white faith in the neutrality of the criminal justice system is the widespread view—documented in recent public opinion polls—that blacks are simply more crime-prone than whites.[42] As an Internal Revenue Service (IRS) investigator interviewed in Studs Terkel's 1992 book *Race: How Blacks and Whites Think and Feel About the American Obsession* described her attitudes, "I'm reverting back to my parents' thinking. Blacks are poor, blacks are crooks, blacks are ADC, watch out for blacks. You're getting on the bus, there's two blacks on the corner, watch out because they're going to rob your purse, stick a knife in you."[43] That hoary perception is now supplemented by new ones, the feeling that blacks are "taking over" and the view that minorities are now granted favored status by those who have power and authority—employers and the media, in particular. One of Terkel's interviewees assumed that a majority of Chicago residents were black—the 1990 census puts the black population of that city at 39.1 percent—and another believed a majority of the city's police officers were African-American, although only 20 percent were.[44] Another says, "Most of the time the news is slanted in favor of the minorities, because that's the popular way to go."[45] For many whites, the criminal justice system is all that stands between them and capitulation to a social world dominated by blacks and the violence and sloth they are presumed to represent.

"The drug problem" is an effective vehicle for summoning this protection, irresistible for political demagoguery. Paul Rosenbaum, the Michigan state legislator who promoted the law mandating a life sentence without parole for possession of more than 650 grams of a hard drug, sold the proposal to his colleagues as a means of repressing and deterring high-level heroin dealers, most of whom—according to news reports on those who were caught—at that time and in that place were not black. But he had to have known that a more likely image for the public considering such a measure would be that of young black males in Detroit, who were continually portrayed in the media as angry, predatory, and, not coincidentally, involved with drugs.[46] Both local and national polls started showing increased concern about crime—often robberies and property offenses that were presumed to be drug-related—about 1975.[47] Drug arrests were on the rise in the late 1970s, with a widening disproportion between blacks and whites; by 1976 blacks were already almost twice as likely as whites to be arrested for drug offenses.[48] The interaction of public opinion, media portrayals of heroin as largely an inner-city drug, and law enforcement attention laid the foundation for the coded message that a tough drug law would help contain unruly blacks.

Even people who would oppose overt discrimination in criminal justice are often willing to live with apparently neutral policies and practices that nonetheless have a disproportionate impact on minorities. Their indifference reflects both the contemporary sentiment—most explicitly articulated in legal contests over affirmative action programs—that only actual prior discrimination by an employer or educational institution justifies "benign" racial preferences, and a more deeply rooted faith in resolutions of social conflict that reward individual merit and demand individual accountability.[49] As long as criminal defendants are not singled out because of their race, and as long as they are guilty or were brought into the criminal justice process on the basis of a reasonable suspicion of their guilt, neither courts nor citizens are likely to be troubled by the overrepresentation of one group or another among them. In this society it is usually not legitimate to consider the possibility that the structural arrangements we have chosen—our commitment to unbridled competition and to very individualistic definitions of rights for human beings—both create disincentives to law-abiding behavior and spotlight the vulnerabilities of minorities and the poor to them.

The dynamics of the drug loitering law in Seattle illustrate the complex influences of race on criminal justice policy. Minority residents (and the AIDS activists) saw the proposed law taking effect in an atmosphere of police hostility to them. Harriett Walden, who organized Mothers Against Police Harassment in 1990, points to the event that galvanized her activism, a time when police stopped her sons on the way to a community festival, took them to the local precinct, and "roughed them up" before letting them go, despite the fact that they had no records and "had no gang clothes or paraphernalia."[50] Such incidents are common, according to Jeri Ware, who chairs Seattle's Human Rights Commission, and have worsened since her youth. "Then I never saw black men spread out on the ground, down on their knees," she says. "The police hide behind the drug thing. . . . One day soon these young people are going to fight back."[51] The rancor extends beyond street-level police-community relations to institutional indifference. Ware complains that the Seattle Police Department resisted the commission's investigation of the department's handling of complaints mandated by a city council resolution passed in tandem with the drug loitering law (and intended to address the concerns of the law's opponents). To the resulting report's conclusion that "the Commission is convinced we are approaching a serious crisis of community confidence in the Police Department" the council responded with what Ware considers inadequate concessions—agreement to appoint an auditor without subpoena power as a substitute for the requested civilian complaint review board, for example.[52]

The responses of the police department, the Seattle City Council, and the mayor to evidence that in its first two years the drug loitering law had been applied in a racially discriminatory manner are perhaps even more telling than the evidence itself. A police official said that the guidelines for arrests now required more evidence of loitering than in the early days of the law.[53] The new chair of the council's Public Safety Committee speculated that the arrest patterns were "to some extent an accident of geography."[54] A representative of the mayor said the ordinance was working and should not be thrown out because of preexisting "tensions between the community and the police."[55] No attempt to deny the racially lopsided impact was made in any official response. In fact, it is hard to escape the conclusion that supporters of the ordinance found that fact no more than a politically inconvenient irrelevance. They rejected a proposal to reimpose a sunset provision on the law, mandating reconsideration of it in two years, and made the ordinance permanent.

One of Seattle's many sources of civic pride is its tolerance. The city's leaders speak of the active local branch of the American Civil Liberties Union with respect, and both blacks and whites say race relations are generally better than in most large American cities. But the city's minority community is relatively small and powerless. It may be that this political fact of life is more relevant than Seattle's vaunted culture of civic liberalism when it comes to the formulation of local drug policy—which, in this case, has more than a tinge of racism.

Norm Rice, Seattle's first African-American mayor—a consensus-oriented former head of the Public Safety Committee on the city council—could not depend on the black community for his political base. When the loitering law was first proposed, he repeatedly stressed that it must not unfairly target minorities. When it came up for re-newal, however, despite strong evidence that most arrested under it had been black and Latino and that many of those charges had been dropped, Rice pushed for re-enactment, as did the white prosecutor, the police department, and the largely white, crime prevention or-ganizations. In general, Rice seemed to have conceded the license of police to "control the streets" even at the cost of minority harassment; he did not join the King County Democratic Party in condemning an April 1991 gang sweep by police that stopped blacks indiscriminately in South Seattle parks.[56]

## BLACK RESPONSES TO RACIALLY DISPARATE IMPACTS

White resistance and black powerlessness are not the only impedi-ments to changing racially biased drug prohibition policies. Minority communities' reactions to aggressive drug enforcement apparently targeted at blacks in inner-city neighborhoods vary. Even blacks may approve a law enforcement strategy that focuses disproportionately on blacks. The greatest margins of victory for the Jackson County anti-drug sales tax came from Kansas City wards where low-income blacks are concentrated. A consultant to the sales tax campaign notes that in meetings with community groups, blacks were more likely to favor strong law enforcement measures rather than prevention or treatment as solutions to the drug problem in their own communi-ties.[57] At one meeting, in response to the consultant's effort to assure the residents that money from the proposed anti-drug sales tax would be used for prevention as well as police and prisons, a woman rose and said, "The only thing I want you to prevent is them getting out."[58] Of another gathering of blacks, held by the county executive to talk about non–law enforcement approaches, he says:

> People were standing up one after another and saying "Wait a minute,
> my biggest problem is that I've got a drug house three doors away, and
> the police come and close it, and a week later the same people come

and open it again. Why are the damn judges letting them out again?"
It turned into a mob almost, the goddamnedest meeting I've ever seen.
People really want a law enforcement solution first. They're willing to
use prevention and treatment *after* we clean up the streets. That's why
the campaign was built around law enforcement . . . additional cops.[59]

This reaction suggests that in some situations black inner-city residents living in close proximity to open drug-dealing and its attendant
violence are prepared to trade off some unwarranted surveillance and
even occasional harassment of young minority males for a measure
of (imagined or real) added protection. And it raises the important
questions of what conditions render black communities willing to
accede to racially differential attention from law enforcement and
what it would take to get those communities to insist on racial neutrality. In the late 1980s the citizens of both Seattle and Kansas City
felt menaced by drugs and invaded by gangs—in Seattle it was the
Crips and Bloods expanding northward from Los Angeles, in Kansas
City Jamaican "posses" began to set up shop in 1986—but the black
community of the latter city was far less ambivalent about law enforcement strategies in the war on drugs that might target them disproportionately. What explains the difference in attitudes?

The behavior and composition of the two cities' police departments
do not provide much of an answer. Law enforcement professionals
around the country regard both departments as exemplars of enlightened, modern policing; since the famous preventive patrol experiments of the early 1970s, the Kansas City department has been a
center for applied police research, and the Seattle department has
acquired, under its present chief, a reputation for its experiments in
community policing, the latest fashion in patrol strategies.[60] Yet local
interviews suggest that in both cities conflicts between police and
minority residents have not been uncommon; although fewer incidents of brutality are alleged and reported in the Kansas City press,
the most important black community organization, the Ad Hoc Group
Against Crime, came into being in 1977 in response to what was
perceived as police indifference to the slaying of several black prostitutes. (Cliff Sargeon, Chairman of Ad Hoc, notes that at the time,
"Police-black community relations were as wide apart as the banks
of the Mississippi River."[61])

The departments are also similar in minority representation among
law enforcement personnel; Seattle's department, with about 9 percent black officers in late 1992, almost reflects the proportion of that
racial group in the general population, while Kansas City lags behind,

with blacks making up 13 percent of sworn officers, less than half the black share of the city's residents.[62] While there are leadership differences in the two cities' departments, at the time of the case studies both cities had relatively progressive (white) police chiefs. Patrick Fitzsimons in Seattle had been there for a decade, both praised and attacked during that period, often seen as detached and unresponsive to the perceived recent crisis of drugs and gangs moving up the coast from California.[63] Larry J. Joiner in Kansas City was perhaps more popular with his officers (he rose through the ranks in the department, while Fitzsimons came to Seattle after twenty-one years in the New York Police Department), and he was succeeded in 1990 by Steven Bishop, whose relationship with black leaders as a division commander had been unusually close, perhaps in part because he took the unusual step of firing officers for excessive use of force.[64] Both chiefs are accused locally of blocking the serious investigation of citizen complaints against police, a sticking point for police-community relations in most cities.

A more complete explanation for the contrast between palpable tensions in police-minority relations in one city and relative harmony in the other can apparently be found in influences outside law enforcement. African-Americans in Kansas City may have greater confidence in police because as a community they have the kind of clout that blacks lack in Seattle. Not only do they represent a much greater share of the city's population—29.6 percent in 1990, as compared with 10.1 percent in Seattle—but the black organization Freedom, Inc. is the city's most powerful political club.[65] Candidates for most local offices routinely seek the tens of thousands of votes it can deliver; it was crucial to the 1991 victory of black Mayor Emanuel Cleaver (another first). The overlap of Freedom, Inc. and the leaders of Ad Hoc also ensures that the latter organization has easy access not only to senior police officials but also to city hall and the county legislature. (This channel of influence is perhaps even more important now than it was when the sales tax was passed in 1989, since the black elite can point to one of its own as mayor.)

The congruence of greater black empowerment and greater willingness to overlook the possibility that the justice system does not operate fairly (even though there is no evidence that its impact is less disproportionately burdensome, or less discriminatory, than in any other large American city) suggests a troubling irony. Greater black political participation in our big cities may not reduce the incidence of racial discrimination in criminal justice if blacks co-opt each other into acquiescence in the trade-off of civil rights and liberties for short-term law enforcement protection.

## AN END TO RACISM?

I have thus far argued that racism in drug prohibition policy is unlikely to be significantly reduced, at least in the short term, not only because of a residue of discriminatory decisions made by police, prosecutors, and judges, but also in light of attitudes outside the criminal justice system. Policymakers pay attention to white anger at what is perceived to be black criminality, the willingness of African-Americans in some situations to live with a measure of discrimination in this area, and the widespread indifference to racially unfair policy outcomes. The media contribute to racist policy directions by the sensationalization of street violence and incivility, editorial rhetoric, and the selection of topics for attention. Political figures, too, perpetuate racial stereotypes and plant racial images into their depictions of the way the social world operates. Finally, interest groups, even those operating from agendas promoting the public good, can have racially divisive influence.

It is hard to escape the conclusion that Seattle's citizen crime prevention groups have contributed, however unwittingly, to racial tension over the drug loitering issue. Initially made up of largely white merchants, the South Seattle Crime Prevention Council (whose parent body was the local chamber of commerce) formed in order to combat commercial burglary and quickly made common cause with police, who told them that the problem they had identified was closely associated with the rise of crack houses and drug use in their neighborhoods.[66] Through their selection of approaches and tactics—determined primarily by resources available to them, including the counsel of police—community organizations slipped into the assumptions that drug abuse was at the core of urban decay, that law enforcement was the appropriate instrumentality for addressing it, and that a focus on the retail drug trade would best meet their immediate needs. The totality of those choices was bound to have a disparate impact on African-Americans and Hispanics.

If awareness of the possibilities for bias in the decisions of police, prosecutors, judges, and probation officers expands, as now appears to be the case, there is hope for reducing discrimination in law enforcement. And political leadership of the right kind, coupled with vigilance by civil rights activists, could undermine at least some of the social and political attitudes that, though outside criminal justice, affect it. But progress in hearts and minds and precincts will not alter the fact that minorities are disproportionately represented in life situations that make them vulnerable—for perfectly appropriate professional reasons—to being the objects of attention for the criminal law. Structural forces like movements of capital and the shift from manufacturing to service jobs as the basis for urban economies have had profound impacts on low-income minorities, making low-level employment opportunities in the illegal drug industry attractive for unskilled inner-city residents, many of whom are black or Hispanic.[67] The urban spaces available to low-income dealers and the need for visible markets to attract buyers from beyond the neighborhood disproportionately expose minority participation in the retail trade to law enforcement attention. As police officials often point out, it is a lot easier to bring in the dealer who is operating from a phone booth on a ghetto street corner than the one who completes his transactions in his suburban study or college dorm or Wall Street office. Both operational and legal problems discourage drug enforcement as a part of routine patrol unless an officer happens upon an open-air market, and many of those are operated by the young, black, inner-city males who have become emblematic of the threat of drugs.

This perspective suggests that one source of racial disparity in drug enforcement (at least at the local level) is embedded in the most fundamental choices the country has made about twentieth-century economic and social development and is therefore likely to be intractable. Constitutional equal protection provides at least a formal remedy for overt biases within and outside the criminal justice system, but it is not (currently, anyway) a basis for claims of unintended disproportionate racial impacts of structural forces.[68] With court orders to keep probationers out of known drug-trafficking areas, loitering penalties aimed at suspected drug buyers and sellers, and the creation of ever-expanding drug-free zones, Seattle has targeted particular aspects of "the drug problem"—street trade, whether in dangerous or relatively harmless substances, and its attendant incivility or violence—that are more likely to implicate blacks than whites. But it does not matter to the courts that Seattle's effort to control its streets constitutes, without discriminatory intent from either police or judges or the political leaders who set standards for them, a kind of selective enforcement. Similarly, Jackson County, in deploying more resources to the investigation and apprehension of drug-trafficking in Kansas City, intensifies the effects of economic and social arrangements that have left more blacks than whites mired in poverty and desperation. But courts will not consider that the anti-drug sales tax, in adding drug enforcement resources at an almost certain cost to revenue for services like education and health, reinforces inequality of condition and thereby contributes to racial inequality.

The political process may prove a more likely avenue for addressing the structural sources of racial inequality.[69] Demands for relief of what used to be called systemic racism are growing in new arenas—among AIDS activists and environmentalists, for instance, as it becomes apparent that both HIV and pollution take an unequal toll on poor minorities.[70] But a challenge to the framework that supports the drug loitering law and the anti-drug tax will be difficult to mount. It will require mobilizing a political will to defy the present tendency to think of social problems as primarily curses brought upon the rest of us by the choices of deviant individuals. The "drug problem" has become a crucible for the construction of dangerous classes. As long as that mentality prevails, it will shield the disproportionate attention paid to minorities by police and courts.

# Chapter 12

# *Drug Prohibition as a Political Resource*

As a rule political figures are fully aware of their own efforts to position themselves to make political use of consensus positions on sensational issues. In a 1990 hearing of the House Subcommittee on Crime on proposed federal death penalty legislation, William J. Hughes (Democrat-N.J.), chairman of the subcommittee, referring to the death penalty as an issue in gubernatorial races, said testily, "The central issue in these campaigns seems to be not whether a particular candidate is for or against the death penalty. Debate focuses, instead, upon which of the candidates has a rightful claim to being the most zealous executioner."[1]

Politicians accuse each other of using the tougher-than-thou position merely as the proverbial political football. Senator Joseph Biden (Democrat-Del.), in 1989 Senate hearings on similar legislation, noted that President Bush had been publicly attacking Congress for not expanding the federal death penalty when, in fact, the previous year Congress had passed the death penalty for killings by drug kingpins and the administration had not yet requested an application of this law and had not proposed to Congress any further death penalty legislation. Bush should "stop putting it in his speeches," Biden complained, "because it is misleading, it is cynical, and it is not accurate."[2] From the perspective of then-President Bush and other cynics, it may not matter much whether get-tough legislation passes or not; its substantive purpose is subsumed in its political utility.

Bush's taunts, of course, escalated into a real "mine's tougher" contest a few months later, when he brought to Congress crime legislation containing provision for a federal death penalty for convicted drug kingpins then subject only to life imprisonment as leaders of continuing criminal enterprises.[3] He didn't have to adopt the slightly riskier strategy of blazing new trails, because that had already been done for him by congressional proposals for the creation of a number of other capital crimes—terrorism, espionage, attempted presidential assassination—where death did not result.

Not all who harness drug-control policy as a political resource have the same motivations. While some carry the banner of prohibition to safeguard their immediate political futures, for others it is simply part of maintaining a general political stance of righteous protectiveness. While the following taxonomy should not be regarded as perfectly comprehensive, nor the categories as always mutually exclusive, those for whom prohibition politics serves as an important vehicle for acquiring or sustaining political power tend to fall into three groups I shall call *true believers, delegates,* and *promoters.*[4]

## TRUE BELIEVERS

One of the difficulties of discerning the degree to which get-tough drug policies are driven primarily by politics rather than policy is that the most ardent policy entrepreneurs are often *true believers*. Their lack of cynicism doesn't keep them from reaping political advantage from their posture, to be sure, but that is not the aim. (In fact, many true believers don't need the boost of advocating tough drug policies. Representatives Gekas, McCollum, and Shaw, the three most active proponents of expanded death penalties in the House, all had safe seats; in 1988 McCollum ran unopposed in both the primary and the general election, while Gekas got 100 percent of the vote.[5])

The relative political disinterest (at least in the short term) of true believers does not necessarily mean, however, that they are wedded to the agenda item of drug abuse—either its moral or medical implications—as the primary source of their support for prohibition policies. The drug problem—or, rather, its political salience—becomes a vehicle for other political and policy interests. (The exception to this rule is the political figure or celebrity whose personal experience of loss attributable to drugs is the driving force behind policy involvement.) For true believers promotion of prohibition policies usually derives from a larger commitment to a substantial role for the state in regulating individual behavior. The motivating force behind that commitment may be moral—based on religious beliefs— or more generally authoritarian, prizing obedience to law as valuable for its own sake or regarding protection from the "dangerous classes" as an abiding political responsibility. In either case, it manifests itself

in decisions beyond the arena of drug policy. The association of prohibition true believers with broader cultural conservatism is apparent
in looking at recent congressional action by Gekas, McCollum, and
Shaw. All three voted against the proposal to allow federal funds to
pay for abortions resulting from rape or incest; all three voted for a
constitutional amendment banning physical desecration of the American flag; all three voted against restricting use of the death penalty
where the defendant can show a pattern of racial discrimination in
previous applications of it.[6] In rating the social conservatism of representatives, according to their roll call votes (with 100 percent the
most conservative), the *National Journal* put Gekas in the eighty-
second percentile in 1990; McCollum was in the eighty-ninth percentile, as was Shaw.[7]

A deep and abiding belief in punishment as a means of restoring
moral balance in society motivates some true believers; it is hard to
imagine that anything but conviction could have prompted Orrin
Hatch (Republican-Utah) when he said on the Senate floor, "Capital
punishment is our society's ultimate recognition of the sanctity of
human life."[8] His counterparts in the House had been pushing for a
comprehensive federal death penalty for several years before the kingpin idea came along. Necessity became the mother of invention when
they met with institutional resistance in the form of the House Judiciary Committee chaired by Peter Rodino, a committed liberal; they
then turned to the drug problem as a political resource. As Representative Gekas put it:

> Since the advent of my congressional service . . . I have used every
> parliamentary device known to mankind, and those in space, if any
> there be, to try to get the full Judiciary Committee and the full House
> to adopt a comprehensive death penalty. It was only through the crisis
> that appeared on the drug scene that permitted us to get to the floor
> and to final adoption of the drug kingpin death penalty statute.[9]

## DELEGATES

Although the boundaries between categories are not always distinct,
dividing those who support harshly prohibitionist policies who are
not true believers into delegates and promoters helps us to understand
something about their motivations.[10] The *delegates* are not actively
seeking political advancement from their prohibitionism—perhaps
because they are doubtful about it on a policy level—but feel that

support is necessary to demonstrate that they are not out of step with their constituencies. (This position need not be solely a political expediency. With such a strong consensus on both the death penalty and drug prohibition, popular sovereignty provides a principled rationale, also.) Like the true believers, delegates may not have immediate political needs that can only be met by prohibitionist postures; they are, rather, constructing themselves as reliable representatives, defending themselves against the charge that they do not share commitments with those whom they serve. Often liberal or moderate in other areas of social policy, they supplement the axiomatic law enforcement thrust with rationales that will fit with the public health problems caused by drugs.

Charles Schumer (Democrat-N.Y.), a generally liberal Brooklyn congressman with a safe seat who opposed the death penalty when he was a New York State Assemblyman, is an interesting example of the delegate who supported the kingpin death penalty provision with a mixture of justifications. As late as the spring of 1991, he was doubtful of the constitutionality of imposing the death penalty on kingpins who had committed no intentional homicide, and uncomfortable with it as a matter of policy. "Even if everything in the President's bill regarding the death penalty became law," he mused in a hearing of the House Subcommittee on Crime and Criminal Justice, which he chairs, "crime and drugs would continue to ravage our streets."[11] But he spoke of the "anguish" of his constituents—who, though solidly Democratic, are increasingly conservative on cultural issues like crime and race.[12] He noted that "my constituents accurately perceive revolving door justice," expressing a feeling of obligation to respond to that anguish with measures that were taking him "in a more conservative direction."[13]

By October, when the death penalty provision was being debated on the House floor, Schumer's support for the provision had crystallized. He argued that the penalty was proportional to the offense because death would surely result from large-scale drug-trafficking, that the constitutional requirement of a morally culpable state of mind in a capital crime was met by the kingpin's probable knowledge that his drugs would kill someone, and that other federal capital crimes that did not include murder (espionage, treason) were justified as threats to national security, an argument that could also apply to illicit drug-trafficking.[14]

During that same debate Schumer made arguments that made very clear that his support of the kingpin death penalty was unrelated to belief in its utility in reducing crime. In referring again to the "anguish" of his constituents, he spoke of their plea to "do something real," and he proffered as response to that plea provisions of the Omnibus Crime Control Act before him that could "do the real job"—those that put cops on the beat, gave drug treatment to prison inmates, and supported "intermediate punishments" like intensive probation for juvenile offenders.[15] He asserted that the general public knows that a measure like the death penalty or limiting the use of habeas corpus "does not make a darn bit of difference to making our streets safer." He nonetheless supported the kingpin death penalty, stressing its moral weight as an expression of society's repugnance for heinous offenses. "I do believe that for some of the very worst offenses the death penalty is an appropriate form of retributive punishment and must be necessary to insure that justice is done," he remarked. "Those who are at the very top of these drug enterprises . . . do indeed deserve society's ultimate approprium [sic], the death penalty."[16] Basing his change of heart on moral rather than utilitarian sources reflects sensitivity to his relatively sophisticated, mostly Jewish constituency, voters who may well understand the empirical doubt about the deterrent effect of the death penalty but are also likely to have strong moral feelings about drugs and street crime—and perhaps a more general anxiety about the return of the "dangerous classes."

Oddly, Schumer's support for the death penalty for drug kingpins may make it easier for him to maintain relatively liberal positions on some other cultural issues, though he denies that he intends it this way.[17] Having paid his dues on capital punishment, he has a buffer that probably makes it easier for him to argue, for example, for retaining a meaningful right of habeas corpus. (Here, too, however, Schumer does not stray too far from his constituents' likely sympathies. He takes the middle position, wishing to retain protection for defendants whose shoddy legal representation might lead to capital convictions, but seeking to reduce the delays that he says constitute abuse of the right.) For this purpose, his stance on the death penalty need not be consistent with his others on social issues. (That it may not be is evident from Representative Gekas's response that he was "astounded" when Schumer was in agreement with him in supporting the death penalty where a defendant accused of murder had acted not with intent to kill but in "reckless disregard" of the possibility that death would result from his conduct.[18]) His constituents can view him as taking on real villains—not impecunious and desperate young blacks selling drugs on the streets of his district but leaders of Medellin cartels. He can simultaneously call for more benign attention to the drug problem, as he did in hosting a "drug summit" in Washington in May 1993, where he called the federal drug funding ratio of 70 percent for law enforcement and only 30 percent for treatment and education an "imbalance."[19] At that meeting he even called for shifting $3 billion away from international interdiction to domestic "demand side" efforts, apparently indifferent to the interdependence of aggressive interdiction practice and the prosecution of the drug kingpins whose capital punishment he endorses.

## PROMOTERS

*Promoters* use tough drug policies more affirmatively (and also more cynically) than Schumer has done, to capture political territory— either along an ideological dimension, appealing to the cultural or religious right, or as part of the creation of an image of leadership. Political need determines the subject of legislative attention and how that attention will be paid, not the other way around. The need may be either collective or individual. In the last twenty years the association of traditionally liberal positions on street crime with Democrats has made the whole party vulnerable, an advantage that Republicans have fully exploited. Republican National Committee Chairman Lee Atwater encouraged Republicans to run on the issue because "almost every Democrat out there running is opposed to the death penalty."[20]

In the search for issues, a position on punishment for drug offenses can help define candidates. For a new congressional representative, or one facing a potentially powerful challenger in the next election, it establishes what one legislative aide calls "tough guy bona fides." As Diane Rust-Tierney of the American Civil Liberties Union points out, "If the public doesn't know much about the candidates, or there doesn't seem to be much difference between them, if one stands up and says, 'I'm for the death penalty,' that's something that sticks in people's minds."[21]

Wes Watkins, a former Oklahoma congressman from the Little Dixie district represented for thirty years by Carl Albert, Speaker of the House from 1971 to 1977, illustrates the use of the death penalty issue for purely promotional purposes. A fighter for economic benefits for his district—water projects, research and technical assistance grants for rural development—Watkins had never served on the congressional committees that deal with social issues. Nonetheless Watkins emerged in 1990 as a strong and visible supporter of an expanded federal death penalty in general and capital punishment for drug kingpins in particular. Testifying before a congressional committee in the spring of that year, he explained his position by equating drug-dealing with killing: "They're just as guilty of murder as if they put a gun to the head of each person that illegal drugs have killed. I think we need to try to address that in some way. They deserve the same consequences in my book."[22] Although this message sounds like the principled commitment of a law enforcement official or cultural conservative, its source was the difficult gubernatorial contest he was waging (which he narrowly lost in a Democratic runoff). Faced with an opponent who had just barely lost the previous election and who supported the popular issue of term limits for state legislators, he mounted the drug warrior's steed. Even in states as rural as Oklahoma—in 1990, 40.6 percent of the population lived outside of a metropolitan area, as compared with a national average of 22.5 percent—the drug problem has symbolic resonance that holds promise for casting its antagonists as public protectors, at least in the short term.[23]

Prohibition politics has collective as well as individual uses, although they may be limited in making partisan distinctions when most members of both major parties are already on record as supporting the basic policy thrust. Conservative Republicans struggling for party influence in a Democratic House in the late 1980s settled on drug policy as a promising way to get prominence, but they had to go beyond general postures of toughness, since there was no dispute about basic policy directions. They created a 1988 task force, which organized them and created opportunities for press conferences and other appearances, developed the drug kingpin death penalty idea, and produced the "user accountability" provisions in that year's bill (providing for loss of certain federal benefits—loan guaranties, professional licenses—to those convicted of state drug offenses), for which the party took credit.

A tough posture on drugs is a serviceable tool for presidents, too, particularly Republicans. Both Nixon and Reagan were promoters, and in September 1989 Bush, casting about for a headline-grabbing issue, chose to devote his first prime-time speech to announcing a new war on drugs. He was rewarded by press responses noting it as "the most visible domestic initiative of his Presidency."[24] The value of the speech was perhaps most evident in the reactions of other politicians; Democrats in Congress, many of whom were known to oppose harsh crime measures like the death penalty, nonetheless generally criticized the proposed program as too little too late. Bush in turn pounced on these reactions; he then had two measures of political gain from his initiative, in casting himself as a protector of the general public and in scoring points against political opponents for being not only soft on drugs but also weak and hypocritical. Democrats were boxed in, foreclosed by popular attitudes from criticizing Bush's toughness, unwilling to endorse the opponent's line; but also not daring to push Bush too hard, for fear of being tarred once again with the "tax-and-spend" label that had contributed to Dukakis' defeat the previous year.

Hitching your political star to as intractable a problem as illicit drugs, especially when resources are limited, carries with it political risks, however. The day after Bush's speech, soundings from the streets of American cities where the real drug war was being waged suggested that those most painfully and pervasively affected by drug abuse dismissed his war as political skirmish. And his critics in Congress immediately pointed out that little money would be spent on treatment programs, that most of the $7.9 billion he cited as commitment for the program did not represent any new effort but was already built into the fiscal 1990 budget. They noted, furthermore, that without new taxes, funds for his war on drugs would have to come from already strapped social programs that might address the underlying causes of rampant drug use in poor urban neighborhoods.[25]

To the general public these comments were mere cavils. In a Gallup poll taken shortly after the speech, 72 percent of respondents said they approved of "the job President Bush is doing in dealing with the drug problem."[26] Bush's advisors were hardly blind to such polls; Lee Atwater, noting the publicity given to the speech in light of the polls of the previous six months showing drugs as the issue of greatest citizen concern, said, "George Bush talking from the bully pulpit on drugs is good for us; every time he uses the bully pulpit it's a winner."[27] It was a winner, too, when the bully pulpit became the battlefield; after Bush invaded Panama in November 1989 to bring Manuel Noriega to stand trial in the United States for drug-trafficking, his approval ratings soared.[28]

Despite a background that would not immediately suggest an affinity for get-tough measures, Paul Rosenbaum, the state legislator who sponsored Michigan's 650 lifer law, also used drug prohibition for promotion purposes. A Democrat, born in the Bronx, educated in Massachusetts and Washington, D.C., he showed considerable sympathy for some liberal positions on social issues, although he represented Battle Creek, a town with a solidly Republican base. (On the personal level, he appears to have had some liberal tendencies, too. One newspaper described his usual appearance in the legislature "in flamboyant orange and blue leisure suits, flowered shirts, and more chains than are in Tiffany showcases."[29]) Previous to his first introduction of the "heroin abuse package" in 1975 he had not been consistently or comprehensively hard-line on drug policy; he opposed capital punishment (because he did not believe in its deterrent effects, he said), supported a bill to decriminalize public drunkenness, which passed, and the 1977 bill to decriminalize marijuana, which didn't. These positions suggest that he was by no means a rigid legalist.

Although Rosenbaum denies it, there is considerable evidence that he promoted his drug proposals at least in part for the immediate political capital he might acquire. A previous Chairman of the House Judiciary Committee, Bob Traxler, had gone on to Congress—perhaps an alluring precedent—and in 1976 Carl Pursell, Chairman of the Judiciary Committee in the state senate, did, too. By 1977, after three years in his job, Rosenbaum was bored, by his own account; at this point his stake in politically popular policies must have risen. He considered running for state attorney general, which would have meant coming up against the Oakland County prosecuting attorney who had organized a ballot initiative opposing "good time" (time off a prison sentence for good behavior). Discarding that option, he decided to run in the Democratic primary for the U.S. Senate, which he lost. His files from that period provide evidence that he hoped his get-tough stance would stand him in good stead in that race. He sent his package of bills to prominent constituents, accompanied by cover notes saying things like, "Maybe we will start to protect the 99 percent decent, God-fearing people in this state, rather than the one percent of the habitual career criminals," with copies sent to assistants who were urged to see if they could raise campaign contributions from the addressees.[30]

Rosenbaum maintains that policy considerations alone drove his interest in tough drug measures. He says, "The FBI and DEA came to me asking me to sponsor a tough new law against drug lords. We went to New York to look at the Rockefeller law [tough mandatory penalties for drug crimes], and then we tried to do the best job we could."[31] But by 1976 skepticism about the 1973 New York drug law's ability to reduce drug trafficking was setting in, and Rosenbaum must have known it. A front-page story in the *New York Times* in late 1975 announced that "New York is experiencing its worst illegal narcotics trafficking problems in five years, according to high law enforcement officials"; and witnesses from the Michigan Department of Public Health testified at 1976 hearings on Rosenbaum's package that preliminary reports showed the law to be ineffective.[32] Lacking deep conviction in the retributive value of harsh penalties, Rosenbaum yielded to the siren song of political opportunity when he sponsored the 650-plus law.


## POLITICAL HARVEST?

A difficult question to answer is how valuable a political resource drug prohibition really is. The evidence from my case studies suggests that support for tough drug policy cannot be counted on to vanquish opponents. Furthermore, those who don't take tough stances aren't necessarily vulnerable to those who do. Several Alaska Democrats on the state legislative committee that blocked a recriminalization bill were tagged as soft on drugs by opponents in the 1988 elections, but they all prevailed nonetheless, while the 1990 Republican candidate for governor who charged the Democrat with being in league with the National Organization for the Reform of Marijuana Laws (NORML) lost, possibly injured by subsequent howls that she had misrepresented the Democrat's position and engaged in dirty tricks.[33] Baltimore Mayor Kurt Schmoke, the only big-city mayor who openly favors decriminalization of drug possession, easily won re-election; his position on drugs never even became an issue in the campaign. Jane Noland, the Seattle City Councilwoman who pushed hardest for the drug loitering law, does not appear to have improved her chances of succeeding Mayor Norm Rice because of it. Paul Rosenbaum proved unable to steer his tough-on-drugs mount through the pack of contenders for the Democratic nomination for senator from Michigan in 1978. Albert Riederer's support of the Jackson County anti-drug sales tax may have cost him as much in criticism of its implementation as it benefited him when the voters approved it; he chose not to run for a fourth term, and some interviewees suggested that one reason for his retirement was that he did not want to have to deal with attacks on his leadership in drug enforcement.

On the other hand, what seems to be a pattern may be explainable by independent influences in most cases. The Alaska legislators had the incumbent's advantage, and the Republican gubernatorial candidate was ultimately swamped by the last-minute third-party candidacy of Walter J. Hickel, a former governor and Secretary of the Interior who promotes and profits from real estate and natural resources development. (In fact, because of the three-way race Hickel won with only 39 percent of the vote, prompting the anti-recrimin-alization wags to print a bumper sticker that said, "Pot Got More Votes than Hickel.") Schmoke has a particular kind of invulnerability by virtue of being African-American and a former prosecutor; his anti-prohibitionism cannot be credibly attacked as part of a strategy to keep blacks down, nor can his views be dismissed as the mean-derings of a visionary. Noland may yet have a political future, and Rosenbaum, with or without help from the drug problem, didn't have enough money for a real shot at one. As for Albert Riederer, he was able to exit his third term as prosecutor with grace, and it may be that his initiative in raising revenue to fight drugs will be what is best remembered after a decent interval if he decides to run for higher office.

That drug prohibition is not a make-or-break issue in individual electoral contests does not mean that politicians regard it as politically irrelevant. Many Michigan state legislators privately felt that Paul Rosenbaum was "demagoguing the issue" of drug offenses, as one of them put it. But the majorities in support of his package of tough penalties were very substantial (84 to 11 in the House, 27 to 7 in the Senate), reflecting a fear that it was risky to go out on the limb of dissent from what was perceived as a consensus position reflecting the public's strongly held moral position and their mounting fears of the "dangerous classes."

Support for prohibition may serve collective political interests more than individual ones. Weighing in on the side of protecting people from dangerous drugs and violence, for instance, is a relatively costless way to restore a bit of piety to political classes that have been damaged by revelations of private culpability and public corruption—or at least to counterbalance such charges. And drug prohibition is a handy tool for one group to differentiate itself from its opponent in a political arena. In 1989 the Republican minority in the Alaska House of Rep-resentatives found common cause (after a period of intraparty wran-gling) in using charges that the recriminalization bill had been stalled in committee for eight years to try to discredit (and eventually unseat) the Democrat majority.[34] To the extent that the attack put the Dem-ocrats on the defensive, it worked; Democratic Governor Steve Cowper felt compelled to respond by considering the inclusion of a recriminalization proposal in his 1990 legislative package, even though most Democrats and a number of Republicans still believed it would violate the state constitution.[35] The governor's tentative endorsement of the measure served another political end of drug prohibition policymaking: It generated media attention that spilled over onto less sexy items on his agenda—funding for the Alaska Marine Highway System, new oil-spill laws—and contributed to an impression of responsible leadership for Cowper's administration and party.

Perhaps drug prohibition is most important as a political resource at the most general level. Get-tough policies reinforce the legitimacy of private morality as a priority topic for public debate. Sin of all kinds has great political salience in this country, to an extent that is often puzzling to Europeans. Otherwise healthy presidential candidacies wither in the exposure of marital indiscretions, and issues like street crime and drugs eclipse concerns about unemployment and nuclear war in public opinion polls. Public policy reflects and shapes this public sensitivity. Among advanced industrial countries we are extremely punitive; we cling to capital punishment where all of western Europe and neighboring Mexico and Canada have abandoned it. And we cast the net of coercion very widely; few Western countries restrict gays in the military or pile civil penalties on top of criminal ones.

That our official moralism doesn't solve many problems is usually irrelevant to its political usefulness. Policymakers know that even in the face of government failure the public will routinely demand more of the same.[36] They profit from this tendency in the short run by not having to defend the failure or the defective theory it reflects. In the long run they benefit, too, because they are relieved of the necessity of considering alternative (and therefore politically risky) ways of ordering the social universe. The politicization of crime and drugs has become the bedrock of what might be called "distraction politics."

The dominant conception of crime in this country has always been an individualistic one—the offense is seen as a product of choice, whether motivated by evil, disease, or despair—that compels responses aimed at individual offenders.[37] In the early 1990s political leaders and the general public were perhaps becoming more aware that social and economic forces may structure a very narrow range of individual choices; at least at the local level, my interviewees knew all too well that young minority males in inner cities were faced with few income-generating possibilities as lucrative as selling drugs. Yet the individualistic approaches still prevail. They are both less costly and less threatening than the alternatives. Law enforcement measures, righteous political rhetoric, and media dramatization of evil will take requisite note of social problems—whatever their sources—to display concern and initiative on the part of policymakers. And they won't demand the mobilization of will and resources necessary either to alter the view of drug-taking and drug-selling as a product of individual pathology or even to achieve the more modest aim of regarding drug dependence as a public health problem rather than a criminal one.

Ironically, as the public and political leaders become more aware of the structural sources of crime, the political utility of harsh punishments may become greater. Responsibility for structural problems in a democracy is by definition collective and cannot be avoided by leaders who recognize them. And yet to acknowledge that responsibility would require either admitting past failures and retiring from the fray or grasping the nettle and demanding fundamental change. Aside from the natural disinclination to avow that they have dedicated their careers to what turn out to be false premises, politicians are unlikely to support radical reform because voters, whose dawning awareness of what is wrong doesn't mean they want to assume the costs of repair, are likely to respond by forcing them into retirement. Reinforcement of old assumptions about the nature of crime through get-tough policies thus becomes an even stronger pillar of political survival. It hardly matters that such offenses as retail drug-dealing threaten to unmask unbridled competition, economic disinvestment, and racial inequality as sources of social disorder.

# CHAPTER 13

# *Drug Prohibition as a Material Resource*

Political scientists sometimes order public policies in a basic three-category typology to improve their analytical understanding of relationships between policy actors and to better predict the course of policymaking.[1] With this perspective policies are seen as either distributive, redistributive, or regulatory.

The key feature of *distributive* policies is subsidy—financial support from government to support or provide incentives for desirable activity, usually private but sometimes public. Farm price supports encourage the growing of crops, government grants make it possible for communities to build, and the state stimulates economic growth by allowing tax deductions for interest paid on home mortgages and investment tax credits. *Redistributive* policies shift resources—income, rights—from one group to another; examples are progressive taxes, public assistance, and the prohibition of racial or gender discrimination in employment. *Regulatory* policies are attempts to protect the public by prohibiting potentially harmful behavior (pollution), mandating beneficial activity (wattage requirements in the workplace), or channeling competition (granting broadcast licenses). Economic activity is usually the target of regulatory policies, but sometimes the focus is on individual behavior—as with "sin taxes," which impose high levies on cigarettes and alcohol to discourage people from using them.

Many policies contain elements of more than one type. At first glance the criminal law, including drug prohibition, seems to be regulatory in nature, protecting the general public by restraining antisocial activities. It is this aspect of its function that gives it fundamental legitimacy. There is an element of redistribution, too, as criminalizing behavior takes rights away from those who have been engaging in it. Least obvious, but nonetheless present indirectly (and sometimes directly, as when government contracts with private companies to construct or run prisons), is a distributive element in crime policy.[2] The federal government makes grants to state and local governments for new police technology or to run special programs for offenders; researchers and professional interest groups play subsystem politics that keep the spigot open; the amount of crime-fighting that can occur is closely related to the amount of money provided. And law enforcement agencies, no more immune to prospects of material gain than other organizations, may generate productive activity for the subsidy it will attract. This tendency calls to mind the comment of Karl Marx—tongue in cheek, presumably—that "The criminal . . . produces the whole of the police and criminal justice, constables, judges, hangmen, juries, etc.; and all these different lines of business, which form equally many categories of the social division of labour, develop different capacities of the human spirit, create new needs and new ways of satisfying them."[3]

The color of money is also a powerful lure for drug policymakers in the 1980s and 1990s, for two reasons. In a pinched time when voters seem unwilling to spend money on many services, drug control is an exception. Furthermore, since the drug trade is illegal, its assets and proceeds can be recycled as revenue to the state, a scarce commodity from an unpopular source unlikely to encounter less resistance than taxes on law-abiding citizens.

It is important to note here that financial motives and the more public-minded aims thought to be appropriate to law enforcement and social service functions need not be mutually exclusive. Anti-drug measures that feather the nests of law enforcement and social service agencies, enhance the business environment, or plump up the public fisc are not usually enacted with the aim of profiting from the suffering of others. The spirit is, rather, one of acknowledging that an ill wind might as well blow somebody some good. In a time of economic squeeze for both private and public sectors, law enforcement professionals, merchants, and providers of health care and social services are likely to seek and accept help where they can find it.


## CIVIL LAW AS CASH COW

It is easy to assume that drug prohibition is solely within the province of the criminal law—either through its substantive sanctions or the narrowing of its procedural protections. But in recent years desperation over drug war failures and the growing prominence more generally of coercion as an instrument of social policy—think of workfare, and Maryland's "healthfare," which lowers a mother's public assistance grant as punishment for not having her children immunized—have enlarged the policy terrain.[4] Drug warriors are increasingly turning to the civil law, where the benign image of privileges withheld and minor fines imposed can conceal more formidable powers.

Not all civil penalties involve money. The "user accountability" provisions of the 1988 federal omnibus drug bill included the possibility of denying some benefits to anyone convicted of a drug offense.[5] (Permanent denial of such benefits as student loans and federal contracts is mandatory for those convicted of three or more drug-trafficking offenses.) Under a program of the U.S. Department of Housing and Urban Development a drug user or dealer can be evicted from public housing even without a criminal conviction.[6] And, as mentioned in Chapter 2, many states, with or without encouragement from the federal government, now add to criminal punishments for convicted drug offenders the suspension of their drivers' licenses.

Other penalties seem calculated to get policy implementers' entrepreneurial juices flowing. One development is the enforcement of the income tax law against drug dealers.[7] And the states are now taxing illicit drugs seized from arrested dealers or users. About half impose hefty levies; a pound of pot in Minnesota, for example, required a $1,590 tax stamp in 1990.[8] The point is not really to collect the tax; when the dealers don't comply with the tax law—as of course they don't—the state can impose fines—or confiscate property, which may be worth much more than the amount of the fine. Some states don't make much use of the law, which suggests that its passage was purely or principally symbolic; others are less passive. Minnesota collected over $2 million from suspected drug dealers between 1987 and 1992.[9]

Asset forfeiture laws are even more common, and the yield is a powerful stimulant to drug enforcement and the organizations that conduct it. Federal law passed in 1970 and expanded several times since then allows law enforcement agencies to seize property of suspected drug offenders—currency, vehicles, real estate—and to keep the proceeds.[10] In fiscal 1991 the federal Asset Forfeiture Program received $644 million in seized assets and shared $279 million from federal forfeitures with state and local law enforcement.[11] By the fall of 1992 almost $2.6 billion in cash and other proceeds had been deposited in the forfeiture fund of the Department of Justice.

The Bush administration also recommended that states adopt similar measures to "sanction both casual users and drug traffickers," and, indeed, most states now have their own programs.[12] Proceeds are sometimes put into a state's general fund; in Missouri they are earmarked for spending on education. But usually forfeiture money is distributed to police departments—occasionally to prosecutors and courts—and may then be shared with informants who supply productive leads to more seizures. The edifice of asset forfeiture has constructed itself; "this reinvestment of forfeiture proceeds in law enforcement has made possible the remarkable growth in federal forfeitures," the Director of the Executive Office for Asset Forfeiture in the Department of Justice said in 1993.[13] Throughout the criminal justice system economic incentives are powerful.

Asset forfeiture is an appealing way to increase law enforcement revenues partly because it is so easy to effect. The usual impediments to confiscating property simply don't apply. While a seizure must be judicially approved under federal regulations—the officer must show probable cause to believe a drug offense is occurring—in many jurisdictions no hearing is required. The practice follows an ancient legal fiction that forfeiture proceedings are brought against a thing, not a person, so the usual due-process requirements of criminal proceedings do not apply.[14] Furthermore, without a costly and complex legal challenge the property usually need not be returned, even when the owner is found to be not guilty of the suspected drug offense; the forfeiture of vehicles suspected of being used in drug deals that remain unproved is common practice in many cities and states.[15] A law enforcement agency need not engage in complicated investigations of high-level dealers to benefit from asset forfeiture laws, either. A ten-month study conducted by *The Pittsburgh Press* found that most property seized was cash or cars of ordinary people, who were either innocent—many were never even charged with a crime—or guilty of only minor offenses.[16]

What appear to be shocking violations of the fundamental fairness that we like to think is associated with deprivations of property by the state are rarely defended with any constitutional rationale.[17] Rather, pragmatism prevails over principle, public concern over judicial philosophy, the fiscal demands of crime control over the intangible social rewards of due process. Concurrent civil and criminal judgments against the property and its owner do not constitute "punishment" in violation of double jeopardy, one court has ruled, because of "[t]he ravages of drugs upon our nation and the billions the government is being forced to spend upon [drug] investigation and enforcement."[18]

Governments are perfectly open about the revenue-raising aims of drug taxes and property seizures. Although the federal government asserts that the fiscal ambition of asset forfeiture is a "by-product" of other objectives supported with crime-control rationales, former Deputy Attorney General George Terwilliger touted the federal asset forfeiture program he supervised as "a blessing to taxpayers, as it enables us to fund part of the cost of law enforcement from the pockets of criminals."[19] As for the drug taxes, the usual rationales for levies on business are easily applied. Drug dealers are engaged in buying and selling within the state, after all; Robert D. Ebel, formerly an official of the Advisory Commission on Intergovernmental Relations, justified the drug taxes in 1990 with the argument that *not* taxing these entrepreneurs would be giving them a tax break just because their business is illegal.[20] Defense lawyers are usually unsympathetic to the economic arguments; they see constitutional protections available to criminal defendants sacrificed for what one called "the frenzied quest for cash."[21]

## CHASING DRUG MONEY

It is easy to understand that quest. In addition to ordinary human greed and the imperative of organizational expansion, tremendous pressure is brought to bear on drug prohibition implementers—by activists, formulators, the media, and the general public—to make more arrests and put more dealers and users in prison. Countering that demand is a reduced supply of resources for those activities. Local law enforcement has suffered most. Although real per-capita expenditures for police rose during the 1960s and early 1970s, they dropped after 1975 and did not rise again for a decade, reflecting the general fiscal crisis in American cities.[22] Even without the ascendance of the drug problem this structural force would have pushed law enforcement officials to develop innovative ways to address their material needs. (In fact, criminal justice inventiveness born of necessity has taken a number of other directions, including the expanded use of computerized arrest records for surveillance of present and past offenders and the development of "intermediate punishments," such as intensive probation—described in Chapter 2—that are cheaper than prison.[23]) The crack invasion, rather than being the *raison d 'être* for law enforcement entrepreneurship, gave it greater legitimacy than ordinary institutional needs could have.

It would be a mistake to say that the Jackson County anti-drug sales tax was conceived and passed solely because the drug problem presented a financial opportunity to drug warriors. But it is certainly the case that those who were running the county were strapped for resources to do the job they had been elected to do; a former county assessor says, "The criminal justice system is very fragmented here, and central to the problem is that we haven't spent any money on it for over a decade."[24] The public clamor for government to "do something" about drug abuse was very sweeping and very intense. It is not surprising that policymakers with pressing material needs should incorporate into such a message a license to solve their own problems as well. It is a pattern that can be observed at other levels in crisis-oriented policymaking—the rush to address the poverty of the inner cities in the 1960s, for example, where the most enduring achievement of community action programs may have been not increased services and better communities but career opportunities they gave to poor people demanding services as "brokers between the ghetto and the society which enclosed it."[25] Wars generate booty, which even honorable combatants are likely to pocket. Savoring it, when the enemy is widely viewed as vicious, may even be done in virtue as well as in triumph.

Jackson County officials were ready to put the spoils of war to both political and operational use. It is axiomatic that both Bill Waris, the county executive, and Albert Riederer, the prosecuting attorney, men with political ambitions, assumed that if they were able to get the taxpayers to agree to let them spend the proceeds of the ¼ percent sales tax, and they spent it in a way that was deemed by the public to be effective, the effort would advance their political fortunes. And there is no question that they needed money from some nontraditional source to do the jobs they had been elected to do, including but not limited to fighting drugs.

The tax revenue was appealing to policymakers beyond the drug enforcement it would buy in large part because it could be used to plug up holes that the fiscal crisis had opened in the dyke of support for public services. Each of the major competitors for the power to spend tax proceeds recognized the other's vulnerability to the prospect of financial gain in the tax. The squabbling between Waris and Riederer over the mechanism of the tax centered less on who had the stronger functional or institutional claim on the new resources than on who would be least likely to deflect the money from its declared purposes. Waris, Riederer alleged, had "a plan to raise general revenues under the banner of fighting drugs."[26] Even for Riederer, who appears to have been far more knowledgeable and concerned about the inner-city drug problem than Waris, institutional needs supplemented specific program objectives as incentives for mounting a drug tax campaign. The former county assessor who first worked for Waris and then for Riederer, managing the early phases of the drug program, only slightly overstates the dilemma both men faced: "We had been tax-starved and we thought we would get something out of this program . . . we were so desperately in need of money that we thought we'd better go along with it, and that's why you don't have any real debate [about the purposes of spending the money]."[27] In fact, the drug policy committee in the county legislature that had been discussing long-range program directions for drug control never met again once the politics of funding became dominant. And despite a campaign that stressed the increase in cops and courts and prison space the tax would provide, Waris contemplated using some of the money for county operating expenses, as Riederer warned he would. But Riederer, too, though genuinely dedicated to programmatic aims, could not resist dipping his finger in the pork barrel; he was criticized even by his supporters for buying more new computers than there were drug prosecutors.[28]

Financial considerations also inhibited possible opposition to the tax. In a time and place where the tax revolt was strong and the voters had to approve every levy, one might expect that both citizens and public service workers would have protested that enacting the anti-drug sales tax would impose a terrible opportunity cost, that voters would be more reluctant in the future to approve additional taxes for schools and parks. Indeed Waris and a county legislator or two did make this point early in consideration of the measure, but it was widely regarded (probably correctly) as self-serving, just part of the contest over which politician would have control of the money.

Others might have made that argument, too, or they might have objected that law enforcement was not the only way to approach drugs—that medical services and drug education could be more effective in reducing drug abuse. Initially, one of the county legislators did express such a concern; he grumbled that people shouldn't have to wait to be arrested before they got help for their drug problem. But by the time the drug tax proposal reached a wider audience, it had been modified enough to still potential voices of dissent. Riederer and his allies made a modest concession—only $3.5 million of the predicted annual yield of $14 million—to those who supported drug treatment or prevention and who, not incidentally, worked in or with programs in community organizations or health centers that would be among the recipients of this largesse.[29] The co-optation extended beyond money to decisionmaking; potential doubters from the social services and medical communities were brought into the fold with invitations to sit on the fiscal commission established to oversee the distribution of funds.

Riederer's cronies who ran the sales tax campaign are unapologetic about using tried-and-true political strategies to deflect possible interest group opposition. Although success seemed likely from the start, they left nothing to chance. Pat Gray, a political consultant who has orchestrated several local tax campaigns, began working for the anti-drug sales tax by going directly to the anti-tax groups and persuading them not to fight the measure but to "sit it out."[30] Then he moved on to other possible opponents. With them he held out the prospect of new support for their activities, the chance to make distributive policy for their own immediate benefit. "We even got the defense attorneys to go along, by making a commitment to them that we'd go down and get some more state money for the defender's office," he crows. "Everybody was taken care of; that's good politics." Steve Glorioso, another consultant, notes, "Some self-interest is always the case in a democracy. You have the Diane Cleavers of this world saying we ought to have more prevention, and by gosh, that's what her agency does. That's normal."[31] (Ms. Cleaver was Mental Health Director of the Swope Parkway Health Center, and also happens to be the mayor's wife. She solicited a contribution for the campaign from her agency and then served on the fiscal commission. Not surprisingly, she did not see the victory of the tax in terms of strategic efforts to build an elite consensus and defuse entrenched interests. There was little concern about an overemphasis on law enforcement, she says, because "there's a lot of feeling about safety, and punishment is a part of safety."[32])

The success of the sales tax conception and campaign in meeting financial and organizational needs of law enforcement (and, to a lesser extent, of the treatment and prevention communities of Kansas City) can be explained in part by an institutional commitment to popular policymaking that was more apparent than real. Democratic participation in a capitalist society is generally a matter of voter choice among competitors for political leadership, while substantive policy choices are made at one remove from the people, by those in whom they have vested power.[33] The exercise of this procedural democracy is often a rather passive exercise requiring that parties or other groups promoting candidates' interests put great energy into shaping voters' preferences. The more active participation of a voter initiative theoretically cuts out the interests of the political elite to arrive at a policy popularly chosen. But the Jackson County anti-drug sales tax, while formally a political decision made directly by the people, was only nominally direct democracy. It was conceived by a political leader and sold to the voters by forces loyal to him. In manipulating possibly dissenting groups as part of the drug tax campaign strategy, Gray and Glorioso were behaving within accepted traditions of representative democracy, mobilizing what are indeed the "normal" interests of those with access to the political leadership. Those traditions were more likely to advance the political and material interests of political leaders than a truly grass-roots referendum would have done.

## SUPPORT YOUR LOCAL MERCHANTS

The resource that prohibition represents in the title of the chapter is deliberately referred to as "material" rather than "financial." The gains that flow from policy change may be less obviously financial than the grants-in-aid and procurement contracts that government provides. In order to encourage business activity government creates the infrastructure within which it can operate—the roads that lead customers to the store, the water for plant machinery—and provides various incentives, like tax credits and accelerated depreciation allowances. To the extent that law enforcement is part of the government's support for a "healthy" business environment, the private sector may be directly served by a number of components of drug prohibition policies. Law enforcement commitment to the policy paves the way for workplace drug-testing, for instance, and the increased discipline it imposes on workers—a significant resource in a time of declining profits.

But in Seattle, drug prohibition provided justification for an intensified police patrol service to shoo addicts and dealers away from retailers' doorways. It is not evident that either downtown merchants or city politicians truly believed that the drug loitering law would reduce the incidence of drugs in the city. But the merchants were able to induce (nonfinancial) public support for their businesses by securing a police commitment to maintaining a favorable commercial environment—a loitering-free "infrastructure," as it were. As long as the drug sales take place somewhere else, the downtown merchants are likely to continue supporting policies that seem unlikely to have much direct effect on drug use. As U.S. military spending, even after the collapse of the Evil Empire, is buoyed by the material benefits it provides to military contractors and local community employment, so is prohibition policy girded in part by the material sustenance it provides to even those actors and interests—like the corporations who conduct random drug tests on their (usually lower-level) employees—who have little real concern about the individual or social harm that the drug problem inflicts. The benefits of keeping Seattle merchants happy count for more than disappointment that the problem has simply been displaced. The drug problem remains essentially unaffected, while the mayor and city council can take credit for supporting their local merchants. In the end, the politics of providing material resources to important constituents fuels the policies of drug prohibition—whether or not the declared objectives of those policies are advanced.

# CHAPTER 14

# *Drugspeak*

Language has many roles in the play of power. One of the most important is to reinforce and reproduce existing policy. More than a record of reality, it *becomes* the reality with which policy formulators and implementers, the media, and the general public fend off policy change.[1] The less successfully the policy meets declared objectives, the more important it becomes to maintain a discourse that supports it.

Many postmodernists propose that language is an autonomous force prior to and constricting individual agency. In this view, the force of language lies not in meta-narratives produced by powerful subjects whose perspectives dominate the political process, but in fragmented, local, diverse "language games" that shift over time and with the social situations of the players.[2] With this perspective, the study of language as power should focus not solely on the ultimate power of the state but also on what Michel Foucault called "infinitesimal mechanisms" that are "invested, colonized, utilized, involuted, transformed, displaced, extended, etc., by ever more general mechanisms and by forms of global domination."[3]

Viewing the discourse of drug prohibition as decentralized and embedded in sources of power less monolithic than the state is useful for understanding its sweep and the role of followers in the policy exchanges that sustain its energy. And it helps to explain the somewhat erratic influence of rhetoric in the five case studies reported in this book. The power of drugspeak as a policy tool depends on local attitudes and conditions, the myriad and fragmented social situations that Foucault would find at the heart of "language games."

At the same time, the postmodernist subversion of the self-aware, active subject does not work very well in the study of many aspects of American politics, including the analysis of policymaking.[4] The discourse of drugs did not fall from the sky. From the days of American drug policymaking in the late nineteenth century, individual and group actors have played major roles in giving it life and force, and today's construction of the dangerous classes as one of Foucault's "general mechanisms" for giving prohibition its vigor must be laid at the door of interest groups, political leaders, and the media. The articulation and dissemination of contemporary drugspeak owe much to presidents, senators, Nancy Reagan, and the early parents' organizations that prodded those leaders. Particular media strategies and presentations are undeniably influential in sustaining the complementary images of weak or evil drug offenders; beleaguered families and neighbors victimized by them; and hard-working, benevolent public servants that serve in the recurring drug wars.[5]

Our punitive drug policies survive not by evidence of their accomplishments, but at least partly by exhortation, threat, and reassurance, continually circulated among political leaders, anti-drug activists, and the media, and consumed (and then passed on) by frustrated citizens.[6] Where drug prohibition is concerned, rhetoric is at least as powerful a policymaking tool as interest group lobbying or political bargaining. It can suppress debate that might alter the public agenda, obviate the mythological pulling and tugging of policy formulation and adoption, and subvert accountability in implementation. And, while it may frighten some young people and occasional users away from drug use, drugspeak is unlikely to be a powerful disincentive for the deprived and desperate people most vulnerable to compulsive use of the most destructive substances.

Although hyperbole and melodramatic language are rarely in short supply in struggles over social policy, drug prohibition language—what William Safire once called "the discourse of drug dudgeon"—is particularly sensational.[7] It is hard to think of another policy area where the vernacular of demonization—we might call it the dangerous classes mentality—is enshrined in formal headings of federal legislation, as in "Title II—Capital Punishment for Drug Kingpins."[8] And the seriousness of the drug problem apparently conveys a boundless license for symbolic drama. When Drug Enforcement Administration officials admitted that the sale of crack cocaine contained in the baggie held up by the president during his 1989 prime-time address on fighting drugs had been staged in Lafayette Park across the street from the White House at the request of White House speech writers, Bush shrugged off the fraud by saying "I think it can happen in any neighborhood, and I think that's what it dramatized."[9]

The term "drugspeak" is deliberately exhaustive. It embraces not only the vernacular of drug enforcement and treatment but a semantic of drug prohibition, from its characterization of a drug-infested society to the braggadocio of political leaders who try to convince the public that reduced cocaine use is a product of the drug wars of the 1980s.

To discuss the rhetorical construction of drug prohibition, I will borrow and extend sociologist Lynn Zimmer's idea of an "anti-drug semantic" that shapes the problematic character of drug-taking and drug users.[10] Drugspeak's pervasive themes also establish the legitimacy of law enforcement as the primary solution to the American drug problem and endorse an unprecedented vigor and reach in applying criminal and civil penalties to those who defy prohibition. The success of drugspeak turns on its ability to make both elites and the general public feel that they are supporting—and sometimes actively participating in—a social movement of great consequence. Images of struggle and unity combine with characterizations of enemies and allies to ritualize public discourse on the subject. Drugspeak suppresses all but the most academic discussion of policy alternatives, deflects attention from items on the shadow agenda, and prevents consideration of the structural sources of the most destructive forms of drug use.

## RHETORIC WITH A PAST

Images of the mind-altering drugs and drug takers we now forswear have varied widely among cultures and eras. Their healing and intoxicating properties have been hailed and sanctified by peasants and priests alike from antiquity to the present.[11] In Shakespeare's England opium was just the poppy that could no longer induce "sweet sleep" when Iago had shaken Othello's trust in Desdemona; 200 years later in that country it was still "a universally prescribed anodyne, cheap and easily obtainable, and regarded with little more suspicion than brandy."[12]

What two British historians call the "problem framework" first developed in England with the mid–nineteenth century public health movement; the moralistic arguments against opium developed later, with the formation of the Society for the Suppression of the Opium Trade and the anti-opium movement it spurred. Shadowing the growing disapproval of opium was the heightened class conflict of the Industrial Revolution and concern, first expressed early in the century, that the drug had become "a cheap species of intoxication" for the lower classes.[13]

In this country the temperance movement, which had millions of adherents by the middle of the nineteenth century, gave Americans a vocabulary with which to assail the physical and moral depredations of drugs. The concept of opium addiction was an easy leap from the paradigm of the alcoholic in the grip of "the habit of intoxication" (though the medical model of alcohol addiction faded from temperance ideology by the 1890s, as pressures for the coercive redress of Prohibition mounted).[14] And the perception of alcohol as a cause of violence, poverty, and property crime in the nineteenth century was easily analogized to opiates, cocaine, and marijuana in the twentieth.[15] But, while opiates were presumed to cause moral degeneration, their consumption was not regarded as shameful, and they were called "God's Own Medicine" by physicians who had little other recourse for easing patients' pain.[16]

The moral and racial messages of drugspeak grew louder in the early twentieth century, presaging more recent fears of the dangerous classes. One of the most direct exploitations of racial fears for the purpose of advancing policy positions came from Hamilton Wright, the Opium Commissioner and first moral entrepreneur of American drug policy. As noted in Chapter 11, this report issued as part of a presidential message to Congress in 1910 ascribed "abnormal crimes" by blacks to "the cocaine vice."[17] Statements like these, combined with others that attributed drug-induced evils to Mexicans smoking marijuana and Chinese smoking opium, helped convince a public already conditioned to regard blacks as inferior and threatened by labor competition from immigrant groups to accept coercive approaches to some kinds of drugs.

The association of drug-taking and criminality took root as officials groped for justifications of increasingly restrictive state and federal drug policies. As Wright pressed for passage of federal legislation to suppress nonmedical sales of cocaine, he inveighed against the cocaine addict as "utterly worthless as a citizen . . . likely soon to join the criminal class."[18] (Wright also demonized the drug user more generally, popularizing the term "dope fiend" and scolding the entire nation by asserting that "Uncle Sam is the worst drug fiend in the world."[19]) Press accounts of violence induced by marijuana fanned the flames of hysteria about that drug that flickered in the late 1920s and burned brightly throughout the 1930s; a 1937 story about a family killed by an ax-wielding son who had previously smoked marijuana was repeated in several national articles about what was now called the "killer weed."[20] The 1936 movie "Reefer Madness" (originally titled "Tell Your Children") carried out the theme.

As Edward Brecher pointed out more than twenty years ago, "Scare publicity has been the second cornerstone of national policy, along with law enforcement, since 1914 [when the Harrison Act was passed]."[21] Negative publicity about marijuana starting in the late 1920s illustrates the uses of rhetoric as a policymaking device. The Federal Bureau of Narcotics, with the zealot Harry J. Anslinger at its helm, mounted a deliberate campaign to build public concern about the "killer-drug," which was not yet in widespread use, to generate support for the Marijuana Tax Act (and for his agency).[22] As a result of planting scare stories in magazines and newspapers, the bureau reported in 1934, "An intelligent and sympathetic public interest, helpful to the administration of the narcotic laws, has been aroused and maintained."[23] By the end of the decade this moral entrepreneurship had seeded a public consciousness of marijuana as epidemic, a moral menace to which youth were particularly vulnerable. It also contributed in the public mind—especially in southern California—to the "Mexican problem," as the Great Depression drove unemployed whites into competition with migrant labor.[24]

The absolutist view of conquering the drug menace—which probably spawned the war metaphor—had its origins in official arrogance and public faith. Although early state drug-control measures were partial, and the Harrison Act of 1914 was a revenue measure intended more to regulate opiate distribution than to repress it, the politicians and the press presented a gullible public with the vision of a problem to be solved with dispatch. Reporting on American efforts to convene another international conference after the Shanghai Commission meeting of early 1909, the *New York Times* announced that the United States was leading "the great powers of the Old World" into a crusade "to drive the opium smoker and opium eater out of existence." Furthermore,

as soon as the crusade against the poppy has been won—and the day of victory may be said to be dawning—the United States will take just as resolute steps to abolish in every civilized land the growing traffic in cocaine, hashheesh [sic], heroin, absinthe, chloral, and other drugs that fasten themselves upon mankind.[25]

Unity in struggle was essential. "To stamp out the use of these drugs among the people will require the best efforts of the National as well as the State Governments," urged the *Times*. "Every physician must be a volunteer in the service, every school teacher, minister, and parent, who realizes the awful importance of the subject, must help." The ingredients of the rhetorical recipe for prohibition—a legacy of the temperance movement and a sign of Progressive Era zeal—had been assembled.

## PROBLEM THEMES OF THE DRUG PROHIBITION SEMANTIC

Drugspeak molds the problematic view of illicit drugs. Creating and maintaining that view require the perception that the negative effects of drugs are both pervasive and profound.

### Drugs Are Everywhere

Giving voice to that perception is the theme of *drugs as ubiquitous and undifferentiated threat*. Its simplest and most common form of expression is description of the geographic sweep of drugs. Senator Arlen Specter (Republican-Penn.), testifying at a congressional hearing in support of the death penalty for kingpins, invoked the menace with what have become common images:

> . . . drugs are rampant on the streets of New York and Miami and Los
> Angeles and Philadelphia and every major city, and they are rampant
> in Lancaster and York and smaller towns, and in farm countries [sic].[26]

The local version of this hyperbole was evident in the campaign for the anti-drug sales tax in Jackson county; the first line on a major piece of campaign literature read, " 'Crack' cocaine is being sold like fast food, on every street in our city."

The national media thrive on this approach; they find it nearly impossible to resist the shock value of drugs infesting not only the crowded, decadent megacities but also the "heartland" and "the remotest corners of America." Beyond the commercial lure of these presentations is also the chance to show that a good reporter will hunt down a story of plague or invasion (both medical and military metaphors are popular) in heretofore healthy and pastoral Columbus or Yakima.[27] These stories can then be aggregated to constitute a new emphasis—how drugs "are eating away at the national fabric of life," as Peter Jennings put it on an ABC special in 1988—that purports to probe not just the scope of the drug problem but its sources. The overview feature aspires to a higher educative function—"to help explain just how wide and deep drugs go," Jennings told his viewers, confusing analysis with description.[28]

Another way of expressing the ubiquity theme is to portray all U.S. institutions as crippled by the presence of drugs. In announcing his 1989 war on drugs, President Bush alluded to their effect on the criminal justice system—"our courts, our prisons, our legal system [all] are stretched to the breaking point"—and the "terribly dangerous" threat they constitute to "our neighborhoods and our families."[29] Taking advantage of the vulnerability of youth, and adults' sense of responsibility to protect them, Bush stressed that for "many kids" drug use begins "before their teens" and suggested that schools, colleges, and workplaces are saturated. Campaign literature for the Jackson County anti-drug sales tax similarly warned that "nine out of ten of our high school seniors know a drug dealer." (Flyers with this language were personalized for different areas of the county but only to the extent that they included the names of the areas. The residents of white, middle-class, suburban Raytown must have been alarmed to read these "facts" about their local schools.)

In the late 1980s both television and the newsweeklies featured depictions of on-the-job and in-school drug use as commonplace activities.[30] Popular magazines carried the alarums of the parents' movement; Peggy Mann asserted in her 1985 book that more than 7 million reprints of her "Marijuana Alert" articles for the *Reader's Digest* were sold.[31] A 1980 *New York Times Magazine* article described parents' concern with high-school students for whom "smoking and comparing joints are a very big part of their daily routine."[32]

The ubiquity theme recognizes no distinctions among drug types, dosages consumed, or frequency of use. It aggregates all kinds of drug experience into a near-universal threat and attributes the threat to the individual agency of dangerous classes. (Alcohol is sometimes included to make the numbers bigger, but excluded if the rhetorical aim is to amplify the sense of deviance.) In 1989 the *Kansas City Times* series called "America Hooked"—even the title carries out the theme,· adapting a word formerly used for opiate addiction to embrace all kinds of use of many different drugs—featured a two-part story about drug use in local schools. Following the anecdotal lead was its principal proposition: that "if you're a kid in school these days chances are your friends or even your parents have used cocaine, crack, marijuana or alcohol, or have experimented with hallucinogenic drugs."[33]

This "classification chaos" presents some strategic problems, however.[34] It is sometimes difficult to convey symbolic warnings that effectively encompass all drugs and all types of use. The slogan for the Jackson County anti-drug sales tax campaign was "Fight Back."

Campaign managers were taken to task for featuring the slogan on most campaign literature with the "I" represented by a vertical hypodermic needle, a symbol of heroin, a feared drug but one that had all but disappeared.

Another danger of lumping all hazards together in a generalized threat is that the audience may turn skeptical of the general argument if it discovers that some of its particulars are false, that most of the illicit drug use creeping into remote and hitherto peaceful corners of American life is casual marijuana use, for instance, and, to a lesser extent, that many users of harder drugs do not become dependent on them. Both prohibition policymakers and anti-drug advocates often address this obstacle with a corollary theme that all use is abuse. Even the National Institute on Drug Abuse, a federal agency supposedly dedicated to the scientific study of drugs and their effects, has defined "drug abuse" as the "nonmedical use of drugs," putting societal evaluations of drug use ahead of epidemiological ones.[35]

Eliminating any distinction between use and abuse is justified with both legalistic and moral arguments, sometimes stated separately but often combined. Former drug czar William Bennett used both. "The simple fact is that drug use is wrong," he said over and over. "And the moral argument, in the end, is the most compelling."[36] But his statement that "the drug crisis is a crisis of authority" and his disregard, in the first "National Drug Control Strategy," of alcohol—a substance that, while legal, provides hedonistic pleasure (and the potential for chronic pain) similar to that of illicit drugs—trumpets a view that the illegality of use, without personal or social damage, constitutes it as abuse.[37]

Not surprisingly, since its focus is on youthful drug use, the parents' movement also equates use and abuse. The National Federation of Parents (NFP) and its local affiliates actively resist distinctions among drug types and various kinds of user behaviors; in 1982 the NFP adopted a resolution rejecting association with any drug prevention or treatment program that advocated or condoned "responsible use."[38] At least when it comes to alcohol, they, too, conflate moral and legal justifications. "Tolerate NO DRUGS," reads the flyer "Guidelines for Parents in Raising Drug-Free Children." "No use of illegal drugs, no illegal use of legal drugs."

The "gateway theory," the idea that a "soft" drug (particularly marijuana) leads users into harder ones, is another motif to support the ubiquity theme that gets around the awkward possibility of much relatively harmless drug use. It is promoted by doctors as well as by politicians and parent groups, often with assertions like that of Robert

DuPont, first director of the National Institute on Drug Abuse, that "up to 50 percent of regular users of marijuana also use heroin."[39] (What does "up to" mean? Who is a "regular user"?) One of the functions of this subtheme is to legitimize as wide a universe of targets for prohibition policy as possible.[40]

The ubiquity theme is salable even where visible manifestations of danger and disease from drugs are missing. In Alaska there is no evidence of anything but fragmentary hard drug use anywhere in the state, yet the recriminalization activists relied on dubious associations of marijuana use with low-weight babies, suicide, and asthma attacks to convey a sense of widespread threat from drugs. In addition to the moral argument—"we need to send our kids a message that drug use is wrong"—their campaign was aimed at parents and suggested that dangerous drugs (marijuana included) were an ever-present menace to their children. Higher-than-average teenage pot use and a grab bag of anecdotes were enough to make the point that, as Marie Majewske put it in an *Anchorage Daily News* column published just before the recriminalization vote, "marijuana is having a tragic impact on our society."[41] President Bush, too, invoked a single threat to suggest a universal one; assigning responsibility for the crack epidemic, he blamed "Everyone who uses drugs. Everyone who sells drugs. And everyone who looks the other way."[42]

## Drugs Subvert National Security

In the universe of political rhetoric it is easy to equate breadth with depth, sliding from the dangers of ubiquity to those of subversion. Anti-drug activists are quick to give voice to the theme of *drugs as national security threat*. Not many have gone as far as Jacques Cousteau, who wrote several years ago that unrestrained drug use would lead to the "destruction of the Western world"—bringing to mind the 1928 radio address of Richmond P. Hobson, a prohibition propagandist of the period, who announced that "upon the [drug] issue hangs the perpetuation of civilization, the destiny of the world and the future of the human race."[43] But in 1989 Defense Secretary Richard Cheney labeled drugs "a direct threat to the sovereignty and security of our country," a politically prudent message to justify greater military involvement in the Andes.[44] And Senator Strom Thurmond (Republican-S.C.) supports the death penalty for drug kingpins, he says, because "large-scale drug trafficking is a pernicious threat to our national security."[45]

Both Reagan and Bush rode this horse, too. In 1986 Reagan issued a top-secret "National Security Decision Directive," a document intended to legitimize military involvement in both drug interdiction at the Mexican border and assistance to other countries' drug-control efforts. Announcement of the directive by then–Vice President Bush, serving as head of the South Florida Task Force of the National Narcotics Border Interdiction System, enhanced the association between drugs and international conflict. "For the first time, the U.S. government specifically states that the international drug trade is a national security concern because of its ability to destabilize democratic allies through the corruption of police and judicial institutions," Bush said.[46] By 1989 President Bush, not content with attributing international instability and all inner-city miseries to drugs, was calling it our "gravest domestic threat . . . the toughest domestic challenge we've faced in decades."[47]

It is not only conservatives who construct the drug problem in very large contexts. In 1990 liberal Representative Pat Schroeder (Democrat-Col.) joined much of the corporate community and publications like *Time* and the *Wall Street Journal* in expressing the fear that "we're all going to be in great trouble in the 21st century, trying to compete" if we don't rid ourselves of the drug problem.[48] Antidrug activists interviewed for my local case studies, whether as the result of hearing or reading the concerns of elites or arriving at them on their own, sounded just like business executives concerned with economic productivity. They used arguments like Schroeder's to justify drug-testing in schools and offices and law enforcement sweeps of neighborhoods where street dealers congregate. My Seattle interviewees believed that nothing less than the economic future of their city was at stake in endorsing a policy that would rout the youthful drug dealers from commercial areas.

Critics of the recent drug war have tended to find a direct link between its ferocious embrace of the subversion theme and the drumbeat of anti-Communism in the 1950s. They suggest that with the collapse of the Evil Empire, illicit drugs and their purveyors are feeding our national addiction to the construction of enemies.[49] Evidence that drugspeak serves both our culture wars and the organizational needs of the military certainly abounds. William Bennett's emphasis on moral absolutes falls into the former category, and it is hard not to be cynical about President Bush's 1990 appeal for increased funding for the military to meet "new threats beyond the traditional East-West Antagonism of the last 45 years. . . . Narcogangsters concern us all, already a threat to our national health and spirit. . . . They must be dealt with by our military in the air, on the land, and in the seas."[50]

But it would be a mistake to isolate the subversion theme as a substitute for the communist scare. The drug threat has competitors, after all, for pride of place in that role—Japanese competition and Islamic terrorism, to name two. It seems likely that drugspeak has simply enabled drug abuse to join the parade of national bugaboos that has tramped through the American twentieth century—the nativism of "the tribal twenties," communism after World War II, perhaps a reprise of xenophobia in the 1990s.[51]

### Drug Dealers Are Devils

Establishing the terrain of the drug problem is not enough, by itself, to win support for a particular policy direction. That requires locating blame. Currently, although many analyses of drug policy point to the impossibility of effective interdiction when demand remains so high, drug prohibition discourse focuses on sale, not use, of illicit drugs.[52] The theme of *drug dealers as devils* is powerful rhetoric for politicians at all levels and an irresistible dramatic—or rather, melodramatic—possibility for media presentations of all kinds. Nancy Reagan's nationally televised statement, part of the Reagans' 1986 announcement of a federal drug war, is typical. "Drug criminals are ingenious," she said. "They work every day to plot a new and better way to steal our children's lives—just as they have done by developing this new drug, crack. For every door we close, they open a new door to death."[53]

Dealers are likened to vampires, animals, terrorists; some such association is invoked to turn even routine activities of distribution and exchange into Mephistophelean bargains for what Bennett called "hollow, degrading, and deceptive pleasure."[54] Hispanic importers are either Colombian drug lords or Mexican "mules," migrant agricultural workers who bring cocaine to their seasonal jobs. Street dealers are usually gang members—an especially useful link if they can be seen as even remotely influenced by the ruthless Crips and Bloods, whose drive-by shootings in Los Angeles supplied the most vivid justification for the kingpin death penalty.

The demons are sometimes disguised. Madison Avenue, through a saturation campaign of strategically located ads sponsored by the Partnership for a Drug-Free America, inverts the threat, making it even more potent for middle-class parents whose children would be unlikely to encounter gang members on suburban blocks. From the back of the phone book an ad captions grinning faces of small children with the question, "Can You Find The Drug Pusher In This Picture?" Below, in smaller type, the Partnership reminds readers that "the frightening thing is, a kid is more likely to be pushed into drugs by some innocent-looking schoolmate."[55]

It should not be assumed that demonizing dealers is limited to the right wing or to corporate America. Jesse Jackson yields to no one in the vigor of his denunciations of those who import and sell drugs. Stopping just short of recommending the death penalty for dealers ("I'm not sure that the state has the moral authority to kill"), he nonetheless called them "purveyors of death" and "terrorists" in a 1989 interview.[56] Charles Rangel, the long-time Democratic congressman from Harlem who in 1990 enjoyed a perfect rating from the American Civil Liberties Union (ACLU) on his congressional performance, takes a similar stance; his biography in *The Almanac of American Politics 1994* says, "Rangel's main emphasis for at least ten years has been denunciation of the drug trade."[57] He has opposed needle exchange programs, sponsored legislation to make the sale of drug paraphernalia a crime, and, as part of a legislative trade-off for more liberal habeas corpus provisions in the omnibus crime bill, voted in 1991 for the death penalty for drug kingpins.[58] (Rangel also sounds the national security threat theme, claiming that drugs have claimed more American casualties than Communism.[59])

Rhetorical excess in labeling dealers and users is not, of course, unique to recent times. Hobson's 1928 radio broadcast called heroin addicts "the living dead," an appellation that survived into the 1960s.[60] But the targets and aims of drugspeak have shifted even since the Nixon-era drug war. In the late 1960s and early 1970s, it was directed more at scaring people out of drug use, describing a ghastly range of effects including moral perversion and physical deterioration. While there was certainly some demonizing of dealers, it did not dominate the discourse; both users and dealers were seen as agents of the drug problem. In the late 1980s and 1990s, however, the anti-drug consensus is stronger, more punitive, and deeply rooted in a general apprehension of the dangerous classes. In the prohibition semantic, users today are principally foils for villain traffickers, the "merchants of death" who have replaced "the walking dead" of earlier demonology.[61] Many Americans would have agreed with Senator Strom Thurmond when he said, in a 1989 Senate hearing on death penalty bills, "We want to get the kingpins, we want to get everybody who deals in drugs, that is what we want."[62]

This demonization of drug dealers is linked to the previous theme, drugs as a threat to national security. Instead of being seen as miscreants whose illegal business victimizes individuals, they are subversives in a campaign against the health and safety of all Americans.[63] Once this social evil is acknowledged as the consequence of their activity, the most severe criminal penalties are justified; arguing for the kingpin death penalty Representative Henry Hyde (Republican-Ill.) likened it to espionage (which he called "death to the country potentially") as "death on the installment plan to an awful lot of people."[64] Retiring Senator Howard Metzenbaum (Democrat-Ohio), a liberal with a history of opposition to the death penalty, nonetheless supported the 1988 kingpin legislation, saying, "As the crisis has grown to extraordinary proportions, so has the need for extraordinary action."[65]

Courts also justify harsh punishments for individual drug dealers with their assessment of the harms done to all of society by drug-trafficking. In a 1978 case that upheld the long sentences for two low-level cocaine sellers, the Second Circuit Court of Appeals concluded, "Measured thus by the harm it inflicts upon the addict, and through him, upon society as a whole, drug dealing in its present epidemic proportions is a grave offense of high rank."[66] The epidemic image also often justifies narrowing criminal procedure rights established by the Constitution, spurring Silas Wasserstrom to entitle a widely read law review article "The Incredible Shrinking Fourth Amendment."[67] The courts engage in "balancing" that stacks the deck, presenting on one side a staggering collective victimization against, on the other, the right of the individual defendant before the court (who is probably guilty) to privacy or due process. Presented that way, the collective interest easily prevails on most occasions.

The prevailing myth that federal jurisdiction extends to conditions that affect us all provides opportunities for sweeping and dramatic castigations at the national level of those who personify those problems. Although state penalties can be harsher than federal ones—the Michigan law is an extreme example—demonization is often less intense closer to home. The contradictions of such intense posturing are simply too apparent when the drug dealers in view may be your relatives or neighbors. Even for anxious parents the image of the dealer as terrorist does not fit the high-school student selling marijuana joints on weekend evenings in the parking lot of the convenience store. As Stuart Scheingold says of street crime control, "At the local level, the concerns are more instrumental, the complex realities of criminality are more insistent, and the myth of crime and punishment is more divisive."[68]

Nonetheless, the drug dealer as the personification of evil was a powerful theme in mobilizing support in Jackson County and Seattle for the anti-drug sales tax and the drug loitering law. In Kansas City the epidemic image—applied to both crack use and violence that erupted in neighborhoods where the drug was sold—provided the background. In 1989 a local organization, supported by many city churches, reported to the county legislature that its members had identified more than 300 crack houses in the area and that more than sixty deaths within the past year could be attributed to drug violence.[69] The local press described such violence as "an everyday occurrence" and the presence of drugs in low-income neighborhoods as a "scourge."[70] The "America Hooked" series described those responsible as "juvenile drug lords [with] easily obtained semiautomatic guns, Uzis, Chinese-made AK-47s, Mac-10s, 9mm pistols and even grenades."[71]

But politicians, the media, and beseiged neighbors also reported a reality more complex than the sensationalism that evidence of Jamaican cocaine gangs provided. Even as they cast some involved in drug-dealing as sybaritic superconsumers, bedecked with gold chains and driving fancy cars, another message was being sent. Local youths in the retail trade were often depicted as mired in poverty and hopelessness, "blank-eyed" as they resorted to violence to defend themselves, more victims than victimizers. In the wake of the early 1989 firebombing that killed several people, church leaders in Kansas City called the drugs and attendant violence that caused it "the evil that has infiltrated our neighborhoods"; but they also noted the "economic blight that breeds drug abuse," and urged attention to drug abuse as a public health problem.[72]

Awareness of the role of social forces in the inner-city drug problem has continued to undercut the demonization of dealers at the local level. By 1992 some Jackson County judges, rebelling at the five-year sentence mandated by state law for first-time drug-dealing, portrayed these offenders with images far removed from the myth of dealers as alien and violent invaders. Defending the practice of suspending such sentences and putting the offenders on probation, Presiding Circuit Judge Jack Gant remarked, "I just don't think the solution is sentencing every teenager to the penitentiary."[73]

Judges, many of whom are appointed or who run for their seats unopposed, may be unique in their ability to resist openly the characterization of dealers as demons. Adherents to the semantic can easily discredit most other opponents. If dealers are devils, set on physical, mental, and moral destruction, the reasoning goes, those who defend their rights and interests must share in their iniquity. When a drug dealer was lured to Lafayette Park so that Bush could demonstrate on national television that crack was sold across the street from the White House, the president grew testy with the uproar over his deception. Rather than debating the appropriateness of the representation, he turned on his critics by saying, "I don't understand. I mean, has somebody got some advocates here for this drug guy?" Often, in fact, those who are skeptical of tactics in the drug war—not just those who openly oppose prohibition—are suspected of being users themselves, motivated solely by self-interest. Majewske cast opponents of the marijuana recriminalization initiative in Alaska as part of the "drug culture."

## SOLUTION THEMES OF THE DRUG PROHIBITION SEMANTIC

Drugspeak contributes more to prohibition than characterizing the scope, nature, and attribution of "the drug problem." It also helps shape policy solutions and mobilizes commitment to them.[74]

The problem themes just discussed construct a simple and abstract foundation for the edifice of law enforcement solutions: Illegal drug use is vast in scope, touching millions and in many ways—all of them problematic. Its nature is evil, defying both divine and state authority, threatening both the social world and individual welfare. Blame can be laid at the feet of callous purveyors and, secondarily, of weak-willed or pathological consumers.

Nonetheless, drugspeak in the form of solution themes is needed to shore up the structure and support its gallery of prohibitionist measures. Beyond the near-universal plea, "Do something!" *what* is to be done is largely the choice of political elites, as is the characterization of the problem. Phrases to fit the themes were made, not brought by the stork: "Just Say No" was hammered into the consciousness of the country by Nancy Reagan and her speechwriters; "zero tolerance" was a catchy name for a Customs Service program; and the "drug-free" school and workplace were ideals turned into policy by presidents and their loyalists from Carter to Clinton.

The drug prohibition semantic therefore includes not only the problem themes but also the specific linguistic innovations of drug warriors promoting solutions on the symbolic terrain. They frame the prohibitionist structure and invoke the dangerous classes as its tenants. More generally, the solution themes hold drug policy in a vise that allows for very little revision.

*Eradicate Drug Use*

The central solution theme in this part of the semantic points toward *eradication as the aim of prohibition*. The eradication theme drives the popular notion of "drug-free" environments and people—schools, job sites, the "drug-free youth" envisioned by parents' groups, the aspiration to a "drug-free America" embraced by the Partnership. Drug use is not to be managed or reduced, but eliminated, the only morally tenable aim if the problem has been cast as an unmitigated and ubiquitous evil.

The war metaphor—as in the "war on drugs" and attendant references to its "troops" and "casualties"—has been an effective carrier of the theme. In this respect it is not different from other public initiatives cast as wars—against poverty, government waste, and so on.[75] The mythology of war posits victory and defeat as the only two outcomes; drug prohibition policy in the United States has embraced that dichotomous posture. A 1990 *New York Times* editorial pointed out that "real wars" are usually fought against well-defined enemies by disciplined warriors backed by national authority and generous funding—the opposite of drug wars, where the nature of the social problem is murky and efforts to conquer it are "tenuously coordinated [and] ill-funded."[76] But perhaps this criticism misses the point; the absolutist image has greatest utility where it can serve to release the unbearable tension of ambiguity.

It can also resolve basic political dilemmas without open conflict. In a liberal democracy, principles of equity and freedom limit the central utilitarianism of the criminal law.[77] But a continuing source of tension is the extent to which we must accept the basically symbolic nature of law enforcement—that few crimes can ever be detected, only a fraction can ever be prosecuted, and problems of proof and process will limit the number of prosecutions that will ever result in conviction and incarceration. Embracing the declared aim of prohibition to bring about a drug-free world tilts the debate toward the utilitarians and invites a buildup of resources and power for police, prosecutors, courts, and corrections. "The call to arms" for law enforcement is that "it is time for the merchants of misery, destruction and death to be put out of business," said a federal court in 1977.[78]

Together with the problem themes of ubiquity and national security threat, the eradication theme justifies both substantive and procedural measures that would otherwise be unthinkable. Bennett's (apparently serious) endorsement in a "Larry King Live" interview of beheading drug dealers merely takes the death penalty proposal backed by Congress one step further. Lower on the penalty scale, the effort to rid commercial areas and school zones of drug offenders in Seattle is geographically extensive enough to reduce significantly the freedom of movement of many probationers and parolees. Tough sanctions that inflict more punishment than is necessary to deter the average potential drug offender—not only life sentences for drug possession, like Michigan's 650-plus law, but also penalties like asset forfeiture that operate outside normal processes of guilt determination and sentencing—have become permissible even though they violate the principle of classical criminology that such punishments are "superfluous and for that reason tyrannical."[79] The narrowing of due-process protections for drug defendants and suspects (and those who live or work near them and are swept with them into the vast field of law enforcement attention) includes preventive detention, warrantless searches, and widespread urine testing in schools and workplaces.[80] Concerned that these developments reduce the criminal law to its purely instrumental function, one legal scholar despairingly asserts the existence of "the drug exception to the criminal law."[81]

"Zero tolerance" reflects the eradication theme, as in Reagan Attorney General Edwin Meese's plea to employers to test most workers for drugs, pursuant to a policy of "zero tolerance of drugs in any place, any time."[82] Originally adopted in early 1988 by the U.S. Customs Service and the Department of Justice as a standard for the arrest and prosecution of anyone caught bringing even small amounts of illegal drugs into the country, "zero tolerance" (William Buckley called it the "bellicose metaphor") has long outlived its original application. Four years after the Customs program was abandoned because it was ineffective and encouraged unconstitutional searches (and perhaps because it was resisted by many prosecutors), the phrase remains a useful justification for surveillance of youth and for drug-screening programs.[83] Bush even adapted it to signal his determination to eradicate the dumping of hazardous wastes.[84]

The "zero tolerance" slogan is popular for several reasons. It underscores the culpability of casual users and repudiates distinctions between their evil and that of addicts and pushers; in his 1989 speech Bush said, "American cocaine users need to understand that our nation has zero tolerance for casual drug use."[85] Like the call for mandatory minimum sentences, it announces that the discretionary authority generally accorded to those who implement policy will be sacrificed to the guarantee of retribution for all law violators. Echoing the larger message of authoritarianism that cultural conservatism transmits, it hints that the present problem is attributable to past tolerance. And it reassures those who believe that what former Attorney General Richard Thornburgh repeatedly called "individual American values" include some reassuring absolutes.

### Appeal to Individual Will

The eradication theme involves a characterization of the task of the state and others with authority in addressing drug use. But prohibition is intended to send its principal message to those who are tempted, and, like the criminal law in general, it speaks to them as individuals poised on the edge of a choice. Harking back to classical criminology (and reflecting the popularity of conservative scholars like James Q. Wilson), which assumed that humans were rational beings whose behavior could be controlled with threats of punishment, the increasingly harsh modern prohibitionist policies are justified as *appeals to individual will*, an approach to altering behavior rather than a single theme of persuasion.[86]

Revitalized theories that explain crime by looking not to social structure but to individual proclivities are predictable in the context of a more general conservatism in American culture and domestic politics. Starting in the 1970s, what one group of criminologists has called "the rhetoric of stability" became a force for resisting 1960s demands for social change and rationalizing the persistence of inequality and the stagnation of the American economy.[87] As unbridled accumulation became increasingly acceptable as the major goal in life, sexual hedonism was rejected, the "traditional values" of family and religion acquired renewed respect, and society's ills were laid at the door of the poor and minorities—and the liberals who championed them. The need for control of certain types of individuals—the "dangerous classes" that I have referred to earlier in this book—drove increasingly punitive criminal justice policies and, by extension, public and private perspectives on how to deal with illicit drugs.

Criminological theories of this period relied on a variety of types of individualistic explanations for crime. For example, the idea of genetic and other predispositions to criminality—cast aside with the waning popularity of positivism in mid-century—became once more at least momentarily respectable when James Q. Wilson and Richard J. Herrnstein's *Crime and Human Nature* posited "constitutional factors" for determining who commits crime and how much of it.[88] In the political arena, however, volitional theories—those that locate the sources of criminality in an individual's rational, nonpathological calculation—are more popular. Casting crime as the product of deliberate choice both stigmatizes wrongdoers and invokes state social control as a protective substitute for the socializing institutions of family and school—which, in this view, are disintegrating. Invoking the aberrant choices of criminals as justification for harsh punishment also apparently serves other important purposes, averting more costly proposals for structural change that might reduce the social disorder we call crime.

The application of the prohibitionist appeal to individual will contains, however, a contradiction. The message is presumably beamed to both those who use and sell drugs and those who may be tempted to use and sell drugs. A certain proportion of the former category, however, use drugs compulsively and are therefore by definition incapable of the rational choice that classical criminological theory presumes them to have.

Use of the deterrence hypothesis is erratic, perhaps more likely in national and state policymaking. The political debate over the 650-plus law in Michigan and the congressional consensus supporting the death penalty for drug kingpins both relied in part on the policy's presumed utility in deterring major drug dealers. Then–Deputy Attorney General William P. Barr maintained in 1991 congressional hearings, for instance, that the existing life sentence for trafficking in large amounts of drugs covered such a large range of behavior that a kingpin already subject to that penalty would have nothing to lose from committing further crimes (short of murder) unless the death penalty were imposed.[89]

But local policymakers adopt prohibitionist policies less because their aim is to affect drug offenders' choices than because they want to control the immediate physical and social environment. Containment was the issue in both Kansas City and Seattle—removing the immediate threat of the drug trade, and only very incidentally persuading those selling drugs that their conduct was reprehensible or destructive or likely to land them in jail. (It should also be noted that there was very little concern expressed in my interviews—either moral or medical—about users and no hypothesis that punishing their suppliers would deter drug-taking.) Proponents of the Seattle loitering law were concerned primarily with removing what City Councilwoman Jane Noland called "the open-air drug markets" from commercial streets, and Jackson County voters with shutting down "crack houses" in residential neighborhoods; first and foremost they wanted to remove the sources of disorder from their communities. Once again Scheingold's observation that the national political arena is more hospitable to punitive and symbolic messages applies; "the politics of criminal process at the national level is more about authority than policy, while the converse is true at the local level."[90]

Appeals to individual will have taken forms other than endorsing harsh punishments for their value as deterrence. Although most senior officials in the national Republican administrations of the 1980s probably believed that the threat of sanctions was the only way to reach dealers, local policymakers and some with national influence have sought to reduce drug use with moral suasion. Nancy Reagan's "drug abuse awareness campaign" with its slogan, "Just Say No," underscored the faith that drug use was chosen behavior that could be unchosen if those who were susceptible could just be convinced that it was wrong or dangerous. Her softer message of dissuasion, which could be adapted for any grass-roots drug prevention project, probably has been at least as effective as the hard-line deterrence philosophy in convincing Americans that conquering illicit drug use is a matter of changing the choices of individuals.[91] Clinton has taken a similar tack, invoking individual and family responsibility as solutions to the nation's violence and drug problems.[92]

Certainly the influence of the "Just Say No" message was strong in the Alaska marijuana recriminalization campaign, spurring the involvement of parents and the apparent salience of an argument that prohibition was needed to counteract the pull of peer pressure on impressionable adolescents. And it legitimized resistance to more complex and ambiguous messages about the implications of drug use. It is no accident that Nancy Reagan and the NFP, with their refusal to condone " 'responsible use' of illicit drugs," made common cause.[93]

Attributing the nation's drug problem to the venality or weakness of individuals does not preclude other suspicions about its sources. While deeply committed religious or political conservatives may find moral arguments as to the sources of drug abuse persuasive, many other Americans give lip service to the moral argument because they see using drugs as a surrogate for societal failures of other kinds—family "breakdown" and street crime, for example. Almost without exception, policymakers and anti-drug activists interviewed for my local case studies saw these problems, in turn, as evidence of systemic difficulty. Viewing structural inequality or insecurity as the root of drug abuse did not, however, suggest to these people remedies aimed at digging up those roots. Individual criminality, whatever its sources, was the problem to be addressed for both users and dealers. Interviewees in both Seattle and Kansas City illustrate Lance Bennett's view that public opinion is not a stable reflection of a general state of consciousness and that people's views arise out of the interaction of their values and their surroundings at a particular moment.[94] Anti-drug activists in both cities were comfortable with the apparent dissonance of believing that inequality and social misery produced drug abuse and spurred the retail drug trade while advocating tough individual penalties and exhortation to address these effects.

### Unify To Fight Drugs

Another solution theme assumes an overarching view of *prohibition as social unity*. It simultaneously harnesses the icons of the cultural right and responds to a near-universal yearning for meaningful participation in ordering the world. Presidents Reagan and Bush used images of American solidarity as invocation to patriotism, though with differences that reflected their views of themselves and the world. For Reagan the war on drugs was a holy one, "our national crusade"; for Bush it was scrappier, "a guerilla war that involves all of us together," fought "from house to house, neighborhood by neighborhood, community by community."[95]

The theme often seems calculated to distract from a lack of substance. In a 1988 letter to Attorney General Edwin Meese, William Von Raab, head of the Customs Service, proposed thirty-eight large and small policy measures. Perhaps to blunt the criticisms that were certain to follow—his proposals were immediately criticized for being gimmicky and unproven as to drug-fighting utility—he noted that they could "help to create a moral climate in which all citizens will feel that they are an active part of the war on drugs."[96] To note cynicism in the use of the theme is not to suggest that solidarity has no practical benefits. A commitment to "the alliance of federal, state and local law enforcement . . . in our war against drugs and violence," stressed by Thornburgh and other federal officials, presumably has at least some crime-control effect.

The national media also called for solidarity, mobilizing TV anchors like Dan Rather and Peter Jennings as the big guns to fire the message. In the 1990 *48 Hours* episode, "Return to Crack Street," Rather reminded viewers that "the war against crack can be won, but not until and unless we have the national will to do it."[97] Nancy Reagan assumed her gentler posture on this one, too; in what she had earlier characterized as "a general call for people to come in and join in the fight against drugs," she pleaded "as a mother" with everyone in "the American family."[98]

At the national level the solidarity theme has the appeal of the distant beacon, abstract and idealized. Locally, it promises an irresistible and immediate opportunity for people to be involved in something bigger than themselves. Neither of the cases of citizen policymaking studied for this book—the initiatives to recriminalize marijuana possession in Alaska and to enact the anti-drug sales tax in Jackson County—truly sprang from the grass-roots, and the impetus for each of them can, in fact, be traced to political and organizational imperatives. Nonetheless, the popular response to those who brought the policies before the voters—the handful of activists, assisted by Republican state legislators, in Alaska; the prosecuting attorney and his friends, in Jackson County—depended, in part, on a feeling that, if unified, ordinary people could "do something." In Alaska, the Republican and Democratic caucuses for the presidential contest of 1988 drew only about 6,500 voters; yet a year later the recriminalization activists had no difficulty getting more than 40,000 petition signatures to put the issue on the 1990 ballot.[99] The sponsors of the sales tax campaign consulted with well-organized community groups—Ad Hoc Group Against Crime and the Kansas City Church/ Community Organization—whose efforts to roust out drug dealers and demand better service from law enforcement were spurred by yearnings for what Cliff Sargeon, Chairman of Ad Hoc, called "empowerment through coalition building."[100]

The invocation of solidarity in fighting drugs at the local level is linked to the current fashion for community policing. In what has become a major redefinition of the urban police function, cops in many cities are now exhorted to see their primary task as maintaining neighborhood order rather than fighting crime.[101] To this end, enlisting the active support of a unified and well-organized community is crucial. Cooperation between state and citizen takes on new value; identification of the decay and incivility that is the target of modern patrol depends on deputizing the eyes and ears of the community. ("It's citizens and law enforcement working together to solve problems that lead to crime," said Attorney General William Barr in early 1992.[102]) If the citizen-deputies are to be reliable, they must submerge differences of perspective—about the potential hazards of a neighborhood condition or, more divisively, who really are the "bad guys" and what should be done about them—into a common orientation that puts unified support of law enforcement first.

Coupling the specter of drugs as a ubiquitous threat and the solidarity theme can enable leaders to convert essentially repressive campaigns into social movements in the public mind. The promise of participation in more than a single initiative or program gave power to Marie Majewske's assertion on the Alaskans for Recriminalization of Marijuana pamphlet that "If we are involved in a WAR on DRUGS . . . then Alaska's marijuana law is the frontline [sic]." Alaskans certainly knew that a vote for pot recriminalization would not constitute a major advance for law and order in a state that had not yet discovered crack and whose principal substance abuse problem was alcohol, especially when the aim of the policy change was as openly symbolic—"we must send a message to youth that drug use is wrong"—as was acknowledged by the activists. But cracking the code of public opinion that supports recriminalization requires an analysis that takes in the meaning of fighting on the "frontline" as well as the significance of changing marijuana policy. The same applies to understanding citizen views of the Jackson County anti-drug sales tax. Kansas City Mayor Emanuel Cleaver (then a city councilman) understood that the act of joining others in protest was as important as what could be accomplished by that act when he commented on grass-roots activism against dealers after drug violence erupted in the inner city early in 1989: "The only thing that comes close to this in my lifetime was the civil rights movement," he said. "Our survival is at stake."[103]

The leaders who emphasize cooperation, unity, and local empowerment seek support for not only the aims but also the methods and results of the "movement." They foster an illusion that participation means control. Occasionally the strategy backfires. Those who heed the call for unity may exercise the power of organization and numbers to become independent of those who mobilized them. Although support for prohibition is strong among followers as well as leaders, the prohibitionist semantic may not be fully effective in regimenting directions within the consensus. The experience of the federal Operation Weed and Seed is instructive.

Begun on a pilot basis in Philadelphia, Trenton, and Kansas City in 1991 and expanded the following year to eight cities, Weed and Seed proposed intensive law enforcement measures to "weed" drug dealers from inner-city areas, followed immediately by social services and community development to "seed" the areas with new opportunity.[104] The watchwords were cooperation and coordination—of federal, state, and local programs, of law enforcement agencies and community groups.

But little money was authorized for the effort.[105] "It's a slogan more than a program," grumbled Alfred Blumstein, then-president of the American Society of Criminology, according to the *New York Times*.[106] Other criminologists and urban experts agreed (including

Jackson County Prosecuting Attorney Albert Riederer), suggesting that the program's expansion was triggered by the beginning of the 1992 presidential campaign.

Out in the targeted cities many recipients were also doubtful, some because funding was so low, some for other reasons. In Kansas City, where Ad Hoc's efforts to rout out drug dealers with bullhorns and housing inspections had caught the attention of the Bush administration, the program was welcome, a reinforcement of local initiative; but in several other cities Weed and Seed polarized community politics. Jack R. Greene, professor of criminal justice at Temple University, notes that most of the federal money was spent on the law enforcement aspect of the program, and that in several cities community groups were pitted against each other for what were trivial amounts of money.[107] In Seattle, ten community organizations joined to ask Mayor Norm Rice to reject the $1.1 million federal grant, saying that police-community relations, already poor, would be worsened by the "weed" portion of the program.[108] In that city the solidarity theme could not paper over a diversity of views on how to fight crime and drugs; the precondition in the affected community of a consensus supporting police simply did not exist.[109]

As with the demonization of drug dealers, the solution themes, with the exception of solidarity, resonate most successfully at the national level. Issue spin doctors give them life, the national media fatten them up, and they are put up for adoption all over the country. In two years of research for this book I never found local innovation in drugspeak, even though drug use as a social condition and core attitudes toward it varied tremendously from site to site. Where the national theme was enthusiastically embraced on the local level, as with the call for solidarity, it was because local perspectives and conditions had reshaped the original idea, as when community and church groups in Kansas City won supporters because they represented a group spirit that seemed concretely protective.

## THE SYMBOLIC VALUE OF DRUGSPEAK

Media repetition, as well as public readiness for colorful contributions to a discourse of anxiety, helps explain the resonance of the prohibition semantic and the vocabulary that decorates it. But drugspeak is first and foremost an arrow in the quiver of political leaders. No conspiracy theory is required to explain the singular commonalities found in pronouncements by presidents, governors, mayors, and legislators at all levels of government. In a time of national suffering and self-doubt when prevailing ideology supports explanations rooted in individual weakness and depravity, politicians who adopt a discourse that captures widespread anxieties and shapes explanations that focus on dangerous classes—people who have always carried some stigma and can now be burdened with more—can be sure of an audience. While not guaranteeing electoral success, the commitment to drugspeak identifies leaders as allies of followers. Even those members of the audience who disagree as a matter of policy with the implications of the prohibition semantic may feel that its use demonstrates dedication to the protection of constituents.

And sometimes it does. Just because drugspeak has political utility does not mean that some of those who capitalize on it are not true believers, particularly when they can relate its message to broader themes of the conservative 1980s. Dick Thornburgh, President Bush's first attorney general, for example, used drugspeak as a springboard for boosting American individualism, touting the American "free market economy" and urging American moral hegemony on the rest of the world. In his fervent sermons he had frequent recourse to virtually all of the themes of the prohibition semantic. He used the ubiquity of the drug problem to justify excluding illicit drug users from the benefits of the Americans with Disabilities Act.[110] Seizing the assets of demonized drug dealers, who were "shrewd and vicious," was "poetic justice." His all-encompassing solution to the drug problem was that "the war on drugs must ultimately be won on the battlefield of values." In a 1991 address he explained that he meant "individual values"—among them "the values of self-respect, of self-reliance, of self-discipline, and, above all, the integrity of the individual mind and spirit functioning as God designed them to function." Supporting the traditional model of volitional criminology, Thornburgh managed also to embrace a sense of the immutability of these "unique American values," a suggestion that their origins could only be found in natural law.

This emphasis has broad implications. The values that should keep us drug-free, in his view, join with others to shore up "the most successful economy ever in the history of the world" and demonstrate that "there are no bounds within which [hate] crimes can be tolerated." Most important, our values convey moral authority "to other societies whose people welcome our example, such as Eastern Europe, and even the Soviet Union, but also to hostile regimes who mistakenly challenge our belief in, and the strength of, our values."[111]

We have heard the echo of the crusade before, whether in the message that the kingpin death penalty is supposed to send to Medellin cartels or in the call to parents to join the pot recriminalization campaign in Alaska. The analogy to a medieval religious campaign is apt. Rhetorical crosses lead the crusaders and beckon to the faithful. Drugspeak provides meaning to devotees and defense against infidels.

*Part IV*

# OTHER VOICES,
# OTHER THEMES

# Chapter 15

# On the European Front

American interest in the more relaxed perspectives on illicit drugs of many European countries—and the sometimes experimental projects that those attitudes have spawned—has grown in the past decade. Anyone who is attentive to drug policy news is aware of the coffee shops in Dutch cities that sell marijuana and hashish, the Swiss experiment (now discontinued) with an open-air drug market in Zurich, widespread needle exchange to prevent HIV transmission in Britain as well as expansion of heroin maintenance in the Liverpool area and elsewhere, and programs in many countries that aim to prevent the spread of AIDS among intravenous drug users by promoting (and often paying for) the exchange of dirty needles for clean ones. Americans who support moving toward some form of drug legalization often hold up these efforts as examples of what we could do here, or at least as evidence that flexibility and innovation are possible within a general policy framework of drug prohibition.

European policy initiatives do, indeed, carry lessons for Americans. One of them is that permissiveness need not encourage the consumption of dangerous drugs. In fact, there appears to be no clear relationship between drug use and drug policy. Cannabis use among the young in the Netherlands—always a fraction of U.S. use—has remained stable since its de facto legalization.[1] (Marijuana possession has remained technically prohibited, but the pragmatic Dutch have simply decided not to enforce the law—providing what one researcher calls "de facto undisturbed access to cannabis"—and have constructed a regulatory scheme that discourages prosecution.[2]) Heroin use declined during the 1980s in Holland, as it did in most western nations.[3] Strict West Germany and relaxed Holland, with very different drug policies, show similar rates of hard drug use. On the other hand, Spain and the Netherlands, the two countries with lenient policies on drug possession, have very different prevalence rates— Spain's is high and Holland's low.[4]

The European innovations may, however, be more instructive for what they tell us about crucial differences in the cultural and political contexts of drug policy in western Europe and the United States than they are for helping us figure out how to address our own problem. The success of alternatives to our punitive approaches—the different treatment of hard and soft drug markets, for instance, in the Netherlands—may depend on the prosperity of a country, or on its level of social and economic benefits. And the policy politics of less harshly prohibitionist approaches may be determined by events and trends that are very specific to the country that has chosen them. While some European countries are identifying dangerous classes of their own—immigrants, who are the target of right-wing political movements in France, Italy, and Germany—drug policy has not become an instrument for repressing them. Finally, in Europe as in the United States, drug policy trends are more complex than they seem at first glance—and likely to become even more so, as the Maastricht Treaty brings local and international policy changes in many areas.[5]

It is easy to reject the gentler approaches found in many European countries—the Netherlands, Britain, Spain, Italy, and, most recently, Germany—by noting that drug policies in Europe are irrelevant because drug problems in those countries are trivial compared to ours. While it is true as a narrow factual observation that a smaller slice of European populations are in thrall to an illicit drug, the comparison doesn't take us very far. Drug deaths, drug seizures, and reports of drug abuse have risen since the mid-1980s in most European countries; some observers characterize the trend as a global epidemic of drug production, trafficking, and consumption.[6] In Germany, for instance, the number of drug deaths increased from 348 in 1986 to 1,480 in 1990, and between 1986 and 1988 the number of new hard drug users known to police more than doubled.[7] Nonetheless, liberalization with respect to the management of drug use continues as a general trend, although there is variation over time and between countries. (Anti-trafficking measures seem to be hardening and deepening everywhere around the world, including in Europe.[8]) In addition, there is no rational basis for the proposition that policy that is effective for a small group will inevitably be unworkable for large ones. In fact, the rationale for demonstration research is precisely the opposite, that mounting a small experiment can show how an idea can be actualized for larger replication.

## DRUG POLICY OVER THERE

It should not be assumed that the wider range of perspectives on drug control across western European precludes tough national stances. Prohibition is the rule in Europe, the same drugs as in the United States are generally included in its sweep, and many countries are embracing greater punitiveness at some levels. In 1990 Italy, a country where the possession of otherwise proscribed drugs "for personal use" had been decriminalized for fifteen years, adopted and enforced a law punishing as a dealer anyone in possession of more than an "average daily dose"—although the voters repudiated the policy by referendum three years later.[9] In 1992 the German Parliament passed a tough new drug bill that aimed at the suppression of organized crime groups that traffic in drugs. Following the directive of Section 5 of the 1988 United Nations Convention against Illicit Traffic in Narcotic Drugs and Psychotropic Substances, which Germany has ratified, it includes a crackdown on money-laundering and authorizes, for the first time in that country, the use of American-style undercover techniques against suspected drug dealers.[10] In Spain, where drug possession has been legal since 1983 (though that may be limited soon), a drug lord can now get a prison sentence of more than twenty-three years.[11] Even in the tolerant Netherlands the central government rejected a 1983 proposal by the Amsterdam City Council for a heroin maintenance program for long-time addicts, and in some Dutch cities drug offenders are being treated somewhat more severely than in the recent past.[12]

The observer of these developments can trace the hand of American law enforcement and the rhetoric of American drug wars in many of them. A member of the Italian Parliament who opposed its 1990 enactment of long drug sentences and "indirect sanctions"—civil penalties like those instituted in the American Anti-Drug Abuse Act of 1988—chided his colleagues for their "sad dependence on the power and the repressive myths of the America of Reagan and Bush."[13] And the new German law is a follow-up of Chancellor Helmut Kohl's 1990 war on drugs ("Rauschgiftbekämpfungsplan"), announced in apparent imitation of the 1989 National Drug Control Strategy of William Bennett, Bush's first drug czar; it even emphasizes the prosecution of yuppies, a favorite theme of Bennett.[14] (The core emphasis of the German bill on targeting drug enterprises recalls the legislative embrace in American legislation of leadership of a "continuing criminal enterprise" as the conceptual basis for finding major drug traffickers suitable candidates for the death penalty.)

U.S. influence on European drug policy is hardly surprising; we have been cajoling or bullying other countries into drug control since the Shanghai Opium Commission of 1909.[15] The moral entrepreneurs of the global prohibitionist regime were unquestionably Americans, starting with Hamilton Wright, who pushed for a worldwide ban on the manufacture of opiates in the early years of the twentieth century.

The most aggressive marketer of the American approach in recent decades has been the Drug Enforcement Administration (DEA). It has representatives in many U.S. embassies, offers free tours of American courts and prisons to European judges, and exercises pressure on other countries through the United Nations to join international efforts at global prohibition of more and more substances. While some countries like Britain have long included the use of informers in their inventory of policing approaches, Ethan Nadelmann, a drug policy specialist at the Woodrow Wilson School of Public and International Affairs at Princeton, points out that DEA training of European law enforcement in the recent past has contributed to the recent adoption of American crime-control icons like the special narcotics squad.[16] Even now, with our many failures in this area, we dominate many aspects of first-world drug policy, purveying our prohibitionist objective and promoting our preferred law enforcement techniques, like buy-and-bust and asset forfeiture. As the French newspaper *Libération* put it in a 1990 special report on drugs, the American DEA is the "spearhead [*fer de lance*] of the world struggle."[17]

But in many European countries, the get-tough American influence has not penetrated beyond a veneer of national rhetoric. Local and regional practice tends to be far more tolerant. Great Britain is one example, combining "political policy"—which is national and harsh—with "service policy"—which is primarily local and regards drug abuse as a "social problem with a medical dimension."[18] Germany is another. Hamburg and Frankfurt, both very hard hit since 1987 by increasing drug deaths and rising cocaine imports, are among a number of cities where local officials and community groups are developing strategies that implicitly or explicitly reject the unbending prohibitionist stance—which is, however, accompanied by a strong declared commitment to prevention and treatment—announced in Bonn. In doing so they are also turning away from what German criminologist Sebastian Scheerer calls "the somber omnipresence of United States criminal policy."[19]

Local authorities in Germany, as well as others in Switzerland and

Spain and France (to say nothing of the better-known pioneers of the Netherlands and Great Britain), are striking out on their own. They have opened "drop-in centers" where committed heroin users can get clean needles and a free lunch, expanded methadone treatment beyond the last-resort use to which it was previously limited in Germany and France, and decriminalized the possession of marijuana for personal use. Although Zurich abandoned its "needle park," it has not backed away from a reform strategy; its efforts are, in fact, more daring and more comprehensive. The city provides a full range of services to hard drug users, including a sizable experiment in heroin maintenance.

More important for the future of such efforts, cities around Europe are making common cause, as in the Frankfurt Resolution. First adopted in November 1990, it committed Amsterdam, Frankfurt, Hamburg, and Zurich to "a permanent exchange of experience and cooperation concerning drug policy" and stated firmly, "Drug use . . . cannot be prevented by drug policy. At its best drug policy can regulate and limit the results of drug use only."[20] This agreement has no official authority but has struck a responsive chord throughout Europe; an additional ten cities in seven countries have signed on since 1990 and fifty-four more have a kind of observer status that enables them to share in information exchange.[21] The resolution recommends needle exchange programs, methadone treatment, experimentation with medically supervised "shooting galleries" and drug maintenance programs, and the legalization of marijuana. Stopping just short of calling for official decriminalization of hard drug use, it concludes that "in connection with drug related problems it is necessary to lay stress on harm reduction and repressive forms of intervention must be reduced to the absolutely necessary minimum."[22] A new organization, European Cities for Drug Policy, has grown up around the resolution; it has now enlisted the help of the American Drug Policy Foundation in creating an international network to support worldwide drug policy reform.

The success of the Frankfurt Resolution in attracting new signatories is powerful evidence that what was, as recently as 1988, a cluster of Dutch and English experiments has become a loose and variegated international movement for drug policy reform. Though diffuse, the movement shares several key principles—that AIDS is a greater threat than drug abuse, that abstinence (at least in the short term) is a pie in the sky for many users, and that diverse reform strategies can coexist as long as they don't perpetuate rigid and coercive measures against users. Adherents attend international annual meetings on "harm reduction," strategize about getting their views into mainstream political discourse, and burrow from within to alter their countries' hard-line attitudes and practice. Even as national leaders talk tough and sign on to increased repression—the 1988 U.N. Convention made it compulsory to prosecute drug consumption—the reform movement's generally low-key mobilization is nurturing a different reality.

It is instructive to look again at Germany, where until recently drug policies have been proudly punitive. Along with the hard-line measures of the new legislation is a provision for allowing prosecutors to drop drug cases without judicial permission. In effect, this modification of Germany's "legality principle," which requires that all arrests lead to the filing of a charge, already exists on the local level. "The law in action is much more elastic than the formal law," says Lorenz Böllinger, Professor of Penal Law and Criminology at the University of Bremen. "Attornies in some judicial districts these days have more leeway to drop prosecutions. We're moving in the direction of Holland."[23] Allowing greater discretion in professional decisions regarding drugs is also driving the increased use of methadone maintenance for heroin addicts. Most ordinary practitioners may now prescribe methadone if they have a patient with a "psychological disorder," normalizing what had been the exceptional and highly visible practice of dispensing it only in clinics (as is the case in the United States).

Not so long ago Holland was the odd country out, both pariah and exemplar for being soft on drugs. Now, however, many drug policymakers and practitioners in Europe view the United States as isolated—in its focus on users as well as dealers and its failure to distinguish between the varying harms of hard and soft drugs. Echoing sentiments of colleagues in France, Germany, and Switzerland, Eddy Englesmann, former head of the Alcohol, Drugs and Tobacco Branch of the Dutch Ministry of Welfare, Health and Cultural Affairs, says, "We don't want to adopt American approaches. What we do is different—what they need may be different."[24]

Perhaps what European countries do is different partly because they have historically been followers, rather than leaders, of prohibitionist crusades. Another explanation may lie in the different social and political contexts of European drug problems. It is an apparent paradox that the concept of the dangerous classes, despite its origins in Europe, has not fueled drug policy there as it has in the United States. Even though in Germany, according to police, foreigners account for much low-level dealing as well as major trafficking, local

policy tends to treat "ant dealing"—where user-dealers sell principally to each other—with the same tolerance as possession.[25] And
the philosophies of harm reduction and normalization—doing what
can be done through social and health services to fend off the medical
and social harms of drug abuse, and doing it in ways that don't isolate
and stigmatize users—could not flourish if moral condemnation of
the larger groups to which users belong found its expression in drug
policy debates.

## BRINGING IT HOME?

Thus far, few rigorous evaluations of European policies have been
conducted, but there are promising indications that some may reduce
drug abuse prevalence. Heroin users in and around Liverpool appear
to be living more settled, productive, safer lives as a result of heroin
maintenance, and the incidence of acquisitive crime in the area has
decreased.[26] Dutch researchers found that the incidence of cocaine
use was relatively low in Amsterdam in the late 1980s, despite a
sharp rise in supply and a drop in price; drug deaths in Holland are
low relative to those of other countries.[27]

Just as significant, these policy developments have gained wide
popular acceptance. In Hamburg, where the mayor has defied the
national punitive orientation by proposing the legalization of heroin
possession, there has been little opposition to the policy of not arresting young users as long as they are not hassling pedestrians, selling
drugs, or spreading AIDS through sharing needles. In Amsterdam the
decriminalization of marijuana and hashish has become so "nor-
malized" (a favorite word of drug reformers) that one of the cannabis-
dispensing coffee shops advertises with a discreet billboard in the
train station. (Nothing more than a modest symbol of the marijuana
leaf on the coffee shop window is allowed to announce the availability
of the drug in individual businesses.) Methadone buses, cruising the
city to provide addicts with maintenance doses, have become a part
of public health routine. In Britain needle exchange has become a
secure institution, believed by researchers there to be reaching most
long-time heroin addicts and slowing the spread of HIV infection.[28]

There are, of course, occasional complaints of some of the side
effects of this permissiveness. Liverpool drug program managers, for
example, told me in 1990 that reports of people being stuck by dis-
carded needles rose after the opening of heroin clinics dispensing the
drug and clean needles. They believed, however, that most of those

needles did not come from their projects, but were purchased illegally on the street. Many drug reformers have concluded that progress will be slow and uneven. In Germany a drug policy group associated with the University of Bremen, sensing a potential backlash, has abandoned the hope that a small, medically supervised "shooting gallery" set up to teach committed heroin users how to inject safely and reduce the chance that they will get and give AIDS would become a model for the state and nation.

If more forgiving drug policies are gaining acceptance in Europe, why are they unlikely to take hold here? While it is difficult to generalize about patterns of culture and politics across many different countries, it appears that the forces that sustain American policy are different enough from the overt and shadow agendas of drug prohibition in a number of other western countries to preclude easy acceptance of even the European reform policies that seem to have measurable impact on the prevalence of drug abuse.

The U.S. tendency to locate the sources of the drug problem in individual pathology or immorality is not nearly as prevalent in many European countries. This is not to suggest that anxiety about drugs is minimal. Public perceptions of danger from drugs are often equivalent to American fears. In France 80 percent of citizens surveyed in a 1989 study said they were afraid of drugs, while in the United States in the same year, 79.5 percent of high-school seniors surveyed reported that they worried about drugs.[29] (Even though only 9 percent of French survey respondents said they had ever encountered illicit drug use, it's no wonder that parents there are fearful. The poster campaign equivalent to that of Partnership for a Drug-Free America features a picture of a gaunt eleven-year-old holding a hypodermic needle that is more lurid than the Partnership's image of the drugged brain as a fried egg.) But drug abuse is far more likely to be regarded as a tragedy than a sin, a product of deprivation rather than of weakness. Protection from it, then, becomes more easily a matter of nurturance rather than punishment. As a public health problem, drug abuse is to be managed with the services (medical, psychological, and social) available for other disabilities.[30]

In some countries this tendency surely reflects long-standing cultural proclivities. Europeans I have interviewed are simply mystified by the moral fundamentalism of William Bennett or the retributive spirit of the former police chief of Los Angeles. Their more easygoing religious traditions contrast sharply with the legacy of American puritan origins, the interdenominational "linking of the American purpose with the Kingdom of God," and the temperance movement's message equating inebriation with corruption of the soul.[31] Differences of perspective on individual responsibility for the drug problem may also be related to larger views of the role of government. Government is more legitimately activist in western Europe; with us it is usually expected to be reactive. Innovation is prized in European democracies; we usually want our system to broker rather than initiate.

Social policy in many of the advanced welfare states of Europe, following the social democratic model, may help to explain why the drug issue does not serve to channel anxieties and hostilities about dangerous classes. In at least those countries, if not more broadly, the separation in social policy between pauper and laborer has long vanished, with generous and universal benefits—for health care and education as well as social insurance and conditions of employment—reinforcing the process. While European class distinctions remain, they do not usually manifest themselves in such visible, material ways as in the United States. Racial hostilities have thus far expressed themselves in open and popular conflict—the riots of the Parisian suburb of Saint-Denis, the violence against immigrants in eastern Germany—rather than through the institutionalized channels of social policy.

A major factor in the re-evaluation of at least some drug policies in several European countries is the advent of AIDS. In Great Britain, for instance, an advisory group of the Department of Health and Social Security concluded in a well-publicized 1988 report, "The spread of HIV is a greater danger to individual and public health than drug misuse. Accordingly, services which aim to minimize HIV risk behavior by all available means should take precedence in development plans."[32] The result has been added resources for intravenous drug users, whether they were prepared to give up their habit or not.

> The central theme of responses to drug problems became harm minimisation for the individual and society, and this has influenced every aspect of policy from prevention aimed at reducing the likelihood of someone trying drugs through to assisting the injecting drug user not to share equipment and to inject in a way least likely to cause major physical damage.[33]

Although the AIDS problem in the United States is much greater than it is in Britain, it is hard to imagine a policy shift here like the one described above. The explanation probably lies in the history of British drug policy, where doctors' views have always had great weight, and in the fifty-year stability of national health and social service systems that, even if supports are frequently inadequate, assume responsibility for the welfare of all citizens. The Rolleston Committee concluded in 1924 that addiction was a disease and should be treated as such, with physicians given discretion to prescribe narcotics to patients addicted to opiates, whether for gradual withdrawal or long-term maintenance.[34] Although the rise of heroin abuse and overprescription of narcotics led to stricter controls in the 1960s, the principle did not change, and the legacy of public health objectives for drug control remains. Medical prescription of otherwise prohibited drugs also signals a public health perspective in other countries; in both Italy and Germany the area of doctors' discretion over treatment of drug abusers (at the local level, once again) has expanded in recent years.

The political systems of many European countries may also make it easier than it is in the United States to abandon the orientation that demonizes dealers and aims at abstinence for users. Parliamentary systems work against the association of one political representative with particular policies, so it is harder to tar a political figure with an unpopular program. Cultural politics are often less intense (though the recent frenzy over immigration in several countries may provide the exception that proves the rule), and public participation in the politics of punishment is far less common than in the United States. Dutch citizens did not mount massive resistance when the city of Amsterdam began sending methadone buses to deliver doses in their neighborhoods, partly because they have more faith in the judgments of their leaders than Americans do, but also because they are less likely to assume that community pressure can be directed at a single office holder who can effect short-term policy change.

The foregoing is not meant to suggest that the policy politics of drug prohibition in these more relaxed European countries is entirely benevolent. When Chancellor Kohl turned to the American model for his proposed war on drugs in 1990—the glossy booklet he issued describing it even resembled the American 1989 Drug Control Strategy—some German cynics saw a geopolitical dimension behind it—that the get-tough rhetoric and substance of his plan were part of an effort to strengthen alliances with the Bush administration. Kohl also gained political capital from his leadership role in establishing a central European police authority (Europol), created in late 1992 and powerfully justified by the specter of increasing international drug-trafficking.[35]

More interesting still is the Italian flip-flop in recent years. There was considerable surprise in Italy when then–Prime Minister Bettino Craxi embraced a set of harsh new proposals that became the 1990 drug law; he had explicitly rejected such an approach only months earlier. During the late 1980s reported heroin deaths in Italy had tripled, giving rise to heated public and parliamentary debate about whether Italy's tolerant drug possession policy should be altered.[36] At the time Craxi announced his new theme publicly he had recently visited the United States, where U.S. Attorney Rudolph Giuliani (now the mayor of New York City) and other influential Republicans had touted the virtues of American drug wars. The Italian debate that took place in the spring of 1990 was widely seen as a way of keeping Craxi's Socialist Party on the front pages for a few months; as a small party whose power depended on the leverage it may have in building a majority coalition, such opportunities were valuable. (Italians sometimes speculate, now that Craxi has been accused of links to the mafia, that his strongly prohibitionist position also reflected an interest in keeping underworld drug profits high.)

Within a year after the passage of the law, it was apparent that it was a programmatic and political disaster. The amount of drugs that constituted an "average daily dose" for purposes of enforcement had been determined to be not more than 100 milligrams of heroin or half a gram of hashish, obviously an absurd administrative decision, given the fact that for many addicts 100 milligrams of heroin—Italy's most problematic drug—is far below the amount needed daily to prevent withdrawal symptoms.[37] Those who went to prison under the law were more likely to be marijuana and hashish users than heroin addicts, who were often diverted to treatment.[38] The additional drug arrests that would not have occurred under the more lenient law were primarily of young people, not large-scale dealers, and prison populations shot up. Yet drug deaths continued to rise; there was simply no indication that more punitive policy had had the deterrent effect that was advertised for the 1990 law.[39] In an atmosphere of high public tension over the issue, the legislation became highly politicized.

If we accept the truism that policy politics reflects the political system that generates it, and we know that party politics is a feature of parliamentary systems, a simple syllogism might conclude that drug policy politics would be driven by party considerations—both interparty competition and internal power struggles—and that has indeed been the case in Italy. In late 1992, on the first day of his accession to the presidency of the lower house of Parliament (and therefore the leadership of the Socialist Party), Giuliano Amato announced that heroin addicts would be released from prison and that the way would be paved for a public referendum on suspending the 1990 law.[40] Less than six months later, on the same day that they interred the country's fifty-year practice of proportional representation in Senate elections, Italian voters threw out the punitive law and returned to their philosophy of tolerance for drug users.[41] In doing so they were repudiating a long-standing campaign of the once-powerful Socialist Party; it is surely not coincidental that the Socialists were among those most tarred by the 1992–93 revelations of widespread corruption in Italian business and government.

European reforms tend in two directions. They may treat hard and soft drug markets separately, as the Dutch system does. And all European countries distinguish trafficking from possession, at least in practice. In the United States, a few states have made both distinctions in a very small way by decriminalizing possession of small amounts of marijuana; but, as the Alaska experience suggests, that innovation may be fragile. In both the separation of markets and the separation of users and dealers it is hard to escape the conclusion that lenience is being proffered, either to a user or to someone involved with marijuana only. The current American tendency to load the baggage of dangerous classes into the vehicle of drug policy—to say nothing of the political and material advantages politicians and bureaucrats realize from supporting prohibition—makes it seem quite unlikely that more than a handful of policy entrepreneurs will be willing to appear to endorse such a perspective. The "zero tolerance" attitude cannot coexist with the philosophy of "normalization" that animates public and political support for the Amsterdam coffee shops.

There is another characterization of much European drug reform that might pave the way for at least marginal changes in American perspectives. The philosophy behind the statement issued by the British Department of Health and Social Security's Advisory Council on the relative priorities of AIDS prevention and drug control is that it is the first duty of public health providers to minimize the greatest risks to public and individual health. The strategy of "harm reduction" (sometimes also called "harm minimization," a term that some believe better encompasses protections of others besides the user, or of society in general) adapts to the reality that many users are unwilling to give up their drug use and considers abstinence from drugs only one goal in dealing with them.[42] Reformers argue that illegal drug use—and the stigma attached to it—should not prevent users from minimizing its risks, and they seek measures that will do that, within the framework of prohibition. British policymakers, even as former

Prime Minister Margaret Thatcher was praising police for conducting rowdy drug raids in pubs, followed this counsel in establishing hundreds of needle exchange schemes around the country. (It is impossible to specify their number because in many cases they are simply integrated in a doctor's medical practice or run informally by a pharmacist.) At Dr. John Marks's clinics in Britain's Merseyside region, heroin users can be maintained on the drug, or switch to smoking heroin (which is safer than shooting up), or exchange dirty needles for clean ones, or learn how to avoid arteries when injecting.

While such drastic departures from current practice are unlikely in the United States, it may be that the idea of harm reduction, seen as a supplement rather than an alternative to law enforcement, can usher in modest reform. The advent of AIDS has forced the acceptance of needle exchange programs in many urban areas. In New York City former Mayor David Dinkins, after having cancelled the city's first legal experiment on taking office in 1990, reversed himself; as of early 1993 two of the newly legal programs were exchanging 13,000 needles for intravenous drug users each week.[43] But it may be that this development, opposed by many as likely to encourage drug use (which is not indicated by other countries' experience), is legitimized only by the threat of AIDS. A better test would be to see whether these projects could be expanded to teach safe methods of injecting or how to recognize and deal with a friend who has taken an overdose.

Furthermore, one of the most important goals of harm reduction programs is to establish and maintain contact with a population group that is generally out of reach of health and social services; medical personnel in a nation without a national system of guaranteed health care do not have the same incentive to find and serve drug abusers. Our demonization of drug dealers and our unwillingness to credit structural forces with driving much involvement with illicit drugs may also severely constrain harm reduction efforts. While prosecution of all kinds of public trafficking is vigorous all over Europe, young people who sell only enough drugs to pay for their own habit are also beneficiaries of much harm reduction policy, even in France, which is otherwise almost as hard-line as the United States. It is hard to envision much sympathy for young user-dealers here, although a tremendous number of the retail dealers in large cities probably fall into that category.

## WHITHER EUROPE?

It is interesting to speculate on whether the tough national rhetoric or the local reformism that characterize a number of European countries will win out in the contest on that continent over directions for drug policy. Europe could go in the direction of harsher and harsher penalties for major traffickers as economic unification makes border control even more difficult.[44] And some instances of drug panic tinged by racial antagonisms are being reported in Europe. In 1989 the British media, police, and politicians, responding to warnings sounded in London by a visiting American DEA official, were, in the words of two leading British drug researchers, "seized by the conviction that Britain was about to suffer a major epidemic of crack use—and that black areas of the inner city would be the epicenter."[45] (Though supply increased modestly, the epidemic never materialized.)

On the other hand, the American pattern of declining use of illicit drugs seems to prevail in most western European countries (though not in the newly liberated east), which may take some of the pressure off political leaders to talk tough on drugs.[46] Furthermore, at least one of the American dangerous classes—youth—is more likely in at least some European nations to be viewed as a class deserving the highest protection, in drug policy as elsewhere; a principal strategy of proponents of the 1993 Italian referendum was to portray the harsh 1990 drug possession law as a killer of youth.[47]

As results from international drug wars are sparse and prisons fill up, pragmatism will perhaps win out over militarism. Statisticians at the French agency OCRTIS (l'Office Central de Répression du Trafic Illicite des Stupéfiants) estimated in 1990 that French police forces were intercepting only 10 to 15 percent of drugs in commercial channels.[48] Though this figure is close to the return that knowledgeable observers report for American efforts, European leaders may have less commitment than we do to sticking with a war that can't be won. On the other hand, political and geopolitical considerations that we cannot anticipate may still drive national policy. It would be a mistake to assume that illegal drugs will always present a less tempting symbolic vehicle in Europe than they have for a century in American political life.

# Chapter 16

# Toward a Kinder,
# Gentler Social Policy?

This book argues that a bundle of concerns—racial and generational fears, political and material needs—play at least as important a role in sustaining the American way of drug prohibition as the medical and social hazards of drug abuse. This conclusion does not preclude the possibility of either marginal or major policy change in the foreseeable future. It does suggest, however, that drug policy reform may come about less as the result of demonstrations that prohibitionist policies do not reduce drug damage than because the concerns of the shadow agenda recede or are refocused on other social conditions.

## WHERE IS DRUG POLICY HEADING?

As a first step toward exploring the future of drug prohibition policy, we can consider the drug policy cases discussed in the preceding chapters. What have been their outcomes? How have they been received by their attentive publics and by those who generate and implement policy? (For purposes of this discussion, an outcome includes both the way the policy has been applied as well as its substantive effects on the condition identified as a problem when the policy was adopted.)

*Federal Kingpin Death Penalty.* For this piece of national policy-making, the outcome at the time this book went to press was not policy but consensus to enact policy. For several years the larger bill to which the provision was attached foundered on conflict over other issues, but in the spring of 1994 it seems possible that crime legislation passed by both the Senate and the House may survive the conference committee. For the moment the kingpin proposal has lost its political utility; attention has shifted to tougher federal penalties for violent crimes and new regional prisons.

It seems unlikely that, if enacted, the penalty will be imposed often or used for the heads of the "continuing criminal enterprise" who have been promised as the targets of the law. There have been few prosecutions under the 1988 statute permitting capital punishment for drug kingpin murderers, and only four cases where death sentences have actually resulted. (The defendants in those cases—a marijuana dealer; young, inner-city gang members; low-level drug distributors—were hardly the moral equivalent of the Colombian drug lords invoked in congressional debate on the objects of the proposed legislation.) If federal prosecutors in the get-tough Republican years 1988–1992 were so wary of kingpin death penalty prosecutions and juries were so reluctant to sentence to death, it seems likely that there will be even fewer impositions of capital punishment for a lesser crime, where no death results, in the foreseeable future.[1] In fact, some who pushed the proposal in Congress conceded as much to reassure their more liberal colleagues that the legislation would not result in the slaughter of inner-city punks who have few income-producing alternatives to selling drugs.

*Michigan 650-plus Law.* By and large, Michigan legislators who voted for the 650-plus law in 1978 seem to have done so because they thought it would ensnare large heroin dealers. But evidence is overwhelming that the law has served up a different kind of defendant; the bulk of people sentenced to life imprisonment under the law are merely couriers in the trade.

*Alaska Pot Recriminalization.* The recriminalization of marijuana possession in Alaska has produced virtually no defendants. The police and the public apparently share a lack of interest in arresting people in their homes and prosecuting them for possessing small amounts of the drug, and the criminal law has always covered other, more problematic situations.

*Jackson County Anti-drug Sales Tax.* Adding $14 million of tax money annually to the war on drugs in Jackson County initially failed to drive up arrests and prosecutions for drug offenses (though that is no longer true). Furthermore, two years after the tax went into effect, neither officials nor anti-drug activists believed that illicit drugs were less available on the streets of Kansas City. In early 1994 the new prosecuting attorney was emphasizing the prevention and education projects funded by the tax, though they were not what the voters initially supported.

*Seattle Drug Loitering Law.* The Seattle loitering law has not resulted in a large number of arrests that could be relied upon to produce solid convictions. While some local merchants say the threat of police action against street dealers has reduced the visibility of drug markets in commercial neighborhoods of Seattle, a city council member who has studied the implementation of the law concluded that the deployment of 100 police officers appointed since the law went into effect has had more impact on the downtown open-air markets than the loitering law.[2] The perception that the law contributes to police harassment of young minority males persists. Policy attention has shifted to panhandling by homeless people.

## Outcomes of the Shadow Agenda

Despite the virtually nonexistent return on taxpayers' investment in drug control in these cases, in none of them is there likely to be a clear repudiation of existing policy or the adoption of a new policy direction. People have simply learned to live with outcomes that, in terms of relief from the condition they publicly identified as problematic, are unsatisfactory.

But if we also acknowledge the shadow agenda, we have to say that in general drug prohibition has not failed. It has, in fact, triumphed—if mostly with the bitter taste extracted from wormwood—as a vehicle for the dangerous classes mentality, a sparkplug of political opportunism, a banner to rally resources.

Looking with this perspective at the cases discussed in this book, indeed, we must conclude that prohibition does have some successes:

- Supporting and voting for the kingpin death penalty presumably helped burnish images of some members of Congress as leaders in assuring security to constituents. Positioned at the extreme end of the range of federal penalties, the proposal lent legitimacy to other, more conventional designations of capital crimes.
- Recriminalizing pot in Alaska made some parents feel empowered to affect their children's futures and to exert their own authority, and it is one strand in the tightening cultural bond between the "last frontier" and the "lower forty-eight." (It probably hasn't hurt the state Republican party either.)

- Riederer's anti-drug sales tax program has ensured organizational and fiscal health for criminal justice at both the county and the city level; in addition, treatment for drug abusers has expanded and funds are available for neighborhood organizers to mobilize communities against drugs and broker local services. Perhaps more important from the point of view of local officials, the availability of a pot of gold has enabled a relatively unconstrained public discussion of directions for future drug- and crime-control efforts—more jail space and an expanded program deferring prosecution for first-time offenders.
- In the cases of both the Michigan 650-plus law and the Seattle drug loitering law, the most important effect—however unintended or inadvertent it may have been—has been to foster and reinforce for many the association between young inner-city black males and the "drug problem." Both in the Midwest and the Northwest, drug prohibition has helped focus, target, and label the often diffuse threat of the "dangerous classes."

What about the future? How might policy directions shift in situations like those examined in this book? Both the federal kingpin death penalty and the 650-plus life sentence are, among other things, harvests of the politician as moral entrepreneur. Among the cultural conflicts that define our society in the late twentieth century, none is more intense than the divisions over standards for individual behavior—what they should be, who is responsible for setting them, how they should be communicated and enforced. As long as issues like "the breakdown of the family" and "moral decline" are flashpoints for significant segments of the electorate, policymakers and implementers will find ways to channel popular anxiety about them into currently salient policy topics. With public concern about violent crime and terrorism apparently on the rise in early 1994, drug prohibition is receding (temporarily?) as a source of symbolic leadership for politicians.

But active or visible efforts to rescind most prohibition policies are unlikely; drug policy reformers envisioning a future of even gradual decriminalization for cocaine and opiates are probably doomed to disappointment. If moderations of prohibitionist impulses appear, it will be through the side window rather than the front door. Concern about mushrooming prison costs and populations, or discomfort with implementing the harsher elements of drug policy, or behind-the-scenes fiddling with the fine points of prohibition—easing access to marijuana for medical uses, for instance, or altering federal guidelines on mandatory minimum sentences for low-level drug dealers—may occur. Riederer now supports spending more money on prevention and education; "that's eventually where the struggle will be won or lost," he told a reporter in 1992.[3] And Seattle-area judges are in the forefront of a movement to soften the state's harsh mandatory sentences for drug offenders.[4] (In this reaction, they are joined by a growing number of federal judges, some of whom are unwilling to sentence in drug cases because they object to the stringency and inflexibility of mandatory sentences.)

At least modest changes may also come about because the social policy ideology of major political leaders dictates a less prohibitionistic approach. Although Clinton publicly expressed support for a "war on drugs," appointed a former police chief as federal "drug czar," and has merely supplemented the Bush law enforcement emphasis with spending proposals for drug treatment and prevention, his administration's generally more forgiving perspective on misfortune and deviance has engendered some optimism among critics of the prohibitionist policies of the 1980s. They noted that Clinton's choice for attorney general, Janet Reno, had supported a Florida program diverting minor drug offenders from prison and was likely to push for abandoning or modifying mandatory sentences for federal drug offenders.[5] That she was notably invisible in the legislative tussle over the 1993 crime bill was discouraging to reformers, but at least the more sympathetic climate in Washington might provide some political access to lonely dissidents, whose ranks have spread beyond ivory-tower academics to include judges, medical groups, and even some law enforcement officials and mayors.

It is also tempting to project that a reduction in racial tensions in American life generally—in the workplace, on urban streets—would render drug policy less susceptible as a vehicle for their expression. It is comforting to consider the possibility that as Seattle works out its future as a world-class city with racial and ethnic diversity as one of its strengths, it will address the impoverishment and alienation of young black males through the development of income-producing alternatives to drug-dealing, rather than through police harassment.

Unfortunately, this last speculative scenario is probably unrealistic —as is suggested by the Kansas City experience, where African-American leaders strongly supported the stepped-up law enforcement that was promised by the anti-drug sales tax. More trusting relations between white and black coupled with a more powerful black presence in American cities might well shore up support for harshly prohibitionist policies because the toll of drug abuse and trafficking in inner-city communities with high concentrations of African-Americans provides symbolic capital for politicians seeking a protective image with those they represent. In addition, blacks may believe, rightly or wrongly, that advocating more permissive approaches to drugs will make them more vulnerable to the stereotype of blacks as being of a lower moral order. (It is not insignificant in this regard that one of the most powerful black politicians in Congress, Representative Charles Rangel (Democrat-N.Y.) from central Harlem, is a committed drug warrior.) The most likely effect of improved race relations on drug policy would probably be not to relax prohibition but to render its application less discriminatory and to expand drug treatment opportunities.

Many drug reformers expect that the prohibitionist consensus is most likely to collapse around the issue of marijuana use. It is certainly true that if there were a clear relationship between the harmfulness of a mind-altering substance and the degree to which its consumption is proscribed and punished, the hemp products (marijuana and hashish) would be outside the realm of prohibition. As Mark Kleiman puts it, "Aside from the almost self-evident proposition that smoking anything is probably bad for the lungs, the quarter century since large numbers of Americans began to use marijuana has produced remarkably little laboratory or epidemiological evidence of serious health damage done by the drug."[6]

But marijuana is a cultural anathema for some groups with political power—parents of minors, religious groups, some doctors. And substantial federal investment has been made in marijuana interdiction, in the southern hemisphere as well as at home. It is hard to imagine either overt or shadow agenda items powerful enough to counter those forces, even for Kleiman's proposal to treat pot-smoking, like alcohol and nicotine, as a "grudgingly tolerated vice" with distribution carefully controlled.[7]

## WHERE SHOULD DRUG POLICY MOVE?

Although this book is about the tenacity of prohibition, not about alternatives to that policy, I feel an obligation to tell readers what I think should be done with this bone I have been worrying for 230 pages. In the prologue I admitted to an initial inability to arrive at coherent policy preferences in the drug area. Some of my early ambivalence lingers despite—or perhaps because of—careful examination of both the overt and shadow agendas of current, failed prohibitionist policies. On the one hand, I am appalled at the excesses of American drug prohibition—our harsh treatment of prisoners of the war on drugs, most of whom are young, poor reminders of the failures of American social and economic policies—and at the violence and corruption that policy direction engenders. On the other hand, I am not yet ready to embrace legalization *by itself* (or decriminalization of the more sweeping kind) of currently illicit drugs other than marijuana. (I do favor the legalization of marijuana, with a regulatory scheme similar to that now provided for alcohol.) In what follows I am presuming a definition of legalization that would eliminate from the Controlled Substances Act proscriptions against nonmedical uses of psychoactive substances and make presently-illicit drugs easily available to adults.

My doubts about legalization are of several kinds.

I begin with the rationalist's analysis of costs and benefits, stressing that for me the values that predominate are medical and social rather than moral: If opiates and cocaine were made even cheaper and more easily available, what would happen to the character and extent of drug abuse? Would some people who are now nonusers experiment with drugs in ways that would prove dangerous to them and destructive of their lives and social environments? Would those who are now casual users escalate to real abuse?

These are obviously complicated questions. Criminologists have warned that studying the causes of crime is a tangled and perhaps foolhardy project.[8] Crime is such a conceptual hodgepodge—it's hard to find commonalities between the corrupt legislator and the street mugger other than the desire for financial gain—and explanations, therefore, tend to be too general to be useful. These difficulties pertain equally to the study of why people use, abuse, manufacture, and distribute drugs. Different drugs have a great variety of effects; types of use vary with the mindset, environment, and previous drug history of the user; and like other businesses, the drug trade operates at several different levels. So for the purposes of discussion I narrow the question to the examination of the most visible, publicly dramatic evidence of a drug culture, the symbol that most commonly generates the greatest heat with the general public—the contemporary urban hard drug scene, with its images of wasted youth, aggressive retail trade, and young black males holding entire inner-city neighborhoods hostage.

I start from a sociological base, with a theory that the use and sale of illicit drugs is instrumental behavior, a means to an end, though not necessarily a fully volitional weighing of costs and benefits.[9] I assume the ends sought by users and dealers are common human desires—for comfort, affection, pleasure, power. I also assume that for the criminal offenders who are most often portrayed in the symbolic drama of the urban drug scene—compulsive users and street dealers—legal means for reaching their goals are often blocked by forces powerful enough that a reasonable but frustrated person could well find illegal means appealing, despite the threat of official punishment and the possibility of physical harm. Social relations and internalized norms obviously play some role in determining which people in the situation described above choose the illegal means and which choose the straight and narrow. But I would argue that those influences are subsequent to determination of a structure of legal and illegal opportunities and subordinate to it.[10]

Within that structure, law enforcement provides one of many kinds of pressure that bring people into treatment and keep them there long enough for it to have an effect.[11] I worry that eliminating this pressure would deflect some abusers from seeking treatment. Legalization would be unlikely to convert abusers to the safer forms of taking drugs—chewing coca leaves instead of sniffing or smoking cocaine, smoking opium instead of injecting heroin—that are not practical in an atmosphere of prohibition.[12]

Again making reference to the structure of influences on crime and drug use, I am also unconvinced that legalization would prevent most of the property crimes currently considered to be drug-related; for many burglars money for drugs is only one of a number of entangled motives for committing acquisitive crime. I also doubt that legalization would bring about the sharp drop in urban violence advertised for it by legalizers. Illegal opportunities multiply with a scarcity of legal opportunity. There is no doubt that the violence of some drug transactions is now a direct consequence of prohibition and that, therefore, traffic-related violence would drop sharply if drugs were legalized. But at the same time legalization would deprive many young inner-city males of one crucial source of income. What will replace that income? If there are no other changes in the structure of legal income opportunities available to this group, legalization will not preclude them from substituting another illegal income-generating activity that, given the availability of firearms in American cities, may be at least as violent. Carjacking and mugging, after all, depend more directly on the threat or use of force than exchanging money for drugs.

Taking a broader perspective, however, I feel that the questions framed by this cost-benefit rationalist's perspective almost beg the larger question of how to reduce the damage of drug abuse. Drug policy did not generate the huge demand for illicit drugs, for the most part, and changing it will not undo the damage done by American patterns of drug use. As I mentioned in the prologue, legalization—conceived as a policy solution to "the drug problem"—has some of the same defects as prohibition: It doesn't address the lives of deprivation or instability of compulsive users (or small-time dealers), and it may distract us from them and from the significance of the latent reasons for the drug war, which would remain after the particular policy of prohibition had vanished.

Americans—both the general public and policymakers—tend to think they can solve social problems by changing only one of life's many conditions; an example of this kind of thinking is the notion that by giving someone a job—of whatever quality—you can get him or her out of poverty. We often say communities are being destroyed by drugs, suggesting that if drug abuse did not exist, the problems of joblessness, family breakdown, infant disease, and poverty would be easily moderated or disappear of their own accord. Only by placing the social stresses that are strongly associated with compulsive use of dangerous drugs squarely at the center of national economic concerns, and shaping broader policies accordingly, will we be able to address comprehensively the harmful consequences of drug use (licit and illicit).

Donald Taft, an influential mid-century criminologist, hypothesizing that a materialistic frontier society harboring deep racial and ethnic conflicts and tolerating many kinds of corruption would be a society with the high criminality of the United States, concluded that "we get the criminals we deserve."[13] It may also be said that we have got the drug problem we deserve. Taft, however, was explaining culture with culture. I prefer to explain culture with structure.

At the moment, ignoring this structure of effects, drug prohibition merely gives citizens and politicians an opportunity to fiddle together while Rome burns. And the legalization proposal holds itself as distant from the forces that drive people to use drugs compulsively and destructively as does our often-cynical reliance on prohibition. After legalization, we would probably still get the drug problem we deserve.

The legalization proposal also overlooks the forces propelling the shadow agenda of prohibition. We should understand that in torpedoing prohibition we would not be vanquishing the racial bias that it may serve or providing alternatives for political and social participation that are more socially meaningful than anti-drug activism.

My reservations about transforming prohibition do not mean I would not modify it substantially. In fact, I would forthrightly recommend legalization if I felt assured it would be instituted as part of a much broader campaign to address the full range of socioeconomic sources of drug abuse. Failing that, I would counsel a gradual de-escalation of prohibition of the kind practiced in the Netherlands, where the basic prohibitionist scheme is still on the books but is rarely enforced against users or small-scale retail dealers of cannabis and (often) harder drugs. While higher priority should be given to public health concerns than to law enforcement, those who do *not* abuse drugs should also be protected by such policies as vigorous prosecution of drug-related behavior that harms others—drugged driving and domestic violence where drugs were involved, for example—and sentence enhancements for crimes committed under the influence of drugs (including alcohol). I would characterize this approach as giving the criminal law a supporting role rather than star billing, closer to the European notion of "harm minimization" than to many of the legalization policies advocated in the United States.

I am aware of many limitations to my policy preference. It doesn't address the violence of drug transactions. And it wouldn't affect the availability of dangerous drugs in dangerous forms in our most troubled communities, though I believe that accomplishing that is simply beyond the scope of drug policy. Keeping in mind the shadow agenda items that support prohibition, I am also concerned that de-escalation might intensify the cultural polarization in this country around issues of behavior. On the other hand, it might also help open up debate on these questions, encouraging education along with exhortation.

Scaling down prohibition could also shift budgetary priorities, an important aim. In Canada, where the spirit of prohibitionism is also strong (a development of the past decade), the allocation of national resources for fighting drugs is, nonetheless, just the reverse of ours —70 percent for prevention and treatment, 30 percent for law enforcement and interdiction.[14]

I would also hope for another change, this time a shift in social thinking rather than public policy. We will not really address problematic drug use until we modify our widespread moral antagonism to the mind-altering experience made possible by psychoactive drugs, and acknowledge that we are deeply and permanently a drug-taking culture. Millions of us consume huge quantities of alcohol, take pills for psychological reassurance, smoke tobacco for the nicotine lift— and many are willing to risk the costs and opprobrium of punishment by choosing their pleasures from among those drugs that the law proscribes. Industry and the media further perpetuate this culture. "In this atmosphere," Todd Gitlin writes, "[the media's] glamorous representations of drugs may well have an added effect of rendering drugs legitimate for some portion of the audience."[15] In American life at the millennium, drug use is not only normal but also, for most people and in certain circumstances, desirable. Our goal should be to become a society of citizens who manage their drug-taking behavior responsibly, not one that seeks and militantly enforces individual or collective abstinence. Rather than the prohibitionist's "zero tolerance," we should aim for deeper understanding and tolerance of the wide range of pleasures and needs that our diverse society pursues.

# Notes

*Preface*

1. *New York Times*, July 17, 1964; *New York Times*, August 9, 1968.
2. *New York Times*, September 15, 1986; *New York Times*, January 21, 1989.

*Prologue*

1. *New York Times*, April 12, 1993. Of the $13 billion federal drug budget for fiscal year 1994, more than $8 billion was allocated for law enforcement, less than $5 billion for public health efforts. Executive Office of the President of the United States, *Budget of the United States Government, FY94* (Washington, D.C.: Government Printing Office, 1993), 47.
2. *New York Times*, January 26, 1994.
3. *New York Times*, February 18, 1993; *New York Times*, August 12, 1993.
4. For a review of research on the relationship between crime fluctuations and the size of police forces, see James Q. Wilson, *Thinking About Crime*, revised edition (New York: Basic Books, 1983), Chap. 4.
5. The best international comparison of incarceration rates estimates that in 1990 the U.S. rate of incarceration per 100,000 population was 455, with South Africa next at 311. Marc Mauer, "Americans Behind Bars: One Year Later," (Washington, D.C.: The Sentencing Project), February 1992, Table 4. Between 1972 and 1990 the clearance rate for FBI index crimes (murder, rape, robbery, aggravated assault, burglary, larceny, and motor vehicle theft) rose slightly, from 20.6 to 21.7 percent, but the violent crime clearance rate dropped, from 48.8 to 43.9 percent. Timothy J. Flanagan and Kathleen Maguire, eds., *Sourcebook of Criminal Justice Statistics 1991* (Washington, D.C.: U.S. Department of Justice, Bureau of Justice Statistics, 1992), Table 4.22. The annual *Sourcebook of Criminal Justice Statistics* is a standard, multiyear source of official data series published by the Bureau of Justice Statistics and other federal agencies, as well as a compilation of public opinion and other surveys, generally national and multiyear. I shall refer often to these volumes; subsequent citations will refer to them as *Sourcebook* with the appropriate year.
6. Bill Clinton and Al Gore, *Putting People First* (New York: Times Books, 1992), 9.
7. This list of basic positions is, of necessity, oversimplified. My list leaves out, for example, what Franklin F. Zimring and Gordon Hawkins call

"cost-benefit specifism," the widely held and important view that some drugs are more harmful than others and that policy positions should reflect the differences in medical and social costs of taking various drugs, as well as different social contexts in which drugs are used. Franklin Zimring and Gordon Hawkins, *Capital Punishment and the American Agenda* (New York: Cambridge University Press, 1986), 9.

8. The National Institute on Drug Abuse estimated that 26,062,000 people used an illicit drug at least once during 1991. A Committee of the Institute of Medicine (a body established under the charter of the National Academy of Sciences) estimated in 1990 that about 5.5 million people need some form of drug treatment. U.S. Department of Health and Human Services, National Institute on Drug Abuse, "National Household Survey on Drug Abuse: Population Estimates 1991," Table 2-A; Dean R. Gerstein and Henrick J. Harwood, eds., *Treating Drug Problems*, Vol. 1. (Washington, D.C.: National Academy Press (Institute of Medicine), 1990), 91.

9. *New York Times*, May 12, 1992.

10. David C. Lewis, "Medical and Health Perspectives on a Failing U.S. Drug Policy," *Daedalus* 121 (Summer 1992):178.

11. See, for example, Ethan A. Nadelmann, "Thinking Seriously About Alternatives to Drug Prohibition," *Daedalus* 121 (Summer 1992):85–132; and Richard Lawrence Miller, *The Case for Legalizing Drugs* (New York: Praeger, 1991).

12. The most cogent recent expression of this view of policy can be found in Deborah A. Stone, *Policy Paradox and Political Reason* (Glenview, Ill.: Scott, Foresman, 1988).

13. The term "policy politics" comes from Stone, *Policy Paradox*, 29.

14. U.S. Department of Justice, *The Nation's Toughest Drug Law: Evaluating the New York Experience* (Washington, D.C.: Government Printing Office, 1978).

15. Stuart Scheingold, *The Politics of Street Crime: Criminal Process and Cultural Obsession* (Philadelphia: Temple University Press, 1991), especially Chap. 5.

16. A very similar definition can be found in Patricia G. Erickson, "Recent Trends in Canadian Drug Policy: The Decline and Resurgence of Prohibitionism," *Daedalus* 121 (Summer 1992), 239–240: "The term 'prohibitionism' includes an array of laws, criminal justice practices and social evaluations that serve to suppress particular forms of drugs, forbidding their use, production, and sale."

17. 42 U.S.C. 12101 *et. seq.* (1991); P.L. 101-516 (1990). With respect to the latter policy, states may also explicitly reject the federal mandate, by a vote of both houses of the state legislature and a statement signed by the governor.

18. Much of the information in the case studies on which this book is based comes from personal interviews I conducted between June and December 1990 and between July 1991 and September 1992. Where quotes and current information are not documented from another source, it

may be presumed that they come from these interviews. Where the name of the interviewee is not provided in the text or a footnote, it is either because that person requested anonymity or because identification did not seem to add anything to the presentation of the information. As a general rule, congressional staff members do not wish to have quotes or "inside" information attributed to them.

19. Interesting discussions of ideology in drug policy abound. See, for example, Jerome L. Himmelstein, *The Strange Career of Marijuana: Politics and Ideology of Drug Control in America* (Westport, Conn.: Greenwood, 1983); and Franklin Zimring and Gordon Hawkins, *The Search for Rational Drug Control* (Cambridge: Cambridge University Press, 1992), Chap. 1.

*Chapter 1*
*Drug Prohibition: More and Less Than Meets the Eye*

1. *Minnesota v. Russell*, 477 N.W.2d 886 (1991).
2. *Ibid.*, 890.
3. A disparity between penalties for crack and cocaine also exists in federal law. See 21 U.S.C. 841(b). Possession of crack is punished 100 times more severely, by weight, than possession of powder cocaine, and over 90 percent of defendants sentenced for federal crack offenses are black, according to the Committee Against the Discriminatory Crack Law, formed to lobby against the present law. *The Drug Policy Letter*, no. 20 (August/September 1993):24.
4. *Minnesota v. Russell*, 888, n. 2.
5. Charles Lindblom, *The Policymaking Process*, second edition (Englewood Cliffs, N.J.: Prentice-Hall, 1980), 43.
6. See Murray Edelman, *The Symbolic Uses of Politics* (Chicago: University of Illinois Press, 1964). Much of my analysis of drug prohibition as symbolic politics is influenced by the work of Edelman, whose books also include *Politics as Symbolic Action* (Chicago: Markham, 1971); *Political Language: Words That Succeed and Policies That Fail* (New York: Academic Press, 1977); and *Constructing the Political Spectacle* (Chicago: University of Chicago Press, 1988).
7. The social construction literature includes Peter L. Berger and Thomas Luckman, *The Social Construction of Reality* (New York: Doubleday, 1966); Herbert Blumer, "Social Problems as Collective Behavior," *Social Problems* 18 (Winter 1971):298–306; Malcolm Spector and John Kitsuse, *Constructing Social Problems* (Hawthorne, N.Y.: Walter de Gruyter, 1987); and Armand L. Mauss, *Social Problems as Social Movements* (Philadelphia: J.B. Lippincott, 1975).
8. Deborah A. Stone, *Policy Paradox and Political Reason* (Glenview, Ill.: Scott, Foresman, 1988), 306.
9. For a history of American criminal punishment, see David J. Rothman, *The Discovery of the Asylum* (Boston: Little, Brown, 1971).
10. Stone, *Policy Paradox*, 106.

11. Emile Durkheim, *The Division of Labor in Society* (New York: Free Press, 1984), 40.
12. U.S. Department of Justice, Bureau of Justice Statistics, "Fact Sheet: Drug Use Trends," May 1992, Tables 3 and 4.
13. Even the most sophisticated journalistic commentators on drug policy define "the drug problem" so broadly as to include any use of illicit substances, and assume that anyone who ever uses a drug has a problem. See, for example, Michael Massing, "Whatever Happened to the 'War on Drugs'?" *New York Review of Books*, June 11, 1992, 42–46.
14. Office of National Drug Control Policy, *National Drug Control Strategy* (Washington, D.C.: Government Printing Office, 1989), 8.
15. Edelman, *The Symbolic Uses of Politics*, 19.
16. See National Institute on Alcohol Abuse and Alcoholism, *Sixth Special Report to the U.S. Congress on Alcohol and Health* (Rockville, Md.: U.S. Department of Health and Human Services, 1987); and U.S. Department of Health and Human Services, Office on Smoking and Health, *The Health Consequences of Smoking: Nicotine Addiction* (Washington, D.C.: Government Printing Office, 1988).
17. Mark A. R. Kleiman, *Against Excess: Drug Policy for Results* (New York: Basic Books, 1992), 203–204.
18. See, for example, the surgeon general's report that concluded that nicotine was addicting and that "the processes that determine tobacco addiction are similar to those that determine addiction to drugs such as heroin and cocaine." Office on Smoking and Health, *The Health Consequences of Smoking*, iii.
19. There is a fundamental political dilemma about defining the drug problem to include alcohol and tobacco, which do the most damage to public health. On the one hand, it seems hypocritical to exclude from the realm of proscribed drugs the dangerous legal ones. On the other hand, to increase controls on use of drugs that are more culturally integrated (or, from another perspective, more likely to be used by the culture's elites) would create a very large group of people defined as deviant, who may develop a collective consciousness that spurs them to successfully challenge the basic project of repressing drug use. Deviance would then become the basis for a social movement, as, for instance, it was for women whose experience of having illegal abortions became fodder for the abortion rights movement in the 1960s.
20. Michael Oreskes, "Drug War Underlines Fickleness of Public," *New York Times*, September 6, 1990; Bush's speech is reported in the *New York Times*, September 6, 1989.
21. See Frederick Lewis Allen, *Since Yesterday: The Nineteen-Thirties in America* (New York: Bantam Books, 1961), especially 65–73.
22. Lindblom, *The Policymaking Process*, 114.
23. John W. Kingdon, *Agendas, Alternatives, and Public Policies* (Boston: Little, Brown, 1984), 153–157.
24. U.S. Department of Health and Human Services, National Institute on Drug Abuse, "National Household Survey on Drug Abuse: Population

Estimates 1991" (Rockville, Md.: National Institute on Drug Abuse, 1991), Table 2-A; U.S. Department of Commerce, Bureau of the Census, *Statistical Abstract of the United States 1992* (Washington, D.C.: Government Printing Office, 1992), Table 13.

25. Edwin Schur, *Narcotic Addiction in Britain and America: The Impact of Public Policy* (Bloomington, Ind.: Indiana University Press, 1962), 70–71.

26. Dean R. Gerstein and Henrick J. Harwood, eds., *Treating Drug Problems*, vol. 1. (Washington, D.C.: National Academy Press (National Institute of Medicine), 1990), 48.

27. Edward Brecher and the editors of *Consumer Reports, Licit and Illicit Drugs* (Boston: Little, Brown, 1972), 6–7.

28. David F. Musto, *The American Disease: Origins of Narcotic Control*, expanded edition (New York: Oxford University Press, 1987), 3.

29. John Helmer, *Drugs and Minority Oppression* (New York: The Seabury Press, 1975), Chap. 2.

30. Arnold H. Taylor, *American Diplomacy and the Narcotics Traffic, 1900–1939: A Study in International Humanitarian Reform* (Durham: Duke University Press, 1969).

31. The Harrison Act did not actually forbid the consumption of cocaine and opiates, but imposed registration and taxation on those who manufactured, imported, and distributed them. The law in fact explicitly provided that a doctor could dispense drugs to patients "in the course of his professional practice only." Treasury Department enforcement, however, as well as a sequence of Supreme Court decisions, enshrined prohibition, prosecuting thousands of doctors for prescribing narcotics and shutting down local clinics that arose to try to keep addicts out of the hands of illegal dealers. The anti-drug zealots of the day were driven at least as much by organizational imperatives—drug control became a growth industry overnight, when possession and sale were criminalized—and by the desire to demonstrate the government's seriousness of purpose as by concern with public health and welfare. Musto, *The American Disease.*

32. Richard Lawrence Miller, *The Case for Legalizing Drugs* (New York: Praeger, 1991), 88–90. Wright was equally concerned about the seduction of white women by the Chinese and their decadent opium-smoking and the tendency he supposedly observed for cocaine to drive African-American males to rape.

33. *Ibid.*, quoted on 88.

34. *Ibid.*, 99; Helmer, *Drugs and Minority Oppression*, Chap. 4.

35. Musto, *The American Disease*, 6–8; H. Wayne Morgan, *Drugs in America: A Social History, 1800–1980* (Syracuse: Syracuse University Press, 1981), 92–93.

36. Musto, *The American Disease*, 231.

37. Miller, *The Case*, 101–102.

38. *Harris Poll*, August 27, 1989, reported in *Sourcebook 1990*, Table 2.92; Joseph E. Jacoby and Christopher S. Dunn, "National Survey on Pun-

ishment for Criminal Offenses, Executive Summary," (Bowling Green, Ohio: Bowling Green State University, 1987), Table 6.

39. See "ABC News-*Washington Post* Poll," May 8–13, 1985, Questions 65–67, as reported in *Sourcebook 1988*, Table 2.98.

40. A notable exception to this rule is Baltimore Mayor Kurt Schmoke, who has repeatedly called for consideration of decriminalizing drug possession. See Kurt Schmoke, "An Argument in Favor of Decriminalization," *Hofstra Law Review* 18 (1990):501–525. More recently and tentatively, the mayors of San Jose, San Francisco, and Oakland joined together to declare their opposition to the drug wars. *San Francisco Chronicle*, May 11, 1993.

*Chapter 2*
*Getting Tough on Illicit Drugs*

1. Frederick B. Artz, *The Mind of the Middle Ages* (New York: Knopf, 1967), 359–360; A. J. Gurevich, *Categories of Medieval Culture* (London: Routledge and Kegan Paul, 1985), 1–25.

2. For historical material on these elements of drug prohibition, see David Musto, *The American Disease: Origins of Narcotic Control*, expanded edition (New York: Oxford University Press, 1987); and John Helmer, *Drugs and Minority Oppression* (New York: The Seabury Press, 1975).

3. Franklin Zimring and Gordon Hawkins, *The Search for Rational Drug Control* (Cambridge: Cambridge University Press, 1992), xiv.

4. U.S. Department of Justice, Bureau of Justice Statistics, "Prisoners in 1992," *Bulletin* (Washington, D.C.: U.S. Department of Justice, May 1993), Table 2.

5. U.S. Department of Justice, Bureau of Justice Statistics, "Correctional Populations in the United States, 1985" (Washington, D.C.: U.S. Department of Justice, December 1987), Table 1.1; U.S. Department of Justice, Bureau of Justice Statistics, "Correctional Populations in the United States, 1990" (Washington, D.C.: U.S. Department of Justice, July 1992), Table 1.1.

6. Federal Bureau of Investigation, *Uniform Crime Reports, Crime in the United States 1980* (Washington, D.C.: Government Printing Office, 1981), Table 24; *Uniform Crime Reports 1990*, Table 24. The annual *Uniform Crime Reports* is a standard, multiyear compilation of official data series collected by local police departments and published by the FBI. I shall refer often to these volumes; subsequent citations will refer to them as *Uniform Crime Reports* with the appropriate year.

7. In federal courts, 13,838 drug defendants were sentenced to imprisonment in 1990, as opposed to 3,479 in 1980. *Sourcebook 1992*, Table 5.38; *Sourcebook 1982*, Table 5.27. There were 27,796 prison sentences imposed in the federal District Courts for all offenses, up from 13,191 in 1980. *Sourcebook 1991*, Table 5.36.

8. *Sourcebook 1990*, Table 6.93. In 1980 there were 24,661 prisoners in federal institutions. *Sourcebook 1990*, Table 6.89.

9. U.S. Department of Justice, Bureau of Justice Statistics, "Drugs, Crime,

and the Justice System: A National Report" (Washington, D.C.: U.S. Department of Justice, December 1992), 195.

10. See the following publications of the U.S. Department of Justice, Bureau of Justice Statistics: "National Judicial Reporting Program, 1988," January 1992; the biennial series of bulletins, "Felony Sentences in State Courts" (1986, 1988, 1990); and the annual series, "National Corrections Reporting Program" (1986–1989).

11. U.S. Department of Justice, Bureau of Justice Statistics, "Felony Sentences in State Courts, 1990," *Bulletin.* (Washington, D.C.: U.S. Department of Justice, March 1993), Table 1; U.S. Department of Justice, Bureau of Justice Statistics, "Felony Sentences in State Courts, 1986," *Bulletin.* (Washington, D.C.: U.S. Department of Justice, February 1989), Table 1.

12. U.S. Department of Justice, Bureau of Justice Statistics, "Prisoners in 1991," *Bulletin*, May 1992, Table 11.

13. Peter Reuter, "Hawks Ascendant: The Punitive Trend of American Drug Policy," *Daedalus* 121, no. 3 (1992):24–25.

14. BJS, "Prisoners in 1992," 1.

15. U.S. Department of Justice, Bureau of Justice Statistics, "Federal Sentencing in Transition, 1986–90," *Special Report*, June 1992, Table 5.

16. BJS, "Drugs, Crime, and the Justice System," 190.

17. *Sourcebook 1991*, Table 5.23. Time served for burglary, for instance, rose by 24 percent; robbery, by 14 percent.

18. Preliminary figures for 1990 showed an average federal prison sentence of ninety months for violent offenses, twenty-two months for property offenses, and eighty-one months for drug offenses. BJS, "Federal Sentencing in Transition," Table 2.

19. National Criminal Justice Association, "A Guide to State Controlled Substances Acts," 1991, cited in BJS, "Drugs, Crime, and the Justice System," 190.

20. U.S. Department of Justice, Bureau of Justice Statistics, "National Corrections Reporting Program, 1986," January 1992, Table 1-8; U.S. Department of Justice, Bureau of Justice Statistics, "National Corrections Reporting Program, 1989," November 1992, Table 1-8. Not surprisingly, the greatest increase was for trafficking offenses, where the mean went from twenty-six months to forty months. It should be noted that these figures understate actual time spent incarcerated because jail time data were not widely available and are therefore not included.

21. BJS, "Felony Sentences in State Courts, 1990," Table 4; BJS, "Felony Sentences in State Courts, 1986," Table 4.

22. *Sourcebook 1991*, Table 5.21.

23. For an excellent journalistic account of this pattern among adolescents, see William Finnegan, "Out There," *The New Yorker*, September 10, 1990, 51–86, and September 17, 1990, 60–90.

24. Among the journalistic accounts of druglords who trade information for lighter penalties is Gerry Fitzgerald, "Dispatches from the Drug War," *Common Cause* 16 (January 1990):13–19.

25. MCL 333.7403(2)(i), MSA 14.15 (7403)(2)(i); 21 U.S.C. 841(b). See also BJS, "Drugs, Crime, and the Justice System," 179, 181.
26. BJS, "Drugs, Crime, and the Justice System," 179.
27. BJS, "National Corrections Reporting Program, 1989," Table 1-12.
28. BJS, "Correctional Populations in the United States, 1990," Table 1.1; U.S. Department of Justice, Bureau of Justice Statistics, "Historical Corrections Statistics in the United States, 1850–1984" (Washington, D.C.: U.S. Department of Justice, December 1986), Tables 7-11 and 7-12.
29. John M. Dawson, "Felons Sentenced to Probation in State Courts, 1986" (Washington, D.C.: U.S. Department of Justice, Bureau of Justice Statistics, November 1990), Table 1.
30. The Department of Justice has estimated that 72,000 people were under intensive supervision in 1990. BJS, "Drugs, Crime, and the Justice System," 182. For a summary of research on the effectiveness of fourteen intensive probation programs in nine states, see Joan Petersilia and Susan Turner, "Evaluating Intensive Supervision Probation/Parole: Results of a Nationwide Experiment," in *Research in Brief* (Washington, D.C.: U.S. Department of Justice, National Institute of Justice, May 1993). A discussion of the political and social implications of this development can be found in Diana R. Gordon, *The Justice Juggernaut: Fighting Street Crime, Controlling Citizens* (New Brunswick, N.J.: Rutgers University Press, 1990), chap. 5.
31. Voncile B. Gowdy, "Intermediate Sanctions," in *Research in Brief* (Washington, D.C.: U.S. Department of Justice, National Institute of Justice, 1993), 1.
32. George B. Vold and Thomas J. Bernard, *Theoretical Criminology* (New York: Oxford University Press, 1986), Chap. 3.
33. Public Law 100-690, Section 5301 (1988), 21 U.S.C. Section 862.
34. According to the Department of Justice, as of late 1991 about 400 convicted drug offenders had been denied federal benefits under the 1988 law. BJS, "Drugs, Crime, and the Justice System," 184.
35. See, for example, Massachusetts General Law c. 90, Section 22(f).
36. 23 U.S.C. Section 104(a)(2), (a)(3), and (c). For a report on states' response to the 1990 amendment to the transportation appropriations bill that used the threat of withholding federal highway funds to coerce the states into passing such legislation, see Diana R. Gordon, "The Drug War Hits the Roads," *The Nation*, May 31, 1993, 735–738.
37. At the national level, the practice is authorized by the Comprehensive Drug Abuse Prevention and Control Act of 1970, 21 U.S.C. 881. The Comprehensive Crime Control Act of 1984 expanded forfeiture to include real property and created an Asset Forfeiture Fund in the Department of Justice, to reserve the proceeds of forfeiture for law enforcement. 28 U.S.C. 524(c)(4).
38. "Statement of Cary H. Copeland, Director and Chief Counsel, Executive Office for Asset Forfeiture, Before the Subcommittee on Legislation and National Security, Government Operations Subcommittee, U.S. House of Representatives, Concerning Asset Forfeiture," June 22, 1993. Law

enforcement officials quite freely admit that an important function of the asset forfeiture program is to finance drug enforcement, though they refute the criticism that the prospect of financial gain drives the identification of opportunities to seize assets. Chapter 13 contains a fuller discussion of this issue.

39. U.S. Department of Justice press release, "Attorney General Thornburgh Shares Drug Booty with Police," April 4, 1990.

40. Roger L. Conner and Patrick C. Burns, "The Winnable War: How Communities Are Eradicating Local Drug Markets," *The Brookings Review* 10 (Summer 1992);29.

41. For criticisms of the use of asset forfeiture in the war on drugs, see Andrew Schneider and Mary Pat Flaherty, "Presumed Guilty: The Law's Victims in the War on Drugs," *The Pittsburgh Press*, August 11–16, 1991; and John Conyers, "Opening Statement, Oversight Hearing on the Department of Justice Asset Forfeiture Program," Subcommittee on Legislation and National Security, Committee on Government Operations, U.S. House of Representatives, September 3, 1992.

42. See Michael F. Zeldin and Roger G. Weiner, "Innocent Third Parties and Their Rights in Asset Forfeiture Proceedings," *American Criminal Law Review* 28 (1991):843–867. Supreme Court decisions have recently strengthened the ability of owners of seized assets to claim their innocence and suggested that some seizures may amount to excessive punishment prohibited by the Eighth Amendment. *U.S. v. A Parcel of Land*, No. 91-781, 61 L.W. 4189 (1993); *Austin v. U.S.*, No. 92-6073, 61 L.W. 4811 (1993). The opinions did not, however, challenge the basic assumptions or routine practices of the policy.

43. See Steven Wisotsky, "Not Thinking Like a Lawyer: The Case of Drugs in the Courts," *Notre Dame Journal of Law, Ethics and Public Policy* 5, no. 3 (1991):651–691.

44. For an overview of Supreme Court decisions "dismantling Fourth Amendment law," see Gerald G. Ashdown, "Drugs, Ideology, and the Deconstitutionalization of Criminal Procedure," *West Virginia Law Review* 95 (Fall 1992):1–54.

45. *U.S. v. Place*, 462 U.S. 696 (1983); *U.S. v. Knotts*, 460 U.S. 276 (1983).

46. *California v. Acevedo*, 111 S.Ct. 1982 (1991).

47. *California v. Hodari D.*, 111 S.Ct. 1547 (1991).

48. *U.S. v. Leon*, 468 U.S. 897 (1984); *Massachusetts v. Sheppard*, 468 U.S. 981 (1984).

49. Ashdown, "Drugs, Ideology, and Deconstitutionalization," 32.

50. See Conner and Burns, "The Winnable War," 26–29.

51. For the early development of the parents' anti-drug movement, see Elizabeth Coleman Brynner, "New Parental Push Against Marijuana," *New York Times Magazine*, February 10, 1980, 36.

52. Representative Charles Schumer (Democrat-N.Y.), Chairman of the Subcommittee on Crime and Criminal Justice of the House Judiciary Committee, estimated in April 1993 that federal law enforcement expenditures for fighting illicit drugs had amounted to $50 billion since

1981. "The 1993 National Summit on U.S. Drug Policy," transcript of meeting on May 7, 1993, available from Columbia Institute, 8 E Street, S.E., Washington, D.C. 20003, 10.

53. U.S. Department of Justice, Bureau of Justice Statistics, "Justice Expenditure and Employment 1982," *Bulletin* (Washington, D.C.: U.S. Department of Justice, August 1985), Table 3; U.S. Department of Justice, Bureau of Justice Statistics, "Justice Expenditure and Employment 1990," *Bulletin* (Washington, D.C.: U.S. Department of Justice, September 1992), Table 7.

54. *Economic Report of the President, 1993* (Washington, D.C.: Government Printing Office, 1993), Table B-41.

55. U.S. Department of Justice, Bureau of Justice Statistics, "Drug Enforcement by Police and Sheriffs' Departments, 1990," *Special Report* (Washington, D.C.: U.S. Department of Justice, May 1992), Tables 3 and 7.

56. U.S. Department of Commerce, Bureau of the Census, *Statistical Abstract of the United States 1991* (Washington, D.C.: Government Printing Office, 1991), Table 653.

57. *New York Times*, May 24, 1992.

58. *Congressional Quarterly Weekly Report*, December 1, 1979, 2728; *Congressional Quarterly Weekly Report*, October 10, 1992, 3168. By mid-1993 the DEA had about 2,800 agents assigned to drug control, in comparison with 1,800 in the FBI. *New York Times*, August 19, 1993.

59. Executive Office of the President of the United States, *Budget of the United States Government, FY94* (Washington, D.C.: Government Printing Office, 1993), 47. In early 1994 the Clinton administration proposed an added $800 million for treatment of chronic drug abuse and a reduction in interdiction funds of about $96 million. *Washington Post*, February 10, 1994.

60. Reuter, "Hawks Ascendant," 21.

61. The quoted description of the program is from U.S. Congress, House of Representatives, Committee on Education and Labor, *Drug Abuse Resistance Education Act of 1990: Report*, 101–572, 2. My speculative conclusion about the implications of law enforcement involvement in DARE is based on comments made by lawyers and social service workers during interviews at the local level.

62. See Zimring and Hawkins, *The Search for Rational Drug Control*, Chap. 7, for a more complete discussion of the implications of national dominance of drug policy.

63. At the end of September 1981, 25 percent of pending criminal cases in U.S. attorneys' offices were drug cases; ten years later they were 37 percent of pending cases. *Sourcebook 1982*, Figure 5.4; *Sourcebook 1991*, Table 5.7; Zimring and Hawkins, *The Search for Rational Drug Control*, 162.

64. See Malcolm M. Feeley and Austin D. Sarat, *The Policy Dilemma: Federal Crime Policy and the Law Enforcement Assistance Administration, 1968–1978* (Minneapolis: University of Minnesota Press, 1980).

65. Harold Lasswell, *Politics: Who Gets What, When, How?* (New York: McGraw-Hill, 1936).
66. Harold Lasswell, *Psychopathology and Politics* (New York: Viking Press, 1960), 1.

*Chapter 3*
*The Kingpin Must Die*

1. NAACP Legal Defense and Education Fund, "Death Row, U.S.A." (New York: NAACP Legal Defense and Education Fund, Winter 1993). There were also eight inmates sentenced to death by the U.S. military.
2. *Sourcebook 1991*, Table 5.46; *Sourcebook 1989*, Table 6.85. This execution figure was low compared with figures from previous and subsequent years (e.g., 1987, with twenty-five executions and 1992, with thirty-one.) Some observers predict that the number will soon begin to rise sharply, as appeals are exhausted and if habeas corpus is further restricted.
3. *Sourcebook 1990*, Table 6.137. Of the 199 executions between January 1973 and April 1993, the greatest number (56) were in Texas, followed by Florida (30), Virginia (21), Georgia (15), and Alabama (10). NAACP LDF, "Death Row," 9.
4. NAACP LDF, "Death Row," 11–41.
5. *Furman v. Georgia*, 408 US 238 (1972). The case did not repudiate capital punishment categorically but found that existing statutes violated broad principles of due process in failing to provide standards for judges and juries in capital cases, creating a risk that the imposition of a death sentence would be arbitrary and capricious.
6. *Sourcebook 1990*, Table 6.138. Data used in the rest of this paragraph are taken from this table. For a review of state executions from the end of the Civil War to the early 1980s, see William J. Bowers, *Legal Homicide: Death as Punishment in America, 1864–1982* (Boston: Northeastern University Press, 1984).
7. For a discussion of regional patterns in the use of the death penalty, see Franklin Zimring and Gordon Hawkins, *Capital Punishment and the American Agenda* (New York: Cambridge University Press, 1986), 30–33.
8. *Coker v. Georgia*, 433 U.S. 584 (1977), 585.
9. *Sourcebook 1990*, Table 6.138. Under civil authority, 1,284 people were executed between 1940 and 1949, 1,064 for murder, 200 for rape, and 20 for other offenses. In the early days of the republic, the federal death penalty was imposed for several offenses not resulting in death—for example, treason, piracy, and counterfeiting.
10. *Coker v. Georgia*, 433 U.S. 584 (1977), 592.
11. *Tison v. Arizona*, 481 U.S. 137 (1987).
12. NAACP LDF, "Death Row," 5.
13. *Penry v. Lynaugh*, 109 S.Ct. 2934 (1989); *Stanford v. Kentucky*, 109 S.Ct. 2969 (1989). But in *Thompson v. Oklahoma*, 487 U.S. 815 (1988), the plurality noted that executing murderers below the age of sixteen would

offend contemporary standards of decency, since there is virtually a national consensus that they are minors "not prepared to assume the full responsibilities of an adult." (They cannot vote or serve on a jury, for example.) Although the outcome of the case rested on a narrower holding—that statutes lacking a minimum age for the death penalty are barred by the Eighth Amendment—it can be said that the Court has whittled away at the execution of minors.

14. *McCleskey v. Kemp*, 481 U.S. 279 (1987).
15. *Herrera v. Collins*, No. 91-7328 (52 Crim. Law Reporter 3029) (1993).
16. *Gregg v. Georgia*, 428 U.S. 153, 179–182.
17. *Sourcebook 1990*, Figure 2.1. Some unpublished research, however, casts doubt on the depth of the support for the death penalty, surveys that find respondents abandoning support for individual sentences as they learn more about the particulars of the crime and the criminal, and surveys that ask respondents to choose between a sentence of death and life imprisonment without possibility of parole. See, for example, Cambridge Survey Research, "An Analysis of Attitudes Toward Capital Punishment in Florida," June 1985, and Craig Haney and Aida Hurtado, "Californians' Attitudes About the Death Penalty," University of California at Santa Cruz, December 1989.
18. *Sourcebook 1990*, Table 2.51.
19. As of January 1994, thirty-eight states had post-*Furman* death penalty statutes.
20. Death Penalty Information Center, "Millions Misspent: What Politicians Don't Say About the High Costs of the Death Penalty," (Washington, D.C.: Death Penalty Information Center, October 1992), 13–14.
21. 49 U.S.C.App. 1473 (1974).
22. *New York Times*, March 15, 1973; *New York Times*, January 31, 1974.
23. *Congressional Quarterly Weekly Report*, October 4, 1986, 2361.
24. *Newsweek*, August 11, 1986, 18. Three weeks later Bush told the *Boston Herald*, "I don't think the death penalty is unreasonable" for major dealers. *Los Angeles Times*, September 2, 1986.
25. *New York Times*, September 15, 1986.
26. *New York Times*, September 2, 1986.
27. *Congressional Quarterly Weekly Report*, September 6, 1986, 2069.
28. *Congressional Quarterly Weekly Report*, September 13, 1986, 2125.
29. *Congressional Quarterly Weekly Report*, September 16, 1986, 1930.
30. *Congressional Record*, September 8, 1988, H7272-7281. The vote was 299 to 111.
31. *Congressional Quarterly Weekly Report*, October 29, 1988, 3145.
32. Anti-Drug Abuse Act of 1988, H.R. 5210; 21 U.S.C. 841(e)(1)(A) and (B).
33. *New York Times*, May 15, 1991.
34. *New York Times*, February 19, 1993.
35. *U.S. v. Juan Raul Garza*, No. CR 93-0009 (S.D. Texas); *U.S. v. Hutching et al.*, No. CR-032-S (E.D. Oklahoma).
36. U.S. Congress, Senate, *Hearings Before the Committee on the Judiciary on*

*S. 32, S. 1225, and S. 1696*, 101st Congress, September 19, 1989, 31 (testimony of Edward S. G. Dennis, Jr., Assistant Attorney General, Criminal Division, U.S. Department of Justice).

37. Comprehensive Violent Crime Act of 1991, H.R. 1400.
38. Anti-Crime Act of 1989, H.R. 3119.
39. *Congressional Quarterly Weekly Report*, July 21, 1990, 2323.
40. *Congressional Quarterly Weekly Report*, October 6, 1990, 3256.
41. U.S. Congress, House of Representatives, *Hearings Before the Subcommittee on Crime and Criminal Justice, Committee on the Judiciary, Selected Crime Issues: Prevention and Punishment*, 102d Congress, May 23, 29, June 12, 26, July 10, 17, and 25, 1991, "Prepared Statement of William Barr, Deputy Attorney General, U.S. Department of Justice," 2, 5–7.
42. See the House debate over these proposals in *Congressional Record*, October 16, 1991, H7950-7959.
43. *Congressional Record*, June 25, 1991, S8547.
44. *Congressional Quarterly Weekly Report*, October 19, 1991, 3078.
45. The bill passed 71 to 26 in the Senate, with only a handful of the opposition—including Senators Daniel Patrick Moynihan (Democrat-N.Y.), Edward M. Kennedy (Democrat-Mass.), and Alan Cranston (Democrat-Calif.)—voting "no" because of the death penalty provisions. *New York Times*, July 12, 1991. The House version passed, 305 to 118. *New York Times*, October 23, 1991.
46. New Jersey Representative Peter Rodino, former Chairman of the House Judiciary Committee and a long-time fighter for liberal positions on social issues (abortion and prayer in schools among them), retired from politics in 1990, after forty-two years in the House, at the age of 81.
47. *New York Times*, November 27 and 28, 1991.
48. See *Congressional Quarterly Weekly Report*, August 14, 1993, 2228.

*Chapter 4*
*The 650 Club*

1. U.S. Sentencing Commission, *Federal Sentencing Guidelines Manual* (St. Paul: West Publishing, 1992), 80.
2. For a journalistic account of the fate of a first-time offender convicted of conspiracy to distribute illicit drugs under the Michigan "650-plus law," see Mike Sager, "The Case of Gary Fannon," *Rolling Stone*, September 3, 1992, 27, and "The State of Michigan vs. Gary Fannon," *Rolling Stone*, September 2, 1993, 51.
3. U.S. Department of Commerce, Bureau of the Census, *Statistical Abstract of the United States 1991* (Washington, D.C.: Government Printing Office, 1991), Table 615.
4. Joe T. Darden, Richard Child Hill, June Thomas, and Richard Thomas, *Detroit: Race and Uneven Development* (Philadelphia: Temple University Press, 1987), 27.
5. *Ibid.*, chap. 2.
6. The population of the city of Detroit dropped from 1,850,000 in 1950 to 1,028,000 in 1990; in 1975, just before the events reported in this

chapter, it was 1,335,000. *Statistical Abstract 1977*, Table 23; *Statistical Abstract 1991*, Table 40. Adding to the general trends of suburbanization and white flight was the movement into the city of southern blacks. Between 1960 and 1990 the proportion of black residents grew from 28.9 percent to 75.7 percent, giving Detroit the highest proportion of black residents among the 100 largest American cities.

7. Darden et al., *Detroit*, 261.
8. "Controlled Substances Act of 1971," 1971 Mich. PA 196.
9. *People v. Lorentzen*, 387 Mich. 167 (1972).
10. *Ibid.*, 176.
11. *People v. Sinclair*, 387 Mich. 91 (1972).
12. *Ibid.*, 133.
13. *Detroit News*, June 7, 1977.
14. *Detroit News*, June 15, 1977.
15. The rate of FBI Index crimes per 100,000 for 1975, as reported by the FBI, was 5.52 times what it had been in 1960. Federal Bureau of Investigation, *Uniform Crime Reports 1960, Crime in the United States* (Washington, D.C.: Government Printing Office, 1961), Table 3; *Uniform Crime Reports 1975*, Table 4. It is important to note that this increase may reflect a surge in crime reporting as much as a crime wave.
16. *Detroit News*, August 31, 1978.
17. *Detroit News*, February 24, 1978.
18. *Detroit News*, January 10, 1977.
19. The life sentence was effectively without possibility of parole, though that provision was part of another bill (House Bill 4195). The legislation as finally enacted is found in Public Health Code sections 333.7401 and 333.7403, Michigan Compiled Laws.
20. *Detroit News*, February 22, 1978.
21. State of Michigan, *1977 Journal of the House*, 754–756.
22. *State News* (Lansing, Michigan), April 7, 1977.
23. An excellent journalistic treatment of the effects of the 650 lifer law is a three-part series by John Castine in the *Detroit Free Press*: "Mandatory Terms Fall Short," March 10, 1990; "Lawmakers Quietly Consider Change," March 11, 1990; "Law's Sponsor Has Second Thoughts," March 12, 1990.
24. Michigan Department of Corrections information sheet prepared for Representative William Bryant, n.d.
25. State of Michigan, House Judiciary Committee, Hearing on House Bill 4024, March 19, 1991, 3.
26. *Statistical Abstract 1991*, Table 27.
27. Castine, *Detroit Free Press*, March 10, 1990.
28. Castine, *Detroit Free Press*, March 12, 1990.
29. House Bill 4024 (1991).
30. Memo to House Judiciary Committee Members from Representative William R. Bryant, March 19, 1991; revised, May 6, 1991. Unpaginated.
31. *Solem v. Helm*, 463 U.S. 277 (1983).
32. *Harmelin v. Michigan*, 111 S.Ct. 2680 (1991).

33. Mich. Const. 1963, Art. I, Section 16.
34. *People v. Bullock*, 440 Mich. 15 (1992).
35. *Ibid.*, 40.
36. *People v. Fluker*, 442 Mich. 890 (1993).

*Chapter 5*
*Just Saying No in Alaska*

1. States that adopted some form of decriminalization include Alaska, Maine, Minnesota, Mississippi, Nebraska, Oregon, California, New York, North Carolina, Ohio, and Colorado. See Eric W. Single, ''The Impact of Marijuana Decriminalization: An Update,'' *Journal of Public Health Policy* 10 (Winter 1989):456–465.
2. U.S. Department of Commerce, Bureau of the Census, *Statistical Abstract of the United States 1991* (Washington, D.C.: Government Printing Office, 1991), Table 26.
3. *Worldmark Encyclopedia of the States* (New York: Worldmark (Harper and Row), 1981), 14; *Statistical Abstract 1991*, Table 27.
4. For documentation of the effects of the construction of the pipeline on drug use in the state, see Bernard Segal, *Drug-Taking Behavior Among School-Aged Youth: The Alaska Experience and Comparisons with Lower-48 States* (New York: Haworth Press, 1990), 8–12. Segal discusses the findings of T. D. Lonner, ''Major Construction Projects and Changing Substance Abuse Patterns in Alaska,'' Center for Alcohol and Addiction Studies, University of Alaska, 1983.
5. *Gray v. State*, 525 P.2d 524 (Alaska 1974).
6. *Ravin v. State*, 537 P.2d 494 (Alaska 1975). The Court neither affirmed nor reversed the decision below, but sent the case back ''for further proceedings'' to ascertain whether Ravin's behavior conformed to the circumstances within which marijuana possession was constitutionally protected.
7. *Ibid.*, 504 and 511.
8. AS 11.71.070 (1990).
9. Margaret R. Porter, Theodore A. Veira, Gary J. Kaplan, Jack R. Heesch, and Ardell B. Collyar, ''Drug Use in Anchorage, Alaska,'' *Journal of the American Medical Association* 223 (1973):657–664, Table 3.
10. If Alaska followed the national trend, there would indeed have been some increased marijuana use after decriminalization, but there was also an even greater increase in use during that period in the states with harsh penalties. Single, ''The Impact of Decriminalization,'' 459. The only firm conclusion seems to be that fluctuations in usage are caused by many different factors. It should be noted that Segal reports research on the effects of the trans-Alaska pipeline construction on drug use that concluded that drug use not only increased while the pipeline was being built but declined after the pipeline was completed in 1978. Segal, *Drug-Taking Behavior*, 8–12.
11. Segal, *Drug-Taking Behavior*, 78. Lifetime experience increased 3.6 percent between 1983 and 1988; the self-report study was conducted with

several thousand (3,609 in 1983, 3,814 in 1988) students in grades 7 to 12 in eight school districts. Segal's comment can be found at 19.

12. *Ibid.*, 119.
13. Letter to author, July 6, 1993.
14. State Office of Alcoholism and Drug Abuse (Alaska), *The Economic Cost of Alcohol and Other Drug Abuse in Alaska, Volume I,* 1989, 16, 18. Researchers warn that admission for alcohol treatment does not mean that drug problems are not also present.
15. State Office of Alcoholism and Drug Abuse (Alaska), *The Economic Cost of Alcohol and Other Drug Abuse in Alaska, Volume II,* 1989, 27.
16. "The Marijuana Report," 9 (Fall 1990).
17. "Anchorage Crime Commission Results," October 1988, mimeo, unpaginated.
18. Charles P. Wohlforth, "Off the Pot," *New Republic,* December 3, 1990, 9; *New York Times,* March 3, 1988.
19. *Anchorage Daily News,* January 31, 1989.
20. *Anchorage Daily News,* January 12, 1989.
21. Interview, July 18, 1991.
22. Interview, July 16, 1991.
23. *Anchorage Times,* November 28, 1989.
24. Unpublished speech by Glenda Straube, campaign manager of Alaskans for Privacy, n.d., 7.
25. *Anchorage Times,* October 11, 1990.
26. "Ballot Proposition #2: 1990 Vote to Recriminalize Marijuana," mimeo, n.d. The initiative prevailed in twenty-one out of twenty-seven districts. It lost in Juneau (yes: 6,019, no: 6,440), the Spenard (yes: 2,699, no: 3,418) and downtown (yes: 3,399, no: 3,746) sections of Anchorage, and the Goldstream (yes: 3,230, no: 3,427) and University (yes: 2,602, no: 3,013) areas of Fairbanks. It also lost—by only 11 votes—in the Fort Yukon district (at the edge of the Arctic Circle), which included a number of villages in the bush.
27. John McPhee, *Coming into the Country* (New York: Farrar, Straus and Giroux, 1977), 79.

*Chapter 6*
*The Taxpayers' Revolt Meets the War on Drugs*

1. U.S. Department of Commerce, Bureau of the Census, *Historical Statistics of the United States: Colonial Times to 1970,* Part 1, Series A 195-209, (Washington, D.C.: Government Printing Office, 1976), 24–35; U.S. Department of Commerce, Bureau of the Census, *Statistical Abstract of the United States 1991* (Washington, D.C.: Government Printing Office, 1991), Tables 26 and 40.
2. Michael Barone and Grant Ujifusa, *The Almanac of American Politics 1992* (Washington, D.C.: National Journal, 1991), 698.
3. *Kansas City Star,* May 23, 1989.
4. *Webster v. Reproductive Health Services,* 492 U.S. 490 (1989).
5. *Ibid.,* 501.

*252*

6. Barone and Ujifusa, *The Almanac of American Politics 1992*, 700.

7. Article X, Sections 16-24, Constitution of Missouri.

8. The St. Louis violent crime rate (including the crimes of murder, rape, robbery, and aggravated assault) was 2,211 per 100,000 population that year, as compared with 2,028 for New York and 1,739 for Los Angeles. Federal Bureau of Investigation, *Uniform Crime Reports 1982, Crime in the United States* (Washington, D.C.: Government Printing Office, 1983), Table 5.

9. *Uniform Crime Reports 1982*, Table 5; *Uniform Crime Reports 1988*, Table 6.

10. *Uniform Crime Reports 1988*, Table 6; *Statistical Abstract 1990*, Table 40.

11. *Kansas City Times*, January 21, 1989.

12. *Kansas City Star*, November 27, 1988.

13. *Kansas City Star*, January 20, 1989.

14. *Kansas City Times*, January 2, 1989.

15. *Kansas City Star*, November 27, 1988.

16. *The Kansas City-Jackson County Star*, October 25, 1989.

17. Interview, September 19, 1991. Much of the factual information in subsequent paragraphs about the Kansas City drug problem and responses to it comes from this interview and others with Riederer (on October 24, 1991, and February 17, 1992) and several other representatives of law enforcement in the city and county. In addition, I have noted newspaper accounts of events, where appropriate.

18. *Kansas City Star*, March 7, 1989.

19. *Kansas City Times*, April 1, 1989; *Kansas City Star*, October 6, 1988.

20. *Kansas City Times*, April 3, 1989.

21. *Kansas City Star*, January 16, 1992.

22. *Kansas City Star*, May 23, 1989.

23. Rev. Stats. Mo., Ch. 613.175 (1989).

24. *Kansas City Times*, August 22, 1989.

25. For the complete wording of the ballot measure, see *Kansas City Times*, September 13, 1989. As passed, it was incorporated into Jackson County law as Ordinance 1795 (1989).

26. *Kansas City Times*, October 14, 1989.

27. The Ad Hoc Group Against Crime, for example, developed a drug prevention and treatment plan for the city's black community. *Kansas City Times*, October 28, 1989.

28. Interview, Steve Glorioso, September 18, 1991.

29. *Kansas City Times*, November 1, 1989.

30. *Kansas City Times*, October 27, 1989.

31. *Kansas City Star*, November 1, 1989.

32. *Kansas City Times*, November 8, 1989.

33. *Statistical Abstract 1991*, Table 454.

34. *Kansas City Times*, November 8, 1989.

35. The *Kansas City Star* conducted a three-month study of the drug program, culminating in a three-part series of articles, published on July 21, 22, and 23, 1991. This paragraph relies heavily on those stories.

36. *Kansas City Star*, July 23, 1991; "Kansas City Illustrated," KCPT-TV, November 29, 1991.
37. "Kansas City Illustrated."
38. "Summary of Key Crime and Drug Proposals" (draft), Campaign for an Effective Crime Policy, November 16, 1992.
39. *Kansas City Star*, March 2, 1992.

*Chapter 7*
*Loitering in Livable Seattle*

1. Seattle Mun. Code, Chap. 12A.20.050 (1990).
2. U.S. Department of Commerce, Bureau of the Census, *Statistical Abstract of the United States 1991* (Washington, D.C.: Government Printing Office, 1991), Table 36; Michael Barone and Grant Ujifusa, *The Almanac of American Politics 1992*, (Washington, D.C.: National Journal, 1990), 1312. Unemployment in 1989 for the metropolitan area was 4.6 percent, as compared with a national average of 5.3 percent. *Statistical Abstract 1991*, Table 637.
3. *Statistical Abstract 1991*, Table 744.
4. Ellen Posner, "A City That Likes Itself: Urban Design," *The Atlantic*, July 1991, 94–100.
5. The unemployment rate for the state was 6.2 percent in 1989, as compared with a national rate of 5.3. *Statistical Abstract 1991*, Table 665.
6. Federal Bureau of Investigation, *Uniform Crime Reports 1991, Crime in the United States* (Washington, D.C.: Government Printing Office, 1992), Table 6; *New York Times*, August 16, 1992.
7. Dan Fleissner, Nicholas Fedan, Ezra Stotland, and David Klinger, "Community Policing in Seattle: A Descriptive Study of the South Seattle Crime Reduction Project," Seattle Police Department, May 1, 1991, 53.
8. These data are extrapolated from U.S. Department of Health and Human Services, Alcohol, Drug Abuse, and Mental Health Administration, "Data from the Drug Abuse Warning Network (DAWN), Annual Data 1989," Statistical series I, no. 9 (Rockville, Md.: National Institute on Drug Abuse, 1990), Table 1.2; and *Statistical Abstract 1990*, Table 36. Drug abuse episodes as a percentage of total emergency room visits (by metropolitan area) and mentions of drug use per 100 emergency room visits (for all causes) also show Seattle to be clustered with cities (or metropolitan areas) of comparable size. See Table 1.1 and App. I, Table I-4.
9. Interview, Kate Godefroy, July 15, 1991.
10. *Statistical Abstract 1991*, Table 40.
11. Seattle Human Rights Commission, "Report of the Seattle Human Rights Commission Regarding the Monitoring and Investigation of Citizen Complaints of Police Harassment," November 8, 1990, 4.
12. Interview, Bob Boruchowitz, July 15, 1991.
13. See Eric Scigliano, "A Chief for All Seasons," *Seattle Weekly*, October 16, 1991, 41–42.

14. For a journalistic summary of this sequence of events, see Eric Scigliano, "The Noland Factor," *Seattle Weekly*, September 4, 1991, 31–33.
15. Interview, Councilman Tom Weeks, July 12, 1991.
16. For an analysis of Rice's victory, see *Seattle Times*, November 19, 1989.
17. Scigliano, "The Noland Factor," 32.
18. Interview, Lucinda Harder, January 2, 1992.
19. Tacoma Mun. Ordinance No. 24167 (1988).
20. Seattle Mun. Code 12A.10.010(B) (1985).
21. *Seattle v. Slack*, 113 Wash.2d 850 (1989).
22. Seattle Mun. Code, Chap. 12A.20.050(C).
23. Letter from Kathleen Taylor to Jane Noland, June 5, 1990.
24. Statement, presented in testimony to the Public Safety Committee of the Seattle City Council, June 19, 1990, first page (document unpaginated).
25. Letter from the Downtown Human Services Council to Jane Noland, June 18, 1990.
26. *Seattle Times*, June 21, 1990.
27. *Seattle Post-Intelligencer*, June 20, 1990.
28. Don Williamson, "Loitering Law: A Day Without Winners," *Seattle Times*, July 3, 1990.
29. *Seattle Post-Intelligencer*, July 11, 1990.
30. Seattle City Council Resolution 28198 (June 25, 1990).
31. "Report of the Seattle Human Rights Commission," 2.
32. "Seattle's Drug War on People of Color," American Civil Liberties Union of Washington, July 1992.
33. *Seattle Times*, August 14, 1992.
34. *Seattle Post-Intelligencer*, August 18, 1992.
35. *Seattle Post-Intelligencer*, August 11, 1993.
36. *Seattle Times*, August 18, 1992. The city attorney's office now provides statistics on arrests and charges to the council. Between January and May 1993 thirty-one arrests were made under the loitering law, twenty-six of them resulting in charges brought. Twenty of those arrested were African-American. City Attorney's Office, "Drug Traffic Loitering Summary Statistics," undated, unpaginated.
37. Seattle Mun. Code, Chap. 12A.12.015 (1987). The Washington drug-free zone law for schools is RCW 69.50.435 (1989).
38. The language describing the proscribed "drug area" is taken from a boiler-plate "Affidavit in Support of the Establishment of Orders to Stay Out of Drug Areas" used in the Municipal Court of Seattle and dated December 5, 1990.

*Chapter 8*
*Drug Prohibition on Demand?*

1. Franklin Zimring and Gordon Hawkins, *The Search for Rational Drug Control* (Cambridge: Cambridge University Press, 1992), xi.
2. Robert Kuttner, *Revolt of the Haves: Tax Rebellions and Hard Times* (New York: Simon and Schuster, 1980).

3. *Sourcebook 1989*, Table 2.47; *Sourcebook 1991*, Table 2.47. These survey figures should be put in context. In 1988 more than half of respondents said they favored the death penalty for rape and attempting to assassinate the president, and 49 percent for hijacking an airplane. Support for capital punishment of drug dealers was also skewed by 47 percent support from older people. If respondents of fifty years and over were eliminated, only about one-third of respondents would have been in favor. The 1990 poll did not give respondents the chance to make judgments about the death penalty for a variety of offenses but was cast as a kind of referendum on the debate going on in Congress. It might be argued that the much stronger support for imposing death on drug dealers found during the period of policy formulation and enactment, when legislators were stating their positions in the most visible forums, reflects, in part, the tendency mentioned above for policymakers to generate public demand as well as to respond to it.

4. See, for example, Arnold A. Gibbs, "Where Are the People's Champions," *Law Enforcement News*, June 15, 1993, 8. Gibbs refers to drug dealers almost offhandedly as "a different class of murderers," a particularly sweeping assumption from one who is assistant chief of police in Miami, a city full of drug dealers, some of whom are undoubtedly sentenced only to probation.

5. George Gallup, Jr., *The Gallup Report*, Report no. 285 (Princeton, N.J.: The Gallup Poll, June 1989), 4, 5.

6. U.S. Department of Health and Human Services, National Institute on Drug Abuse, "National Household Survey on Drug Abuse: Population Estimates 1991."

7. *Ibid.*, Table 17.

8. *Sourcebook 1990*, Table 2.4.

9. *Ibid.*, Tables 2.3, 2.25, and 2.89.

10. U.S. Department of Justice, Bureau of Justice Statistics, "Criminal Victimization in the United States, 1990" (Washington, D.C.: U.S. Department of Justice, February 1992), Table 6.

11. *Sourcebook 1988*, Table 2.107.

12. *Sourcebook 1990*, Table 2.29; *Sourcebook 1988*, Table 2.42.

13. *Sourcebook 1990*, Table 2.90.

14. *Sourcebook 1989*, Table 2.2.

15. *New York Times*, November 22, 1991.

16. For disjunctions between the experience of crime and the apprehension of it, see Stuart A. Scheingold, *The Politics of Law and Order: Street Crime and Public Policy* (New York: Longman, 1984); Wesley G. Skogan and Michael G. Maxfield, *Coping with Crime: Individual and Neighborhood Reactions* (Beverly Hills: Sage, 1981); Arthur Stinchcombe, Rebecca Adams, Carol A. Heimer, Kim Lane Scheppele, Tom W. Smith, and D. Garth Taylor, *Crime and Punishment: Changing Attitudes in America* (San Francisco: Jossey-Bass, 1980).

17. *Sourcebook 1988*, Table 2.28.

18. *Sourcebook 1990*, Tables 2.20 and 2.21. This trend has been noted at

least since the late 1970s. See James Garofalo, "Public Opinion About Crime: The Attitudes of Victims and Nonvictims in Selected Cities" (Washington, D.C.: U.S. Department of Justice, National Criminal Justice Information and Statistics Service, 1977), 15–16.

19. Anchorage Chamber of Commerce, "Anchorage Crime Commission Results" (Anchorage: Anchorage Chamber of Commerce, October 1988), unpaginated.

20. *Detroit News,* March 11, 1977, June 5, 1977, and May 19, 1978.

21. *Detroit News,* June 5, 1977, and June 15, 1977.

22. *Detroit News,* May 3, 1977, and July 28, 1978.

23. *Detroit News,* May 24, 1978.

24. *Detroit News,* August 31, 1978.

25. In 1989, for example, eighty-seven medical examiners reporting 7,162 drug abuse–related deaths in twenty-seven metropolitan areas attributed only 5 deaths (0.07 percent of the total) to marijuana alone, as compared with 28, or 3.9 percent, for aspirin alone. U.S. Department of Health and Human Services, Alcohol, Drug Abuse, and Mental Health Administration, "Data from the Drug Abuse Warning Network (DAWN), Annual Data 1989," Statistical series I, no. 9 (Rockville, Md.: National Institute on Drug Abuse, 1990), Table 3.10. There is a continuing dispute about whether marijuana can kill. Mark Kleiman points out that even the very rare attributions of death to marijuana that show up in some medical examiner reports are inconclusive, labeled "drug-related," rather than "drug-induced." See Mark A. R. Kleiman, *Marijuana: Costs of Abuse, Costs of Control* (New York: Greenwood Press, 1989), 12.

26. Federal Bureau of Investigation, *Uniform Crime Reports 1991, Crime in the United States* (Washington, D.C.: Government Printing Office, 1992), Tables 4.1 and 29.

27. Mark Kleiman's 1989 study of marijuana policy found that in 1982 about 40 percent of the federal drug enforcement budget was spent on arrest, prosecution, and incarceration in marijuana cases, and that this amount increased by 23 percent (in constant dollars) between 1982 and 1986, to $636 million. Kleiman, *Marijuana,* 85, 153. In 1988 then–Attorney General Edwin Meese announced (in a U.S. Department of Justice press release, July 13) a "comprehensive national strategy for ridding America of domestically grown marijuana," enlisting not only the Drug Enforcement Administration and Department of Justice, but also the Bureau of Land Management, the Fish and Wildlife Service, and the National Guard. Federal zeal is also evident in more recent adventures like Operation Green Sweep, which sent U.S. troops in military helicopters flying low over the King Range in northern California in late July 1990, purportedly to eradicate marijuana gardens on federal land but also conducting surveillance of private homes and gardens. See declarations filed with complaint in *Drug Policy Foundation v. Bennett,* Northern District of California, No. C-90-2278 FMS (August 20, 1990).

28. See Institute of Medicine, *Marijuana and Health* (Washington, D.C.: National Academy Press, 1982); the estimate of 20 million yearly marijuana users comes from "National Household Survey 1991," Table 3-A.

29. Mark A. R. Kleiman, *Against Excess: Drug Policy for Results* (New York: Basic Books, 1992), 253. There are, of course, contrary views, the most common of which blends the physical, mental, and social effects into an "a motivational syndrome," which is said to rob pot-smoking teen-agers of their ambitions and cost them dearly in adult achievement. See Robert L. DuPont, Jr., *Getting Tough on Gateway Drugs: A Guide for the Family* (Washington: American Psychiatric Press, 1984), 76–78.

30. *Los Angeles Times*, September 6, 1990.

31. U.S. Department of Justice press release, July 13, 1988.

32. *Sourcebook 1990*, Table 2.87.

33. Kleiman, *Marijuana*, 80.

34. Peter Reuter, "Prevalence Estimation and Policy Formulation," *The Journal of Drug Issues* 23, no. 2 (1993):173. Reuter bases his conclusion that "total drug consumption is dominated by the small share of all users who use heavily" on prevalence estimates derived from the National Household Survey of Drug Abuse and the High School Senior Survey sponsored by the National Institute on Drug Abuse.

35. U.S. Department of Commerce, Bureau of the Census, *Statistical Abstract of the United States 1991* (Washington, D.C.: Government Printing Office, 1991), Table 204; M. E. Hilton, "Drinking Patterns and Drinking Problems in 1984: Results from a General Population Survey," *Alcoholism: Clinical and Experimental Research* 11, no. 2 (1987), 167–175.

36. *Sourcebook 1990*, Table 3.82.

37. *Sourcebook 1990*, Table 3.74.

38. *Sourcebook 1990*, Tables 3.104 and 3.106.

39. U.S. Department of Justice, Bureau of Justice Statistics, "Profile of State Prison Inmates 1986," *Bulletin* (Washington, D.C.: U.S. Department of Justice, January 1988), Table 12; U.S. Department of Justice, National Institute of Justice, "Drug Use Forecasting—Drugs and Crime 1990: Annual Report" (Washington, D.C.: U.S. Department of Justice, August 1991), 16–17.

40. For a discussion of the complexities of separating out alcohol as an autonomous cause of automobile accidents, disease, and interpersonal violence, see Dean R. Gerstein, "Alcohol Use and Consequences," in *Alcohol and Public Policy: Beyond the Shadow of Prohibitions*, edited by Mark H. Moore and Dean R. Gerstein (Washington, D.C.: National Academy Press, 1981), 182–224; and James J. Collins, "Alcohol and Interpersonal Violence: Less Than Meets the Eye," in *Pathways to Criminal Violence: Contemporary Perspectives*, edited by Neil Allen Wiener and Marvin E. Wolfgang (Newbury Park, Calif.: Sage, 1989), 49–67.

41. U.S. Department of Justice, Bureau of Justice Statistics, "Profile of Jail Inmates, 1989," *Bulletin* (Washington, D.C.: U.S. Department of Justice, April 1991), Table 14.

42. The general tendency should not be overstated. The study of jail inmates

found that a few murders, rapes, and assaults (7.7 percent of the total of all offenses) were committed to obtain money for drugs, and that 20 percent of burglars said they were under the influence of alcohol when they committed their offense; furthermore, 36.4 percent of those who committed "other property" offenses were affected by alcohol, as opposed to 6.8 percent of those under the influence of drugs. This brings to mind the scene in the 1967 movie "Cool Hand Luke" where Paul Newman lands in jail for lopping off the heads of parking meters while on a binge.

43. *Uniform Crime Reports 1982*, Table 1; *Uniform Crime Reports 1991*, Table 2. These trends should be regarded with some caution. The National Crime Victimization Survey Report, which relies on interviews with a representative sample of American households rather than on resident reports of crime incidents to police, found violent crime (excluding murder, which obviously cannot be measured by victimization surveys) essentially unchanged ( − 0.54 percent) in the same period. U.S. Department of Justice, Bureau of Justice Statistics, "Criminal Victimization in the United States, 1991," December 1992, Table 1.

44. U.S. Department of Health and Human Services, "Data from the Drug Abuse Warning Network (DAWN) 1989" Table 2.15.

45. *Ibid.*, Table 3.06a.

46. Dorothy P. Rice, Sander Kelman, Leonard S. Miller, and Sarah Dunmeyer, *The Economic Costs of Alcohol and Drug Abuse and Mental Illness: 1985* (Rockville, Md.: U.S. Department of Health and Human Services, Alcohol, Drug Abuse, and Mental Health Administration, 1990), 23.

47. *Ibid.*, Table 1.

48. *Ibid.*, 24.

49. U.S. Department of Health and Human Services, "Data from the Drug Abuse Warning Network (DAWN), 1989," Table 3.16. We have no trend data for crack deaths, either. Cocaine deaths were, however, apparently rare before the 1980s. See Lester Grinspoon and James Bakalar, *Cocaine: A Drug and Its Social Evolution* (New York: Basic Books, 1976), 111–116.

50. U.S. Department of Justice, National Institute of Justice, "Drug Use Forecasting, Third Quarter 1991" (Washington, D.C.: U.S. Department of Justice, July 1992), 4–7.

51. "National Household Survey 1991," Table 5-A.

52. For a variety of ways of looking at the trend data from the late 1970s to the late 1980s, see *Sourcebook 1990*, Tables 3.77–3.85.

53. The Office of National Drug Control Policy reports that federal budget authority for drug treatment and research has almost doubled between 1989 and 1992. Office of National Drug Control Policy, *National Drug Control Strategy"* (Washington, D.C.: Government Printing Office, 1992), 59. President Clinton's 1993 drug strategy, however, included cuts for drug prevention and treatment programs.

54. *Anchorage Daily News*, January 31, 1989.

55. Interview, January 2, 1992.

## Chapter 9
### Beyond Drug Abuse: Three Other Agenda Items

1. Stuart A. Scheingold, *The Politics of Street Crime: Criminal Process and Cultural Obsession* (Philadelphia: Temple University Press, 1991), 5.
2. *Griswold v. Connecticut*, 381 U.S. 479 (1965).
3. See Armand L. Mauss, *Social Problems as Social Movements* (Philadelphia: J.B. Lippincott, 1975), 3–37.
4. The political scientist E. E. Schattschneider put it slightly differently when he said, "The definition of the alternatives is the supreme instrument of power." E. E. Schattschneider, *The Semisovereign People: A Realist's View of Democracy in America* (Hinsdale, Ill.: Dryden Press, 1975), 66. I mean to suggest agenda-setting as a phenomenon that includes determination of the setting within which alternatives are chosen or excluded. What Schattschneider would have called the "mobilization of bias" thus inheres in structural patterns of group and institutional behavior, rather than in the competition of conflicts. See Stephen Lukes, *Power: A Radical View* (London: Macmillan, 1974).
5. Harold Lasswell, *Psychopathology and Politics* (New York: Viking Press, 1960), 50.
6. Robert Eyestone, *From Social Issues to Public Policy* (New York: Wiley, 1978), 10.
7. Office of National Drug Control Policy, "Needle Exchange Programs: Are They Effective?" Bulletin no. 7, July 1992, 1.
8. Murray Edelman, *Constructing the Political Spectacle* (Chicago: University of Illinois Press, 1988), 27–28.
9. Roger W. Cobb and Charles D. Elder, *Participation in American Politics: The Dynamics of Agenda-Building*, second edition (Baltimore: Johns Hopkins University Press, 1983), 85–87.
10. Eyestone, *From Social Issues to Public Policy*, 135–152.
11. See Charles O. Jones, *An Introduction to the Study of Public Policy*, third edition (Monterey, Calif.: Brooks-Cole, 1984), 30.
12. For two analyses of perspectives on drugs that rely on some version of this contest, see Franklin Zimring and Gordon Hawkins, *The Search for Rational Drug Control* (Cambridge: Cambridge University Press, 1992), Chap. 1; and Peter Reuter, "Hawks Ascendant: The Punitive Trend of American Drug Policy," *Daedalus* 121, no. 3 (1992):15–52. A third group sometimes injects itself into the policy debate, those for whom the principal significance of drugs in American life is not the ingestion of drugs but the selective prohibition of them, which they believe generates violence, public corruption, and property crime that, taken together, constitute a social ill at least as serious as drug abuse. I'm not examining this problem definition here because what interests me for the moment is how people turn their perceptions of conditions in the social world around them into political demand, not how people develop critiques of policy.
13. See Zimring and Hawkins, *The Search for Rational Drug Control*, 10–15.

14. An exception to this is Representative Charles Schumer, whose position on the death penalty for drug kingpins is discussed in Chapter 12.
15. *Sourcebook 1991*, Table 2.83.
16. *Sourcebook 1991*, Table 2.84.
17. *Sourcebook 1990*, Table 2.92.
18. Joseph E. Jacoby and Christopher S. Dunn, "National Survey on Punishment for Criminal Offenses: Executive Summary" (Bowling Green, Ohio: Bowling Green State University, 1987), Table 2.
19. *Ibid.*, Tables 4 and 6.
20. *Sourcebook 1990*, Table 2.94; *Sourcebook 1991*, Table 2.88.
21. *Sourcebook 1991*, Table 2.89.
22. See John W. Kingdon, *Agendas, Alternatives, and Public Policies* (Boston: Little, Brown, 1984), 153–157.
23. See Clarence Lusane, *Pipe Dream Blues: Racism and the War on Drugs* (Boston: South End Press, 1991), 45–46; and Dorothy Roberts, "Punishing Drug Addicts Who Have Babies: Women of Color, Equality and the Right to Privacy," *Harvard Law Review* 104 (1991):1419. Median sentence length for drug-trafficking offenses (new court commitments to state prisons) in 1989, the last year for which data are available, was thirty-six months for whites and forty-eight months for blacks. U.S. Department of Justice, Bureau of Justice Statistics, "National Corrections Reporting Program, 1989" (Washington, D.C.: U.S. Department of Justice, November 1992), Table 1-7.
24. For an argument that forces of orthodoxy and progressivity, generated by religious groups, are locked in a struggle for the soul of American social values, see James Davison Hunter, *Culture Wars: The Struggle to Define America* (New York: Basic Books, 1991).
25. The rate of change in state and local government revenues (in constant 1982 dollars) for the country as a whole dropped off sharply, from an average annual increase during the 1966–1973 business cycle of 6.5 percent, to 1.9 percent during the 1973–1979 cycle, and remained low, at 2.1 percent, during the 1979–1989 cycle. *Economic Report of the President, 1991* (Washington, D.C.: Government Printing Office, 1991), Tables B-82 and B-3.
26. *Ibid.*, Table B-94.
27. U.S. Department of Commerce, Bureau of the Census, *Historical Statistics of the United States: Colonial Times to 1970*, part 2, series V (Washington, D.C.: Government Printing Office, 1976), 20–30.

*Chapter 10*
*Controlling the Dangerous Classes*

1. S. Francis Milsom, *The Historical Foundations of Common Law* (London: Butterworths, 1969), 13.
2. William Chambliss, "A Sociological Analysis of the Law of Vagrancy," *Social Problems* 12 (Summer 1964):67–77.
3. Christopher Hill, *The Century of Revolution, 1603–1714* (New York: W. W. Norton, 1961), 23–28.

4. Frances Fox Piven and Richard Cloward, *Regulating the Poor: The Functions of Public Welfare* (New York: Pantheon, 1971), 12–14.

5. A racial element fed the creation of the category, as it was carved out of the larger subordinated group of workers. A French sociologist comments:

> For the first time [in early nineteenth-century Paris] those aspects typical of every procedure of racialization of a social group right down to our own day are condensed in a single discourse: material and spiritual poverty, criminality, congenital vice (alcoholism, drugs), physical and moral defects, dirtiness, sexual promiscuity and the specific diseases which threaten humanity with 'degeneracy'. . . . Through these themes, there forms the phantasmatic equation of 'labouring classes' with 'dangerous classes', the fusion of a socioeconomic category with an anthropological and moral category, which will serve to underpin all the variants of sociobiological (and also psychiatric) determinism, by taking pseudo-scientific credentials from the Darwinian theory of evolution, comparative anatomy and crowd psychology, but particularly by becoming invested in a tightly knit network of institutions of social surveillance and control.

Etienne Balibar, " 'Class Racism,' " in *Race, Nation, Class*, edited by Etienne Balibar and Immanuel Wallerstein (London: Verso, 1991), 209.

6. Louis Chevalier, *Laboring Classes and Dangerous Classes* (Princeton, N.J.: Princeton University Press, 1973).

7. Antoinette Wills, *Crime and Punishment in Revolutionary Paris* (Westport, Conn.: Greenwood Press, 1989), 99.

8. Chevalier, *Laboring Classes*, 8–9.

9. Douglas Hay, "Property, Authority and the Criminal Law," in *Albion's Fatal Tree: Crime and Society in Eighteenth-Century England*, edited by Douglas Hay, Peter Linebaugh, John G. Rule, E. P. Thompson, and Cal Winslow (New York: Pantheon, 1975), 25.

10. The 1888 English translation of the Communist Manifesto uses the term "dangerous class" as a translation for "lumpen proletariat" in the German editions. Karl Marx and Frederick Engels, *Collected Works: Volume 6, 1845–1848* (New York: International Publishers, 1976), 494. The concept of the lumpen proletariat as Marx and Engels developed it differs from the "dangerous class" as popularly used in that it does not include criminality as a major element. It does, however, suggest a threat to bourgeois society by its very existence as a "passive rotting mass thrown off by the lowest layers of old society."

11. Michael Katz, *The Undeserving Poor: From the War on Poverty to the War on Welfare* (New York: Pantheon, 1989), 14.

12. Robert H. Bremner, *From the Depths: The Discovery of Poverty in the United States* (New York: New York University, 1956), 5–6. A refinement on this association was the distinction between poverty and pauperism, the latter being the condition of poverty dependent on public relief,

which acquired a morally negative connotation almost as soon as poor laws were enacted. Katz, *The Undeserving Poor*, 13. Gertrude Himmelfarb describes the explicit institutionalization of this distinction in England in the Royal Commission report of 1834 on the reform of the poor laws and the subsequent New Poor Law, which intensified the stigma of pauperism. *The Idea of Poverty: England in the Early Industrial Age* (New York: Random House, 1983), 159–174.

13. It has been suggested that the attitudes of Progressive reforms that gave rise to modern police forces in the early twentieth century helped shape perspectives on drug-taking as criminal—an attention to underworld associations of lower-class drug users rather than how their drug use met needs similar to those of users who were middle-class women and physicians. The association of "pleasure drug use" with lower class and minority people weakened the developing medical perspective and strengthened the criminal one; "the compassionate impulse to comfort the wretched became more and more a determination to administer a good swift kick to the wayward." Dean R. Gerstein and Henrick J. Harwood, eds. *Treating Drug Problems*, Vol. 1. (Washington, D.C.: National Academy Press (Institute of Medicine), 1990), 48.

14. Charles Loring Brace, *The Dangerous Classes of New York, and Twenty Years Work Among Them* (New York: Wynkoop and Hallenbeck, 1872), 28–29.

15. Frank Browning and John Gerassi, *The American Way of Crime: From Salem to Watergate* (New York: Putnam, 1980), 266–278.

16. David Musto, *The American Disease: Origins of Narcotic Control*, expanded edition (New York: Oxford University Press, 1987), 245.

17. The particularly ferocious association of criminality and foreignness after World War I is discussed in John Higham, *Strangers in the Land: Patterns of American Nativism, 1860–1925* (New Brunswick: Rutgers University Press, 1988). Higham cites (p. 268) a Wyoming statute, passed in the early 1920s, that provided that aliens could not possess "any dirk, pistol, shot gun, rifle, or other fire arm, bowie knife, dagger, or any other dangerous or deadly weapon."

18. Murray Edelman, *Constructing the Political Spectacle* (Chicago: University of Illinois Press, 1988), 74.

19. Ellen Willis, "Hell No, I Won't Go," *Village Voice*, September 19, 1989, 29.

20. The position that the legalization proposal is racist is a corollary of the view, held even by some African-American leaders, that through a white "conspiracy," drugs were "deliberately and systematically brought into the black communities" to suppress or even exterminate them. Testimony of Dr. Lorraine Hale, U.S. Congress, House of Representatives, "Intravenous Drug Use and AIDS: The Impact on the Black Community," *Hearing Before the Select Committee on Narcotics Abuse and Control*, 100th Congress, 1st session, September 25, 1987, 39. See also Clarence Lusane, *Pipe Dream Blues: Racism and the War on Drugs* (Boston: South End Press, 1991), 13.

21. Michel Foucault, *Discipline and Punish* (New York: Pantheon, 1977), 7.
22. Address of Arnold I. Burns, Deputy Attorney General, before the 1986 Office of Labor-Management Standards Managers' Conference, U.S. Department on Labor, New Orleans, Louisiana, November 17, 1986, 8.
23. British writers also note a linkage between traditional concepts of the "dangerous classes" and modern concerns about disruptive youth, and the extent to which drugs symbolize their unmanageability. See Virginia Berridge and Griffith Edwards, *Opium and the People: Opiate Use in Nineteenth-Century England* (New Haven: Yale University Press, 1987), 237.
24. Wiley B. Sanders, ed., *Juvenile Offenders for a Thousand Years* (Chapel Hill: University of North Carolina Press, 1970), 41.
25. Herbert Asbury, *The Gangs of New York: An Informal History of the Underworld* (New York: Paragon House, 1927), 238–239.
26. Federal Bureau of Investigation, *Uniform Crime Reports 1990, Crime in the United States* (Washington, D.C.: Government Printing Office, 1991), Table 27. The number of persons between the ages of ten and nineteen dropped more than 10 percent between 1980 and 1990, from 39,468,000 to 34,981,000. U.S. Department of Commerce, Bureau of the Census, *Statistical Abstract of the United States 1992* (Washington, D.C.: Government Printing Office, 1992), Table 12.
27. *Statistical Abstract 1992*, Table 718.
28. For data on public confidence in public schools, the Supreme Court, organized religion, etc., see Harris and Gallup polls from the early 1970s through 1991, synthesized in *Sourcebook 1991*, Tables 2.4, 2.5, 2.7, and 2.37; and Seymour Martin Lipset and William Schneider, *The Confidence Gap: Business, Labor and Government in the Public Mind* (New York: The Free Press, 1983).
29. For an interesting discussion of "moral panics," with a focus on attitudes toward youth culture in Britain, see Stanley Cohen, *Folk Devils and Moral Panics: the Creation of the Mods and Rockers* (London: MacGibbon and Kee, 1972).
30. *Statistical Abstract 1991*, Table 128.
31. Anchorage Chamber of Commerce, "Anchorage Crime Commission Results" (Anchorage: Anchorage Chamber of Commerce, October 1988), unpaginated.
32. The statewide survey undertaken by Hellenthal Associates, Anchorage, found 38.2 percent of 606 adults interviewed by phone in support of keeping the possession of small amounts of marijuana in the home legal, while 59.9 percent favored making it illegal. A consultant report prepared for Alaskans for Privacy stated that "voters are inclined by a ratio of 2-to-1 to vote for the initiative," and the Anchorage survey on which it was based found that out of 103 adults surveyed, 44 believed that the existing Alaska law allowing possession in the home of less than four ounces of marijuana has caused "harm" to Alaska. (The unpublished and incomplete nature of materials prepared for this political contest makes it difficult to comply with scholarly citation standards. Data from the Hellenthal Associates survey appear to be on page

6, but no survey title is provided. Only the executive summary and selected data tabulations for the Alaskans for Privacy survey are available. They are in my possession.)

33. *Anchorage Times*, October 11, 1990.

34. James O. Eastland, "Introduction" to U.S. Congress, Senate, *Hearings Before the Subcommittee To Investigate the Administration of the Internal Security Act and Other Internal Security Laws, Senate Judiciary Committee* (hereinafter *Hearings*, 93d Congress), 93d Congress, 2d session, May 9, 17, 16, 20, 21; June 13, 1974, xi.

35. See Senate, *Hearings*, 93d Congress.

36. Elizabeth Coleman Brynner, "New Parental Push Against Marijuana," *New York Times Magazine*, February 10, 1980, 36.

37. Jan Skirrow and Edward Sawka, "Alcohol and Drug Prevention Strategies—An Overview," *Contemporary Drug Problems* 14 (Summer 1987):167.

38. Brochures and newsletters on the approach and activities of the National Federation of Parents for Drug-Free Youth are available from NFP National Office, 9551 Big Bend, St. Louis, MO 63122-6519.

39. "Marijuana: What Parents Must Learn," NFP brochure, not dated or paginated.

40. Brynner, "New Parental Push," 53.

41. *Anchorage Times*, September 27, 1989.

42. News release, office of Senator Frank Murkowski (not dated, but probably September 1989).

43. *New York Times*, February 3, 1990.

44. *Statistical Abstract 1991*, Table 450; *Statistical Abstract 1977*, Table 814.

45. National Federation of Parents for Drug-Free Youth, "Guidelines for Organizing a Parent Group in Your Neighborhood," unpaginated, n.d.

46. *New Perspectives Quarterly* (Summer 1989):4. For a trenchant analysis of Bennett's perspective as expressed in the "National Drug Control Strategy, 1989," see Franklin Zimring and Gordon Hawkins, *The Search for Rational Drug Control* (Cambridge: Cambridge University Press, 1992), 3–10.

47. *Sourcebook 1991*, Table 2.2.

48. Quoted in Skip Hollandsworth, "Straight Rides over Kids Again . . . And Some Say They Love It," in *Drug Prohibition and the Conscience of Nations*, edited by Arnold S. Trebach and Kevin B. Zeese (Washington, D.C.: Drug Policy Foundation, 1990), 168. Straight closed down in June 1993, victim of declining enrollments and inquiry into its practices in several states, according to the Drug Policy Foundation. *Drug Policy Letter*, August/September 1993, 27.

49. For examples of both perspectives, see selections in Oscar Handlin, ed., *Immigration as a Factor in American History* (Englewood Cliffs, N.J.: Prentice-Hall, 1959), especially Charles F. Read, "Lorenzo Papanti, Teacher of Dancing," 133–135, and Mary R. Coolidge, "Chinese Immigration," 169–171.

50. "The Waterhouse Posse," *Kansas City Star* (Sunday magazine), November 27, 1988.
51. *Ibid.*
52. See *Detroit News*, June 5, 1977, and July 28, 1978.
53. *Congressional Record*, October 16, 1991, H7958.
54. A 1991 article in *Volunteers in Prevention*, a publication of the parent-led drug prevention network, is entitled "Profile of the Enemy" and names the ACLU, National Organization for the Reform of Marijuana Laws (NORML), and the Drug Policy Foundation, which it says "supports legalizing crack and other drugs." (The 1987/1988 biennial report of the foundation says, "The Foundation is not a legalization organization, even though many in the Foundation support outright legalization.")
55. Howard S. Becker, *Outsiders: Studies in the Sociology of Deviance* (New York: Free Press, 1973), 9.
56. Letter from Lynda Adams, *Anchorage Times*, April 28, 1988.
57. "Drug Policy and the Intellectuals," a speech given by William J. Bennett, Director, Office of National Drug Control Policy, Kennedy School of Government, Harvard University, December 11, 1989.
58. Interview, April 2, 1992.
59. Letter to the Editor, *The Northeast Detroiter*, from Paul A. Rosenbaum, March 1, 1978. Subject Files, State Archives, Bureau of History, Michigan Department of State, MS 78: Accession #126 (Box 945).
60. See Jerome H. Skolnick, "Rethinking the Drug Problem," *Daedalus* 121 (Summer 1992):141–142.
61. "Kansas City Illustrated," KCPT-TV, November 29, 1991.
62. Interview, January 3, 1992.
63. Interview, Lucinda Harder, January 2, 1992.
64. For a description of the role of moral entrepreneurs, see Becker, *Outsiders*, Chap. 8.
65. Interview, July 18, 1991.
66. Charles P. Wohlforth, "Off the Pot," *New Republic*, December 3, 1990, 10.

*Chapter 11*
*The Ambiguous Significance of Race*

1. Norval Morris, "Race and Crime: What Evidence Is There That Race Influences Results in the Criminal Justice System?" *Judicature* 72 (August-September 1988):113.
2. Jerome G. Miller, "Hobbling a Generation: Young African American Males in the Criminal Justice System of America's Cities: Baltimore, Maryland," (Alexandria, Va.: National Center on Institutions and Alternatives, September 1992), 3.
3. Clarence Lusane, *Pipe Dream Blues: Racism and the War on Drugs* (Boston: South End Press, 1991), 4.
4. Jim Baumohl, "The 'Dope Fiend's Paradise' Revisited: Notes from Research in Progress on Drug Law Enforcement in San Francisco, 1875–

1915," *The Drinking and Drug Practices Surveyor* 24 (June 1992): 3–12. For the significance of race in American drug history, see David Musto, *The American Disease: Origins of Narcotic Control,* expanded edition (New York: Oxford University Press, 1987).

5. John Helmer, *Drugs and Minority Oppression* (New York: The Seabury Press, 1975), 13.

6. Musto, *The American Disease,* 283, n. 15.

7. Federal Bureau of Investigation, *Uniform Crime Reports 1991, Crime in the United States* (Washington, D.C.: Government Printing Office, 1992), Table 43. The estimate of the fifteen to twenty-four population is extrapolated from U.S. Department of Commerce, Bureau of the Census, *Statistical Abstract of the United States* (Washington, D.C.: Government Printing Office, 1991), Table 12.

8. *Washington Post,* May 17, 1992.

9. Extrapolated from U.S. Department of Justice, Bureau of Justice Statistics, "National Corrections Reporting Program, 1989," (Washington, D.C.: U.S. Department of Justice, November 1992), Table 1-5.

10. *Uniform Crime Reports 1985,* Table 45; *Uniform Crime Reports 1990,* Table 44.

11. Extrapolated from U.S. Department of Justice, Bureau of Justice Statistics, "National Corrections Reporting Program, 1987" (Washington, D.C.: U.S. Department of Justice, April 1992), Table 1-5.

12. U.S. Department of Health and Human Services, Alcohol, Drug Abuse, and Mental Health Administration, "National Household Survey on Drug Abuse: Population Estimates 1991" (Rockville, Md.: National Institute on Drug Abuse, 1991), Tables 2-D and 2-B; U.S. Department of Health and Human Services, Alcohol, Drug Abuse, and Mental Health Administration, "Annual Emergency Room Data 1990: Data from the Drug Abuse Warning Network (DAWN)" (Rockville, Md.: National Institute on Drug Abuse, 1991), Table 2.01.

13. "National Household Survey 1991," Tables 2-B, 2-C, and 2-D.

14. Jerome G. Miller, "Search and Destroy: The Plight of African American Males in the Criminal Justice System," Alexandria: National Center on Institutions and Alternatives, September 1992. Manuscript.

15. Jerald G. Bachman, John M. Wallace, Jr., Candace L. Kurth, Lloyd D. Johnston, and Patrick M. O'Malley, "Drug Use Among Black, White, Hispanic, Native American, and Asian American High School Seniors (1976–1989): Prevalence, Trends and Correlates" (Ann Arbor, Mich.: Institute for Social Research, University of Michigan, 1990), Table 4. It should perhaps be noted that while the high-school survey does not, by definition, reach young people who have dropped out of high school, blacks are probably not substantially overrepresented among that group. In 1989, 14.6 percent of whites eighteen to twenty-one years old, and 17.4 percent of blacks, were not high-school graduates. *Statistical Abstract 1991,* Table 258.

16. "Household Survey 1991," Tables 2-D and 2-B.

17. "Household Survey 1991," Tables 20-B, 20-D, 21-B, and 21-D.

18. "Household Survey 1991," Tables 2-A and 2-D.
19. "Household Survey 1991," Tables 5-A and 5-D.
20. Lusane, *Pipe Dream Blues*, 25. The figures for the number of young African-American male crack users are extrapolated from "Household Survey," Table 5-D, assuming the proportion of male and female users to be the same for the eighteen to thirty-five age group as for the using population as a whole; the figure for the general population of African-American males in that age group is extrapolated from *Statistical Abstract 1991*, Table 12, assuming the number of African-American males to be half of the total of males and females in that age group.
21. "Household Survey 1991," 10.
22. Bachman et al., "Drug Use," 43–46.
23. "Household Survey 1991," 10; Bachman et al., "Drug Use," 39.
24. For evidence of declining use among all groups, see Bachman et al., "Drug Use," Figure 1; and U.S. Department of Health and Human Services, Alcohol, Drug Abuse, and Mental Health Administration, "National Household Survey on Drug Abuse: Highlights 1990" (Rockville, Md.: National Institute on Drug Abuse, 1991), 13–18.
25. Alfred Blumstein, "On the Racial Disproportionality of United States' Prison Populations," *Journal of Criminal Law and Criminology* 73, no. 3 (1982):1259–1281; Joan Petersilia, "Racial Disparities in the Criminal Justice System," R-2947-NIC (Santa Monica, Calif.: RAND Corporation, 1983).
26. Stephen Klein, Joan Petersilia, and Susan Turner, "Race and Imprisonment Decisions in California," *Science* February 16, 1990, 812–816. The crimes for which race was insignificant as a predictor of the in/out decision were assault, robbery, burglary, theft, and forgery. The researchers also found that race played no role in predicting the length of prison sentence for any of the crimes studied.

    An analysis conducted by the *San Jose Mercury News* of dispositions for 2,290 first offenders convicted of sale or transportation of drugs in California is also instructive in this area. Twelve percent of Hispanics were sentenced to prison, as opposed to jail or probation, while 8 percent of blacks and only 6 percent of whites got prison terms. *San Jose Mercury News*, December 8, 1991.
27. Theodore G. Chiricos and William D. Bales, "Unemployment and Punishment: An Empirical Assessment," *Criminology* 29, no. 4 (1991):701–724; Texas study cited in Miller, "Search and Destroy," 16.
28. U.S. Sentencing Commission, "Mandatory Minimum Penalties in the Federal Criminal Justice System" (Washington, D.C.: U.S. Sentencing Commission, August 1991), 76.
29. *Ibid.*, 82.
30. *Ibid.*, 14.
31. Blacks charged with federal offenses of all kinds are somewhat more likely than whites to be detained pending trial. *Sourcebook 1991*, Table 5.9. In 1988 a thirteen-state survey found that among juvenile defendants charged with drug offenses, 25 percent of whites and 52 percent

of blacks were detained pending disposition. *Sourcebook 1991*, Table 5.93.

32. Allen E. Liska and Mark Tausig, "Theoretical Interpretations of Social Class and Racial Differentials in Legal Decision-Making for Juveniles," *Sociological Quarterly* 20 (Spring 1979):205.

33. *Philadelphia Inquirer*, November 1, 1992.

34. I have been told this so often in so many places by so many victims that I do not feel the usual scholarly impulse to cite published sources. My most credible sources are African-American male students at City College of New York (about 40 percent of the student body is black), who tell me with astonishing frequency of being stopped and frisked for drugs (and weapons) when they are on perfectly innocent errands. They are most likely to be harassed when traveling in groups without women present, and four young males out on the town on Saturday night in certain neighborhoods in New York City are more likely than not to be stopped. (Students have told me that they don't even go out in groups of more than two on weekend nights for this reason; one recently told me that in the course of driving across Brooklyn with a friend to a party on a weekend night he was stopped three times by police.) That the law enforcement attention is triggered by race appears virtually certain because it occurs no matter how well-dressed my students are or how clean and new their car is. See also Tracey Maclin, "Black and Blue: African-Americans and Police," *Reconstruction* 2, no. 1 (1992):13–16.

35. *The Detroit News*, April 26, 1990.

36. An overview article on Drug Enforcement Administration profiles for drug traffickers is Charles L. Becton, "The Drug Courier Profile: 'All seems infected that th'infected spy, as all looks yellow to the jaundic'd eye,' " *North Carolina Law Review* 65, no. 3 (1987):417–480.

37. *Orlando Sentinel*, August 23, 1992.

38. *Delaware v. Prouse*, 440 U.S. 648 (1979), 661.

39. See, for example, *The Washington Post*, May 12, 1992; *USA Today*, December 20, 1989, and December 20, 1990; *Dallas Times Herald*, August 19, 1990; *The Philadelphia Inquirer*, November 1, 1992; *Albany Times Union*, May 17, 18, and 19, 1991; *San Jose Mercury News*, December 8, 9 and 10, 1991. A collection of news articles from around the country on racial disparities and criminal justice is available from The Sentencing Project in Washington, D.C.

40. Sacramento Superior Court Presiding Judge James Ford likened the effect of drug penalties on blacks to the impact of Jim Crow laws. *Sacramento Bee*, December 10, 1990.

41. *Washington Post*, May 1, 1992.

42. See Tom W. Smith, "Ethnic Images," GSS Topical report no. 19 (Chicago: National Opinion Research Center, University of Chicago, December 1990).

43. Studs Terkel, *Race: How Blacks and Whites Think and Feel About the American Obsession* (New York: The New Press, 1992), 45.

44. *Statistical Abstract 1991*, Table 40; Terkel, *Race*, 142, 235.

45. Terkel, *Race*, 104.

46. A background factor here is probably the larger sense, mentioned earlier, that blacks were intruding on white rights and privilege. Blacks made up over 60 percent of the city of Detroit in the late 1970s, at least triple their share of the city's population immediately after World War II, and tremendous resentment was directed at blacks for the city's decay, much of which was actually caused by corporate migration to the suburbs and government policies of disinvestment in Detroit. See Joe T. Darden, Richard Child Hill, June Thomas, and Richard Thomas, *Detroit: Race and Uneven Development* (Philadelphia: Temple University Press, 1987), especially Chap. 2.

47. George Gallup, Jr., *The Gallup Report*, Report no. 124, (Princeton, N.J.: The Gallup Poll, October 1975), 15.

48. Arrests of blacks for drug violations made up 21.8 percent of the total in 1976, while they constituted only 11.5 percent of the national population. Extrapolated from *Statistical Abstract 1977*, Tables 296 and 24.

49. One of the clearest statements of the requirement of "prior discrimination" (since modified and qualified in some respects) can be found in *Wygant v. Jackson Board of Education*, 476 U.S. 267 (1986). Race-conscious remedies for minorities and justice system disparities are, of course, conceptually very different. In one case, the issue is setting the standard for distributing benefits, and in the other it is the obverse, putting restrictions on the reach of repressive mechanisms. But in the public mind these problems are corollary, linked by the common presumption that individual merit and desert take precedence over what Derrick Bell calls "the equality policy choice." Derrick Bell, *Race, Racism and American Law*, third edition (Boston: Little, Brown, 1992), 61.

50. Interview, Harriett Walden, January 16, 1992.

51. Interview, Jeri Ware, January 8, 1992.

52. Seattle Human Rights Commission, "Report of the Seattle Human Rights Commission Regarding the Monitoring and Investigation of Citizen Complaints of Police Harassment," November 8, 1990, 20.

53. *Seattle Times*, July 15, 1992.

54. *Ibid.*

55. *Seattle Post-Intelligencer*, August 18, 1992.

56. *Seattle Times*, April 25, 1991.

57. Readers may remember that in Chapter 8, I discussed evidence that nationally blacks are not likely to have as punitive attitudes as whites. While Kansas City in 1990 might be an exception to the general rule, it is also possible that beleaguered community residents might voice their support for harsh treatment of crack dealers among them and still respond to a questionnaire in support of more pacific approaches. For the "situational perspective" on understanding public opinion, see W. Lance Bennett, *Public Opinion in American Politics* (New York: Harcourt Brace Jovanovich, 1980).

58. Interview, Steve Glorioso, September 18, 1991.

59. *Ibid.*
60. George L. Kelling, Tony Pate, Duane Dickman, and Charles E. Brown, *The Kansas City Preventive Patrol Experiment* (Washington, D.C.: The Police Foundation, 1974); U.S. Department of Justice, National Institute of Justice, "Community Policing in Seattle: A Model Partnership Between Citizens and Police" (Washington, D.C.: U.S. Department of Justice, August 1992).
61. Interview, Cliff Sargeon, September 19, 1991.
62. As of November 1, 1992, 110 of law enforcement (as opposed to civilian) personnel in the Seattle Police Department were black, out of a total of 1,232. Personal communication from Seattle Police Department, taken from the internal "EEO Job Category Report," January 1993. As of January 1, 1993, 148 of law enforcement personnel in the Kansas City Police Department were black, out of a total of 1,138. Personal communication from Kansas City Police Department, taken from the internal "Law Enforcement Breakdown by Ethnic Group Report," January 1993.
63. For an even-handed profile of former Seattle Chief of Police Pat Fitzsimons, see Eric Scigliano, "A Chief for All Seasons," *Seattle Weekly*, October 16, 1991.
64. An interview with Joiner appeared in *Law Enforcement News*, January 15, 1989.
65. *Statistical Abstract 1991*, Table 40.
66. Dan Fleissner, Nicholas Fedan, Ezra Stotland, and David Klinger, "Community Policing in Seattle: A Descriptive Study of the South Seattle Crime Reduction Project," Seattle Police Department (1991), 60.
67. For an analysis of the relationship between economic organization and urban employment problems, see William Julius Wilson, *The Truly Disadvantaged: The Inner City, the Underclass, and Public Policy* (Chicago: University of Chicago Press, 1987), 100—104.
68. See *McCleskey v. Kemp*, 481 U.S. 279 (1987), where the Supreme Court ruled that racial disparity in imposing the death penalty did not create a constitutionally significant risk of bias in an individual case unless the statute under which the defendant had been sentenced had been passed "to further a racially discriminatory purpose."
69. Derrick Bell points out, however, that Congress has failed to approve the Racial Justice Act, which would have required the Supreme Court to set aside a death sentence where the defendant provided convincing evidence of racial disparity in capital sentencing in the jurisdiction where the sentence was imposed. Bell, *Race*, 337—338.
70. Evidence that both grass-roots and professional groups are beginning to focus on inequality of condition appeared in prominent articles on two successive days in the *New York Times*. See "Pollution-Weary Minorities Try Civil Rights Tack," January 11, 1993, A1; and "Commission Says Racism Contributes to AIDS Spread," January 12, 1993, A14.

*Chapter 12*
*Drug Prohibition as a Political Resource*

1. U.S. Congress, House of Representatives, *Hearings Before the Subcommittee on Crime, the Committee on the Judiciary, on Federal Death Penalty Legislation*, 101st Congress, 2d session, March 14, 1990, 1.
2. U.S. Congress, Senate, *Hearings Before the Committee on the Judiciary on S.32, S.1225, and S.1696*, 101st Congress, 1st session, September 19, 1989, 24.
3. Comprehensive Violent Crime Act of 1991, H.R. 1400.
4. These are types of prohibition advocates, categorized by their relationship to the policies they are advocating—not to be confused with the three types of policy roles played by those involved in controlling the dangerous classes first introduced in Chapter 9.
5. Michael Barone and Grant Ujifusa, *The Almanac of American Politics 1992* (Washington, D.C.: National Journal, 1991), 264, 1087.
6. *Ibid.*, 1087, 264, 283.
7. *Ibid.*, 1086, 264, 283.
8. *Congressional Record*, June 25, 1991, S8544.
9. U.S. Congress, House of Representatives, *Hearings Before the Subcommittee on Civil and Constitutional Rights of the Committee on the Judiciary on H.R. 4618, H.R. 105, H.R. 596, H.R. 1197, H.R. 1464, H.R. 1477, H.R. 2196, Title I of 2709, and Titles I and II of H.R. 3119*, 101st Congress, 2d session, May 9, 1990, 475.
10. My use of the term "delegate" is based loosely on the concept of a representational style where the legislator follows the implicit or explicit instructions of those represented, in contrast to the Burkean ideal of the representative as trustee, who acts on the basis of judgment and conscience. See Ross J.S. Hoffman and Paul Levack, eds., *Burke's Politics* (New York: Knopf, 1959).
11. U.S. Congress, House of Representatives, *Hearings Before the Subcommittee on Crime and Criminal Justice, Committee on the Judiciary*, 102d Congress, 1st session, May 29, 1991, 60.
12. *Ibid.*, 111.
13. *Ibid.*, 166.
14. *Congressional Record*, October 16, 1991, H7958.
15. *Ibid.*, H7895-7896.
16. *Ibid.*, H7958.
17. Interview, April 19, 1993.
18. *Congressional Record*, October 16, 1991, H7956.
19. "The 1993 National Summit on U.S. Drug Policy," transcript of meeting on May 7, 1993, available from Columbia Institute, 8 E Street, S.E., Washington, DC 20003, 10.
20. Quoted in Death Penalty Information Center, "Millions Misspent: What Politicians Don't Say About the High Costs of the Death Penalty" (Washington, D.C.: Death Penalty Information Center, October 1992), 10. Such blatant exploitation of the drug problem as fodder for political

attacks is not new. Nixon's advisers urged him to wage a symbolic war against street crime and drugs, proposing law enforcement measures that liberal Democrats would find unpalatable, enabling them to be cast as "soft on crime." Edward Jay Epstein, *Agency of Fear: Opiates and Political Power in America* (New York: G. P. Putnam, 1977), Chap. 5.

21. Interview, April 2, 1992.
22. *Hearings Before the Subcommittee on Civil and Constitutional Rights*, May 9, 1990, 481.
23. *Statistical Abstract 1991*, Table 35.
24. *New York Times*, September 6, 1989.
25. *New York Times*, September 7, 1989.
26. *Sourcebook 1989*, Table 2.89.
27. Elizabeth Drew, "Letter from Washington," *The New Yorker*, October 2, 1989, 104.
28. *New York Times*, January 19, 1990.
29. *Michigan State News*, May 4, 1978.
30. Letters to various constituents from Paul A. Rosenbaum, 1978. Michigan State Archives (Box 945).
31. Interview, October 15, 1991.
32. *New York Times*, December 8, 1975. The findings on the New York drug law were issued in Joint Committee on New York Drug Law Evaluation, *The Nation's Toughest Drug Law: Evaluating the New York Experience* (New York: The Association of the Bar of the City of New York, 1977).
33. *Anchorage Daily News*, January 31, 1989.
34. *Anchorage Times*, November 2, 1989.
35. *Anchorage Daily News*, October 29, 1989.
36. Murray Edelman, *Political Language: Words That Succeed and Policies That Fail* (New York: Academic Press, 1977), 149.
37. For a discussion of individualistic and structural concepts of crime, see Stuart A. Scheingold, *The Politics of Street Crime: Criminal Process and Cultural Obsession* (Philadelphia: Temple University Press, 1991), 4–7.

*Chapter 13*
*Drug Prohibition as a Material Resource*

1. Many scholars have conceptualized policy types. See Theodore J. Lowi, "American Business, Public Policy, Case Studies, and Political Theory," *World Politics* 16, no. 4 (1964):677–715; and Randall B. Ripley, *Policy Analysis in Political Science* (Chicago, Ill.: Nelson-Hall, 1985), Chap. 3. While the typologies often include additional categories, the analytical essentials are contained in only three.
2. For a first-rate analysis of the distributive aspects of criminal justice policy, see Malcolm M. Feeley and Austin D. Sarat, *The Policy Dilemma: Federal Crime Policy and the Law Enforcement Assistance Administration, 1968–1978* (Minneapolis: University of Minnesota Press, 1980).
3. Karl Marx, *Theories of Surplus Value, Part I* (Moscow: Progress Publishers, 1963), 387.

4. Mimi Abramovitz and Frances Fox Piven, "Scapegoating Women on Welfare," *New York Times*, September 2, 1993.
5. 21 U.S.C. Section 862 (1988).
6. U.S. Department of Justice, Bureau of Justice Statistics, "Drugs, Crime, and the Justice System: A National Report" (Washington, D.C.: U.S. Department of Justice, December 1992), 184.
7. "Taxation of Drug Traffickers' Income: What the Drug Trafficker Profiteth, the IRS Taketh Away," *Arizona Law Review* 33 (1991):701–729.
8. *New York Times*, December 23, 1990.
9. Personal communication from the Minnesota Department of Revenue, Tax Research Division, February 9, 1993.
10. 21 U.S.C. Section 881.
11. U.S. Department of Justice, *Annual Report of the Department of Justice Asset Forfeiture Program 1991* (Washington, D.C.: U.S. Department of Justice, 1991).
12. Office of National Drug Control Policy, *National Drug Control Strategy*, (Washington, D.C.: Government Printing Office, September 1989), 125.
13. Cary H. Copeland, "Statement of Cary H. Copeland Before the Subcommittee on Legislation and National Security, Government Operations Subcommittee, U.S. House of Representatives, Concerning Asset Forfeiture," June 22, 1993, 1.
14. See *U.S. v. A Parcel of Land with a Building Located at 40 Moon Hill Road, Northbridge, Mass.*, 884 F.2d 41 (1989).
15. See *U.S. v. U.S. Currency in the Amount of $228,536*, 895 F.2d 908 (1990).
16. "Presumed Guilty: The Law's Victims in the War on Drugs," *The Pittsburgh Press*, August 11–16, 1991.
17. "Real Property Forfeitures as a Weapon in the Government's War on Drugs: A Failure To Protect Innocent Ownership Rights," *Boston University Law Review* 72 (1992):217–242.
18. *U.S. v. A Parcel of Land*, 44.
19. *Annual Report, 1991*, 1; "DAG Terwilliger Issues Changes To Strengthen the Justice Department's Asset Forfeiture Program," U.S. Department of Justice press release, January 15, 1993.
20. *New York Times*, December 23, 1990.
21. "Presumed Guilty," August 11, 1991.
22. See U.S. Department of Commerce, Bureau of the Census, *Compendium of Government Finances* (Washington, D.C.: Government Printing Office, 1962, 1967, 1972, 1977, 1982, 1987); also U.S. Department of Justice, Bureau of Justice Statistics, "Justice Expenditure and Employment 1990," *Bulletin* (Washington, D.C.: U.S. Department of Justice, September 1992), Figure 1.
23. Diana R. Gordon, *The Justice Juggernaut: Fighting Street Crime, Controlling Citizens* (New Brunswick, N.J.: Rutgers University Press, 1990), Chap. 5.
24. Interview, John Kelley, September 19, 1991.
25. Peter Marris and Martin Rein, *Dilemmas of Social Reform: Poverty and Community Action in the United States*, second edition (London: Routledge and Kegan Paul, 1972), 269.

26. *Kansas City Times*, September 12, 1989.
27. Interview, John Kelley, September 19, 1991.
28. *Kansas City Star*, July 21, 1991.
29. Much of the $1.5 million allocated for the deferred prosecution program also went toward drug treatment, as well as some of the jail money.
30. Interview, September 17, 1991.
31. Interview, September 18, 1991.
32. Telephone interview, October 1, 1991.
33. See Joseph A. Schumpeter, *Capitalism, Socialism, and Democracy* (New York: Harper and Brothers, 1942), especially Chap. XXII.

*Chapter 14*
*Drugspeak*

1. Murray Edelman, *Political Language: Words That Succeed and Policies That Fail* (New York: Academic Press, 1977), 4.
2. Jean-Francois Lyotard, *The Post-Modern Condition: A Report on Knowledge* (Minneapolis: University of Minnesota, 1984).
3. Michel Foucault, *Power/Knowledge: Selected Interviews and Other Writings, 1972–1977* (New York: Pantheon, 1980), 99.
4. Pauline Marie Rosenau, *Post-Modernism and the Social Sciences* (Princeton, N.J.: Princeton University Press, 1992), 52.
5. Edelman, *Political Language*, 149.
6. For an account of earlier constructions of the U.S. drug problem, see Armand L. Mauss, *Social Problems as Social Movements* (Philadelphia: J.B. Lippincott, 1975), Chap. 7.
7. William Safire, "Drug War Lingo," *New York Times*, September 24, 1989.
8. H.R. 3119 (1989).
9. *New York Times*, September 23, 1989.
10. Lynn Zimmer, "The Anti-Drug Semantic," paper presented at the Drug Policy Foundation conference, 1992. The author identifies, in anti-drug literature and media presentations since the late 1970s, a number of themes that are "designed to discourage personal use and create an atmosphere of intolerance toward use by others." She argues that evidence of the success of the semantic can be found in both the intensity of the drug wars at all levels of government and the institutional embrace of the anti-drug message by the entertainment and advertising industries.
11. Religious, medicinal, and recreational uses of cannabis over thousands of years are described in Gabriel G. Nahas, *Marihuana—Deceptive Weed* (New York: Raven Press, 1973), Chap. 1. For evidence that judges, worshipers, and state legislatures (but not in Oregon) can still view peyote as a legitimate component of religious observance in drug-fighting societies, see *Employment Div., Oregon Dept. of Human Resources v. Smith*, 494 U.S. 872 (1990). Sociologist Harry Levine reminds us that no less a puritan than Cotton Mather called alcohol, the most popular and enduring psychoactive drug, "the good creature of God." Harry Gene Levine, "The Discovery of Addiction: Changing Conceptions of

Habitual Drunkenness in America," *Journal of Substance Abuse Treatment* 2 (1985):44.

12. *Othello*, III, iii, 330–333; Aileen Ward, "Foreword," in *Confessions of an English Opium Eater and Other Writings*, by Thomas De Quincey (New York: Carroll and Graf, 1966), ix.

13. Virginia Berridge and Griffith Edwards, *Opium and the People: Opiate Use in Nineteenth-Century England* (New Haven: Yale University Press, 1987). The quoted material (p. 107) is taken from a contemporary medical journal. Berridge and Edwards note, however (p. 109), that "it was the sobering and not the 'stimulant' effect of the drug which most consumers expected. The distinction between 'medical' and 'non-medical' use was impossible to draw, and it was easy enough for observers to substitute moral judgment (the 'bad use' of opium) for cultural sensibility."

14. Levine, "The Discovery of Addiction," 48.

15. Harry Gene Levine, "The Good Creature of God and the Demon Rum: Colonial American and 19th Century Ideas About Alcohol, Crime and Accidents," in *Alcohol and Disinhibition: Nature and Meaning of the Link*, edited by Robin Room and Gary Collins (Rockville, Md.: U.S. Department of Health and Human Services, National Institute on Alcohol Abuse and Alcoholism, 1983), 132–139.

16. Edward M. Brecher and the editors of Consumer Reports, *Licit and Illicit Drugs* (Boston: Little, Brown, 1972), 8.

17. John Helmer, *Drugs and Minority Oppression* (New York: The Seabury Press, 1975), 12.

18. *New York Times*, July 25, 1909.

19. *New York Times*, March 15, 1911.

20. Howard S. Becker, *Outsiders: Studies in the Sociology of Deviance* (New York: Free Press, 1973), 142.

21. Brecher, *Licit and Illicit Drugs*, 523.

22. For discussions of the campaign mounted against marijuana in the 1920s and 1930s, see Jerome L. Himmelstein, *The Strange Career of Marijuana: Politics and Ideology of Drug Control in America* (Westport, Conn.: Greenwood, 1983); and David Musto, *The American Disease: Origins of Narcotic Control*, expanded edition (New York: Oxford University Press, 1987), Chap. 9. Musto does not believe the Federal Bureau of Narcotics created the scare campaign, but Anslinger himself described extensive activities speaking and writing for popular audiences about "this evil weed of the fields and rivers and roadsides." Quoted in John Rublowsky, *The Stoned Age: A History of Drugs in America* (New York: Putnam, 1974), 107–107, from Harry J. Anslinger and Fulton Oursler, *The Murderers* (New York: Farrar, Straus and Cudahy, 1961).

23. Becker, *Outsiders*, 140.

24. Helmer, *Drugs and Minority Oppression*, 69.

25. *New York Times*, July 25, 1909.

26. U.S. Congress, House of Representatives, *Hearings Before the Subcommittee on Crime, Committee on the Judiciary, on Federal Death Penalty Leg-*

*islation*, 101st Congress, 2d session, March 24 and May 23, 1990, 235.

27. *New York Times*, August 27, 1989. The *New York Times* published a three-part series entitled "Cocaine Reaches the Heartland," between August 27 and 29, followed the next day by a front-page story (with photograph of the president, the attorney general, the secretary of defense, the White House chief of staff, the CIA director, and the drug czar) on the drug violence in Colombia, presumably prelude to announcement a week later of the latest war on drugs. The Yakima story was Susan Beck, Pamela Brown, and D. M. Osborne, "The Cocaine War in America's Fruit Bowl," *The American Lawyer 12*, (March 1990): 82–89.

28. "Drugs: A Plague on the Land," ABC News Special, April 10, 1988.

29. *New York Times*, September 6, 1989.

30. See, for example, *Time*, March 17, 1986, 52–61; *Newsweek*, March 17, 1986, 58–65; and "End of the Line," NBC-TV, January 7, 1987.

31. Peggy Mann, *Marijuana Alert* (New York: McGraw-Hill, 1985), v.

32. Elizabeth Coleman Brynner, "New Parental Push Against Marijuana," *New York Times Magazine*, February 10, 1980, 37.

33. *Kansas City Times*, May 29, 1989.

34. Brecher, *Licit and Illicit Drugs*, 526.

35. Louise G. Richards, "Demographic Trends and Drug Abuse, 1980–1995," (Rockville, Md.: Department of Health and Human Services, National Institute on Drug Abuse, May 1981), 4.

36. William Bennett, "Should Drugs Be Legalized?" *Reader's Digest*, March 1990, 94.

37. William Bennett, "Restoring Authority," in "Moralism and Realism in the Drug War," *New Perspectives Quarterly* 6 (Summer 1989):4. For a trenchant analysis of Bennett's legalistic perspective, see Franklin Zimring and Gordon Hawkins, *The Search for Rational Drug Control* (Cambridge: Cambridge University Press, 1992), 15–21.

38. National Federation of Parents, "The History of the National Federation of Parents," unpaginated, n. d.

39. Robert L. DuPont, Jr., *Getting Tough on Gateway Drugs: A Guide for the Family* (Washington, D.C.: American Psychiatric Press, 1984), 62.

40. The purpose of these comments is not to suggest that no "gateway" relationship exists but that the idea of such a relationship has become, in the words of Mark Kleiman, "little more than a magical incantation." He provides an intelligent discussion of the logical implications and limitations of this concept in *Against Excess: Drug Policy for Results* (New York: Basic Books, 1992), 259–264.

41. *Anchorage Daily News*, October 27, 1990.

42. *New York Times*, September 6, 1989.

43. Cousteau is quoted in Zimmer, "The Anti-Drug Semantic," 17. Hobson's NBC broadcast is reproduced in Musto, *The American Disease*, 191. His remarks are a useful reminder that this theme, too, is not new. Twenty years ago Mississippi Senator Eastland even applied it to marijuana use; he wrote, "If the epidemic is not rolled back, our society may be largely taken over by a 'marijuana culture'. . . . Such a society could not long

endure." James O. Eastland, "Introduction," U.S. Congress, Senate, *Hearings Before the Subcommittee to Investigate the Administration of the Internal Security Act and Other Internal Security Laws, Senate Judiciary Committee*, 93d Congress, 2d session, May 9, 17, 16, 20, 21; June 13, 1974, xii.

44. Quoted in Peter Dale Scott and Jonathan Marshall, *Cocaine Politics: Drugs, Armies and the CIA in Central America* (Berkeley: University of California, 1991), 2.
45. *Congressional Record*, June 24, 1991, S8498.
46. *New York Times*, June 8, 1986.
47. *New York Times*, September 6, 1989.
48. Quoted in Zimmer, "The Anti-Drug Semantic," 19. A typically sweeping allegation of this kind is the assertion of *Time* (March 17, 1986, 52) that drugs used on the job are "sapping the energy, honesty and reliability of the American labor force even as competition from foreign countries is growing even tougher."
49. Morris J. Blachman and Kenneth E. Sharpe, "The War on Drugs: American Democracy Under Assault," *World Policy Journal* (Winter 1989–90):135.
50. Quoted in Mathea Falco, "Foreign Drugs, Foreign Wars," *Daedalus* 121 (Summer 1992):5.
51. John Higham, *Strangers in the Land: Patterns of American Nativism, 1860–1925* (New Brunswick: Rutgers University Press, 1988), Chap. 10.
52. James A. Inciardi describes the demonized image of the drug user that prevailed in the thirties: " 'Dope fiends,' as they were called, were sex-crazed maniacs, degenerate street criminals, and members of the 'living dead'. 'Narcotics,' including marijuana and cocaine, reportedly ravaged the human body; they destroyed morality; addicts were sexually violent and criminally aggressive; they were weak and ineffective members of society; addiction was contagious since users had a mania for perpetuating the social anathema of drug taking; and finally, once addicted, the user entered into a lifetime of slavery to drugs." *The War on Drugs: Heroin, Cocaine, Crime, and Public Policy* (Palo Alto, Calif.: Mayfield, 1986), 100. Although the rhetorical emphasis has, in general, shifted from users to dealers, there are still notable recent demonizations of users, as when Nancy Reagan said, in a speech opening the 1987 White House conference on drugs, that an illicit drug user was "an accomplice to murder." *New York Times*, March 1, 1987.
53. *Washington Post*, September 15, 1986.
54. Office of National Drug Control Policy, *National Drug Control Strategy* (Washington, D.C.: Government Printing Office, 1989), 9.
55. For a critique of Partnership ads, see Richard Blow, "This Is the Truth, This Is the Partnership for a Drug-Free America, This Is What the Partnership for a Drug-Free America Does to the Truth," *Washington City Paper*, December 6–12, 1991, 29–34.
56. "Drug Use Is a Sin," in "Moralism and Realism in the Drug War," *New Perspectives Quarterly* 6 (Summer 1989), 9.

57. Michael Barone and Grant Ujifusa, *The Almanac of American Politics 1994* (Washington, D.C.: National Journal, 1993), 899.
58. *Congressional Record*, October 16, 1991, H7959. He voted against it, however, when it was put forward as a separate amendment in 1990. *Congressional Record*, October 4, 1990, H8859.
59. Quoted on an ABC special in 1988, he said, "Take a body count of how many people we've lost to Communism, and a body count of how many people we've lost to drug addiction. And I'll tell you how to measure national security." "Drugs: A Plague On The Land."
60. For a description of Hobson's activities and influence, see Edward Jay Epstein, *Agency of Fear: Opiates and Political Power in America* (New York: G. P. Putnam, 1977), Chap. 1.
61. "Merchants of death" is what former Representative Lawrence Coughlin (Republican-Penn.) called traffickers in a 1990 House floor debate on the kingpin death penalty. *Congressional Record*, October 4, 1990, H8858. "The walking dead" was Justice William O. Douglas's phrase (probably adapted from Hobson's term, possibly tongue in cheek), in *Robinson v. California*, 370 U.S. 660 (1962), 672. Steven Wisotsky, in a law review article on how judicial opinions reflect popular views on drugs, suggests that Douglas was either embracing the common rhetoric or recording an awareness of its currency. "Not Thinking Like a Lawyer: The Case of Drugs in the Courts," *Notre Dame Journal of Law, Ethics and Public Policy* 5, no. 3 (1991), 664.
62. U.S. Congress, Senate, *Hearings Before the Committee on the Judiciary on S. 32, S. 1225, and S. 1696*, 101st Congress, 1st session, September 19, 1989, 31.
63. Thurmond calls them "individuals who choose to undermine our Nation's health and safety." *Congressional Record*, June 24, 1991, S8498.
64. *Congressional Record*, October 16, 1991, H7958.
65. Senate, *Hearings*, 1989, 8.
66. *Carmona v. Ward*, 576 F.2d 405, 411 (1978). Steven Wisotsky identifies two problems with this trend. As Justice Marshall pointed out, in dissenting from the denial of certiorari in this case, "To rationalize [defendant's] sentences by invoking all evils attendant on or attributable to widespread drug trafficking is simply not compatible with a fundamental premise of the criminal justice system, that individuals are accountable only for their own criminal acts." *Cromona v. Ward*, 439 U.S. 1091, 1096 (1979). In addition, the harms recited were in large part direct results of the *illegality* of the drugs—the violence of black market transactions, the high prices of drugs that lead users to commit property crimes, the corruption of police that are tempted by high drug profits. Wisotsky, "Not Thinking Like a Lawyer," 673–676.
67. Silas J. Wasserstrom, "The Incredible Shrinking Fourth Amendment," *American Criminal Law Review* 21, no. 3 (1984):257–401.
68. Stuart A. Scheingold, *The Politics of Street Crime: Criminal Process and Cultural Obsession* (Philadelphia: Temple University Press, 1991), 25.
69. *Kansas City Times*, April 18, 1989.

70. *Kansas City Star*, January 20, 1989.
71. *Kansas City Times*, January 21, 1989.
72. *Ibid.*
73. *Kansas City Star*, September 8, 1992.
74. See Joel Best, ed., *Images of Issues: Typifying Contemporary Social Problems*, (New York: Aldine de Gruyter, 1989), xix–xx.
75. The similarity in these wars goes beyond their aims. They seem always to attack problems after the fact and in spasms, without an overall plan and little attention given to prevention. See Paul Light, "An End to the War on Waste," *The Brookings Review* 11 (Spring 1993):48.
76. *New York Times*, February 25, 1990.
77. Herbert L. Packer, *The Limits of the Criminal Sanction* (Palo Alto: Stanford University Press, 1968), 16.
78. *United States v. Miranda*, 442 F.Supp.786 (S.D.Fla. 1977).
79. Cesare Beccaria, *On Crimes and Punishments* (Indianapolis: Bobbs-Merrill, 1963), 43. Quoted in George B. Vold and Thomas J. Bernard, *Theoretical Criminology* (New York: Oxford University Press, 1986), 23. For a discussion of proportionality in criminal punishment, see H.L.A. Hart, *Punishment and Responsibility: Essays in the Philosophy of Law* (Oxford: Clarendon, 1968), 161–173.
80. See Steven Wisotsky, *Beyond the War on Drugs: Overcoming a Failed Policy* (Buffalo, N.Y.: Prometheus Books, 1990), Chap. 7.
81. *Ibid.*, 125. This is not the first time, of course, that the drug problem has been held to justify measures that would usually be considered constitutionally excessive or unfair. See Epstein, *Agency of Fear*.
82. *Law Enforcement News*, May 15, 1988.
83. The expansiveness of the term had its down side as far as the administration was concerned. Cartoonists had a field day with it. One compared the Customs program with Reagan's tolerance of his possibly corrupt attorney general, Edwin Meese. *Atlanta Constitution*, June 5, 1988.
84. *Los Angeles Times*, September 1, 1988.
85. *New York Times*, September 6, 1989.
86. For summaries of eighteenth-century and contemporary versions of classical criminology, see Vold and Bernard, *Theoretical Criminology*, Chap. 2.
87. J. Robert Lilly, Francis T. Cullen, and Richard A. Ball, *Criminological Theory: Context and Consequences* (Newbury Park, Calif.: Sage, 1989), Chap. 7. The term "the rhetoric of stability" is found on p. 187.
88. James Q. Wilson and Richard J. Herrnstein, *Crime and Human Nature* (New York: Simon and Schuster, 1985), 69.
89. U.S. Congress, House of Representatives, *Hearings Before the Subcommittee on Crime and Criminal Justice, Committee on the Judiciary, Selected Crime Issues: Prevention and Punishment*, 102d Congress, 1st session, May 23, 29, June 12, 26, July 10, 17 and 25, 1991, "Prepared Statement of William Barr, Deputy Attorney General, U.S. Department of Justice," 7.
90. Scheingold, *The Politics of Street Crime*, 23.

91. According to the Reagan White House, Mrs. Reagan "was instrumental in the establishment of thousands of parent and youth groups, including 12,000 Just Say No clubs." White House Office of Public Affairs, "The Reagan Record on the Crusade for a Drug-Free America," June 6, 1988, 5.
92. *New York Times*, November 14, 1993.
93. Judy Arendsee, "The History of the National Federation of Parents," unpaginated, n.d. Available from National Federation of Parents for Drug-Free Youth, 11159-B South Towne Square, St. Louis, MO 63123.
94. W. Lance Bennett, *Public Opinion in American Politics* (New York: Harcourt Brace Jovanovich, 1980), 13–14.
95. Reagan said, in his 1986 announcement of an intensified drug war, "When we all come together, united—striving for this cause—then those who are killing America and terrorizing it with slow but sure chemical destruction will see that they are up against the mightiest force for good that we know." *Washington Post*, September 15, 1986. Bush's statement was part of a speech he made as Vice President, when he was in charge of international drug interdiction policy, and is taken from White House, "The Reagan Record on the Crusade for a Drug-Free America," June 6, 1988, 35.
96. *Los Angeles Times*, May 28, 1988.
97. Quoted in Ralph Brauer, "The Drug War of Words," *The Nation*, May 21, 1990, 705.
98. *Washington Post*, September 14, 1986; *New York Times*, September 15, 1986.
99. Estimates for turnout in the 1988 caucuses are from the *New York Times*, March 3 and 12, 1988.
100. Interview, September 19, 1991.
101. Malcolm Sparrow, Mark H. Moore, and David Kennedy, *Beyond 911: A New Era for Policing* (New York: Basic Books, 1990).
102. "Statement of William P. Barr, Attorney General, Before the Select Committee on Narcotics Abuse and Control, U.S. House of Representatives, Concerning Operation Weed and Seed," May 20, 1992.
103. *Kansas City Star*, February 12, 1989.
104. *New York Times*, July 20, 1992.
105. Barr announced that Bush proposed spending more than $500 million on the program in fiscal year 1993 (as part of the urban aid bill that he subsequently vetoed), but critics said only $11 million had actually been committed. "Barr Announces Large Increases for Justice Department's FY 1993 Violent Crime Budget," U.S. Department of Justice press release, n.d., 2.
106. *Ibid.*
107. Telephone interview, February 26, 1993.
108. *Seattle Post-Intelligencer*, September 15, 1992.
109. Seattle did eventually accept the grant, after a long negotiation with the federal government in which the local officials got an agreement that two-thirds of the money would go to social services and only one-

third to law enforcement. But once again a law enforcement issue revealed tensions over police conduct, race, and tolerance in Seattle. Eric Scigliano, "Send No Cash," *Seattle Weekly*, December 23, 1992, 14.

110. "Statement Before the Committee on the Judiciary, U.S. House of Representatives, Concerning H.R. 2273 and S. 933, Americans with Disabilities Act of 1989," October 12, 1989. The following commentary on Thornburgh's use of drugspeak is based on a reading of speeches, public statements, and congressional testimony between fall 1989 and spring 1991. See, for example, "Law Enforcement in the 1990s: Dawn of a New Decade," keynote address to the California Police Chiefs Association, February 4, 1991; "An Anti-Crime Coalition for America's Communities," keynote address to the opening assembly of the Attorney General's Summit on Law Enforcement Responses to Violent Crime: Public Safety in the Nineties, March 4, 1991; and "Values and Law in a New World Order," address given to the fifty-fourth annual Supreme Court Day banquet, Drake University School of Law, Des Moines, Iowa, March 9, 1991.

111. It is perhaps significant that these last remarks were made in a speech given just a few weeks after what he called the "uplifting events" of the Gulf War, which Thornburgh says showed that Bush meant it "when he said we would fight 'for a world where the rule of law, not the law of the jungle, governs the conduct of nations.' "

## Chapter 15
## On the European Front

1. A study by the Dutch Ministry of Health, Welfare and Cultural Affairs found that between 1976, when penalties for the use of marijuana and hashish were officially reduced, and 1985, "3% of young people aged 15 and 16 and 10% of the 17 and 18 age group had occasionally (that is, on one or several occasions) used hashish or marijuana. In 1985 these figures were 2% and 6%, respectively." Govert F. van de Wijngaart, "A Social History of Drug Use in the Netherlands: Policy Outcomes and Implications," *The Journal of Drug Issues* 18, no. 3 (1988):488.

2. Peter Cohen, *Drugs as a Social Construct* (Amsterdam: Universiteit van Amsterdam, 1990), 23.

3. Henk Jan Van Vliet, "Separation of Drug Markets and the Normalization of Drug Problems in the Netherlands: An Example for Other Nations?" *The Journal of Drug Issues* 20, no. 3 (1990):466.

4. Karl-Heinz Reuband, "Drug Use and Drug Policy: A Cross-National Comparison," Zentralarchiv für Empirisches Sozialforschung, Universistät zu Köln, 1990, Manuscript, Table 2.

5. For a recent report on competitive trends, see Peter Reuter, Mathea Falco, and Robert MacCoun, *Comparing Western European and North American Drug Policies: An International Conference Report* (Santa Monica, Calif.: RAND Corporation, 1993).

6. A recent analysis of the global drug trade in the early nineties is Stephen

Flynn, "Worldwide Drug Scourge," *The Brookings Review* 11 (Winter 1993):6–11 and (Spring 1993):36–39. For a summary report on international patterns in drug traffic and demand, see the United Nations publications, "Report of the International Narcotics Control Board," various years, available from the U.N. Sales Section, New York or Geneva. An assessment of drug abuse increases in countries in all regions of the world at the beginning of the present "epidemic" can be found in Division of Narcotics Drugs of the United Nations Secretariat, "Review of Drug Abuse and Measures To Reduce the Illicit Demand for Drugs by Region," *Bulletin on Narcotics* XXXIX, no. 1 (1987):3–30.

7. *Innenpolitik* Nr. I (1991), 3; Karl-Heinz Reuband, "Drug Abuse Trends in West Germany," in *Epidemiologic Trends in Drug Abuse* (Rockville, Md: U.S. Department of Health and Human Services, National Institute on Drug Abuse, 1990), III-1. As with figures on police reports in the United States, caution must be used in interpreting the data on drug users, since it is difficult to disentangle the extent to which the trend may reflect increases in reporting as sensitivity to the drug problem rises.

8. See Nicholas Dorn, Karim Murji, and Nigel South, *Traffickers: Drug Markets and Law Enforcement* (London: Routledge, 1992).

9. Legge 26 giugno 1990, no. 162. For the text of the bill and a collection of news articles commenting on its passage, see Consiglio Regionale del Piemonte, Servizio Documentazione, "Droga," Dossier no. 4, July 1990.

10. Gesetz zur Bekämpfung des illegalen Rauschgifthandels und anderer Erscheinungsformen der Organisierten Kriminalität BGB1.I 1302, 1305, vom 15.7.1992.

11. Francis Caballero, *Droit de la Drogue* (Paris: Dalloz, 1989), 671.

12. Govert F. van de Wijngaart, "Competing Perspectives on Drug Use: The Dutch Experience," doctoral dissertation, Rijksuniversiteit, Utrecht, 1990, 30; René, Mole and Franz Trautman, "The Liberal Image of the Dutch Drug Policy," *The International Journal on Drug Policy* 2, no. 5 (1991):16–21.

13. Marco Taradash, "Editoriale," *CORAnews*, no. 58, March 19, 1990, 2.

14. Der Bundesminister für Jugend, Familie, Frauen and Gesundheit, Der Bundesminister des Innern, "Nationaler Rauschgiftbekämpfungsplan: Massnahmen der Rauschgiftbekämpfung und der Hilfe für Gefährdete und Abhängige," June 1990.

15. David Musto, *The American Disease: Origins of Narcotic Control*, expanded edition (New York: Oxford University Press, 1987), 35–37.

16. Ethan A. Nadelmann, "The D.E.A. in Europe: Drug Enforcement in Comparative and International Perspective," March 1990, manuscript.

17. "Drogue: La Guerre Mondiale," *Libération*, May 1990, 3.

18. David Turner, "Pragmatic Incoherence: The Changing Face of British Drug Policy," in *Searching for Alternatives: Drug Control Policy in the United States*, edited by Melvyn B. Krauss and Edward P. Lazear (Stanford: Hoover Institution Press, 1991), 186.

19. Personal interview, September 24, 1990. Much of this chapter is based

on interviews with drug policy researchers and officials of private and public drug-control agencies in Germany, Britain, the Netherlands, France, and Italy during the academic year 1990–1991 and the summer of 1993. For discussions of the increasing drug abuse in German cities, see "Der Stoff versaut das Land," *Der Spiegel* 28 (June 1990):32–41; increasing drug deaths in western Europe are documented in Reuband, "Drug Use."

20. "Frankfurt Resolution," November 1990, mimeographed document, first page (unpaginated). Reproduced in proceedings for the conference, "European Cities at the Centre of Illegal Trade in Drugs," Frankfurt am Main, November 20–22, 1990.

21. Information provided by the Drug Policy Foundation, Washington, D.C. The more recent signatory cities are Arnhem, Rotterdam, and Venlo (Netherlands); Basel and Lucerne (Switzerland); Kallithea (Greece); the Province of Teramo (Italy); Charlerol (Belgium); Zagreb (Croatia); and Ljubljana (Slovenia).

22. "Frankfurt Resolution," second and third pages.

23. Interview, June 9, 1993.

24. Interview, September 18, 1990.

25. See the contributions of Dr. Karlheinz Gemmer to "1st Conference: European Cities at the Centre of Illegal Trade in Drugs," Frankfurt am Main, 1991, 29–60.

26. Cindy Fazey, "The Evaluation of the Liverpool Drug Dependency Clinic" (Liverpool: Mersey Regional Health Authority, 1987); Howard Parker and Russell Newcombe, "Heroin Use and Acquisitive Crime in an English Community," *British Journal of Sociology* 38, no. 3 (1987):331–350.

27. Peter Cohen, *Cocaine Use in Amsterdam in Non-Deviant Subcultures* (Amsterdam: Instituut voor Sociale Geografie, Universiteit van Amsterdam, 1989), 15–16; Frits Rüter, "The Pragmatic Dutch Approach to Drug Control: Does It Work?" 1988, lecture.

28. See G. V. Stimson, "Risk Reduction by Drug Users with Regard to HIV Infection," *International Review of Psychiatry* 3, no.3/4 (1991):401–415.

29. *Le Monde*, July 4, 1990. The article reports on a study issued by L'Institute des Hautes Études de la Sécurité Intérieure. The U.S. high-school senior survey was conducted by the Institute for Social Research, University of Michigan; data are from *Sourcebook 1989*, Table 2.60.

30. Servizi Studi del Parlamento, *Aspetti e problemi della tossicodependenza*, vol. 1, Rome 1989, 105–110.

31. James Davison Hunter, *Culture Wars: The Struggle To Define America* (New York: Basic Books, 1991), 71; Harry Gene Levine, "The Discovery of Addiction: Changing Conceptions of Habitual Drunkenness in America," *Journal of Substance Abuse Treatment* 2 (1985):47.

32. Advisory Council on the Misuse of Drugs, "AIDS and Drug Misuse, Part 1" (London: Her Majesty's Stationery Office, 1988), 17.

33. Turner, "Pragmatic Incoherence," 186.

34. See The Second Report of the Interdepartmental Committee, Ministry of Health, Scottish Home and Health Department, *Drug Addiction* (London: Her Majesty's Stationery Office, 1965).

35. *New York Times*, December 12, 1992.

36. *New York Times*, October 8, 1989.

37. Giancarlo Arnao, "Il buco della legge," *CORAnews*, no. 58, March 19, 1990, 4.

38. "Osservatorio sull'Attuazione della Legge 162/90 sulla Droga: a Quasi un Anno dalla Approvazione della Legge Quale Bilancio?" Partito Democratico della Sinistra, Roma, April 23, 1991.

39. Drug deaths went from 809 in 1988 and 973 in 1989 to 1,152 in 1990. The strict new law was enforced for half of 1990. CORA (Coordinamento Radicale Antiproibizionista), "Osservatorio delle Leggi sulla Droga," Rapporto 3 September 1991:16. This report's statistics are taken from the monthly bulletin of the National Institute of Statistics (Istituto Nazionale di Statistica).

40. *La Repubblica*, November 8–9, 1992.

41. *La Repubblica*, April 20, 1993.

42. For a discussion of the concepts of harm minimization and harm reduction, see Nicholas Dorn, "Clarifying Policy Options on Drug Trafficking: Harm Minimization is Distinct from Legalization" in *The Reduction of Drug-Related Harm*, edited by P. A. O'Hare, R. Newcombe, A. Matthews, *et al.* (London: Institute for the Study of Drug Dependence), 108–121.

43. *New York Times*, February 18, 1993.

44. For reports on the policy directions of individual European countries, see Nicholas Dorn, Jorgen Jepsen, and Ernesto Savona, eds., *Euro-Narc*, in press.

45. Nicholas Dorn and Nigel South, "After Mr. Bennett and Mr. Bush: U.S. Foreign Policy and the Prospects for Drug Control," in *Global Crime Connections*, edited by Frank Pearce and Michael Woodiwiss (London: Macmillan, 1993), 76.

46. Peter Reuter makes the point that the number of first users appears to be declining in many European countries and that the resulting aging of the drug-abusing population may explain the increase in drug deaths better than the hypothesis of a greater number of users. Peter Reuter, "Drugs: The Threat and the Response," Ditchley conference report no. D91/4, 1991, 4.

47. One poster in favor of repeal of the 1990 law, for example, read "Drugs don't kill; the law does" ("La droga non uccide la legge sì"). Another bore the legend "Free of prison, free of drugs" ("Liberi dal carcere, liberi dalla droga") and showed youthful hands reaching out from between prison bars.

48. "France, Les As des Stups Voués au Coupisolé," from the special report on drugs, "Drogne: La Guerre Mondiale," *Libération*, May 1990, 36.

*Chapter 16*
*Toward a Kinder, Gentler Social Policy?*

1. For the purpose of discussing policy outcome, I am omitting consideration of whether the death penalty for kingpin drug trafficking where no death results would be held to be cruel and unusual punishment prohibited by the Eighth Amendment, a distinct possibility.
2. Mary Bruno "Outsider on the Inside," *Seattle Weekly*, December 9, 1992, 21.
3. *Kansas City Star*, September 8, 1992.
4. Eric Scigliano, "Hard Time," *Seattle Weekly*, October 21, 1992, 14.
5. "The Drug Policy Letter," 19 (June/July 1993):2–3.
6. Mark A. R. Kleiman, *Against Excess: Drug Policy for Results* (New York: Basic Books, 1992), 253.
7. *Ibid.*, 277–280.
8. Norval Morris and Gordon Hawkins, *The Honest Politician's Guide to Crime Control* (Chicago, University of Chicago Press, 1970), 45–50.
9. For the distinction between instrumental and expressive behavior, see Talcott Parsons, *The Social System* (Glencoe, Ill.: The Free Press, 1951), Chap. 2. A good discussion of the distinction between traditional deterrence theory and a looser notion of the human will that leads to the choice of crime as "a sense of option" can be found in David Matza, *Becoming Deviant* (Englewood Cliffs, N.J.: Prentice-Hall, 1969), 116.
10. The classic statement of this position is Robert K. Merton, "Social Structure and Anomie," in *Social Theory and Social Structure*, by Robert K. Merton (New York: Free Press, 1967), Chap. VI.
11. For a discussion of the contribution of various forces to motivation for treatment, see Dean R. Gerstein and Henrick J. Harwood, eds., *Treating Drug Problems*, vol. 1 (Washington, D.C.: National Academy Press (Institute of Medicine), 1990), 109–113.
12. Some drug historians believe that users have often substituted more concentrated (and therefore more dangerous) forms of a drug for relatively benign ones as the proscription of their original drug of choice made it more expensive and exposed users to prosecution. For an account of the switch from smoking opium to injecting heroin or morphine, see David T. Courtwright, *Dark Paradise: Opiate Addiction in America Before 1940* (Cambridge: Harvard University Press, 1982), 83–86.
13. Donald Taft, *Criminology* (New York: Macmillan, 1956), 28.
14. Patricia G. Erickson, "Recent Trends in Canadian Drug Policy: The Decline and Resurgence of Prohibitionism," *Daedalus* 121 (Summer 1992):248.
15. Todd Gitlin, "On Drugs and Mass Media in America's Consumer Society," in *Youth and Drugs: Society's Mixed Messages*, edited by Hank Resnik (Rockville, Md.: U.S. Department of Health and Human Services, Office for Substance Abuse Prevention, 1990), 47.

# BIBLIOGRAPHY

Abramovitz, Mimi, and Frances Fox Piven. "Scapegoating Women on Welfare." *New York Times*, September 2, 1993.

Advisory Council on the Misuse of Drugs. "AIDS and Drug Misuse, Part 1." London: Department of Health and Social Security, 1988.

Allen, Frederick Lewis. *Since Yesterday: The Nineteen-Thirties in America.* New York: Bantam Books, 1961.

Anchorage Chamber of Commerce. "Anchorage Crime Commission Results." Anchorage: Anchorage Chamber of Commerce, October 1988.

Arnao, Giancarlo. "Il buco della legge." *CORAnews*, no. 58, (March 19, 1990), 4.

Artz, Frederick B. *The Mind of the Middle Ages.* New York: Knopf, 1967.

Asbury, Herbert. *The Gangs of New York: An Informal History of the Underworld.* New York: Paragon House, 1927.

Ashdown, Gerald G. "Drugs, Ideology, and the Deconstitutionalization of Criminal Procedure." *West Virginia Law Review* 95 (Fall 1992):1–54.

Austin, Gregory A. *Perspectives on the History of Psychoactive Substance Use.* Rockville, Md.: National Institute on Drug Abuse, 1978.

Bachman, Jerald G., John M. Wallace, Jr., Candace L. Kurth, Lloyd D. Johnston, and Patrick M. O'Malley. "Drug Use Among Black, White, Hispanic, Native American, and Asian American High School Seniors (1976–1989): Prevalence, Trends and Correlates." Ann Arbor, Mich.: Institute for Social Research, University of Michigan, 1990.

Balibar, Etienne. " 'Class Racism.' " In *Race, Nation, Class,* edited by Etienne Balibar and Immanuel Wallerstein. London: Verso, 1991.

Barone, Michael, and Grant Ujifusa. *The Almanac of American Politics 1992.* Washington, D.C.: National Journal, 1991.

———. *The Almanac of American Politics 1994.* Washington D.C.: National Journal, 1993.

Baumohl, Jim. "The 'Dope Fiend's Paradise' Revisited: Notes from Research in Progress on Drug Law Enforcement in San Francisco, 1875–1915." *The Drinking and Drug Practices Surveyor* 24 (June 1992):3–12.

Beccaria, Cesare. *On Crimes and Punishments.* Indianapolis: Bobbs-Merrill, 1963.

Beck, Susan, Pamela Brown, and D.M. Osborne. "The Cocaine War in America's Fruit Bowl." *The American Lawyer* 12 (March 1990): 82–89.

Becker, Howard S. *Outsiders: Studies in the Sociology of Deviance.* New York: Free Press, 1973.

Becton, Charles L. "The Drug Courier Profile: 'All seems infected that th'infected spy, as all looks yellow to the jaundic'd eye.' " *North Carolina Law Review* 65, no. 3 (1987):417–480.

Bedau, Hugo Adam, ed. *The Death Penalty in America*, third edition. Oxford: Oxford University Press, 1982.

Bell, Derrick. *Race, Racism and American Law*, third edition. Boston: Little, Brown, 1992.

Benjamin, Daniel K., and Roger Leroy Miller. *Undoing Drugs: Beyond Legalization*. New York: Basic Books, 1991.

Bennett, W. Lance. *Public Opinion in American Politics*. New York: Harcourt Brace Jovanovich, 1980.

Bennett, William. "Restoring Authority in "Moralism and Realism in the Drug War." *New Perspectives Quarterly* 6 (Summer 1989):4–7.

———. "Should Drugs Be Legalized?" *Reader's Digest*, March 1990, 94.

Berger, Peter L., and Thomas Luckman. *The Social Construction of Reality*. New York: Doubleday, 1966.

Berridge, Virginia, and Griffith Edwards. *Opium and the People: Opiate Use in Nineteenth-Century England*. New Haven: Yale University Press, 1987.

Best, Joel, ed. *Images of Issues: Typifying Contemporary Social Problems*. New York: Aldine de Gruyter, 1989.

Blachman, Morris J., and Kenneth E. Sharpe. "The War on Drugs: American Democracy Under Assault." *World Policy Journal* 7 (Winter 1989–90):135–163.

Blow, Richard. "This Is the Truth, This Is the Partnership for a Drug-Free America, This Is What the Partnership for a Drug-Free America Does to the Truth." *Washington City Paper*, December 6–12, 1991, 29–34.

Blumer, Herbert. "Social Problems as Collective Behavior." *Social Problems* 18, no. 3 (Winter 1971):298–306.

Blumstein, Alfred. "On the Racial Disproportionality of United States' Prison Populations." *Journal of Criminal Law and Criminology* 73, no. 3 (1982):1259–1281.

Bowers, William J. *Legal Homicide: Death as Punishment in America, 1864–1982*. Boston: Northeastern University Press, 1984.

Brace, Charles Loring. *The Dangerous Classes of New York, and Twenty Years Work Among Them*. New York: Wynkoop and Hallenbeck, 1872.

Brauer, Ralph. "The Drug War of Words." *The Nation*, May 21, 1990.

Brecher, Edward M., and the editors of *Consumer Reports*. *Licit and Illicit Drugs*. Boston: Little, Brown, 1972.

Bremner, Robert H. *From the Depths: The Discovery of Poverty in the United States*. New York: New York University, 1956.

Browning, Frank, and John Gerassi. *The American Way of Crime: From Salem to Watergate*. New York: Putnam, 1980.

Bruno, Mary. "Outsider on the Inside." *Seattle Weekly*, December 9, 1992.

Brynner, Elizabeth Coleman. "New Parental Push Against Marijuana." *New York Times Magazine*, February 10, 1980.

Der Bundesminister für Jugend, Familie, Frauen and Gesundheit, Der Bundesminister des Innern. "Nationaler Rauschgiftbekämpfungsplan:

Massnahmen der Rauschgiftbekämpfung und der Hilfe für Gefährdete und Abhängige," June 1990.

Caballero, Francis. *Droit de la Drogue*. Paris: Dalloz, 1989.

Castine, John. "Mandatory Terms Fall Short," "Lawmakers Quietly Consider Change," "Law's Sponsor Has Second Thoughts." *Detroit Free* Press, March 10–12, 1990.

Chambliss, William. "A Sociological Analysis of the Law of Vagrancy." *Social Problems* 12 (Summer 1964):67–77.

Chevalier, Louis. *Laboring Classes and Dangerous Classes*. Princeton, N.J.: Princeton University Press, 1973.

Chiricos, Theodore G., and William D. Bales. "Unemployment and Punishment: An Empirical Assessment." *Criminology* 29, no. 4 (1991):701–724.

Clinton, Bill, and Al Gore. *Putting People First*. New York: Times Books, 1992.

Cobb, Roger W., and Charles D. Elder. *Participation in American Politics: The Dynamics of Agenda-Building*, second edition. Baltimore: Johns Hopkins, 1983.

Cohen, Peter. *Cocaine Use in Amsterdam in Non-Deviant Subcultures*. Amsterdam: Instituut voor Sociale Geografie, Universiteit van Amsterdam, 1989.

———. *Drugs as a Social Construct*. Amsterdam: Universiteit van Amsterdam, 1990.

Cohen, Stanley. *Folk Devils and Moral Panics: The Creation of the Mods and Rockers*. London: MacGibbon and Kee, 1972.

Collins, James J. "Alcohol and Interpersonal Violence: Less Than Meets the Eye." In *Pathways to Criminal Violence*, edited by Neil Alan Wiener and Marvin E. Wolfgang. Newbury Park, Calif.: Sage, 1989:49–67.

Conner, Roger L., and Patrick C. Burns. "The Winnable War: How Communities Are Eradicating Drug Markets." *The Brookings Review* 10 (Summer 1992):26–29.

Conyers, John. "Opening Statement, Oversight Hearing on the Department of Justice Asset Forfeiture Program." Subcommittee on Legislation and National Security, Committee on Government Operations, U.S. House of Representatives. September 3, 1992.

Copeland, Cary H. "Statement of Cary H. Copeland Before the Subcommittee on Legislation and National Security, Government Operations Subcommittee, U.S. House of Representatives, Concerning Asset Forfeiture," June 22, 1993.

CORA (Coordinamento Radicale Antiproibizionista). "Osservatorio delle Leggi sulla Droga." *Rapporto* 3 (September 1991).

Courtwright, David T. *Dark Paradise: Opiate Addiction in America Before 1940*. Cambridge: Harvard University Press, 1982.

Darden, Joe T., Richard Child Hill, June Thomas, and Richard Thomas. *Detroit: Race and Uneven Development*. Philadelphia: Temple University Press, 1987.

Dawson, John M. "Felons Sentenced to Probation in State Courts, 1986." Washington, D.C.: U.S. Department of Justice, Bureau of Justice Statistics, November 1990.

Death Penalty Information Center. "Millions Misspent: What Politicians

Don't Say About the High Costs of the Death Penalty." Washington, D.C.: Death Penalty Information Center, October 1992.

Dorn, Nicholas. "Clarifying Policy Options on Drug Trafficking: Harm Minimization is Distinct from Legalization." In *The Reduction of Drug-Related Harm*, edited by P.A. O'Hare, R. Newcombe, A. Matthews, et al. London: Institute for the Study of Drug Dependence, 1992.

Dorn, Nicholas, Jorgeu Jepson and Ernesto Sarona, eds., *Euro-Narc*, in press.

Dorn, Nicholas, Karim Murji, and Nigel South. *Traffickers: Drug Markets and Law Enforcement*. London: Routledge, 1992.

Dorn, Nicholas, and Nigel South. "After Mr. Bennett and Mr. Bush: U.S. Foreign Policy and the Prospects for Drug Control." In *Global Crime Connections*, edited by Frank Pearce and Michael Woodiwiss. London: Macmillan, 1993:72–90.

Drew, Elizabeth. "Letter from Washington." *The New Yorker*, October 2, 1989.

"Drogue: La Guerre Mondiale." *Libération*, May 1990.

DuPont, Robert L., Jr. *Getting Tough on Gateway Drugs: A Guide for the Family*. Washington, D.C.: American Psychiatric Press, 1984.

Durkheim, Emile. *The Division of Labor in Society*. New York: Free Press, 1984.

*Economic Report of the President, 1991*. Washington, D.C.: Government Printing Office, 1991.

*Economic Report of the President, 1993*. Washington, D.C.: Government Printing Office, 1993.

Edelman, Murray. *Constructing the Political Spectacle*. Chicago: University of Illinois Press, 1988.

———. *Political Language: Words That Succeed and Policies That Fail*. New York: Academic Press, 1977.

———. *Politics as Symbolic Action*. Chicago: Markham, 1971.

———. *The Symbolic Uses of Politics*. Chicago: University of Illinois Press, 1964.

Epstein, Edward Jay. *Agency of Fear: Opiates and Political Power in America*. New York: G.P. Putnam, 1977.

Erickson, Patricia G. "Recent Trends in Canadian Drug Policy: The Decline and Resurgence of Prohibitionism." *Daedalus* 121 (Summer 1992):239–267.

Executive Office of the President of the United States. *Budget of the United States Government, FY94*. Washington, D.C.: Government Printing Office, 1993.

Eyestone, Robert. *From Social Issues to Public Policy*. New York: Wiley, 1978.

Falco, Mathea. "Foreign Drugs, Foreign Wars." *Daedalus* 121 (Summer 1992):1–14.

Fazey, Cindy. "The Evaluation of the Liverpool Drug Dependency Clinic." Liverpool: Mersey Regional Health Authority, 1987.

Federal Bureau of Investigation. *Uniform Crime Reports, Crime in the United States*. Washington, D.C.: Government Printing Office, 1982–1992.

Feeley, Malcolm M., and Austin D. Sarat. *The Policy Dilemma: Federal Crime Policy and the Law Enforcement Assistance Administration, 1968–1978*. Minneapolis: University of Minnesota Press, 1980.

Finnegan, William. "Out There." *The New Yorker*, September 10, 1990, 51–86 and September 17, 1990, 60–90.

Fitzgerald, Gerry. "Dispatches from the Drug War." *Common Cause* 16 (January 1990):13–19.

Flanagan, Timothy J., and Kathleen Maguire, eds. *Sourcebook of Criminal Justice Statistics 1989*. Washington, D.C.: U.S. Department of Justice, Bureau of Justice Statistics, 1990.

Flanagan, Timothy J., and Kathleen Maguire, eds. *Sourcebook of Criminal Justice Statistics 1991*. Washington, D.C.: U.S. Department of Justice, Bureau of Justice Statistics, 1992.

Flanagan, Timothy J., and Maureen McLeod, eds. *Sourcebook of Criminal Justice Statistics 1982*. Washington, D.C.: U.S. Department of Justice, Bureau of Justice Statistics, 1983.

Fleissner, Dan, Nicholas Fedan, Ezra Stotland, and David Klinger. "Community Policing in Seattle: A Descriptive Study of the South Seattle Crime Reduction Project." Seattle Police Department, 1991.

Flynn, Stephen. "Worldwide Drug Scourge." *The Brookings Review* 11 (Winter 1993):6–11 and (Spring 1993):36–39.

Foucault, Michel. *Discipline and Punish*. New York: Pantheon, 1977.

―――. *Power/Knowledge: Selected Interviews and Other Writings, 1972–1977*. New York: Pantheon, 1980.

Gallup, George, Jr. *The Gallup Report*. Report no. 124. Princeton, N.J.: The Gallup Poll, October 1975.

Gallup, George, Jr. *The Gallup Report*. Report no. 285. Princeton, N.J.: The Gallup Poll, June 1989.

Garofalo, James. "Public Opinion About Crime: The Attitudes of Victims and Nonvictims in Selected Cities." Washington, D.C.: U.S. Department of Justice, National Criminal Justice Information and Statistics Service, 1977.

Gerstein, Dean R. "Alcohol Use and Consequences." In *Alcohol and Public Policy: Beyond the Shadow of Prohibition*, edited by Mark H. Moore and Dean R. Gerstein. Washington, D.C.: National Academy Press, 1981:182–224.

Gerstein, Dean R., and Henrick J. Harwood, eds. *Treating Drug Problems*, Vol. 1. Washington, D.C.: National Academy Press (Institute of Medicine), 1990.

Gibbs, Arnold A. "Where Are the People's Champions?" *Law Enforcement News*, June 15, 1993.

Gitlin, Todd. "On Drugs and Mass Media in America's Consumer Society." In *Youth and Drugs: Society's Mixed Messages*, edited by Hank Resnik. Rockville, Md.: U.S. Department of Health and Human Services, Office for Substance Abuse Prevention, 1990:31–52.

Goode, Erich. "The American Drug Panic of the 1980s: Social Construction or Objective Threat?" *Violence, Aggression and Terrorism* 3, no. 4 (1989):327–348.

Gordon, Diana R. "The Drug War Hits the Roads." *The Nation*, May 31, 1993, 735–738.

————. *The Justice Juggernaut: Fighting Street Crime, Controlling Citizens*. New Brunswick, N.J.: Rutgers University Press, 1990.

Gowdy, Voncile B. "Intermediate Sanctions." In *Research in Brief*. Washington, D.C.: U.S. Department of Justice, National Institute of Justice, 1993.

Greenberg, David F., and Drew Humphries. "The Cooptation of Fixed Sentencing Reform." *Crime and Delinquency* 26, no. 2 (1980):206–225.

Grinspoon, Lester, and James Bakalar. *Cocaine: A Drug and Its Social Evolution*. New York: Basic Books, 1976.

Gurevich, A.J. *Categories of Medieval Culture*. London: Routledge and Kegan Paul, 1985.

Gusfield, Joseph R. *The Culture of Public Problems: Drinking-Driving and the Symbolic Order*. Chicago: University of Chicago Press, 1981.

Handlin, Oscar, ed. *Immigration as a Factor in American History*. Englewood Cliffs, N.J.: Prentice-Hall, 1959.

Hart, H.L.A. *Punishment and Responsibility: Essays in the Philosophy of Law*. Oxford: Clarendon, 1968.

Hay, Douglas. "Property, Authority and the Criminal Law." In *Albion's Fatal Tree: Crime and Society in Eighteenth-Century England*, edited by Douglas Hay, Peter Linebaugh, John G. Rule, E. P. Thompson, and Cal Winslow. New York: Pantheon, 1975.

Helmer, John. *Drugs and Minority Oppression*. New York: The Seabury Press, 1975.

Higham, John. *Strangers in the Land: Patterns of American Nativism, 1860–1925*. New Brunswick: Rutgers University Press, 1988.

Hill, Christopher. *The Century of Revolution, 1603–1714*. New York: W. W. Norton, 1961.

Hilton, M. E. "Drinking Patterns and Drinking Problems in 1984: Results from a General Population Survey." *Alcoholism: Clinical and Experimental Research* 11, no. 2 (1987):167–175.

Himmelfarb, Gertrude. *The Idea of Poverty: England in the Early Industrial Age*. New York: Random House, 1983.

Himmelstein, Jerome L. *The Strange Career of Marijuana: Politics and Ideology of Drug Control in America*. Westport, Conn.: Greenwood, 1983.

Hoffman, Ross J.S., and Paul Levack, eds. *Burke's Politics*. New York: Knopf, 1959.

Hollandsworth, Skip. "Straight Rides over Kids Again . . . And Some Say They Love It." In *Drug Prohibition and the Conscience of Nations*, edited by Arnold S. Trebach and Kevin B. Zeese. Washington, D.C.: Drug Policy Foundation, 1990:166–175.

Hunter, James Davison. *Culture Wars: The Struggle To Define America*. New York: Basic Books, 1991.

Inciardi, James A. *The War on Drugs: Heroin, Cocaine, Crime, and Public Policy*. Palo Alto, Calif.: Mayfield Publishing, 1986.

Institute of Medicine. *Marijuana and Health*. Washington, D.C.: National Academy Press, 1982.

Interdepartmental Committee, Ministry of Health, Scottish Home and Health

Department. *Drug Addiction.* London: Her Majesty's Stationery Office, 1965.

Jacoby, Joseph E., and Christopher S. Dunn. "National Survey on Punishment for Criminal Offenses, Executive Summary." Bowling Green, Ohio: Bowling Green State University, 1987.

Joint Committee on New York Drug Law Evaluation. *The Nation's Toughest Drug Law: Evaluating the New York Experience.* New York: The Association of the Bar of the City of New York, 1977.

Jones, Charles O. *An Introduction to the Study of Public Policy,* third edition. Monterey, Calif.: Brooks-Cole, 1984.

Kaplan, John. *The Hardest Drug: Heroin and Public Policy.* Chicago: University of Chicago, 1983.

———. *Marijuana: The New Prohibition.* New York: Pocket Books, 1971.

Katz, Michael. *The Undeserving Poor: From the War on Poverty to the War on Welfare.* New York: Pantheon, 1989.

Kelling, George L., Tony Pate, Duane Dickman, and Charles E. Brown. *The Kansas City Preventive Patrol Experiment.* Washington, D.C.: The Police Foundation, 1974.

Kingdon, John W. *Agendas, Alternatives, and Public Policies.* Boston: Little, Brown, 1984.

Kleiman, Mark A.R. *Against Excess: Drug Policy for Results.* New York: Basic Books, 1992.

———. *Marijuana: Costs of Abuse, Costs of Control.* New York: Greenwood Press, 1989.

Klein, Stephen, Joan Petersilia, and Susan Turner. "Race and Imprisonment Decisions in California." *Science,* February 16, 1990, 812–816.

Kuttner, Robert. *Revolt of the Haves: Tax Rebellions and Hard Times.* New York: Simon and Schuster, 1980.

Lasswell, Harold. *Politics: Who Gets What, When, How?* New York: McGraw-Hill, 1936.

———. *Psychopathology and Politics.* New York: Viking Press, 1960.

Levine, Harry Gene. "The Discovery of Addiction: Changing Conceptions of Habitual Drunkenness in America." *Journal of Substance Abuse Treatment* 2 (1985):41–57.

———. "The Good Creature of God and the Demon Rum: Colonial American and 19th Century Ideas About Alcohol, Crime and Accidents." In *Alcohol and Disinhibition: Nature and Meaning of the Link,* edited by Robin Room and Gary Collins. Rockville, Md.: U.S. Department of Health and Human Services, National Institute on Alcohol Abuse and Alcoholism, 1983:111–171.

Lewis, David C. "Medical and Health Perspectives on a Failing U.S. Drug Policy." *Daedalus* 121 (Summer 1992):165–194.

Light, Paul. "An End to the War on Waste." *The Brookings Review* 11 (Spring 1993):48.

Lilly, J. Robert, Francis T. Cullen, and Richard A. Ball. *Criminological Theory: Context and Consequences.* Newbury Park, Calif.: Sage, 1989.

Lindblom, Charles. *The Policymaking Process,* second edition. Englewood Cliffs, N.J.: Prentice-Hall, 1980.

Lipset, Seymour Martin, and William Schneider. *The Confidence Gap: Business, Labor and Government in the Public Mind.* New York: The Free Press, 1983.

Liska, Allen E., and Mark Tausig. "Theoretical Interpretations of Social Class and Racial Differentials in Legal Decision-Making for Juveniles." *Sociological Quarterly* 20 (Spring 1979):197–207.

Lowi, Theodore J. "American Business, Public Policy, Case Studies, and Political Theory." *World Politics* 16, no. 4 (1964):677–715.

Lukes, Stephen. *Power: A Radical View.* London: Macmillan, 1974.

Lusane, Clarence. *Pipe Dream Blues: Racism and the War on Drugs.* Boston: South End Press, 1991.

Lyotard, Jean-Francois. *The Post-Modern Condition: A Report on Knowledge.* Minneapolis: University of Minnesota, 1984.

Maclin, Tracey. "Black and Blue: African-Americans and Police." *Reconstruction* 2, no. 1 (1992):13–16.

Maguire, Kathleen, and Timothy J. Flanagan, eds. *Sourcebook of Criminal Justice Statistics 1990.* Washington, D.C.: U.S. Department of Justice, Bureau of Justice Statistics, 1991.

Mann, Peggy. *Marijuana Alert.* New York: McGraw-Hill, 1985.

Marris, Peter, and Martin Rein. *Dilemmas of Social Reform: Poverty and Community Action in the United States,* second edition. London: Routledge and Kegan Paul, 1972.

Marx, Karl, *Theories of Surplus Value, Part I.* Moscow: Progress Publishers, 1963.

Marx, Karl, and Frederick Engels. *Collected Works: Volume 6, 1845–1848.* New York: International Publishers, 1976.

Massing, Michael. "Whatever Happened to the 'War on Drugs'?" *New York Review of Books,* June 11, 1992.

Matza, David. *Becoming Deviant.* Englewood Cliffs, N.J.: Prentice-Hall, 1969.

Mauer, Mark. "Americans Behind Bars." Washington, D.C.: The Sentencing Project, February 1992.

Mauss, Armand L. *Social Problems as Social Movements.* Philadelphia: J.B. Lippincott, 1975.

McPhee, John. *Coming into the Country.* New York: Farrar, Straus and Giroux, 1977.

Meese, Edwin, III. "Building a Drug Free Future." Preface to "Toward a Drug Free America: A Report from the National Drug Policy Board." n.d. (probably June 1988).

Merton, Robert K. "Social Structure and Anomie." In *Social Theory and Social Structure,* by Robert K. Merton. New York: Free Press, 1967.

Miller, Jerome G. "Hobbling a Generation: Young African American Males in the Criminal Justice System of America's Cities: Baltimore, Maryland." Alexandria, Va.: National Center on Institutions and Alternatives, September 1992.

———. "Search and Destroy: The Plight of African American Males in the

Criminal Justice System." Alexandria: National Center on Institutions and Alternatives, September 1992. Manuscript.

Miller, Richard Lawrence. *The Case for Legalizing Drugs*. New York: Praeger, 1991.

Milsom, S. Francis. *The Historical Foundations of Common Law*. London: Butterworths, 1969.

Mole, René, and Franz Trautman. "The Liberal Image of the Dutch Drug Policy." *The International Journal on Drug Policy* 2, no. 5 (1991):16–21.

Moore, Mark H., and Dean R. Gerstein, eds. *Alcohol and Public Policy: Beyond the Shadow of Prohibition*. Washington, D.C.: National Academy Press, 1981.

Morgan, H. Wayne. *Drugs in America: A Social History, 1800–1980*. Syracuse: Syracuse University Press, 1981.

Morris, Norval. "Race and Crime: What Evidence Is There That Race Influences Results in the Criminal Justice System?" *Judicature* 72 (August–September 1988):111–113.

Morris, Norval, and Gordon Hawkins. *The Honest Politician's Guide to Crime Control*. Chicago, University of Chicago Press, 1970.

Musto, David. *The American Disease: Origins of Narcotic Control*, expanded edition. New York: Oxford University Press, 1987.

NAACP Legal Defense and Education Fund. "Death Row, U.S.A.," New York: NAACP Legal Defense and Education Fund, Winter 1993.

Nadelmann, Ethan A. "The D.E.A. in Europe: Drug Enforcement in Comparative and International Perspective." Princeton, N.J.: Woodrow Wilson School of Public and International Affairs, March 1990. Manuscript.

———. "Thinking Seriously About Alternatives to Drug Prohibition." *Daedalus* 121 (Summer 1992):85–132.

Nahas, Gabriel G. *Marihuana—Deceptive Weed*. New York: Raven Press, 1973.

National Commission on Marijuana and Drug Abuse. *Drug Use in America: Problem in Perspective*. Washington, D.C.: Government Printing Office, 1973.

National Institute on Alcohol Abuse and Alcoholism. *Sixth Special Report to the U.S. Congress on Alcohol and Health*. Rockville, Md.: U.S. Department of Health and Human Services, 1987.

Office of National Drug Control Policy. *National Drug Control Strategy*. Washington, D.C.: Government Printing Office, 1989.

Office of National Drug Control Policy. *National Drug Control Strategy*. Washington, D.C.: Government Printing Office, 1992.

Office of National Drug Control Policy. "Needle Exchange Programs: Are They Effective?" Bulletin no. 7, July 1992.

Oreskes, Michael. "Drug War Underlines Fickleness of Public." *New York Times*, September 6, 1990.

"Osservatorio sull'Attuazione della Legge 162/90 sulla Droga: a Quasi un Anno dalla Approvazione della Legge Quale Bilancio?" Partito Democratico della Sinistra. Roma, 1991.

Packer, Herbert L. *The Limits of the Criminal Sanction*. Palo Alto: Stanford University Press, 1968.

Parker, Howard, and Russell Newcombe. "Heroin Use and Acquisitive Crime in an English Community." *British Journal of Sociology* 38, no. 3 (1987):331–350.

Parsons, Talcott. *The Social System.* Glencoe, Ill.: The Free Press, 1951.

Petersilia, Joan. "Racial Disparities in the Criminal Justice System." R-2947-NIC. Santa Monica, Calif.: RAND Corporation, 1983.

Petersilia, Joan, and Susan Turner. "Evaluating Intensive Supervision Probation/Parole: Results of a Nationwide Experiment." In *Research in Brief.* Washington, D.C.: U.S. Department of Justice, National Institute of Justice, May 1993.

Piven, Francis Fox, and Richard Cloward. *Regulating the Poor: The Functions of Public Welfare.* New York: Pantheon, 1971.

Porter, Margaret R., Theodore A. Veira, Gary J. Kaplan, Jack R. Heesch, and Ardell B. Collyar. "Drug Use in Anchorage, Alaska." *Journal of the American Medical Association* 223 (1973):657–664.

Posner, Ellen. "A City That Likes Itself: Urban Design." *The Atlantic*, July 1991, 94–100.

Reuband, Karl-Heinz. "Drug Abuse Trends in West Germany." In Rockville, Md.: *Epidemiologic Trends in Drug Abuse.* U.S. Department of Health and Human Services, National Institute on Drug Abuse, 1990:III-1–III-14.

Reuband, Karl-Heinz. "Drug Use and Drug Policy: A Cross-National Comparison." Zentralarchiv für Empirisches Sozialforschung, Universistät zu Köln, 1990. Manuscript.

Reuter, Peter. "Drugs: The Threat and the Response." Ditchley Conference report no. D91/4. Santa Monica, Calif.: Rand Corporation, 1991:4.

———. "Hawks Ascendant: The Punitive Trend of American Drug Policy." *Daedalus* 121, no. 3 (1992):15–52.

———. "Prevalence Estimation and Policy Formulation." *The Journal of Drug Issues* 23, no. 2 (1993):167–184.

Reuter, Peter, Mathea Falco, and Robert MacCoun. *Comparing Western European and North American Drug Policies: An International Conference Report.* Santa Monica, Calif.: RAND Corporation, 1993.

Rice, Dorothy P., Sander Kelman, Leonard S. Miller, and Sarah Dunmeyer. *The Economic Costs of Alcohol and Drug Abuse and Mental Illness: 1985.* Rockville, Md.: U.S. Department of Health and Human Services, Alcohol, Drug Abuse and Mental Health Administration, 1990.

Richards, Louise G. "Demographic Trends and Drug Abuse, 1980–1995." Rockville, Md.: Department of Health and Human Services, National Institute on Drug Abuse, May 1981.

Ripley, Randall B. *Policy Analysis in Political Science.* Chicago, Ill.: Nelson-Hall, 1985.

Roberts, Dorothy. "Punishing Drug Addicts Who Have Babies: Women of Color, Equality and the Right to Privacy." *Harvard Law Review* 104 (1991):1419–1482.

Rosenau, Pauline Marie. *Post-Modernism and the Social Sciences.* Princeton, N.J.: Princeton University Press, 1992.

Rothman, David J. *The Discovery of the Asylum.* Boston: Little, Brown, 1971.

Rublowsky, John. *The Stoned Age: A History of Drugs in America*. New York: Putnam, 1974.

Rüter, Frits. "The Pragmatic Dutch Approach to Drug Control: Does It Work?" University of Amsterdam, 1988. Lecture.

Safire, William. "Drug War Lingo." *New York Times*, September 24, 1989.

Sager, Mike. "The Case of Gary Fannon." *Rolling Stone*, September 3, 1992.

———. "The State of Michigan vs. Gary Fannon." *Rolling Stone*, September 2, 1993.

Sanders, Wiley B., ed. *Juvenile Offenders for a Thousand Years*. Chapel Hill: University of North Carolina Press, 1970.

Schattschneider, E.E. *The Semisovereign People: A Realist's View of Democracy in America*. Hinsdale, Ill.: Dryden Press, 1975.

Scheingold, Stuart A. *The Politics Of Law and Order: Street Crime and Public Policy*. New York: Longman, 1984.

———. *The Politics of Street Crime: Criminal Process and Cultural Obsession*. Philadelphia: Temple University Press, 1991.

Schmoke, Kurt. "An Argument in Favor of Decriminalization." *Hofstra Law Review* 18 (1990):501–525.

Schneider, Andrew, and Mary Pat Flaherty. "Presumed Guilty: The Law's Victims in the War on Drugs." *The Pittsburgh Press*, August 11–16, 1991.

Schumpeter, Joseph A. *Capitalism, Socialism, and Democracy*. New York: Harper and Brothers, 1942.

Schur, Edwin. *Narcotic Addiction in Britain and America: The Impact of Public Policy*. Bloomington, Ind.: Indiana University Press, 1962.

Scigliano, Eric. "A Chief for All Seasons." *Seattle Weekly*, October 16, 1991.

———. "Hard Time." *Seattle Weekly*, October 21, 1992.

———. "The Noland Factor." *Seattle Weekly*, September 4, 1991.

———. "Send No Cash." *Seattle Weekly*, December 23, 1992.

Scott, Peter Dale, and Jonathan Marshall. *Cocaine Politics: Drugs, Armies and the CIA in Central America*. Berkeley: University of California, 1991.

Segal, Bernard. *Drug-Taking Behavior Among School-Aged Youth: The Alaska Experience and Comparisons with Lower-48 States*. New York: Haworth Press, 1990.

Servizi Studi del Parlamento. *Aspetti e problemi della tossicodependenza*, Vol. 1. Rome, 1989.

Siegal, Ronald K. *Intoxication: Life in Pursuit of Artificial Paradise*. New York: Dutton, 1989.

Single, Eric W. "Impact of Marijuana Decriminalization: An Update." *Journal of Public Health Policy* 10 (Winter 1989):456–465.

Skirrow, Jan, and Edward Sawka. "Alcohol and Drug Prevention Strategies—An Overview." *Contemporary Drug Problems* 14 (Summer 1987):147–241.

Skogan, Wesley G., and Michael G. Maxfield. *Coping with Crime: Individual and Neighborhood Reactions*. Beverly Hills: Sage, 1981.

Skolnick, Jerome H. "Rethinking the Drug Problem." *Daedalus* 121 (Summer 1992):133–159.

Smith, Tom W. "Ethnic Images." GSS topical report no. 19. Chicago: National Opinion Research Center, University of Chicago, December 1990.

Sparrow, Malcolm, Mark H. Moore, and David Kennedy. *Beyond 911: A New Era for Policing*. New York: Basic Books, 1990.

Spector, Malcolm, and John Kitsuse. *Constructing Social Problems*. Hawthorne, N.Y.: Walter de Gruyter, 1987.

State Office of Alcoholism and Drug Abuse (Alaska). *The Economic Cost of Alcohol and Other Drug Abuse in Alaska, Volumes I and II*. 1989.

Stimson, G.V. "Risk Reduction by Drug Users with Regard to HIV Infection." *International Review of Psychiatry* 3, no. 3/4 (1991):401–415.

Stinchcombe, Arthur, Rebecca Adams, Carol A. Heimer, Kim Lane Scheppele, Tom W. Smith, and D. Garth Taylor. *Crime and Punishment: Changing Attitudes in America*. San Francisco: Jossey-Bass, 1980.

"Der Stoff versaut das Land." *Der Speigel* 28 (June 1990):32–41.

Stone, Deborah A. *Policy Paradox and Political Reason*. Glenview, Ill.: Scott, Foresman, 1988.

Taft, Donald. *Criminology*. New York: Macmillan, 1956.

Taradash, Marco. "Editoriale." *CORAnews*, no. 58, March 19, 1990.

Taylor, Arnold H. *American Diplomacy and the Narcotics Traffic, 1900–1939: A Study in International Humanitarian Reform*. Durham: Duke University Press, 1969.

Terkel, Studs. *Race: How Blacks and Whites Think and Feel About the American Obsession*. New York: The New Press, 1992.

Terry, Charles E., and Mildred Pellens. *The Opium Problem*. New York: Bureau of Social Hygiene, 1928.

Thornburgh, Dick. "An Anti-Crime Coalition for America's Communities." Address, Attorney General's Summit on Law Enforcement Responses to Violent Crime: Public Safety in the Nineties, Washington, D.C., March 4, 1991.

———. "Law Enforcement in the 1990s: Dawn of a New Decade." Address, California Police Chiefs Association, Anaheim, Calif., February 4, 1991.

———. "Statement Before the Committee on the Judiciary, U.S. House of Representatives, Concerning H.R. 2273 and S. 933, Americans with Disabilities Act of 1989," October 12, 1989.

———. "Values and Law in a New World Order." Address, Drake University School of Law, Des Moines, Iowa, March 9, 1991.

Trebach, Arnold, and Kevin Zeese. "Preface." In *Drug Prohibition and the Conscience of Nations*, edited by Arnold S. Trebach and Kevin B. Zeese. Washington, D.C.: Drug Policy Foundation, 1989.

Turner, David. "Pragmatic Incoherence: The Changing Face of British Drug Policy." In *Searching for Alternatives: Drug Control Policy in the United States*, edited by Melvyn B. Krauss and Edward P. Lazear. Stanford: Hoover Institution Press, 1991:175–190.

United Nations. "Report of the International Narcotics Control Board." 1989–1991.

United Nations Secretariat, Division of Narcotic Drugs. "Review of Drug

Abuse and Measures To Reduce the Illicit Demand for Drugs by Region." *Bulletin on Narcotics* 39, no. 1 (1987):3–30.

U.S. Congress, House of Representatives, Committee on Education and Labor. *Drug Abuse Resistance Education Act of 1990: Report.* n.d.

U.S. Congress, House of Representatives. *Hearing Before the Select Committee on Narcotics Abuse and Control*, 100th Congress, 1st session, September 25, 1987.

U.S. Congress, House of Representatives. *Hearings Before the Subcommittee on Civil and Constitutional Rights of the Committee on the Judiciary on H.R. 4618, H.R. 105, H.R. 596, H.R. 1197, H.R. 1464, H.R. 1477, H.R. 2196, Title I of 2709, and Titles I and II of H.R. 3119*, 101st Congress, 2d session, May 9, 1990.

U.S. Congress, House of Representatives. *Hearings Before the Subcommittee on Crime, Committee on the Judiciary, on Federal Death Penalty Legislation*, 101st Congress, 2d session, March 24 and May 23, 1990.

U.S. Congress, House of Representatives. *Hearings Before the Subcommittee on Crime and Criminal Justice, Committee on the Judiciary*, 102d Congress, 1st session, May 29, 1991.

U.S. Congress, House of Representatives. *Hearings Before the Subcommittee on Crime and Criminal Justice, Committee on the Judiciary, Selected Crime Issues: Prevention and Punishment*, 102d Congress, 1st session, May 23, 29, June 12, 26, July 10, 17, and 25, 1991.

U.S. Congress, Senate. *Hearings Before the Committee on the Judiciary on S. 32, S. 1225, and S. 1696*, 101st Congress, 1st session, September 19, 1989.

U.S. Congress, Senate. *Hearings Before the Subcommittee To Investigate the Administration of the Internal Security Act and Other Internal Security Laws, Senate Judiciary Committee*, 93d Congress, 2d session, May 9, 17, 16, 20, 21; June 13, 1974.

U.S. Department of Commerce, Bureau of the Census. *Compendium of Government Finances.* Washington, D.C.: Government Printing Office, 1962, 1967, 1972, 1977, 1982, 1987.

U.S. Department of Commerce, Bureau of the Census. *Historical Statistics of the United States: Colonial Times to 1970*, parts 1 and 2. Washington, D.C.: Government Printing Office, 1976.

U.S. Department of Commerce, Bureau of the Census. *Statistical Abstract of the United States.* Washington, D.C.: Government Printing Office, 1973–1992.

U.S. Department of Health and Human Services, Alcohol, Drug Abuse, and Mental Health Administration. "Annual Emergency Room Data 1990: Data from the Drug Abuse Warning Network (DAWN)." Rockville, Md.: National Institute on Drug Abuse, 1991.

U.S. Department of Health and Human Services, Alcohol, Drug Abuse, and Mental Health Administration. "Data from the Drug Abuse Warning Network (DAWN), Annual Data 1989." Statistical series I, no. 9. Rockville, Md.: National Institute on Drug Abuse 1990.

U.S. Department of Health and Human Services, National Institute on Drug Abuse. "National Household Survey on Drug Abuse: Population Estimates 1991." Rockville, Md.: National Institute on Drug Abuse, 1991.

U.S. Department of Health and Human Services, Office on Smoking and Health. *The Health Consequences of Smoking: Nicotine Addiction.* Washington, D.C.: Government Printing Office, 1988.

U.S. Department of Justice. *Annual Report of the Department of Justice Asset Forfeiture Program 1991.* Washington, D.C.: U.S. Department of Justice, 1991.

U.S. Department of Justice. *The Nation's Toughest Drug Law: Evaluating the New York Experience.* Washington, D.C.: Government Printing Office, 1978.

U.S. Department of Justice, Bureau of Justice Statistics. "Capital Punishment 1991." *Bulletin.* Washington, D.C.: U.S. Department of Justice, October 1992.

U.S. Department of Justice, Bureau of Justice Statistics. "Correctional Populations in the United States, 1985." Washington, D.C.: U.S. Department of Justice, December 1987.

U.S. Department of Justice, Bureau of Justice Statistics. "Correctional Populations in the United States, 1990." Washington, D.C.: U.S. Department of Justice, July 1992.

U.S. Department of Justice, Bureau of Justice Statistics. "Criminal Victimization in the United States, 1990." Washington, D.C.: U.S. Department of Justice, February 1992.

U.S. Department of Justice, Bureau of Justice Statistics. "Criminal Victimization in the United States, 1991." Washington, D.C.: U.S. Department of Justice, December 1992.

U.S. Department of Justice, Bureau of Justice Statistics. "Drug Enforcement by Police and Sheriffs' Departments, 1990." *Special Report.* Washington, D.C.: U.S. Department of Justice, May 1992.

U.S. Department of Justice, Bureau of Justice Statistics. "Drugs, Crime, and the Justice System: A National Report." Washington, D.C.: U.S. Department of Justice, December 1992.

U.S. Department of Justice, Bureau of Justice Statistics. "Fact Sheet: Drug Use Trends." Washington, D.C.: U.S. Department of Justice, May 1992.

U.S. Department of Justice, Bureau of Justice Statistics. "Federal Sentencing in Transition, 1986–90." *Special Report.* Washington, D.C.: U.S. Department of Justice, June 1992.

U.S. Department of Justice, Bureau of Justice Statistics. "Felony Sentences in State Courts, 1986." *Bulletin.* Washington, D.C.: U.S. Department of Justice, February 1989.

U.S. Department of Justice, Bureau of Justice Statistics. "Felony Sentences in State Courts, 1988." *Bulletin.* Washington, D.C.: U.S. Department of Justice, December 1990.

U.S. Department of Justice, Bureau of Justice Statistics. "Felony Sentences in State Courts, 1990." *Bulletin.* Washington, D.C.: U.S. Department of Justice, March 1993.

U.S. Department of Justice, Bureau of Justice Statistics. "Historical Corrections Statistics in the United States, 1850–1984." Washington, D.C.: U.S. Department of Justice, December 1986.

U.S. Department of Justice, Bureau of Justice Statistics. "Justice Expenditure and Employment 1982." *Bulletin*. Washington, D.C.: U.S. Department of Justice, August 1985.

U.S. Department of Justice, Bureau of Justice Statistics. "Justice Expenditure and Employment 1990." *Bulletin*. Washington, D.C.: U.S. Department of Justice, September 1992.

U.S. Department of Justice, Bureau of Justice Statistics. "National Corrections Reporting Program, 1986." Washington, D.C.: U.S. Department of Justice, January 1992.

U.S. Department of Justice, Bureau of Justice Statistics. "National Corrections Reporting Program, 1987." Washington, D.C.: U.S. Department of Justice, April 1992.

U.S. Department of Justice, Bureau of Justice Statistics. "National Corrections Reporting Program, 1988." Washington, D.C.: U.S. Department of Justice, April 1992.

U.S. Department of Justice, Bureau of Justice Statistics. "National Corrections Reporting Program, 1989." Washington, D.C.: U.S. Department of Justice, November 1992.

U.S. Department of Justice, Bureau of Justice Statistics. "National Judicial Reporting Program, 1988." Washington, D.C.: U.S. Department of Justice, January 1992.

U.S. Department of Justice, Bureau of Justice Statistics. "National Update." Washington, D.C.: U.S. Department of Justice, January 1992.

U.S. Department of Justice, Bureau of Justice Statistics. "Prisons and Prisoners in the United States." Washington, D.C.: U.S. Department of Justice, April 1992.

U.S. Department of Justice, Bureau of Justice Statistics. "Prisoners in 1982." *Bulletin*. Washington, D.C.: U.S. Department of Justice, April 1983.

U.S. Department of Justice, Bureau of Justice Statistics. "Prisoners in 1991." *Bulletin*. Washington, D.C.: U.S. Department of Justice, May 1992.

U.S. Department of Justice, Bureau of Justice Statistics. "Prisoners in 1992." *Bulletin*. Washington, D.C.: U.S. Department of Justice, May 1993.

U.S. Department of Justice, Bureau of Justice Statistics. "Probation and Parole in 1981." *Bulletin*. Washington, D.C.: U.S. Department of Justice, August 1982.

U.S. Department of Justice, Bureau of Justice Statistics. "Probation and Parole in 1990." *Bulletin*. Washington, D.C.: U.S. Department of Justice, November 1991.

U.S. Department of Justice, Bureau of Justice Statistics. "Profile of Jail Inmates 1989." *Bulletin*. Washington, D.C.: U.S. Department of Justice, April 1991.

U.S. Department of Justice, Bureau of Justice Statistics. "Profile of State Prison Inmates 1986." *Bulletin*. Washington, D.C.: U.S. Department of Justice, January 1988.

U.S. Department of Justice, Bureau of Justice Statistics. "State and Federal

Prisoners, 1925–85." *Bulletin.* Washington, D.C.: U.S. Department of Justice, October 1986.

U.S. Department of Justice, National Institute of Justice. "Community Policing in Seattle: A Model Partnership Between Citizens and Police." Washington, D.C.: U.S. Department of Justice, August 1992.

U.S. Department of Justice, National Institute of Justice. "Drug Use Forecasting—Drugs and Crime 1990: Annual Report." Washington, D.C.: U.S. Department of Justice, August 1991.

U.S. Department of Justice, National Institute of Justice. "Drug Use Forecasting, Third Quarter 1991." Washington, D.C.: U.S. Department of Justice, July 1992.

U.S. Department of Justice, National Institute of Justice. *Research in Brief.* Washington, D.C.: U.S. Department of Justice, January 1993.

U.S. Sentencing Commission. *Federal Sentencing Guidelines Manual.* St. Paul: West Publishing, 1992.

U.S. Sentencing Commission. "Mandatory Minimum Penalties in the Federal Criminal Justice System." Washington, D.C.: U.S. Sentencing Commission, August 1991.

van de Wijngaart, Govert F. "A Social History of Drug Use in the Netherlands: Policy Outcomes and Implications." *The Journal of Drug Issues* 18, no. 3 (1988):481–495.

———. "Competing Perspectives on Drug Use: The Dutch Experience." Doctoral dissertation, Rijksuniversiteit, Utrecht, 1990.

Van Vliet, Henk Jan. "Separation of Drug Markets and the Normalization of Drug Problems in the Netherlands: An Example for Other Nations?" *The Journal of Drug Issues* 20, no. 3 (1990):463–471.

Vold, George B., and Thomas J. Bernard. *Theoretical Criminology.* New York: Oxford University Press, 1986.

Ward, Aileen. "Foreword." In *Confessions of an English Opium Eater and Other Writings,* by Thomas De Quincey. New York: Carroll and Graf, 1966.

Wasserstrom, Silas J. "The Incredible Shrinking Fourth Amendment." *American Criminal Law Review* 21, no. 3 (1984):257–401.

Williamson, Don. "Loitering Law: A Day Without Winners." *Seattle Times,* July 3, 1990.

Willis, Ellen. "Hell No, I Won't Go." *Village Voice,* September 19, 1989.

Wills, Antoinette. *Crime and Punishment in Revolutionary Paris.* Westport, Conn.: Greenwood Press, 1989.

Wilson, James Q. *Thinking About Crime,* revised edition. New York: Basic Books, 1983.

Wilson, James Q., and Richard J. Herrnstein. *Crime and Human Nature.* New York: Simon and Schuster, 1985.

Wilson, William Julius. *The Truly Disadvantaged: The Inner City, the Underclass, and Public Policy.* Chicago: University of Chicago Press, 1987.

Wisotsky, Steven. *Beyond the War on Drugs: Overcoming a Failed Policy.* Buffalo, N.Y.: Prometheus Books, 1990.

———. "Not Thinking Like a Lawyer: The Case of Drugs in the Courts."

*Notre Dame Journal of Law, Ethics and Public Policy* 5, no. 3 (1991):651–691.

Wohlforth, Charles P. "Off the Pot." *New Republic*, December 3, 1990, 9–10.

Zeldin, Michael F., and Roger G. Weiner. "Innocent Third Parties and Their Rights in Asset Forfeiture Proceedings." *American Criminal Law Review* 28 (1991):843–867.

Zimmer, Lynn. "The Anti-Drug Semantic." Paper presented at Drug Policy Foundation conference, 1992. Department of Sociology, Queens College, City University of New York.

Zimring, Franklin, and Gordon Hawkins. *Capital Punishment and the American Agenda*. New York: Cambridge University Press, 1986.

———. *The Search for Rational Drug Control*. Cambridge: Cambridge University Press, 1992.

# Index

drug prohibition (*cont*).
  marijuana and, 104–6, 257*n*27
  market interpretation of policy process and, 97
  military funding and, 192
  modification of policy, difficulty of, 27–28
  morality issue, 116–17
  origins of, 24–26, 241*n*31
  overt agendas of proponents, 116–18
  persistence despite failure, 7–8, 184
  probation system and, 34
  public health issue, 116–17
  public's acceptance of unsatisfactory outcomes, 227
  public's concern about drugs and, 22, 30, 99–103
  rationalist perspective on drug policy and, 7
  as reflection of larger culture, 29–30
  rightist cultural agenda and, 28
  semantic of, *see* drugspeak
  state drug policies, 32–33, 34
  sustaining forces of, 17–18, 26
  supply and demand, focus on, 37–38
  user types, failure to distinguish between, 105–6, 189–90
  "war on drugs," 9, 22, 26, 29
  *see also* sentencing of drug offenders; shadow agenda of prohibitionist policy; *specific laws*
drug raids, 149, 269*n*34
drugspeak, 9–10, 11, 275*n*10
  advertising and, 193–94
  anti-drug sales tax and, 188, 189–90, 195–96, 204, 205
  demonization of users and sellers, 29, 184, 186–87, 193–97, 278*n*52
  "drug–free" concept, 27, 197, 198
  elements of, 185

  eradication theme, 198–200
  false claims, consequences of, 190
  gateway theory, 190–91, 277*n*40
  historical perspective on, 185–88, 194
  individual will, appeals to, 200–203
  kingpin death penalty and, 195
  marijuana recriminalization and, 191, 202, 204–5
  media and, 188, 203, 277*n*27
  as national-level phenomenon, 206
  "national security threat" theme, 191–93, 194–95
  political utility, 183–84, 206–7
  problem themes, 188–97
  racial aspects, 186
  scare publicity, 187, 276–22
  solidarity theme, 203–6, 281*n*95
  solution themes, 197–206
  survival of prohibitionist policies and, 184
  symbolic value, 184, 206–8
  ubiquity theme, 188–91, 204–5
  war metaphor, 10, 22, 198
drug-taking behavior, responsible management of, 234–35
drug users, *see* user types
drunk driving laws, 110
Dukakis, Michael, 136, 167
DuPont, Robert, 191
Durkheim, Emile, 19, 124

Eastland, James O., 277*n*43
Ebel, Robert D., 177
Edelman, Murray, 126
Edwards, Don, 137, 138, 150
electronic monitoring, 34
Ellis, Johnny, 110
Englesmann, Eddy, 216
English, Glenn, 50
English-only movement, 134
"eradication of drug use" theme, 198–200
European Cities for Drug Policy, 215

European drug policy, 11–12, 27,
211
AIDS and, 217, 219–20
cities, cooperation among, 215
cultural and political contexts,
212, 216–17
dangerous classes and, 216–17
differentiation in, 222
drug use, impact on, 211–12,
217, 282*n*1
future prospects, 224
"harm reduction" strategy, 222–
23, 234
legal reforms, 216
moralistic attitudes, absence of,
218–19
prohibitionism in, 213, 220–22
public attitude toward, 217–18,
222
scope of drug problem and, 212
social/medical orientation, 214–
15, 217, 218, 219–20
U.S. influence on, 213–14
exclusionary rule, 37
expenditures for drug control, 39,
245*n*52

Federal Bureau of Investigation
(FBI), 38
Federal Bureau of Narcotics, 187
Federal Crime legistration, 3, 48–
49
federalization of law enforcement,
39–40
fetal alcohol syndrome, 110
Fitzsimons, Patrick, 156
Florida, 147, 150
formulators, 137–38, 141
Foucault, Michel, 127, 183
France, 123, 218, 223, 224
Frankfurt Resolution, 215
Freedom, Inc., 81, 156
*Furman v. Georgia* (1972), 45,
247*n*5
future of drug policy, 12, 26–28
alternatives to prohibition, 230–
35

de-escalation of prohibition, proposal for, 233–34
drug-taking behavior, responsible
management of, 234–35
in Europe, 224
legalization of drugs, 231–33
moderation of prohibitionist policies, chances of, 27, 228–30
race relations and, 157–59, 229–
30

Gant, Jack, 196
Gates, Daryl, 104
gateway theory, 190–91, 277*n*40
Gekas, George W., 50, 51, 52, 161,
162, 164
Gephardt, Richard, 74
Germany, 211, 212, 213, 214,
216–17, 218, 220
Gibbs, Arnold A., 256*n*4
Gitlin, Todd, 234
Giuliani, Rudolph, 221
global drug trade, 282*n*6
Glorioso, Steve, 180, 181
Goldwater, Barry, ix
Gray, Pat, 180, 181
Great Britain:
current drug policies, 214, 217–
18, 219–20, 222–23, 224
past drug policies, 24, 185–86
Poor Law of 1601, 122
Greene, Jack R., 206
*Gregg v. Georgia* (1976), 46–47

habeas corpus, right of, 164
Hackley, Jack, 81
Hancock, Mel, 75
Hanley, Alyce, 66, 69–70, 101,
140
Harder, Lucinda, 111
Harmelin, Ronald, 61
"harm reduction" strategy, 27,
222–23, 234
Harrison Act of 1914, 10, 24–25,
39, 187, 241*n*31
hashish, 63, 67, 230
Hasson, Kenneth, 61–62

lumpen proletariat, 262*n*10
Lusane, Clarence, 146

*McCleskey v. Kemp* (1987), 271*n*68
McCollum, Bill, 51–52, 161, 162
McPhee, John, 72
Majewske, Marie, 67, 69–70, 101,
 110, 129, 130, 131, 191, 197,
 204
mandatory minimum sentences, 33,
 138, 148, 150, 229
Mann, Peggy, 189
marijuana, 20, 23, 24, 117
 dangers of, 104, 230, 257*n*25,
  258*n*29
 decriminalization and prevalence
  of use, 65–67, 251*n*10
 European policies on, 211, 215,
  217, 221
 future policy developments, 230,
  231
 gateway theory, 190–91, 277*n*40
 hysteria about, 186–87
 liberal attitudes of 1970s, 56–57,
  63, 64–65
 moral issues, 104–5
 penalties for marijuana involvement, 105
 prohibitionist policy on, 104–6,
  257*n*27
 racial aspects of drug prohibition
  and, 25
 racial patterns of use, 145–46
 young people and, 129–33
marijuana recriminalization, 7, 63
 activists' role, 140–41
 alcohol anomaly, 110
 Bennett's participation, 71, 132–
  33
 conservative social agenda and,
  140–41
 crime concerns, 67, 103
 demand-response dynamic, 98–
  99
 demographic changes and, 63–
  64
 diffuse concern about drugs

transformed into specific advocacy of prohibition policy, 101
 drugspeak and, 191, 202, 204–5
 enforcement of, 72
 implementers' role, 139
 initiative campaign, 69–72,
  252*n*26
 "legal" status of marijuana in
  1970s and 1980s, 64–65
 legislative initiatives, 68–69
 liberals and, 136–37
 outcomes of, 72, 226, 227
 political aftermath, 169–71
 political aspects, 131
 prevalence of use concerns, 65–
  67
 privacy rights and, 64–65, 136–
  37
 public support for, 68, 264*n*32
 youthful behavior, focus on,
  129–30, 132–33
market interpretation of policy process, 97
Marks, John, 223
Marshall, Thurgood, 279*n*66
Martin, Terry, 69, 70
Martinez, Robert, 115, 131
Marx, Karl, 174
material aspects of drug prohibition, 120–21, 173–74, 228
 anti-drug sales tax, 177–81
 asset forfeiture, 35–36, 175–77,
  244*nn*37, 38, 245*n*42
 commercial environment of business districts, 88–89, 181–82
 drug loitering law, 88–89, 181–
  82
 law enforcement's material
  needs, 177–81
 tax law used against drug dealers, 175, 177
 treatment/prevention services
  and, 179–80
media, drugspeak and, 188, 203,
 277*n*27
Meese, Edwin, 104–5, 199, 203,
 257*n*27

Switzerland, 214, 215
Symblic politics, 4, 22–23
 death penalty, 48

Taft, Donald, 233
taxes to support drug enforcement,
 *see* anti-drug sales tax
tax law used against drug dealers,
 175, 177
Taxpayers' Defense League, 81
tax revolt movement, 98
Taylor, Kathleen, 90
temperance movement, 186
Terkel, Studs, 151
Terwilliger, George, 177
Texas, 148
Thatcher, Margaret, 223
Thompson, Richard, 62
*Thompson v. Oklahoma* (1988),
 247*n*13
Thornburgh, Dick, 36, 200, 203,
 207, 282*n*111
"three strikes and you're out" sentencing proposal, 3
Thurmond, Strom, 191, 194
tobacco, 21, 240*nn*18, 19
Traxler, Bob, 168
true believers prohibition policies,
 161–62

"ubiquitous nature" of drug problem, 188–91, 204–5
"user accountability" concept, 35,
 52, 166, 175
user types, 9–10
 failure to distinguish between,
 105–6, 189–90

violence, drug-related, 6
vocabulary of drug policy, *see*
 drugspeak
Von Raab, William, 203

Wagstaff, Bob, 71, 72
Walden, Harriett, 152–53
Ware, Jeri, 153
Waris, Bill, 178, 179
war on drugs, *see* drug prohibition
warrant requirements, 37
Washington Supreme Court, 89
Wasserstrom, Silas, 195
Waterhouse posse, 76, 135
Watkins, Wes, 165–66
Weed and Seed program, 205–6,
 281*nn*105, 109
Weeks, Tom, 91
Welborn, Jack A., 62
Whipple, Rachel, 139
Wilson, James Q., 200
wiretap authority in investigating
 drug crimes, 59
Wisotsky, Steven, 279*n*66
work ethic, 123, 132–33
workplace drug-testing, 181
Wright, Hamilton, 25, 143, 186,
 214, 241*n*32

young people:
 adults' apprehension about, 128–
 29
 authoritarian approach to problems of, 133
 crime rate among, 128
 as dangerous class, 127–33
 drug programs targeting, 130–32
 high-school seniors, drug use by,
 145, 146–47
 marijuana and, 129–33
 work ethic and, 132–33

"zero tolerance" slogan, 197, 199–
 200
Zimmer, Lynn, 185, 275*n*10
Zimring, Franklin, 39, 98